Usability Inspection Methods

Usability Inspection Methods

Edited by

JAKOB NIELSEN
SunSoft

and

ROBERT L. MACK
IBM T. J. Watson Research Center

John Wiley & Sons, Inc.
New York • Chichester • Brisbane • Toronto • Singapore

Publisher: Katherine Schowalter

Editor: Diane D. Cerra

Associate Managing Editor: Maureen B. Drexel

Designations used by companies to distinguish their products are often claimed as trademarks. In all instances where John Wiley & Sons, Inc. is aware of a claim, the product names appear in initial capital or all capital letters. Readers, however, should contact the appropriate companies for more complete information regarding trademarks and registration.

This text is printed on acid-free paper.

This publication is designed to provide accurate and authoritative information in regard to the subject matter covered. It is sold with the understanding that the publisher is not engaged in rendering legal, accounting, or other professional service. If legal advice or other expert assistance is required, the services of a competent professional person should be sought.

Library of Congress Cataloging-in-Publication Data

Nielsen, Jakob, 1957-
    Usability inspection methods / Jakob Nielsen, Robert L. Mack.
        p.   cm.
    Includes bibliographical references and index.
    ISBN 0-471-01877-5 (alk. paper)
    1. User interfaces (Computer systems)   2. Human-computer
interaction.   I. Mack, Robert L., 1949- . II. Title.
QA76.9.U83N55   1994
005.1'4—dc20   93-48412
                                                               CIP

Printed in the United States of America
10 9 8 7 6 5 4 3 2 1

About the Editors

Jakob Nielsen is a distinguished engineer in the human factors engineering department of SunSoft, a Sun Microsystems business. Dr. Nielsen's earlier affiliations include the IBM User Interface Institute at the T. J. Watson Research Center in Yorktown Heights, NY and the Technical University of Denmark, and Bellcore (Bell Communications Research). His interests include usability engineering, hypertext, and next-generation user interfaces. Nielsen coined the term "discount usability engineering," and was the co-inventor of the heuristic evaluation method described in this book. He is the "Methods and Tools" editor for the ACM *interactions* user interface magazine and on the editorial boards for *Behaviour & Information Technology*, the *Hypermedia* journal, *Interacting with Computers*, the *International Journal of Human-Computer Interaction*, and the *International Journal of Human-Computer Studies*. Nielsen is vice chair for publications of the Association for Computing Machinery Special Interest Group on Computer-Human Interaction (ACM SIGCHI).

Robert L. Mack is a Research Staff Member at the IBM Thomas Watson Research Center in New York. He manages a Usability Engineering group in the Computer Science Department. Dr. Mack's research interests have focussed on advanced user interface technologies, and development of methods for supporting usability engineering. Advanced interface technologies include touch interfaces and speech recognition, IBM's Common User Access graphical user interface guidelines, and most recently interface techniques for multimedia information management. Usability engineering methods include qualitative user interface methods such as thinking aloud, competitive benchmarking, and usability inspection methods. Many of these research interests have been pursued in the context of working with IBM Development groups, and as a member of the IBM User Interface Institute between 1985 and 1992. Mack has taught courses on usability engineering and user interface design within IBM for a number of years.

Acknowledgments

This book was inspired by the workshop on usability inspection methods we organized at the ACM *CHI'92* conference (Association for Computing Machinery conference on Computer-Human Interaction). The book is not a proceedings of the workshop in the traditional sense since all authors reworked their papers considerably based on the discussions at the workshop as well as recent research results. Also, a few of our authors were not at the workshop and a few of the workshop participants were unable to contribute chapters for this book.

In addition to the authors represented in the book, we would like to thank Brigham Bell, Thomas M. Lanzetta, and Allan MacLean for their contributions to the *CHI'92* workshop on usability inspection. The discussions at the workshop helped all of us refine our understanding of the various inspection methods and of the deeper issue of the relation between inspections and other aspects of usability.

Jakob Nielsen and Robert L. Mack

Contents

Preface

Jakob Nielsen

SunSoft

Robert L. Mack

IBM T. J. Watson Research Center

Usability inspection is the generic term for a range of usability engineering methods that have seen explosive growth since the first two, heuristic evaluation and cognitive walkthroughs, were formally presented at lectures during the ACM *CHI'90* conference on computer-human interaction in Seattle on April 4, 1990. Over the next two years, it was realized that several additional usability methods were fairly similar to heuristic evaluation and cognitive walkthroughs. For a workshop at the *CHI'92* conference two years later in Monterey, we decided to use "usability inspection" as the generic term for all these methods. At the time of the 1992 workshop, the initial research results had solidified sufficiently to allow us to build up a conceptual understanding of usability inspection. We also had participants from industry representing the first practical applications of the methods. After the workshop, industrial use has kept growing very rapidly, to the extent that we now can claim inspection methods to be a major, established part of usability engineering.

The expansion in practical use of usability inspection methods has taken place mostly over the very short period of four years since the presentation of the early research papers. Granted that early research activities happened a few years before the formal presentation of the results and that some development projects used usability-inspection-like methods without calling them that, the rapid spread of usability is still very impressive when compared to most other examples of technology transfer. For example, it took about twenty years from the invention of the mouse until its appearance as a standard element of a popular personal computer and another ten years or so from the introduction of that first mouse-based personal computer to the time when the majority of computer users had a mouse. We can only speculate on the reasons for the much faster technology transfer of usability inspection methods from the research labs to widespread industrial use, but some of the major reasons seem to be:

- Many companies have just recently realized the urgent need for increased usability activities to improve their user interfaces. Since usability inspection methods are cheap to use and do not require special equipment or lab facilities, they may be among the first methods tried.

- The knowledge and experience of interface designers and usability specialists need to be broadly applied; inspections represent an efficient way to do this. Thus, inspections serve a similar function to style guides by spreading the expertise and knowledge of a few to a broader audience.

- Usability inspection methods present a fairly low hurdle to practitioners who want to use them. In general, it is possible to start using simple usability inspection after a few hours; inspection methods can be used in many different stages of the system development lifecycle.

- Usability inspection can be integrated easily into many established system development practices; it is not necessary to change the fundamental way projects are planned or managed in order to derive substantial benefits from usability inspection.

- Usability inspection provides instant gratification to those who use it; lists of usability problems are available immediately after the inspection and thus provide concrete evidence of aspects of the interface that need to be improved.

Book Structure

This book has five main parts. The first part (Chapter 1) is simply the overview chapter by Mack and Nielsen. It is intended to summarize the various usability inspection methods presented in the remaining chapters and outline the main issues covered by the book. If you only have time to read one chapter, this might be it.

The second part consists of Chapters 2 to 6 and covers specific inspection methods in depth. This part is organized according to a rough formality scale, with the most informal methods first and the more formal methods last. In Chapter 2, Nielsen describes the heuristic evaluation method which is perhaps the most informal method described in this book. Bias describes the pluralistic walkthrough method in Chapter 3 as a way to integrate evaluation perspectives from users, developers, human factors experts, and others. In Chapter 4, Wixon, Jones, Tse, and Casaday describe several inspection and design review methods they have developed over the years and offer a framework for understanding and conducting inspections. In Chapter 5, Wharton, Rieman, Lewis, and Polson describe the cognitive walkthrough method with its fairly detailed prescription for how to perform an inspection. Finally, in Chapter 6, Kahn and Prail describe formal usability inspections as a way of integrating several of the other methods into a coherent framework.

The third part of the book contains chapters that compare usability inspection with user testing as well as comparing various different usability inspection methods. Chapter 7 by Desurvire and Chapter 8 by Karat report on case studies where the same user interfaces were evaluated using multiple methods including usability inspection and usability testing. The purpose of the research studies was to compare the relative effectiveness of the evaluation methods and understand the methods' strengths and weaknesses. The results have implications for both practitioners and researchers. The research results from these studies provide valuable insights into the relative merits of the various methods and at what points in the development cycle the different methods can be used for optimal effect. Chapter 9 by Bradford and Chapter 10 by Brooks take a step back and consider the use of inspection and user testing in the broader context of product development and the system lifecycle, with Bradford reporting on a case study of methods used early in the development lifecycle and Brooks discussing ways of maximizing the market impact of the methods.

The fourth part of the book consists of Chapter 11 by Jeffries and Chapter 12 by Mack and Montaniz. The main goal of usability inspection is to derive lists of usability problems; these chapters consider how the concept of "usability problems" is related to the larger issues of improving user interface designs and how one should analyze problem reports from the inspectors.

The fifth part of the book looks at fundamental issues that may point towards future methodological developments. In Chapter 13, Wharton and Lewis discuss the role of psychological theory in inspection methods, and in

Chapter 14, Blatt and Knutson review several prototypes they have built to provide computer support to guide interface designers.

Finally, the comprehensive bibliography provides the necessary references for readers to access the extensive research literature summarized and discussed in this book.

Audience

The main audience for this book is user interface practitioners who are searching for cost-effective ways to improve their user interface designs. The book is structured with this reader in mind, starting out with descriptions of simple "discount usability engineering" methods like heuristic evaluation that can be learned very quickly and that can be immediately applied to the reader's current project, almost no matter what stage it is in. Later chapters describe progressively more formal inspection methods that may take a little longer to learn, but offer additional benefits. In addition to the method definition chapters, practitioners should also read the chapters comparing inspection methods and user testing; they should benefit from the recommendations for when to use what methods. The remaining chapters of the book are also written in a way that should help practitioners do their job better. But realistically speaking, we know that many practitioners want to start working with their new knowledge as soon as possible and the early chapters do make this possible.

The second audience for the book is researchers in the field of human-computer interaction (HCI) who are interested in recent developments in usability engineering in which inspection methods play a very prominent role. Researchers should benefit also from the introductory chapters defining the various methods and the comparative chapters with their interesting research results addressing the relative merits of the methods. Researchers may improve their conceptual understanding of usability problems and problem reports as fundamental aspects of usability engineering by reading the chapters about these topics. Also, they should find inspiration for further research in the chapters on psychological theory and computerized aids.

Finally, a third audience is students and professors in user interface design programs. These readers may choose individual chapters to supplement their main textbook for a basic course covering all of HCI, or they may use the entire book as a virtual textbook for an advanced course in usability inspection methods. In any case, usability inspection methods are so important in modern usability engineering that nobody can claim to have a complete education in the HCI field without exposure to at least a few inspection methods.

Jakob Nielsen and Robert L. Mack
February 1994

List of Contributors

Randolph G. Bias
IBM Corporation
11400 Burnet Road
Austin, TX 78758
bias@ausvm1.vnet.ibm.com

Louis Blatt
NCR Consulting Design Group
500 Tech Parkway
Atlanta, GA 30313
louis.blatt@atlantaga.ncr.com

Janice Bradford
Hewlett-Packard Laboratories
Measurement Systems Department
3500 Deer Creek Road, Bldg 26U
Palo Alto, CA 94304-1317
janice@hpljbw.hpl.hp.com

Patricia Brooks
Bell-Northern Research
P.O. Box 3511, Dept. OK15
Station C
Ottawa, K1Y 4H7

Canada
brooks@bnr.ca

George Casaday
Digital Equipment Corporation
110 Spit Brook Road, zk01-2/c21
Nashua, NH 03062-2698
casaday@vaxuum.enet.dec.com

Heather Desurvire
Citibank
c/o Carmina Serrano
909 Third Avenue 31st Floor
New York, NY 10043
ccorp!apple!heather@uunet.UU.NET or heather@acm.org

Robin Jeffries
SunPro, Sun Microsystems
2550 Garcia Avenue
Mountain View, CA 94043
Robin.Jeffries@Eng.Sun.com

Sandra Jones
Boston College
33 Puritan Road
Arlington, MA 02174
joness@bcvms.bc.edu

Michael J. Kahn
Hewlett-Packard
Human Factors Engineering, 48NA
19483 Pruneridge Avenue
Cupertino, CA 95014
michael_kahn@hpg200.hp.com

Clare-Marie Karat
IBM T.J. Watson Research Center
30 Saw Mill River Road
Hawthorne, New York 10532
ckarat@watson.ibm.com

James F. Knutson
NCR Consulting Design Group
500 Tech Parkway
Atlanta, GA 30313
jim.knutson@atlantaga.ncr.com

Clayton Lewis
University of Colorado at Boulder
Department of Computer Science
Campus Box 430
Boulder, CO 80309
clayton@cs.colorado.edu

Robert L. Mack
IBM T. J. Watson Research Center, Hawthorne
PO Box 704
Yorktown Heights, NY 10598
maier@watson.ibm.com

Frank Montaniz
Cheyenne Software Inc.
3 Expressway Plaza
Roslyn Heights, NY 11577
frankm@chey.com

Jakob Nielsen
SunSoft
2550 Garcia Avenue
Mountain View, CA 94043-1100
jakob.nielsen@eng.sun.com

Amanda Prail
Hewlett-Packard
Human Factors Engineering
19483 Pruneridge Avenue
Cupertino, CA 95014
amanda_prail@hpg200.hp.com

Peter Polson
University of Colorado at Boulder
Department of Psychology
Campus Box 345
Boulder, CO 80309
ppolson@clipr.colorado.edu

John Rieman
University of Colorado at Boulder
Department of Computer Science
Campus Box 430
Boulder, CO 80309
rieman@cs.colorado.edu

Linda Tse
Independent Consultant
14 South London Street
Nahsua, NH 03062
linda@magman.mv.com

Cathleen Wharton
University of Colorado at Boulder
Department of Computer Science and Institute of Cognitive Science
Campus Box 430
Boulder, CO 80309
cwharton@cs.colorado.edu

Dennis Wixon
Digital Equipment Corporation
110 Spit Brook Road
Nashua, NH 03062
wixon@usable.enet.dec.com

Usability Inspection Methods

Chapter 1   *Executive Summary*

Robert L. Mack

IBM T. J. Watson Research Center

Jakob Nielsen

SunSoft

This chapter provides an overview of the main usability inspection methods, with reference to the chapters that treat individual issues in more depth.

1.1   *Definition of Usability Inspection*

Usability inspection is the generic name for a set of methods based on having evaluators inspect or examine usability-related aspects of a user interface. Usability inspectors can be usability specialists, but they can also be software development consultants with special expertise (e.g., knowledge of a particular interface style for graphical user interfaces), end users with content or task knowledge, or other types of professionals. The different inspection methods have slightly different goals (see Section 1.2), but normally, usability inspection is intended as a way of evaluating user interface designs. In usability inspection, the evaluation of the user interface is based on the considered judgment of the inspector(s). The individual inspection methods vary as to how this judgment is derived and on what evaluative criteria inspectors are expected to base their judgments. In general, the defining characteristic of usability inspection is the reliance on judgment as a source of evaluative feedback on specific elements of a user interface.

We can contrast inspections to other kinds of evaluation methods. The four basic ways of evaluating user interfaces are: *automatically* (usability measures computed by running a user interface specification through evaluation software); *empirically* (usability assessed by testing the interface with real users); *formally* (using exact models and formulas to calculate usability measures); and *informally* (based on rules of thumb and the general skill, knowledge, and experience of the evaluators). Usability inspections correspond to the latter category of informal methods.

With the current state of the art, automatic methods do not work and formal methods are very difficult to apply and do not scale up well to complex, highly interactive user interfaces. Empirical methods are the main way of evaluating user interfaces, with user testing probably being the most commonly used method. Often, real users can be difficult or expensive to recruit in order to test all aspects of all the versions of an evolving design. In this respect, inspection methods are a way to "save users." Several studies of usability inspection methods have discovered that many usability problems are overlooked by user testing, but that user testing also finds problems that are overlooked by inspection. This suggests that the best results are achieved by combining empirical tests and inspections. The relationship between usability inspection and user testing is discussed in many chapters, and in particular, by Desurvire (Chapter 7), Karat (Chapter 8), and Brooks (Chapter 10).

We coined the term "usability inspection" in reference to function and code inspection methods that have long been used in software engineering for debugging and improving code (Ackerman et al. 1989; Fagan 1976, 1986; Freedman and Weinberg 1990; Russell 1991; Stevens 1989; Weller 1993). Admittedly, most usability inspection methods that began to appear in the published HCI literature around 1990 were developed without much explicit connection to the achievements in the program inspection field. The main exception to this historical fact is the formal usability inspection method described by Kahn and Prail (Chapter 6), which was explicitly intended to leverage off developers' program inspection methods.

1.2   Inspection Objectives

Typically, a usability inspection is aimed at finding usability problems in an existing user interface design, and then using these problems to make recommendations for fixing the problems and improving the usability of the design. This means that usability inspections are normally used at the stage in the usability engineering cycle when a user interface design has been generated and its usability (and utility) for users needs to be evaluated.

Identifying Usability Problems

Usability problems can be defined as aspects of a user interface that may cause the resulting system to have reduced usability for the end user. Usability is a fairly broad concept that basically refers to how easy it is for users to learn a system, how efficiently they can use it once they have learned it, and how pleasant it is to use. Also, the frequency and seriousness of user errors are normally considered to be constituent parts of usability. Thus, a user can find an interface element to be problematic for many reasons: It might make the system harder to learn; it might make it slower for users to perform their tasks; it may cause usage errors; or it may simply be ugly or otherwise unpleasing. Much of the work of usability inspection is concerned with classifying and counting the number of usability problems found in an inspection. Such analyses depend on the exact definition of what constitutes a usability problem and judgments as to how different phenomena might constitute manifestations of a single, underlying problem. It is difficult to make these distinctions, but often common sense is sufficient to determine what constitutes a usability problem. From the general definition of usability problem, one can say that any aspect of the design where a change would lead to improved system measures on one or more usability measures should be counted as a usability problem.

Usability Engineering Lifecycle

Identifying user interface problems, either in testing or through inspections is important, but it is only a part of a larger process. After the list of usability problems has been generated, a development team must redesign the user interface in order to fix as many of the problems as possible. To do so involves further types of information and analyses; these begin to point to a larger usability engineering context. We will discuss the role of inspections in the larger context of usability engineering in later sections, especially in Section 1.5. The following three points provide an overview of the use of inspection problem reports for influencing design.

- Fixes and other redesign suggestions must be generated. Usability inspection methods are generally better at finding problems than at driving the design of improved user interfaces, so additional considerations based on other usability methods may be needed for this stage. Typically, usability problem reports do contain suggestions for redesigns as noted by Jeffries (Chapter 11) and Desurvire (Chapter 7). In many cases it is also obvious just from knowing about a usability problem how it can be fixed. Furthermore, some inspection methods recommend including meetings of teams of developers and usability specialists (Wixon et al., Chapter 4; Kahn and Prail, Chapter 6) where redesign solutions can be hashed out.

- Effective use of a list of usability problems typically requires that these problems be prioritized with respect to the severity of each problem. As discussed in several chapters, most notably Brooks (Chapter 10), priorities are necessary to avoid expending disproportionate efforts on fixing usability problems that may not matter much to users anyway. Severity ratings are normally derived from an estimate of the expected user or market impact of each usability problem. In general, severity ratings are not a mainstream characteristic of usability inspection methods, but Nielsen (Chapter 2), Karat (Chapter 8), and Desurvire (Chapter 7) do give some examples of how to rate usability problems.

- Finally, it is necessary to get an estimate of the software cost associated with implementing the suggested redesigns. Several software engineering methods exist for estimating the programming cost. Although they may not be highly accurate, they can still provide useful information for the rough cost-benefit analysis that will be needed to make the final decision as to what usability problems can be fixed. Severe usability problems will normally be fixed no matter what their cost. It is often possible to fix many less severe problems that involve modest changes to the code. These trade-offs should not be considered part of the usability inspection method itself: It is preferable to have problem reports point out even those usability problems the inspector may judge to be too expensive to fix, because it is sometimes possible for design teams to develop alternative and much cheaper redesign suggestions.

Team Building and Education

Another objective of usability inspection methods can be the communication of information among the members in group inspection methods (Wixon et al., Chapter 4). As noted by Kahn and Prail (Chapter 6), there are considerable educational benefits to be gained as inspectors without usability expertise are made aware of the usability problems found by inspection. This exposure to additional usability concerns seems to be an effective way to increase developers' appreciation for the user-oriented perspectives in software development.

Usability inspection can also be used in traditional courses since the discussion of lists of usability problems is a good way to make usability issues and problems concrete for the students. Nielsen (Chapter 2) describes ways in which instructors can use usability inspection to provide rapid training of students in user interface design classes.

1.3   *Inspection Methods*

Usability inspection is the generic term for several methods, including at least the following eight:

- *Heuristic evaluation* (Chapter 2) is the most informal method and involves having usability specialists judge whether each dialogue element conforms to established usability principles. These principles are normally referred to as the heuristics (see Table 2.2 on page 30 for a sample list of heuristics) and give the method its name.

- *Guideline reviews* are inspections where an interface is checked for conformance with a comprehensive list of usability guidelines. However, since guideline documents contain on the order of 1,000 guidelines, guideline reviews require a high degree of expertise and are fairly rare in practice. This book does not contain a specific example of guideline reviews, but the method can be considered as somewhat of a cross between heuristic evaluation and standards inspection.

- *Pluralistic walkthroughs* (Chapter 3) are meetings where users, developers, and human factors people step through a scenario, discussing usability issues associated with dialogue elements involved in the scenario steps.

- *Consistency inspections* (Chapter 4) have designers representing multiple projects inspect an interface to see whether it does things in a way that is consistent with their own designs. Thus, consistency inspections are aimed at evaluating consistency across the family of products that has been evaluated by an inspection team.

- *Standards inspections* (Chapter 4) have an expert on some interface standard inspect the interface for compliance. Thus, standards are aimed at increasing the degree to which a given interface is in the range of other systems on the market that follow the same standards.

- *Cognitive walkthroughs* (Chapter 5) use a more explicitly detailed procedure to simulate a user's problem-solving process at each step in the human-computer dialogue, checking to see if the simulated user's goals and memory for actions can be assumed to lead to the next correct action.

- *Formal usability inspections* (Chapter 6) are intended to be very similar to the code inspection methods with which many software developers are already familiar. In this method, the various participants have well-defined responsibilities: A moderator is appointed to manage both individual and focused inspections, and the full team inspection meeting; a design owner is responsible for design and redesigns; the inspectors have the job of finding problems; and a scribe records all defects and issues identified during the meeting. Inspections are performed through a six-step process: planning, a kickoff meeting, a preparation phase where inspectors review the interface individually, the main inspection review when the inspectors' lists of usability problems are merged, and a follow-up phase where the effectiveness of the inspection process itself is assessed.

- *Feature inspections* focus on the function delivered in a software system; for example, whether the function as designed meets the needs of intended end users. Feature inspections can involve not only evaluation of a function, but can also involve the design of that function. Feature inspections are not discussed in any depth in this book, although several chapters refer to the need for inspections to focus on the usefulness of interface function, and not simply the usability of the interface, as an implementation of that function (e.g., Desurvire, Chapter 7). Another example referred to in this book is programming walkthroughs, discussed briefly by Wharton et al. (Chapter 5) as a variation of cognitive walkthroughs. The objective of the programming walkthrough is to design a programming language, starting from general attributes of the language, and elaborating the goals, subgoals, and actions required to accomplish a specific programming task. Programming walkthroughs are also discussed in depth in Bell (1992), and Bell et al. (1994).

1.4   Inspection Methodology Issues

Choosing a usability inspection method requires consideration of several methodology issues, beginning with the objectives of the inspection. Nearly all chapters discuss one or more of these issues. Moreover, inspection objectives are typically driven by development constraints, as much as by the appropriateness of a method for some usability-related objective. In this section we provide a brief summary of these methodology issues and pointers to chapters that focus discussion on them. We also recommend Chapter 4 by Wixon et al. for its suggested "lens of inspection" metaphor for making methodology decisions (see Figure 4.1 on page 80).

Objectives

We have already identified the high-level objectives of inspections: Identify potential usability problems and provide design-relevant information that can contribute to improving the usability of a product. In a software development context, however, these high-level objectives must be resolved into more specific objectives. Section 1.3 summarized several possible inspection methods, but selecting one of them requires a more specific objective. Objectives also often involve taking into account development constraints and trade-offs. Establishing clear objectives can only come with experience, informed by the experience of others as conveyed, for example, in case studies. All the chapters in this book discuss the importance of having clear objectives, but Chapter 10 by Brooks, Chapter 4 by Wixon et al., and Chapter 6 by Kahn and Prail, in particular, provide useful discussions and examples about the relation between the objectives of usability inspections and broader development contexts.

Inspection Framework

How does a usability inspection participant actually evaluate an interface? Each inspection method we summarized in Section 1.3 uses somewhat different guidelines. Heuristic inspections use heuristics that are derived from usability guidelines and principles. Examples are described in Chapter 2 by Nielsen, Chapter 8 by Karat, and Chapter 7 by Desurvire. Inspections based on evaluating conformity to an interface style, of course, adapt relevant guidelines in the form of checklists or heuristics. Examples are discussed in Chapter 4 by Wixon et al. These chapters also discuss variations in these heuristics which can reflect differences among users, the systems under evaluation, the user tasks involving those systems, and the objectives of the inspection in terms of what information the development team needs (again, see Chapter 10 by Brooks and Chapter 4 by Wixon et al.).

Cognitive walkthrough guidelines represent a clear contrast with interface guidelines and heuristics, at least on the surface. Cognitive walkthroughs are typically cast in the form of questions about the relationship between task goals attributed to users, and the interface actions needed to accomplish them (at least the actions the software designer intended). Chapter 13 by Wharton and Lewis and Chapter 6 by Kahn and Prail discuss the rationale and examples for such principles in depth; additional discussion can be found in Chapter 12 by Mack and Montaniz. These questions about goals and actions are generic, but are answered in the context of the specific task scenarios, appropriate for the users and task domain for which the interface is designed. Many variations in the specific form of cognitive walkthrough questions have been tried, and Chapter 6 by Kahn and Prail, Chapter 8 by Karat, Chapter 12 by Mack and Montaniz, and, of course, Chapter 5 by Wharton et al. provide or point to examples.

Deciding what guidelines to adopt is really deciding what usability inspection method to choose. This level of decision must be made by broader considerations, including the relative effectiveness of results provided by the method and how easy methods are to learn and use. These issues are further discussed later in the chapter.

Scenarios

Should inspectors evaluate an interface in terms of specific end-user tasks, or should they be encouraged to interact with the interface with more general and open-ended instructions? Most of the chapters that discuss applications of specific inspection methods make the case for asking inspectors to use specific task scenarios in their inspection. The rationale is that scenarios, properly chosen, represent how the system is intended to be used by end users. In this context, properly chosen means representative of end-user tasks or chosen explicitly to expose inspectors to particular aspects of the interface. Asking inspectors to evaluate the system in terms of task scenarios provides a task-oriented perspective on the interface. This perspective is essential for cognitive walkthroughs because task scenarios represent a structure and flow of goals and actions whose obviousness is precisely what inspectors are supposed to evaluate.

On the other hand, as Nielsen argues in Chapter 2, there are advantages to giving inspectors more open-ended instructions for evaluating a system. Real users will not necessarily be given explicit task scenarios. They will generate their own goals and combine exploration, inference, and training to map them into interface actions. Moreover, giving inspectors specific scenarios, while it controls their focus, also constrains what they might try doing with the system, and hence what they might discover. To the extent that inspectors create their own task-orientation, they will explore the interface through scenarios anyway.

The use of scenarios involves the obvious trade-off between ensuring that inspectors inspect an interface in terms of a specific focus and task flow that a usability specialist cares about, and allowing a potentially more open-ended and inspector-driven exploration and exposure to an interface. Scenarios ensure that certain interface features are evaluated. Controlled comparisons across users or other conditions are possible. When scenarios are not prescribed, there is potentially more opportunity for inspectors to explore more diverse aspects of the interface, although this depends on the instructions inspectors are given, and how complex the interface is. Inspectors who are not given specific scenarios typically explore the interface in terms of meaningful tasks of their own choice. As we suggested, the range of tasks that might be spontaneously carried out depends on how much inspectors are encouraged to explore and how task-oriented they are. Of course, in some cases, a system under inspection may have a limited set of tasks associated with it and scenario-driven inspection is constrained. Desurvire (Chapter 7) and Nielsen (Chapter 2) both discuss examples involving phone-based interface prototypes.

For the evaluation of very complex domain-specific systems, scenarios can be created from actual user task data to help the inspectors understand how users are expected to interpret and act on the interface. The scenario can thus supply the domain knowledge needed to operate the system that the inspectors may not have and allow them to perform their evaluation even when they are not domain specialists themselves (Bradford, Chapter 9; Nielsen, Chapter 2).

Inspector Experience

Who should carry out inspections? What experience and skills should inspectors have? Several chapters compare inspections carried out by groups with different types of expertise. Nielsen (Chapter 2), Desurvire (Chapter 7), and Karat (Chapter 8) discuss these questions for heuristic evaluation; and Kahn and Prail (Chapter 6), Mack and Montaniz (Chapter 12), and Wharton et al. (Chapter 5) discuss them for cognitive walkthroughs. Not surprisingly, experience with usability guidelines, user testing, and the design of user interfaces, leads to more effective usability inspection problem reporting. This is compared to inspectors who are software developers but lacking interface or usability expertise, or inspectors who are not experts in either software development or usability.

Who should do inspections could also depend on other objectives for inspection. One original objective, discussed by Wharton et al. (Chapter 5), was to allow usability specialists to conduct inspections themselves, as a way to leverage usability expertise and as an alternative for laboratory testing involving end users. Another objective, also discussed by Wharton et al., is to give software developers who might not have experience with usability issues or usability testing, experience with a user-centered perspective on interfaces. Yet another objective, exemplified in Nielsen's heuristic evaluation method, is to have nonexperts, perhaps even end users, carry out inspections, but to do so with much less control and formality; hence, less cost than would be entailed by formal user testing.

Clearly, there is considerable discretion in deciding who should do inspections, depending on the objectives of inspection. A mix of expertise and experience provides an opportunity to take advantage of fresh perspectives on the part of nonexperts and the more thoughtful evaluations likely to result from usability experts. The trade-offs here are obviously in time and effort at finding, training, and engaging inspectors from these different groups.

Individual or Group Inspection

Should individuals carry out inspections or should they be conducted by groups? Nielsen (Chapter 2), Wharton et al. (Chapter 5), and Desurvire (Chapter 7) make the case for individual inspections where the inspectors work independently of each other before their inspection reports are combined (though Wharton et al. also support the possibility of cognitive walkthroughs in group sessions). The rationale is to ensure that individuals have an opportunity to form their own intuitions about an interface and to feel free to make evaluations without being influenced by other opinions. Individual inspections can also be carried out by individuals at will, without the overhead of organizing group meetings.

On the other hand, there are advantages to having teams of more than one individual carry out inspections. Bias (Chapter 3), Desurvire (Chapter 7), Karat (Chapter 8), and Wixon et al. (Chapter 4) discuss these advantages in their chapters. People can reinforce each other, helping each other to notice problems that might not be seen individually. Conversely, there may be value to some level of critical evaluation of problems, if the problems that are "filtered out" are indeed implausible. Problem predictions that are not plausible end-user problems are potential false positives, and Jeffries (Chapter 11) discusses examples in more depth.

In fact, both individual and group inspections can be carried out in different phases of an inspection or as part of follow-on design activities. Nielsen (Chapter 2) discusses group debriefing of individual inspectors as one way of creating a group perspective on inspection problems, following a phase of individual inspections. Beyond the inspection (or end-user testing) process itself, the results of usability testing or inspection are typically presented to, and analyzed by, the larger design team. In this context it can be useful for the group as a whole to walk through interface screens in a scenario-driven way. Group design walkthroughs with a usability focus are an important type of design activity in a development project. Bias (Chapter 3), Kahn and Prail (Chapter 6), and Wixon et al. (Chapter 4), discuss group walkthroughs with this aim. (In Chapter 12, Mack and Montaniz also allude to examples of group design review and analysis, not otherwise discussed in this book: Karat and Bennett 1992a, b; Mack 1992.)

The trade-off in having both individual and group inspections is, of course, time. If time and inspectors are scarce, it may be necessary to make a decision about individual or group inspections. There are no clear-cut guidelines. It should be noted, however, that inspection results, like the results of user testing, must be analyzed beyond their raw form, in order to simplify them and derive implications for design. At some point, these follow-on analyses inevitably involve the larger development team.

Usability of Methods

Inspection methods need to be learned and applied efficiently. Existing inspection methods do differ in these two respects. One of the main motivations for heuristic evaluation is that it is relatively easy to learn and to apply. One of the main criticisms of cognitive walkthroughs is that the approach is not as easy to learn or to apply. This has led to several variations in the method; Chapter 5 by Wharton et al. discusses this evolution. Kahn and Prail (Chapter 6), and Mack and Montaniz (Chapter 12) also discuss potentially simpler variants.

The learnability and usability of an inspection technique is an important goal. With experience on the part of the HCI community, more efficient (and effective) methods will likely evolve. The cognitive jogthrough reported by Rowley and Rhoades (1992) may be an example (see also Wharton et al., Chapter 5). Of course, the effort to learn and to use a method could trade off with the effectiveness of the method in producing useful results. Currently, it is fair to say that the simpler technique, heuristic evaluation, is also the more effective in situations where the two techniques have been compared. However, it may be just as appropriate to view an inspection technique analogous to more traditional methods of usability testing and data analysis. A real mastery of empirical testing methods does require a degree of training and certainly experience with experimental design, data analysis, and so on. Analogously, cognitive walkthrough methods may require experience and only achieve their full potential over the long term. The cognitive walkthrough procedure takes time to learn, but once internalized, it can be applied efficiently (see Wharton et al., Chapter 5). For trained usability professionals, such an investment may be acceptable. For other professionals, such as software developers, this may not be the case. Finally, as Wharton et al. suggest there may be other objectives and results for which cognitive walkthroughs are better suited, such as generating design or interfaces.

1.5   Usability Inspection and the Usability Engineering Lifecycle

The preceding section discussed important methodological issues for choosing and adapting usability inspection methods, which motivated many of the discussions in the chapters of this book. Ultimately, however, we are interested in how usability inspection methods contribute to the larger context of usability engineering which certainly includes many other kinds of contributions by usability and software human factors specialists. This section continues to discuss methodology issues, but in the larger context. It is in this larger context that the objectives of usability inspection will be determined; hence, what specific method will be selected and where the results of inspections will be relevant. Consequently, the focus is on the validity of inspection data with respect to "real users'" experience, usefulness of data in influencing design, and the relationship between inspections, design and prototyping, and user testing.

Validity of Inspection Results

Ideally, we would want to answer many of the aforementioned methodology decisions by simply asking what set of decisions lead to the most effective results. Unfortunately, this turns out to be a difficult question to answer. The validity of inspection results can mean different things, but basically it is the answer to the question: How predictive are they of end-user problems? The answer to this question is important because ultimately we want to know how seriously to take problems identified by inspections, with respect to making recommendations for modifying software. Careful comparisons are hard to carry out and to interpret.

Jeffries (Chapter 11), Mack and Montaniz (Chapter 12), Nielsen (Chapter 2), Desurvire (Chapter 7) and Karat (Chapter 8) discuss in some depth the qualitative characteristics of concrete examples of usability problem reports and how well they predict (or fail to predict) end-user problems. We ask this question when inspection problem reports are obtained in place of user testing. We assume that problem reports predict problems that end users of the software are likely to actually have in laboratory testing. And the laboratory results are assumed, of course, to be representative of users' experience in the context of their work. The validity of inspection problem reports is analogous to the question of validity we have when we try to infer the usability of products in the marketplace from laboratory testing of usability involving representative end users.

In general, validity is defined relative to the criteria that are chosen to compare methods and results. The validity of results is related not to an absolute criteria, but to the goals and purpose of the work. This seems like a truism, but one often loses sight of it when discussing efficiency and validity which are sometimes treated as absolutes without mentioning a frame of reference.

The first comprehensive comparison of inspection techniques was done by Jeffries, Miller, Wharton, and Uyeda (1991). Their paper forms the background to several other comparisons reported in Chapter 7 by Desurvire, Chapter 8 by Karat (see also Karat et al. 1992), and Chapter 12 by Mack and Montaniz (see also Montaniz and Mack 1993). Jeffries et al. (1991) compared heuristic evaluation, cognitive walkthroughs, guideline-based inspection methods, and laboratory user testing. It is very difficult in any comparison to ensure that different inspection method and inspection group conditions are really comparable, but in general, the heuristic evaluation method resulted in problem reports that appeared to be better predictors of end-user problems (discovered in the laboratory testing) than cognitive walkthroughs or guideline-based inspections. Studies described by Desurvire and Karat in Chapters 7 and 8 report results consistent with the Jeffries et al. (1991) findings. In general, inspection problem reports typically do not predict end-user problems as well as we might wish, in order to confidently substitute inspection for end-user testing. Aggregated inspection problem predictions rarely do better than 30 to 50 percent of end-user problem types. Heuristic inspections appear to result in more overall predictions and better predictions of end-user problem types than cognitive walkthroughs. This is a broad generalization and the relative effectiveness of methods depends on many more specific factors, including the training and experience of inspectors, the type and severity of problem identified. The chapters by Desurvire (Chapter 7), Karat (Chapter 8), and Wharton et al. (Chapter 5) present in depth analyses of these interactions.

When considering the effectiveness of problem reports as problem predictions, not all problems are of equal interest. Identifying severe problems is especially important, and Jeffries (Chapter 11), Desurvire (Chapter 7), Karat (Chapter 8), Mack and Montaniz (Chapter 12), and Nielsen (Chapter 2) offer valuable suggestions on how to define severity, how to effectively classify the severity of problems, and how likely inspection techniques will identify severe problems. Severity is generally a derived measure based on how frequently a problem occurs and what impact it has on the user. Problems may be a nuisance, easily recoverable from, or may result in total task failure and extreme frustration for end users. These distinctions can be captured in severity ratings and, in some cases, in a qualitative analysis of problem content. There are no standards for analyzing severity, as Desurvire (Chapter 7) observes, but the chapters indicated above provide in-depth discussions of this important attribute of problem report content, as well as pointers to related literature.

Desurvire (Chapter 7), Jeffries (Chapter 11), and Mack and Montaniz (Chapter 12) discuss qualitative attributes of usability problems (predicted and observed in end-user testing) that may help explain misses or the failure of inspection problem reports to predict end-user problems. For example, in the case of inspections that are based on scenarios, it is possible that the problems end users have drive them into parts of an interface that create new tasks (and potential problems) which inspection participants do not experience in their more constrained situation. In effect, inspectors and end users are "evaluating" overlapping, but also partially incomparable sets of user task scenarios. Desurvire (Chapter 7), and Mack and Montaniz (Chapter 12) also distinguished different types of problems in terms of psychological function, noting that some types of problems may be easier for inspectors to infer and describe than others. For example, perceptual-motor problems involving the use of a mouse pointing device differ from seemingly more cognitive errors like choosing a wrong menu option. The former problems may not be obvious to inspectors unless they have experienced such problems themselves or observed them in others. Usability specialists with behavioral training or testing experience surely have an advantage here.

Nielsen (Chapter 2) offers a contrasting perspective on the predictability of inspection reports. Predicting end-user problems is highly desirable, of course, but if we grant that inspections are intended to substitute for testing, and that therefore we are not going to also collect end-user test data, we face a different problem in assessing the effectiveness of inspections. In this case we are interested in the relationship between number of inspections (and inspectors), and the number of problem types we can discover. This relationship has been the focus of Nielsen's work with heuristics evaluations, and is discussed in depth in his chapter. The good news for the "discount usability" perspective is that between four and five evaluators appear to be sufficient in most cases to identify 80 percent of the total usability problems we are likely to identify, in some asymptotic sense, with many more inspectors (and presumably would identify in end-user testing).

In addition to explaining the failure of inspection problem reports to predict end-user problems, we also need to account for problem predictions that do not correspond to end-user problems. These are false positives; Jeffries devotes much of Chapter 11 to discussing them. The issue for developers is whether and how to respond to predicted problems that do not occur for end users in a testing situation.

Finally, the validity of inspection problems, taken as end-user problems is the same question we must always ask with respect to more traditional end-user testing done in the laboratory. Inspections that do not use end users involve additional assumptions about how inspector intuitions (expressed in their problem reports) relate to "real" end-user problems. As Brooks (Chapter 10) quite effectively points out, however, usability problems are not the only thing a development team needs to worry about. She suggests that we assess the effectiveness of inspection methods and end-user testing against the insight they provide not only for usability, but also for the overall satisfaction customers ultimately come to have with the product in the workplace. Enhancing usability is important but not enough.

Effectiveness of Inspection Problem Information

Even more important than predicting end-user problems, is the effectiveness of inspection problem reports in improving the usability of an interface. This impact begins, of course, with a list of problem reports. Fixes and other redesign suggestions must be generated. Typically, usability problem reports do contain suggestions for redesigns as noted by Jeffries (Chapter 11) and Desurvire (Chapter 7); knowing about a usability problem is often sufficient to find an obvious way to fix it. However, usability inspection methods are generally better at finding problems than at driving the design of improved user interfaces, so additional considerations based on other usability methods may be needed for this stage. These considerations are also likely to require the involvement of the larger design team and additional methods that go beyond inspection procedures per se.

Several chapters, especially those of Desurvire (Chapter 7), Jeffries (Chapter 11), Kahn and Prail (Chapter 6), and Mack and Montaniz (Chapter 12), discuss qualitative characteristics of inspection report content and its relation to influencing interface design change. Inspectors often explicitly describe specific improvements or preferences in giving reports; these may be directly relevant to making potential design improvements. It can also be useful to encourage inspectors to describe potential problems in behavioral terms that describe possible underlying causes and consequences. These attributes of problem report content can provide useful clues for a design team about why problems occur and what to do about them. Similarly, it is useful when inspectors can make judgments about the potential severity of problems, whether in terms of quantitative ratings or in qualitative terms of describing the specific consequence of a user problem (e.g., losing data). Severity judgments can help to organize and prioritize problems. Jeffries' discussion in Chapter 11 of what makes an effective problem report is especially recommended.

Effective use of recommendations derived from usability problems typically requires that these problems be prioritized with respect to the severity of each problem and the cost estimated for implementing the suggested design change. As Brooks (Chapter 10) points out, priorities are necessary to avoid expending disproportionate efforts on fixing usability problems which may not matter much to users anyway. We discussed how problem severity can be analyzed in the preceding section. In general, severity ratings are not a mainstream characteristic of usability inspection methods. Severity ratings are normally derived from an estimate of the expected user or market impact of each usability problem; Nielsen (Chapter 2), Karat (Chapter 8), and Desurvire (Chapter 7) do give some examples of how to rate usability problems.

Another issue in problem analysis, discussed at length by Bradford (Chapter 9) and Jeffries (Chapter 11), is that software design problems are not always simple, but may involve larger design concepts that require more analysis and integration of results and implications across multiple interface features. A particular problem report may focus on a specific interface feature or issue, but on more careful examination, may point to larger issues or be correlated with other problem descriptions. In one example discussed at the workshop on which this book is based, an inspector predicted that some users might lose track of a newly created folder on a graphical windowing desktop. There was a visual discontinuity between the creation dialog and the desktop environment on which the newly created folder appeared, and the desktop was cluttered. This specific potential problem actually raised a more general question of how users find documents and folders on the desktop of this particular system. Inferring multiple views of a problem and synthesizing commonalities across superficially different problems requires the skills of a usability specialist.

Tackling these larger design issues also requires a good working relationship with the larger design and development team. These relationships are discussed by Brooks (Chapter 10), Kahn and Prail (Chapter 6), and Wixon et al. (Chapter 4). As Desurvire (Chapter 7) and Brooks (Chapter 10) point out, inspection data may not have the same surface credibility as user test data. For example, showing a video of a test user in a laboratory evaluation can be quite persuasive. It can be a challenge to establish the same kind of credibility for inspection data. Involving the design team in usability evaluations and inspections can be an effective way to increase the credibility of usability evaluations, as several contributors state, notably Bias (Chapter 3), Kahn and Prail (Chapter 6), and Wixon et al. (Chapter 4). Bias's "pluralistic walkthrough," involving end users, developers, and usability specialists in inspection teams is one promising possibility.

When to Use Inspection Methods

Given that usability inspections are part of a larger development process, it is also important to consider under what conditions inspections are appropriate or most effectively applied. With a few exceptions, such as feature inspection (discussed on page 6) inspection methods are not suited for use in the very early phases of the usability engineering lifecycle where no user interface design has been designed or implemented. During these early stages, methods like task analysis, competitive analysis, scenario writing, and envisioning can be used (Nielsen 1993a), but it is impossible to inspect and evaluate what does not yet exist. Similarly, inspection methods are poorly suited for usability engineering very late in the cycle, when the system has been released to the customers and the goal is to have them actually use it and get ideas for future versions. At this point, field studies, interaction logging, and the analysis of user-support calls are more appropriate than inspection methods.

In general, usability inspection methods require the existence of an interface design. They do not necessarily require this design to be *implemented,* however. Many inspection methods lend themselves to the evaluation of interface specifications because the methods do not require the inspector to actually *use* the system for anything. This means that inspections can be done relatively early in the design stage, especially compared to end-user usability testing (Bradford, Chapter 9).

Usability inspection methods are well suited as part of an iterative design process where they can be combined with other usability evaluation methods like user testing. A research result that has been replicated several times (Jeffries et al. 1991; Desurvire, Chapter 7; Karat, Chapter 8; Nielsen, Chapter 2) is that user testing and usability inspection have a large degree of nonoverlap in the usability problems they find. Consequently, it will pay off to use both methods in combination. A typical strategy is to apply a usability inspection method first to clean up the interface as much as possible, then to subject the revised design to user testing.

Cost-Benefit of Usability Inspection

Underlying decisions about what inspection method or method variant to use are trade-offs about time and resources. The cost and benefit of usability inspection, compared to end-user testing, or doing nothing, for that matter, is emerging as an important issue in the HCI community for planning and justifying the application of usability engineering methods in software development. Nielsen (Chapter 2) and Karat (Chapter 8) discuss the issue briefly in the context of usability inspections and provide pointers to more in-depth discussion (see Bias and Mayhew 1994).

Heuristic evaluation methods, for example, were originally motivated by Nielsen's "discount usability" perspective: Usability engineering activities are often difficult to justify and carry out in a timely way, but many activities can be done quickly and cheaply, and produce useful results. The methodology decisions we sketched in this section turn less on what is "correct" than on what can be done within development constraints. After all, with sufficient resources we would likely simply aim for rapid prototyping and end-user testing.

In contrast to the "discount usability engineering" perspective, cognitive walkthroughs appear more formal and "expensive." Learning the technique requires some exposure to psychological concepts and models of human problem solving and goal-oriented activity. The procedure itself involves a systematic question and answer protocol. With experience, the underlying concepts procedural formalities can be internalized and efficiently applied.

The language of goals, actions, and task breakdown has considerable face validity in thinking about human-computer interaction, and the usability of user interfaces (see Wharton and Lewis, Chapter 13). The attractiveness of cognitive walkthrough for many practitioners likely lies in the fact that it bases itself on this perspective. The effectiveness of cognitive walkthroughs may be better judged in terms of long-term use and experience by specialists, and in the context of software design, in contrast to software evaluation.

The ultimate trade-off, as Nielsen notes in Chapter 2 (see also Nielsen 1994a), may be between doing *no* usability-related assessment of a developing product and doing *some* kind, however limited in scope or formality. We suspect that most methodology decisions, however unsatisfactory they might appear from some ideal perspective, will nonetheless result in an inspection process that will produce useful insights into the usability of an interface and contribute to improving that interface.

Virtually all usability inspection methods perform detailed evaluation of individual dialogue elements in a single user interface design. An exception is consistency inspection where the elements of two or more interface designs are compared in order to ensure that similar things are done the same way. Another exception is heuristic estimation (Nielsen and Phillips 1993; Polson et al. 1992b) where the overall usability characteristics of an user interface are assessed. A typical application of heuristic estimation is where some other usability method has found a usability problem with the interface design, but where the fix would be too expensive to implement without further justification. Heuristic estimation can then be used to estimate the time users would take to complete typical tasks with the interface and with the proposed revised design, resulting in task analysis that can serve as input to a cost-benefit analysis to determine whether the change should be implemented.

1.6   Research Directions

The methodological issues discussed in the preceding sections point to possibilities for direct methodological research. First, much work is needed to improve methods with respect to making more and better problem predictions and streamlining the inspection process (this is especially true of cognitive walkthroughs). One way to improve inspection methods would be to better understand the process of making inspections.

As suggested by Mack and Montaniz (Chapter 12), sensitivity to potential problems probably is driven largely by inspectors' own difficulties in using various interfaces, the likelihood of inspectors having similar problems, and inspectors' skill at reflecting on and generalizing these personal experiences. Similarly, in Chapter 2 Nielsen notes the similarity between usability inspection and having problems as a participant in an empirical end-user test. Research might be directed at finding ways to help inspectors become more aware of their own experience and generalizing it for purposes of making inspection judgments, as Desurvire suggests (Chapter 7). Can we provide tools or training that encourage problem report content that is informative with respect to describing concrete problems, problem severity, and possible design improvements? A better understanding of how users learn or accomplish goals with software tools may yet suggest more effective heuristics or evaluation frameworks. Analyzing the effectiveness of inspection guidelines may help. For example, Nielsen (Chapter 2) performed a factor analysis of a database of 249 usability problems to discover a set of heuristics that provided as broad explanations as possible of these problems. Cognitive theory may contribute here, as Wharton and Lewis argue in Chapter 13.

A second direction would directly tackle the question raised by several contributors, especially Brooks (Chapter 10), of how valid inspection data are with respect to the larger real-world context of software under inspection. What do inspections (or empirical data) really predict? Are schemes for characterizing problem severity valid in the marketplace? Answers to these questions bear on the cost-benefit justification for testing or inspections, on possibilities for improving inspection methods, or even for specifying what methods are best suited for what evaluation or design questions. A longitudinal study that focused on problems or feedback in terms specific enough to assess the relevance of earlier feedback during development, would be invaluable.

A third area of research would be to improve the way inspection data are analyzed and how results may be used more effectively in the larger development cycle. Design and evaluation should be, and typically are, tightly linked; this relationship needs to be understood and supported.

Programming walkthroughs, mentioned earlier as an example of feature inspections (see Bell et al. 1994) suggest the possibility and value of closely integrating the evaluative and generative design capabilities of inspections. We suspect that many early design activities involve a close interleaving of generation and evaluation, sharing many of the attributes of cognitive and programming walkthroughs. Mack and Montaniz (Chapter 12) discuss examples of such design activities briefly, alluding to group design methods involving scenario-driven usability walkthroughs developed by Bennett (1984), and Karat and Bennett (1992a, 1992b). A recent example from our own (Mack's) laboratory involved taking seriously the often made recommendation to write a user manual for new software before a line of code is written. We wrote a quick reference guide for new users of a speech recognition interface for a graphical windowing environment (see J. Karat 1994), and used it to guide early interface design. We walked the design team through progressively more concrete versions of the design guide, comparing handwritten sketches of the designer's initial interface ideas against questions and tasks we thought were plausible for end users learning to use the system. We found this technique to be extremely useful in both evaluating design ideas and generating new ones. We did not use cognitive walkthroughs explicitly, but the language of goals and goal-action matches and mismatches was quite natural in this context.

Finally, we believe that there is a need to develop tools for cumulating, organizing, and helping to apply information based on inspections, not only within a single product development cycle but also across multiple products. Several chapters, especially Bradford (Chapter 9) and Jeffries (Chapter 11), suggested a need for methods of analyzing usability feedback, from inspections or from end-user testing, in more integrative ways for purposes analyzing broader design issues and trade-offs. We see promise in integrating design rationale schemes such as QOC (MacLean et al. 1991a, 1991b; see also MacLean and McKerlie 1994) with the analysis of design implications of inspection data. The QOC technique (an acronym for Question, Option and Criteria) lays out a space of design questions (or issues), and develops for each one a decision tree of design (or implementation) options associated with criteria that might be used for deciding among options. Important design issues and decision criteria can be raised by the results of empirical tests and inspections. The generation of design criteria for selecting among options might also be driven by inspection data. Issues can be compared and trade-offs made potentially more easily.

Blatt and Knutson (Chapter 14) discuss software tools under development at NCR that are intended to provide such criteria to give software developers access to usability and user interface design expertise and experience across multiple products. This online repository would include interface and usability guidelines, examples of usable design from previous products, and guidelines and support for conducting inspections and empirical testing.

1.7 Conclusions

The chapters in the book represent a wide range of applied experience with usability inspection methods and their role in the larger usability inspection context. Usability engineers who are considering adopting such methods, or who want to reflect on and refine similar methods already being used, should find these chapters very informative. Usability inspections are not yet a substitute for user testing, but appear to be quite effective for generating useful insight into the usability of a developing interface where end-user testing simply cannot be done quickly enough or with sufficient scope to answer all the usability questions that come up in a development process. Still, there is much room for improving these methods, and practitioners and HCI researchers are invited to take the opportunity to build on the solid work represented in this volume.

Chapter 2   *Heuristic Evaluation*

Jakob Nielsen
SunSoft

Most usability engineering methods can contribute substantially to the usability of the resulting interface *if only they were used* during the project lifecycle. But even the best method will have zero impact on the product if it does not get used. Unfortunately, experience has shown that many developers find many usability methods to be intimidating, too expensive, and too difficult and time-consuming to use (Nielsen 1994a). In order to overcome this problem, I have long advocated the use of so-called discount usability engineering (Nielsen 1989b, 1990b) with methods that are cheap, fast, and easy to use. Heuristic evaluation is one of the main discount usability engineering methods. It is easy (can be taught in a half-day seminar); it is fast (about a day for most evaluations); and it is as cheap as you want it. Even though the results of using heuristic evaluation improve with the more you know and the more carefully you apply the method, one of its virtues is that the "intimidation barrier" is very low, leading to immediate gratification.

2.1   How to Conduct a Heuristic Evaluation

Heuristic evaluation (Nielsen and Molich 1990; Nielsen 1992a) is a usability engineering method (Nielsen 1993a) for finding the usability problems in a user interface design so that they can be attended to as part of an iterative design process. Heuristic evaluation involves having a small set of evaluators examine the interface and judge its compliance with recognized usability principles (the "heuristics").

In general, heuristic evaluation is difficult for a single individual to do because one person will never be able to find all the usability problems in an interface. Luckily, experience from many different projects has shown that different people find different usability problems. Therefore, it is possible to improve the effectiveness of the method significantly by involving multiple evaluators. Figure 2.1 shows an example from a case study of heuristic evaluation where 19 evaluators were used to find 16 usability problems in a voice response system allowing customers access to their bank accounts (Nielsen 1992a). Each of the black squares in Figure 2.1 indicates the finding of one of the usability problems by one of the evaluators. The figure clearly shows that there is a substantial amount of nonoverlap between the sets of usability problems found by different evaluators. It is certainly true that some usability problems are so easy to find that they are found by almost everybody, but there are also some problems that are found by very few evaluators. Furthermore, one cannot just identify the best evaluator and rely solely on that person's findings. First, as further discussed in Section 2.5 on page 58, it is not necessarily true that the same person will be the best evaluator every time. Second, some of the hardest-to-find usability problems (represented by the leftmost columns in Figure 2.1) are found by evaluators who do not otherwise find many usability problems. Therefore, it is necessary to involve multiple evaluators in any heuristic evaluation (see the section titled "Determining the Number of Evaluators" on page 32 for a discussion of the best number of evaluators). My recommendation is normally to use three to five evaluators since one does not gain that much additional information by using larger numbers.

Heuristic evaluation is performed by having each individual evaluator inspect the interface alone. Only after all evaluations have been completed are the evaluators allowed to communicate and have their findings aggregated. This procedure is important in order to ensure independent and unbiased evaluations from each evaluator. The results of the evaluation can be recorded either as written reports from each evaluator or by having the evaluators verbalize their comments to an observer as they go through the interface. Written reports have the advantage of presenting a formal record of the evaluation, but require an additional effort by the evaluators and the need to

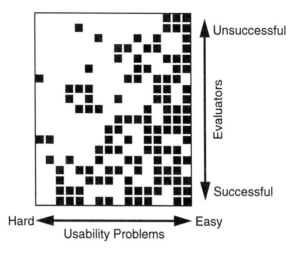

Figure 2.1 *Illustration showing which evaluators found which usability problems in a heuristic evaluation of a banking system. Each row represents one of the 19 evaluators and each column represents one of the 16 usability problems. Each square shows whether the evaluator represented by the row found the usability problem represented by the column: The square is black if this is the case and white if the evaluator did not find the problem. The rows have been sorted in such a way that the most successful evaluators are at the bottom and the least successful are at the top. The columns have been sorted in such a way that the usability problems that are the easiest to find are to the right and the usability problems that are the most difficult to find are to the left.*

be read and aggregated by an evaluation manager. Using an observer adds to the overhead of each evaluation session, but reduces the workload on the evaluators. Also, the results of the evaluation are available fairly soon after the last evaluation session since the observer only needs to understand and organize one set of personal notes, not a set of reports written by others. Furthermore, the observer can assist the evaluators in operating the interface in case of problems, such as an unstable prototype, and help if the evaluators have limited domain expertise and need to have certain aspects of the interface explained.

In a user test situation, the observer (normally called the "experimenter") has the responsibility of interpreting the user's actions in order to infer how these actions are related to the usability issues in the design of the interface. This makes it possible to conduct user testing even if the users do not know anything about user interface design. In contrast, the responsibility for analyzing the user interface is placed with the evaluator in a heuristic evaluation session, so a possible observer only needs to record the evaluator's comments about the interface, but does not need to interpret the evaluator's actions.

Two further differences between heuristic evaluation sessions and traditional user testing are the willingness of the observer to answer questions from the evaluators during the session and the extent to which the evaluators can be provided with hints on using the interface. For traditional user testing, one normally wants to discover the mistakes users make when using the interface; the experimenters are therefore reluctant to provide more help than absolutely necessary. Also, users are requested to discover the answers to their questions by using the system rather than by having them answered by the experimenter. For the heuristic evaluation of a domain-specific application, it would be unreasonable to refuse to answer the evaluators' questions about the domain, especially if nondomain experts are serving as the evaluators. On the contrary, answering the evaluators' questions will enable them to better assess the usability of the user interface with respect to the characteristics of the domain. Similarly, when evaluators have problems using the interface, they can be given hints on how to proceed in order not to waste precious evaluation time struggling with the mechanics of the interface. It is important to note, however, that the evaluators should not be given help until they are clearly in trouble and have commented on the usability problem in question.

Typically, a heuristic evaluation session for an individual evaluator lasts one or two hours. Longer evaluation sessions might be necessary for larger or very complicated interfaces with a substantial number of dialogue elements, but it would be better to split up the evaluation into several smaller sessions, each concentrating on a part of the interface.

During the evaluation session, the evaluator goes through the interface several times and inspects the various dialogue elements and compares them with a list of recognized usability principles. These heuristics are general rules that seem to describe common properties of usable interfaces (see Table 2.1 and Table 2.2 for two possible sets of heuristics). In addition to the checklist of general heuristics to be considered for all dialogue elements, the evaluator obviously is also allowed to consider any additional usability principles or

Simple and natural dialogue
Speak the users' language
Minimize the users' memory load
Consistency
Feedback
Clearly marked exits
Shortcuts
Precise and constructive error messages
Prevent errors
Help and documentation

Table 2.1 *Original list of usability heuristics. This specific list was developed by the author and Rolf Molich (Molich and Nielsen 1990), but it is similar to other usability guidelines. Each heuristic is discussed in considerable detail in (Nielsen 1993a). The last heuristic, help and documentation, was added in 1991.*

results that come to mind that may be relevant for any specific dialogue element. Furthermore, it is possible to develop category-specific heuristics that apply to a specific class of products as a supplement to the general heuristics. One way of building a supplementary list of category-specific heuristics is to perform competitive analysis and user testing of existing products in the given category and try to abstract principles to explain the usability problems that are found (Dykstra 1993).

In principle, the evaluators decide on their own how they want to proceed with evaluating the interface. A general recommendation would be that they go through the interface at least twice, however. The first pass would be intended to get a feel for the flow of the interaction and the general scope of the system. The second pass then allows the evaluator to focus on specific interface elements while knowing how they fit into the larger whole.[1]

---

[1] This two-pass approach is similar in nature to the phased inspection method for code inspection (Knight and Myers 1993). In theory, it should be possible to extend the phased inspection approach fully to heuristic evaluation and have evaluators conduct several passes through the interfaces, each time looking for violations of a single heuristic. In practice, however, such a multi-pass approach would be tedious, and it would seem unnatural to evaluators to "overlook" usability problems that were not related to the one issue they were supposed to inspect for in a given pass.

- *Visibility of system status:* The system should always keep users informed about what is going on, through appropriate feedback within reasonable time.
- *Match between system and the real world:* The system should speak the users' language, with words, phrases, and concepts familiar to the user, rather than system-oriented terms. Follow real-world conventions, making information appear in a natural and logical order.
- *User control and freedom:* Users often choose system functions by mistake and will need a clearly marked "emergency exit" to leave the unwanted state without having to go through an extended dialogue. Support undo and redo.
- *Consistency and standards:* Users should not have to wonder whether different words, situations, or actions mean the same thing. Follow platform conventions.
- *Error prevention:* Even better than good error messages is a careful design which prevents a problem from occurring in the first place.
- *Recognition rather than recall:* Make objects, actions, and options visible. The user should not have to remember information from one part of the dialogue to another. Instructions for use of the system should be visible or easily retrievable whenever appropriate.
- *Flexibility and efficiency of use:* Accelerators—unseen by the novice user—may often speed up the interaction for the expert user to such an extent that the system can cater to both inexperienced and experienced users. Allow users to tailor frequent actions.
- *Aesthetic and minimalist design:* Dialogues should not contain information which is irrelevant or rarely needed. Every extra unit of information in a dialogue competes with the relevant units of information and diminishes their relative visibility.
- *Help users recognize, diagnose, and recover from errors:* Error messages should be expressed in plain language (no codes), precisely indicate the problem, and constructively suggest a solution.
- *Help and documentation:* Even though it is better if the system can be used without documentation, it may be necessary to provide help and documentation. Any such information should be easy to search, focused on the user's task, list concrete steps to be carried out, and not be too large.

Table 2.2 *Revised set of usability heuristics derived from a factor analysis of 249 usability problems (Nielsen 1994c).*

Since the evaluators are not *using* the system as such (to perform a real task), it is possible to perform heuristic evaluation of user interfaces that exist on paper only and have not yet been implemented (Nielsen 1990c). This makes heuristic evaluation suited for use early in the usability engineering lifecycle.

If the system is intended as a walk-up-and-use interface for the general population or if the evaluators are domain experts, it will be possible to let the evaluators use the system without further assistance. If the system is domain-dependent and the evaluators are fairly naive with respect to the domain of the system, it will be necessary to assist the evaluators to enable them to use the interface. One approach that has been applied successfully is to supply the evaluators with a typical usage scenario (Carroll 1994; Carroll and Rosson 1990; Clarke 1991; Nielsen 1990c, 1994b), listing the various steps a user would take to perform a sample set of realistic tasks (as further discussed in Section 2.2 on page 36. Such a scenario should be constructed on the basis of a task analysis of the actual users and their work in order to be as representative as possible of the eventual use of the system.

The output from using the heuristic evaluation method is a list of usability problems in the interface with references to those usability principles that were violated by the design in each case in the opinion of the evaluator. It is not sufficient for evaluators to simply say that they do not like something; they should explain *why* they do not like it with reference to the heuristics in Table 2.1 or 2.2 or to other usability results. The evaluators should try to be as specific as possible and should list each usability problem separately. For example, if there are three things wrong with a certain dialogue element, all three should be listed with reference to the various usability principles that explain why each particular aspect of the interface element is a usability problem. There are two main reasons to note each problem separately: First, there is a risk of repeating some problematic aspect of a dialogue element, even if it were to be completely replaced with a new design, unless one is aware of all its problems. Second, it may not be possible to fix all usability problems in an interface element or to replace it with a new design, but it could still be possible to fix *some* of the problems if they are all known.

Heuristic evaluation does not provide a systematic way to generate fixes to the usability problems or a way to assess the probable quality of any redesigns. However, because heuristic evaluation aims at explaining each observed usability problem with reference to established usability principles, it will often be fairly easy to generate a revised design according to the guidelines provided by the violated principle for good interactive systems. Also, many usability problems have fairly obvious fixes as soon as they have been identified.

For example, if the problem is that the user cannot copy information from one window to another, then the solution is obviously to include such a copy feature. Similarly, if the problem is the use of inconsistent typography in the form of upper/lower case formats and fonts, the solution is obviously to pick a single typographical format for the entire interface. Even for these simple examples, however, the designer has no information to help design the exact changes to the interface (e.g., how to enable the user to make the copies or on which of the two font formats to standardize).

One possibility for extending the heuristic evaluation method to provide some design advice is to conduct a debriefing session after the last evaluation session. The participants in the debriefing should include the evaluators, any observer used during the evaluation sessions, and representatives of the design team. The debriefing session would be conducted primarily in a brainstorming mode and would focus on discussions of possible redesigns to address the major usability problems and general problematic aspects of the design. A debriefing is also a good opportunity for discussing the positive aspects of the design, since heuristic evaluation does not otherwise address this important issue.

Heuristic evaluation is explicitly intended as a "discount usability engineering" method (Nielsen 1989b, 1990b, 1993a, 1994a). Independent research (Jeffries et al. 1991) has indeed confirmed that heuristic evaluation is a very efficient usability engineering method. One recent case study found a benefit-cost ratio for a heuristic evaluation project of 48: The cost of using the method was about $10,500 and the expected benefits were about $500,000 (Nielsen 1994a). As a discount usability engineering method, heuristic evaluation is not guaranteed to provide "perfect" results or to find every last usability problem in an interface.

Determining the Number of Evaluators

In principle, individual evaluators can perform a heuristic evaluation of a user interface on their own, but the experience from several projects indicates that fairly poor results are achieved when relying on single evaluators. Averaged over six projects (Molich and Nielsen 1990; Nielsen and Molich 1990; Nielsen 1992a), single evaluators found only 35 percent of the usability problems in the interfaces. However, since different evaluators tend to find different problems, it is possible to achieve substantially better performance by aggregating the evaluations from several evaluators. Figure 2.2

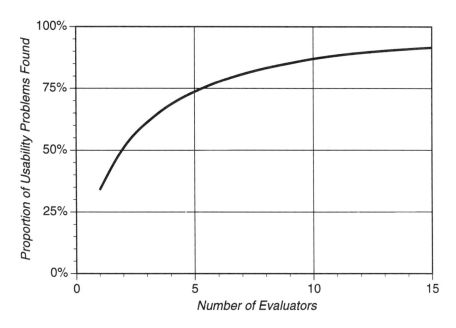

Figure 2.2 *Curve showing the proportion of usability problems in an interface found by heuristic evaluation using various numbers of evaluators. The curve represents the average of six case studies of heuristic evaluation (Nielsen 1992a).*

shows the proportion of usability problems found as more and more evaluators are added. The figure clearly shows that there is a nice payoff from using more than one evaluator. It would seem reasonable to recommend the use of about five evaluators, but certainly at least three. The exact number of evaluators to use would depend on a cost-benefit analysis. More evaluators should obviously be used in cases where usability is critical or when large payoffs can be expected due to extensive or mission-critical use of a system.

Nielsen and Landauer (1993) present such a model based on the following prediction formula for the number of usability problems found in a heuristic evaluation:

$$\text{ProblemsFound}(i) = N(1 - (1-\lambda)^i) \qquad \textbf{(EQ 1)}$$

where ProblemsFound(i) indicates the number of different usability problems found by aggregating reports from i independent evaluators, N indicates the total number of usability problems in the interface, and λ

indicates the proportion of all usability problems found by a single evaluator. In six case studies (Nielsen and Landauer 1993), the values of λ ranged from 19 percent to 51 percent with a mean of 34 percent. The values of N ranged from 16 to 50 with a mean of 33. Using this formula results in curves very much like that shown in Figure 2.2, though the exact shape of the curve will vary with the values of the parameters N and λ, which again will vary with the characteristics of the project.

In order to determine the optimal number of evaluators, one needs a cost-benefit model of heuristic evaluation. The first element in such a model is an accounting for the cost of using the method, considering both fixed and variable costs. Fixed costs are those that need to be paid no matter how many evaluators are used; these include time to plan the evaluation, get the materials ready, and write up the report or otherwise communicate the results. Variable costs are those additional costs that accrue each time one additional evaluator is used; they include the loaded salary of that evaluator as well as the cost of analyzing the evaluator's report and the cost of any computer or other resources used during the evaluation session. Based on published values from several projects the fixed cost of a heuristic evaluation is estimated to be between $3,700 and $4,800 and the variable cost of each evaluator is estimated to be between $410 and $900.

The actual fixed and variable costs will obviously vary from project to project and will depend on each company's cost structure and on the complexity of the interface being evaluated. For illustration, consider a sample project with fixed costs for heuristic evaluation of $4,000 and variable costs of $600 per evaluator. In this project, the cost of using heuristic evaluation with i evaluators is thus $(4,000 + 600i)$.

The benefits from heuristic evaluation are mainly due to the finding of usability problems, though some continuing education benefits may be realized to the extent that the evaluators increase their understanding of usability by comparing their own evaluation reports with those of other evaluators. For this sample project, assume that it is worth $15,000 to find each usability problem, using a value derived by Nielsen and Landauer (1993) from several published studies. For real projects, one would obviously need to estimate the value of finding usability problems based on the expected user population. For software to be used in-house, this value can be estimated based on the expected increase in user productivity; for software to

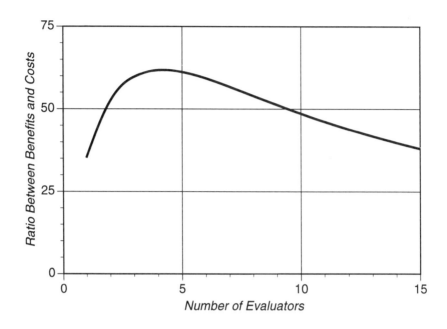

Figure 2.3 *Curve showing how many times the benefits are greater than the costs for heuristic evaluation of a sample project using the assumptions discussed in the text. The optimal number of evaluators in this example is four, with benefits that are 62 times greater than the costs.*

be sold on the open market, it can be estimated based on the expected increase in sales due to higher user satisfaction or better review ratings (Nielsen 1993c). Note that real value only derives from those usability problems that are in fact fixed before the software ships. Since it is impossible to fix all usability problems, the value of each problem found is only some proportion of the value of a fixed problem.

Figure 2.3 shows the varying ratio of the benefits to the costs for various numbers of evaluators in the sample project. The curve shows that the optimal number of evaluators in this example is four, confirming the general observation that heuristic evaluation seems to work best with three to five evaluators. In the example, a heuristic evaluation with four evaluators would cost $6,400 and would find usability problems worth $395,000.

2.2   Case Study: Evaluating a Highly Domain-Dependent System

This section presents detailed information about the use of heuristic evaluation to find usability problems in a rather complex telephone company application. Most uses of heuristic evaluation have concerned interfaces for broader categories of users, such as online information services or word processors, but as this example shows, it is also possible to use the method for interfaces that are intended for very specialized user populations.

The Integrating System

The domain-specific interface that was evaluated for this study was a prototype user interface for a system for internal telephone company use; it will be called the Integrating System in this chapter. Understanding the details of the Integrating System is fairly complicated and requires extensive knowledge of telephone company concepts, procedures, and databases. Since a detailed explanation is not necessary to understand the generally applicable lessons from the study, the Integrating System will only be outlined here. Briefly, the Integrating System provides a graphical user interface to access information from several backend systems in a uniform manner, despite the differences between the backend systems. The Integrating System can be used to resolve certain problems when data inconsistencies require manual intervention by a technician because the computer systems cannot determine which information is correct. The traditional method for resolving these problems involves having the technician compare information across several of these databases by accessing them through a number of traditional alphanumeric terminal sessions. The databases reside on different computers and have different data format and user interface designs, so this traditional method is somewhat awkward and requires the technicians to learn a large number of inconsistent user interfaces.

Performing this task involves a large amount of highly domain-specific knowledge about the way the telephone system is constructed and the structure of the different databases. Technicians need to know where to look for what data and how the different kinds of data are related. Also, the individual data items themselves are extremely obscure for people without detailed domain knowledge.

It should be noted that, even though it might seem possible in theory to avoid many of the underlying data inconsistencies by use of various well-known computer science techniques, maintaining consistency has proven very difficult because of the complexity and opportunity for human error involved in the application. The real-world systems underlying this application involve a large number of databases that have been in place for a long time with literally billions of data elements which cannot easily be changed, thus making some solution like the Integrating System necessary.

At the time of the usability study reported here, the Integrating System was prototype software that was not yet connected to the multitude of backend computers holding the real databases. Therefore, the system could not be used to freely access data but could only provide access to the information needed to resolve one particular request for manual assistance for one given problem. On the basis of a task analysis of the way real technicians resolved similar problems, a sample problem had been defined together with a series of steps a technician could go through to resolve it. Users had access to most of the functionality of the full Integrating System system, but could only retrieve the data that had been determined as relevant to the sample problem. Requests for any other data resulted in an error message. In other words, users of the prototype were restricted to working within a simple, prespecified usage scenario (Nielsen 1990c), but they could vary the sequence in which they initiated the various steps.

It should be emphasized that the user interface evaluated in this study was indeed an experimental prototype. Although it was developed by a highly skilled, experienced team, it was nevertheless *expected* to contain usability problems.[2] Indeed, the number of interface problems found was not unusual: Such problems are unavoidable without evaluation; iterative design is a necessary part of the usability engineering lifecycle (Nielsen 1993b). Finding as many usability problems as possible in the prototype stage of a project makes them considerably easier and cheaper to fix then than if the problems were to be discovered in later phases of the lifecycle (or not at all!).

---

[2] The presence of several such problems in the interface should not be taken as a sign that its designers were not competent or were insensitive to usability. Most of the evaluators were impressed by the general quality of the prototype user interface. The focus of the present discussion is the problems in the interface rather than its positive aspects, but readers should not interpret this focus as implying that the interface was not in other ways quite good.

The Evaluators

The evaluators were 11 usability specialists who had not been involved with the design of the prototype interface. Only one of the evaluators had a real understanding of the domain; the other 10 had no knowledge of the domain. To assess the evaluators' domain knowledge, they were asked to indicate their level of understanding of 17 system-related terms on a 1 to 3 scale in which 1 = does not know term, 2 = has some idea of its meaning, and 3 = knows the meaning of the term. As a control, the questionnaire also contained an eighteenth term with no meaning; this term was rated an average of 1.1, indicating that it was indeed unknown to the evaluators and that they did not overestimate their own knowledge. The evaluators gave the terms a mean rating of 1.9 when excluding the rating of the meaningless control term. This rating indicates that the evaluators did not have sufficient understanding of the central concepts of the system to be able to use it without help.

One should note the potential problems in using this term assessment method for the purpose of checking whether the terminology in a user interface is understandable. People who claim not to know a term probably do not know it. In contrast, people who claim that they do know a term may only *think* they know it, but in fact may be thinking about a related term with a different meaning. For the purpose of the current study, however, we were aware that the terminology in the system was somewhat obscure to non-specialists but could assume that it was familiar to the highly trained technicians who would be the intended real users. In contrast to traditional usability studies, the purpose of the questionnaire was therefore not to assess the terminology but to assess the evaluators.

Procedure for the Heuristic Evaluation

The heuristic evaluation consisted of four phases: a pre-evaluation training session, the actual evaluation, a debriefing session to discuss the outcome of the evaluation, and a severity rating phase during which the evaluators assessed the severity of the usability problems that had been found in the evaluation session. The first three phases were compressed into two days of real time, ensuring that a list of the usability problems found in the interface could be made available to the project developers at the end of the second day.

Briefing on the Method, the Domain, and the Scenario

Since the evaluators knew much too little about the domain to be able to use the system without help, the actual heuristic evaluation was preceded by a short (90 minutes) training session. First, the evaluators were given a general introduction to the heuristic evaluation method and were reminded of the set of heuristics. Since the evaluators were all usability specialists,[3] it was not necessary to teach these well-known usability principles as such; so, the presentation was mostly intended to provide a shared terminology for referring to usability problems and to ensure that the evaluators considered a broad spectrum of usability concerns when judging the interface.

The evaluators were then given a lecture on the domain being addressed by the Integrating System and were told about the general concepts of resolving database inconsistencies. Obviously, such a short lecture could in no way make the evaluators experts in this complicated domain, but it could at least give them some notion of the purposes of the system.

After the lecture on the domain, the evaluators were given a presentation on the specific scenario they were going to go through with the system. To ensure that the evaluators approached the Integrating System user interface from a fresh and unbiased perspective, they were not shown any screen-dumps of the actual system, nor were they told of the specific interaction techniques involved in using it. The presentation of the scenario covered each step in the resolution of the sample problem with respect to the underlying semantics of the steps and the domain-related reasons for the steps. For each step, the scenario explained what information had been retrieved by the previous step, how a technician would analyze that information, and what further action would be needed as a result of that analysis. For example, one step involved looking up further information about telephone numbers that had been found in a previous step to be associated with two addresses of interest. The scenario contained a total of seven such steps.

---

[3] No official certification exists to determine whether a person is a usability specialist. The evaluators in this study were employed with usability as the only or major part of their job description and had an average of seven years experience in the human-computer interaction field.

The Actual Evaluations

For the actual heuristic evaluation sessions, each evaluator conducted his or her evaluation individually and independently of the other evaluators. The evaluators were asked not to discuss the evaluation results until all evaluators had completed their evaluations. This procedure was intended to ensure unbiased evaluations from all evaluators.

Each evaluator was given one hour to perform the evaluation and was asked to evaluate the interface in two passes: first, by stepping through the prespecified usage scenario, and second by performing a more detailed analysis of individual dialogue elements. The reliance on the usage scenario was intended to expose the evaluators to the flow of the system and to give them as realistic a feel for the use of the system as possible, given that they did not really understand the domain of the system.

The list of steps in the scenario was made available to the evaluators for use during the evaluation session. The scenario description highlighted the specific actions that needed to be taken at each stage without explaining how these actions were to be achieved in the interface. Given the information in the scenario, all the evaluators were able to complete a session with the system, going through all the steps necessary to resolve the sample problem.

The evaluators were asked to find as many usability problems in the interface as possible, including both major and minor problems. They were asked to explicitly identify each problem to the observers who made a note of the problems for further analysis. In contrast to traditional usability testing, the observers were not charged with the responsibility of interpreting the comments since the evaluators pointed out the specific elements of the user interface they wanted changed.

The evaluators were also asked to state what established usability principle was violated by each usability problem and to classify the problem as either major or minor. The evaluators were generally not very good at providing this information during the evaluation session where they were more focused on inspecting the interface and finding new usability problems. Occasionally, the observers interrupted an evaluator to ask for more explicit references to established usability principles and the severity classification for a usability problem, but these interruptions were quickly abandoned as they seemed to interfere too much with the evaluators' work flow when finding usability problems. It appears that finding usability problems and the more detailed analysis of such problems are two different processes that should not be interleaved in a single session. Instead of the elicitation of severity classifications during the evaluation session, information about the severity of the usability problems was gained from a later survey of the evaluators, as discussed in a later section.

The evaluation sessions were observed by two specialists who made notes of the usability problems identified by the evaluators. These notes avoided the need for the evaluators to write reports listing the usability problems they had found; thus the evaluation process was speeded up since the aggregated list of usability problems was available immediately after the end of the last evaluation session.

One observer (the author) was a specialist in the heuristic evaluation method and one observer was a specialist in the Integrating System application and a member of the development team. Two observers were used since we were uncertain about the potential difficulties involved in managing the evaluation sessions; this study was our first attempt at using the heuristic evaluation method for the evaluation of a highly domain-specific interface. It turned out that the evaluation sessions ran smoothly; therefore, there should be no need to allocate more than a single observer for future studies. It is important, though, that the observer has a good understanding of the application so that the observer can answer the evaluators' questions during the evaluation sessions.

On the other hand, though, it was valuable to have a member of the development team present during the evaluation sessions. General insights gained during the observations were used later to formulate a new way of looking at certain aspects of the system. These insights were aimed at improvements in the overall interface and interaction flow rather than fixing a specific usability problem.

Debriefing

After the completion of all 11 evaluation sessions, a one-hour debriefing session was conducted with three of the evaluators, the two observers, and two additional members of the development team. All evaluators had been invited to the debriefing, but most were prevented from coming for practical reasons. The principal content of this session was a discussion of the general characteristics of the interface as well as speculations on potential improvements to address some of the major usability problems that had been found.

A major shortcoming of the heuristic evaluation method is that it identifies usability problems without indicating how they are to be fixed. In general, ideas for appropriate redesigns have to appear magically in the heads of the designers on the basis of their sheer creative powers without special assistance from the method. Of course, in practice, the identification of a usability problem often implies an appropriate and sometimes even obvious solution.

The debriefing session indicated one possible approach towards modifying the heuristic evaluation method to include advice for the redesign phase. Several of the usability problems were discussed in more or less of a brainstorming mode, leading to several ideas for redesigns. The brainstorming format was not followed completely, however, as critical and comparative comments were allowed.

A major outcome of the debriefing session was an idea for a higher-level redesign of the interface to make it more object-oriented. This single redesign would have the potential to fix eight of the ten most severe usability problems as well as several other problems. The prototype interface treated query outputs as a plain text event, even though they were highly formatted and consisted of a predetermined number of fields with specific meaning. An alternative, more object-oriented, interface design could recognize the individual data elements on the screen as user-oriented objects, even though they had been produced as output from external database queries. Instead of the function-oriented construction of new queries into which data could be pasted, the object-oriented view would concentrate on the data and allow users to apply further queries to any selected data. For example, one possible redesign would have users select a data field and pop up a list of those external databases for which a query for that datatype would be meaningful. Thus, at the same time, the interface would be simplified (by only presenting the relevant databases) and several steps and usability problems in the construction of the query could be avoided.

Similar insights as to the need for a more object-oriented interface could have been derived either from first principles concerning graphical user interface design (Nielsen et al. 1992), a careful task analysis of the users' true information needs rather than their current work practices, or some forms of user testing. It is notable that the debriefing provided similarly concrete design ideas converting the more abstract theoretical principles into a practical opportunity for achieving a redesigned interface.

Usability Problems

Forty usability problems were found in the part of the user interface that was actually covered by the usage scenario. These problems will be referred to as the "core" usability problems, since they are related to that part of the user interface that was evaluated in depth. The user interface included a few additional features that were not part of the usage scenario; these features were not subjected to nearly the same degree of scrutiny. Such a focus on part of a user interface in an early evaluation exercise is acceptable as long as one remembers to study the remaining parts more closely later. Also, the part of the user interface that is being studied should be a fairly large and preferably important part of the overall interface. These conditions were met in our case.

One example of a major core usability problem was that the window containing the systems' responses would not automatically scroll when new information had been retrieved. It was thus possible for new information to be invisible, causing the users to wait too long before acting on it. An example of a minor problem was that the input field in a certain dialog box did not automatically get the input focus when the box appeared on the screen. Thus, users had to waste a small amount of time on clicking in the field before they could start typing.

In addition to the 40 "core" usability problems in the part of the user interface covered by the scenario, four usability problems were found in other parts of the interface that were not subjected to intensive evaluation. Since these parts of the interface were not part of the scenario, they were not evaluated by all the evaluators, but only by those who chose to explore additional parts of the system. One example of a noncore usability problem was that the Find Text function was case-sensitive, so that searches for FOO, Foo, and foo would give different results. Users may not always remember what case was used for certain text, so a case-insensitive search would be better. Since the Find Text function was not part of the scenario, most evaluators never used it; thus, it was not evaluated exhaustively.

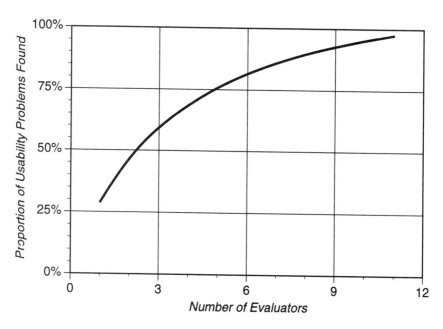

Figure 2.4 *Graph showing the number of core usability problems in the Integrating System found by aggregating the findings of 1 through 11 evaluators.*

The statistical analyses of the usability problems that are reported below have been limited to the core usability problems since they were the only ones that were investigated systematically. The only exception is the estimation of the benefits from the heuristic evaluation, where all 44 problems are taken into account. The four noncore usability problems were indeed discovered as a result of the study and therefore do contribute to the practical benefits from the use of the method.

The mean number of core usability problems found by a single evaluator was 11.5 or 29 percent, confirming the aforementioned result that one cannot rely on having a single person perform heuristic evaluation (Nielsen and Molich 1990). Figure 2.2 shows the number of usability problems that would have been found by using various numbers of evaluators from 1 to 11.

In addition to the usability problems, four minor programming errors (bugs) were discovered during the heuristic evaluation. These problems cannot be classified as usability problems as such, even though bugs obviously do impact usability negatively. The main conclusion from the discovery of bugs during the heuristic evaluation is that users always find new ways to exercise a program; therefore, a debugging process cannot be completed without exposing the software to use outside the development team.

A further lesson from the bugs is that prototype software is notoriously prone to crashing and that one should be prepared to reboot the system during any interface testing. In fact, the Integrating System prototype was very robust for a prototype and only crashed once during the 11 hours of evaluation sessions. We had made sure to have the programmers stand by using a rotating scheme that guaranteed that one of them would always be available. Recovery from the one crash therefore took only about five minutes.

User Testing

One cannot expect heuristic evaluation to address all usability issues when the evaluators have no knowledge of the actual users and their tasks, since these two aspects are critical elements in usability engineering. Therefore, we supplemented the heuristic evaluation with a small scale user test. We conducted formal user testing with four users and also had one of the users' managers use the system. In retrospect, we regret not having taken the manager through a regular test, since we got several interesting ideas from observing her use of the system.

The user test was performed as a thinking-aloud study (Lewis 1982; Nielsen 1992b, 1993a) in which the users were asked to verbalize their thoughts while using the system. The same sample scenario as that used for the heuristic evaluation was used for the user test since the prototype only contained the data necessary to handle these specific tasks.

Seventeen of the 40 core usability problems that had been found by heuristic evaluation were confirmed by the user test. The correlation between the number of users observed having a problem and the heuristic evaluators' mean severity rating of that problem is .46 which is reasonably high (and significant at $p < .01$), lending some credence to the validity of the severity ratings. Of course, .46 is not an extremely high correlation, but there are other factors to take into account when calculating the severity of a usability problem than just how many users experience the problem. One obvious additional variable is the impact of the problem on the users and their work, which could not be measured in this test of a prototype.

One can discuss whether the 23 core problems that were not observed in the user test are in fact valid "problems" since they could not be seen to bother the real users. As argued elsewhere (Nielsen 1992a), such problems can indeed be very real, but their impact may just have too short a duration to be observable in a standard user test. Problems that have the effect of slowing users down for 0.1 second or so simply cannot be observed unless data from a very large number of users is subjected to statistical analysis, but they can be very real and costly problems nevertheless. Also, some problems may occur too infrequently to have been observed with the small number of users tested here. Finally, some problems were related to deviations from graphical user interface standards. Such deviations can be expected to impact users who have previous experience with standards-compliant interfaces or who shift between using several standards-compliant systems. However, none of the test users had any previous experience with graphical user interfaces and could not be expected to be impacted by the deviations from the standard. It would therefore be impossible to find these usability problems by user testing with these users, but they are still usability problems.

A very interesting result from the user testing was the discovery of four new usability problems that had not been found in the heuristic evaluation. Three of the problems were similar to those found by heuristic evaluation. For example, one of the new problems related to the case sensitivity of one of the query features, just as the heuristic evaluation had found a problem with the case sensitivity of the Find Text feature. These two case sensitivity problems are examples of exactly the same underlying phenomenon (a description error, to use Norman's terminology [Norman 1983]).

One problem was very different from those found by heuristic evaluation, however. The prototype interface produced standard error messages in separate dialog boxes when the user performed database queries for records that were not in the database. Even though this behavior is appropriate for most traditional database uses, it is suboptimal for the particular task supported by the Integrating System. Knowing that a certain record is *not* in the database is actually important information for the task of resolving data inconsistencies; the feedback message that something could not be found should therefore appear in the normal system response window integrated with other information retrieved from the databases. Dialog boxes containing error messages are normally dismissed by the user and do not remain visible to remind the user of the problem.

The fact that four new problems were found shows the value of running tests with real users to supplement heuristic evaluations. The problem that missing data is interesting information rather than an error condition is obvious in hindsight, but could probably not have been predicted by domain-ignorant usability specialists. It is truly a domain-specific usability problem, so the discovery of this problem by user testing is an indication of the need to use multiple usability engineering methods to supplement each other.

2.3   Severity Ratings

In addition to the simple list of usability problems that were found in an interface, heuristic evaluation can be used to assess the relative severity of the individual usability problems. Such severity ratings can then be used to allocate the most resources to fix the most serious problems and also provide a rough estimate of the need for additional usability efforts. If the severity ratings indicate that several disastrous usability problems remain in an interface, it will probably be unadvisable to release it. But one might decide to go ahead with the release of a system with several usability problems if they are all judged as being cosmetic in nature.

The severity of a usability problem is a combination of three factors:

- The *frequency* with which the problem occurs: Is it common or rare?
- The *impact* of the problem if it occurs: Will it be easy or difficult for the users to overcome?
- The *persistence* of the problem: Is it a one-time problem that users can overcome once they know about it or will users repeatedly be bothered by the problem?

Finally, of course, one needs to assess the *market impact* of the problem since certain usability problems can have a devastating effect on the popularity of a problem, even if they are "objectively" quite easy to overcome. Even though severity has several components, it is common to combine all aspects of severity in a single severity rating as an overall assessment of each usability problem in order to facilitate prioritizing and decision-making.

It is difficult to get good severity estimates from the evaluators during the evaluation session when they are more focused on finding new usability problems. Also, as noted previously, each evaluator will only find a small number of the usability problems, so a set of severity ratings of only the problems found by that evaluator will be incomplete. Instead, severity ratings can be collected by sending a questionnaire to the evaluators *after* the actual evaluation sessions, listing the complete set of usability problems that have been discovered, and asking them to rate the severity of each problem. Since each evaluator has only identified a subset of the problems included in the list, the problems need to be described in reasonable depth, possibly using screendumps as illustrations. The descriptions can be synthesized by the evaluation observer from the aggregate of comments made by those evaluators who had found each problem (or, if written evaluation reports are used, the descriptions can be synthesized from the descriptions in the reports). These descriptions allow the evaluators to assess the various problems fairly easily even if they have not found them in their own evaluation session. Typically, evaluators need only spend about 30 minutes to provide their severity ratings. It is important to note that each evaluator should provide individual severity ratings independently of the other evaluators.

Often, the evaluators will not have access to the actual system while they are considering the severity of the various usability problems. It is possible that the evaluators can gain additional insights by revisiting parts of the running interface rather than relying on their memory and the written problem descriptions. At the same time, there is no doubt that the evaluators will be slower at arriving at the severity ratings if they are given the option of interacting further with the system. Also, scheduling problems will sometimes make it difficult to provide everybody with computer access at convenient times if special computer resources are needed to run a prototype system or if software distribution is limited due to confidentiality considerations.

The 0 to 4 rating scale shown in Table 2.3 was used in the "Integrating System" case study for rating the severity of the usability problems.

Since any individual evaluator typically has personally found only a small fraction of the total set of usability problems, it is reasonable to ask to what extent the evaluators' judgments might be biased. One might expect the evaluators to rate their "own" problems as more severe than the problems that had been found by others but that they had overlooked themselves. In the

0 I don't agree that this is a usability problem at all

1 Cosmetic problem only—need not be fixed unless extra time is available on project

2 Minor usability problem—fixing this should be given low priority

3 Major usability problem—important to fix, so should be given high priority

4 Usability catastrophe—imperative to fix this before product can be released

Table 2.3 *Five-point rating scale for the severity of usability problems found by heuristic evaluation.*

case study, it turned out, however, that any given evaluator's severity rating of a usability problem was essentially independent of whether that evaluator had found that problem. When separating out the effect of the total number of evaluators finding each problem, the remaining partial correlation between the severity judgments from an individual evaluator and whether that evaluator found the problem was only .09. There was a positive correlation of .33 between the evaluators' ratings and the number of evaluators having found each problem. Since the individual evaluators did not know how many other evaluators had found each problem, they would have no way of letting their severity judgments depend on this number. Therefore, the correlation between the severity ratings and the overall probability of finding the problems is due to the well-established phenomenon that the more severe usability problems are found more frequently by heuristic evaluation (Nielsen 1992a).

Reliability of the Severity Judgments

The average correlation between the severity ratings provided by any two evaluators is .24. Kendall's coefficient of concordance between the eleven evaluators is $W = .31$, which is statistically significant ($\chi^2 = 132.3$, df $= 39$, $p < .01$) and thus indicates that the agreement is not just chance. Also, of the 55 pair-wise comparisons between evaluators, only 4 have negative correlations, whereas the remaining 51 are positive ($p < .001$).

Even though the statistics indicate better than random agreement between evaluators, the inter-rater reliability is still very low compared to the standards of most respected rating methods. Basically, the reliability of the severity ratings from single evaluators is so low that it would be advisable not to base any major investments of development time and effort on such single ratings. On the other hand, the better-than-random agreement between evaluators means that it is possible to use the mean of the severity judgments from several evaluators and get much more reliable results. It is a fairly simple task for an evaluator to produce severity ratings for an interface which is known to that evaluator from a heuristic evaluation session; the evaluators in the case study presented here spent about half an hour each on doing so. Therefore, it would seem reasonable to ask for severity judgments from all or at least most evaluators.

The Spearman-Brown formula for estimating the reliability of combined judgments from several evaluators is

$$r_{n-n} = \frac{n \cdot r_{1-1}}{1 + (n-1) \cdot r_{1-1}} \qquad \text{(EQ 2)}$$

Figure 2.5 shows a plot of the way the reliability of the mean severity estimate increases as more evaluators are added.

The standard error of measurement for the true underlying value of a rating derived as the mean of n ratings is

$$\sigma_\infty = \sigma_n \cdot \sqrt{1 - r_{n-n}} \qquad \text{(EQ 3)}$$

where r_{n-n} is the reliability of a group of n raters and σ_n is the standard deviation of the mean of the n ratings which again is

$$\sigma_n = \frac{\sigma_1}{\sqrt{n}} \qquad \text{(EQ 4)}$$

if the individual ratings can be assumed to be independent variables. This assumption of independence obviously only holds if the evaluators perform their evaluations separately (as was done in this study) and do not discuss the usability problems before giving their severity judgments.

Combining equations 2 to 4 gives the standard error of measurement shown in Figure 2.5. Since the severity judgments are fairly close to following a normal distribution as shown in Figure 2.6, the normal distribution can be

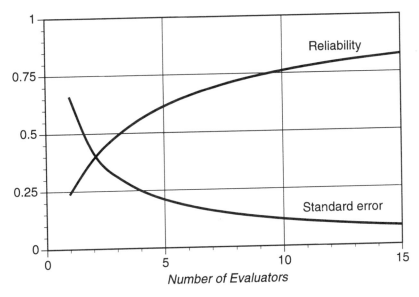

Figure 2.5 *The upper curve shows the reliability of the severity estimates as a function of the number of evaluators used. The lower curve shows the standard error of measurement (in rating units from the 0-4 scale) for the underlying true mean severity value when measured by the mean of the ratings from that number of evaluators. Values for more than one evaluator are plotted according to the Spearman-Brown formula.*

used to calculate confidence intervals for the severity estimates. The standard deviation of the complete set of severity ratings adjusted for means is 0.75 which can be used for a general estimate of σ_1.

Because of the low reliability of the severity ratings and the high standard deviation for the individual ratings, the probability of having a single evaluator provide an estimate that is within ±0.5 rating units of the true severity of a problem is only 55 percent. In other words, almost half of the time the absolute rating will be substantially different from the "true" rating (that would result from having an infinite number of evaluators). On the other hand, combining the estimates of several evaluators considerably improves the confidence intervals for the mean estimate. With just two evaluators, one has a 77 percent chance of getting within ±0.5 of the "true"

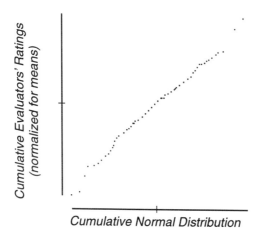

Cumulative Normal Distribution

Figure 2.6 *Probability (percentile vs. percentile) plot comparing the distribution of the severity ratings minus their means and the normal distribution. The plot is close to a straight line, indicating that the severity ratings follow a distribution close to the normal distribution.*

severity, and the probability is 95 percent with four evaluators. Figure 2.7 shows how the probability of getting within ±0.5 and ±0.25 goes up with the number of evaluators.

Severity estimates for usability problems have two possible practical applications: First, one needs to know the absolute need for usability improvements in order to determine the need for continued usability efforts and to consider the extent to which an increased usability engineering budget or delays in product introduction is warranted. Second, given a specific budget for usability activities and the need to move on in the product lifecycle within a given timeframe, one needs to set relative priorities for which problems to fix first.

For the first application of estimating the absolute severity of the usability problems in an interface, it may be sufficient to estimate the severity of each usability problem with an uncertainty of ±0.5 rating units. The length of a ±0.5 interval is of course one unit; it would be difficult to interpret the meaning of subjective usability severities with a much finer resolution than that. For example, any cost-benefit estimate of the potential fixing of usability problems has to include estimates of the programming effort

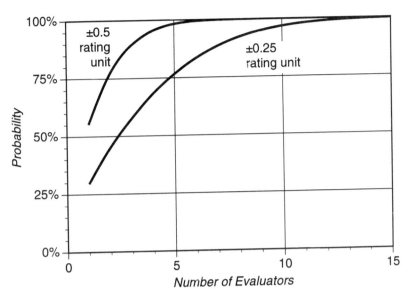

Figure 2.7 *Probability for having the mean severity rating from sets of 1 through 15 evaluators be within an interval of ±0.5 and ±0.25 rating unit of the true severity of a usability problem.*

needed to implement a redesign as well as an estimate of the usability of the new design. Neither value can be estimated with great precision in any case, so it would be a wasted effort to measure the severity of the usability deficiencies in the old design with extremely narrow confidence intervals.[4]

For the second application of deciding the relative severity of the usability problems in order to prioritize them, estimates from more evaluators will be needed for tight confidence intervals, since one is comparing two average scores, each of which has been estimated with some uncertainty.

One way of addressing the accuracy of relative severity estimates is to consider the probability with which a usability problem can be assigned to its proper decile or its neighboring decile. Deciles divide the total space of problems into 10 groups sorted by severity. For example, the first decile contains the 10 percent least severe usability problems and the tenth decile

---

[4] It would be valuable to have externally valid data to calibrate the subjective rating scale with respect to the economic impact of fixing usability problems of various severities.

contains the 10 percent most severe problems (that is, those rated as the 91 to 100 percent most severe). Allowing an estimate to fall within the neighboring deciles as well as the true decile would mean, for example, that we could count a claim that a particular usability problem was among the 71 to 80 percent most severe as being close enough as long as the problem in fact was among the 61 to 90 percent most severe. Obviously, allowing assignment to neighboring deciles implies a fairly low precision, since one can only be sure of having estimated the relative severity of a usability problem to within a group of 30 percent of the total set of usability problems. On the other hand, such fairly low precision is probably about as good as one needs, given that the final decision of which usability problems to fix also involves estimates of the value of possible redesigns and the programming cost of such redesigns.

The probability of assigning usability problems to their proper decile or its neighboring decile can be estimated under the assumption that the severity estimates are normally distributed (as supported by Figure 2.6) with standard errors for the various number of evaluators as shown in Figure 2.5. These probabilities have been calculated for each of the 40 core usability problems; Figure 2.8 shows the result averaged over all 40 problems. As can be seen from this figure, relative severity estimates are quite poor, with the probability of getting within one decile of the correct one being only 42 percent for a single evaluator. Six evaluators are needed for achieving an 81 percent probability of getting within one decile, and eleven evaluators are needed to reach the 95 percent level of confidence.

In some cases, less precise relative severity estimates may be adequate. Figure 2.8 also shows the probabilities for estimating within the correct quartile or its neighboring quartile. Quartiles divide the set of usability problems into 1 to 25 percent, 26 to 50 percent, 51 to 75 percent, and 76 to 100 percent severity intervals. Getting within one quartile of the correct one means that the least severe 25 percent of the problems will never be estimated within the top 50 percent, and the most severe 25 percent of the problems will never be estimated within the bottom 50 percent. In other words, one can be assured that fixing the problems that are estimated as the top 50 percent will take care of all the 25 percent most severe problems. Also, this level of precision makes sure that one will never rate one of the least severe 25 percent of the problems as more important than one of the most severe 25 percent of the problems.

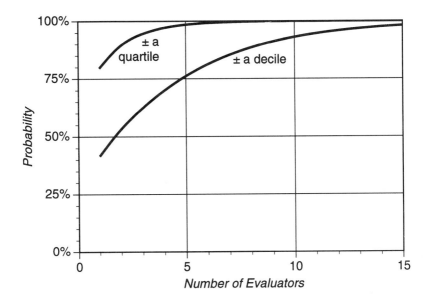

Figure 2.8 *Probability of having the mean severity rating from sets of 1 through 15 evaluators assign a usability problem to the correct quartile or decile or the neighboring quartile or decile, respectively.*

As can be seen from Figure 2.8, it is much easier to get within one quartile of correct than to get within one decile; the 94.5 percent confidence level is reached with as little as three evaluators. Even with this more liberal relative severity requirement, one should still be wary of using estimates from single evaluators, since they would get it wrong 20 percent of the time.

Based on these considerations, one can definitely conclude that severity ratings from a single evaluator are too unreliable to be trusted. As more evaluators are asked to judge the severity of usability problems, the quality of the mean severity rating increases rapidly, and ratings from three or four evaluators would seem to be satisfactory for many practical purposes.

2.4 Characteristics of Usability Problems Found by Heuristic Evaluation

Heuristic evaluation is a good method for finding both major and minor problems in a user interface. As one might have expected, major problems are slightly easier to find than minor problems, with the probability for finding a given major usability problem at 42 percent on the average for single evaluators in six case studies (Nielsen 1992a). The corresponding probability for finding a given minor problem was only 32 percent.

Even though major problems are easier to find, this does not mean that the evaluators concentrate exclusively on the major problems. In case studies of six user interfaces (Nielsen 1992a), heuristic evaluation identified a total of 59 major usability problems and 152 minor usability problems. Thus, it is apparent that the lists of usability problems found by heuristic evaluation will tend to be dominated by minor problems,[5] which is one reason severity ratings form a useful supplement to the method. Even though major usability problems are by definition the most important ones to find and to fix, minor usability problems are still relevant. Many such minor problems seem to be easier to find by heuristic evaluation than by other methods. One example of such a minor problem found by heuristic evaluation was the use of inconsistent typography in two parts of a user interface. The same information would sometimes be shown in a serif font (like this one) and sometimes in a sans serif font (like this one), thus slowing users down a little bit as they have to expend additional effort on matching the two pieces of information. This type of minor usability problem could not be observed in a user test unless an extremely careful analysis were performed on the basis of a large number of videotaped or logged interactions, since the slowdown is very small and would not stop users from completing their tasks.

Usability problems can be located in a dialogue in four different ways: at a single location in the interface, at two or more locations that have to be compared to find the problem, as a problem with the overall structure of the interface, and finally as something that *ought* to be included in the interface

---

[5] Using the average probabilities for finding major and minor problems, the number of major usability problems found by a single evaluator in the six case studies would be 25 and the number of minor problems would be 49. Thus, there would have been about twice as many minor problems as major problems included in each evaluation report.

but is currently missing. An analysis of 211 usability problems (Nielsen 1992a) found that the difference between the four location categories was small and not statistically significant. In other words, evaluators were approximately equally good at finding all four kinds of usability problems. However, the interaction effect between location category and interface implementation *was* significant and had a very large effect. Problems in the category "something missing" were slightly easier to find than other problems in running systems, but much harder to find than other problems in paper prototypes. This finding corresponds to an earlier, qualitative, analysis of the usability problems that were harder to find in a paper implementation than in a running system (Nielsen 1990c). Because of this difference, one should look harder for missing dialogue elements when evaluating paper mock-ups.

A likely explanation of this phenomenon is that evaluators using a running system may tend to get stuck when needing a missing interface element (and thus notice it), whereas evaluators of a paper "implementation" just turn to the next page and focus on the interface elements found there.

Alternating Heuristic Evaluation and User Testing

Even though heuristic evaluation finds many usability problems that are not found by user testing, it is also the case that it may miss some problems that can be found by user testing. Evaluators are probably especially likely to overlook usability problems if the system is highly domain-dependent and they have little domain expertise. In the case study of the Integrating System discussed in Section 2.2, several additional usability problems were found by user testing, including some that were so domain-specific that they would have been virtually impossible to find without user testing.

Since heuristic evaluation and user testing each finds usability problems overlooked by the other method, it is recommended that both methods be used. Because there is no reason to spend resources on evaluating an interface with many known usability problems only to have many of them come up again, it is normally best to use iterative design between uses of the two evaluation methods. Typically, one would first perform a heuristic evaluation to clean up the interface and remove as many "obvious" usability problems as possible. After a redesign of the interface, it would be subjected to user testing both to check the outcome of the iterative design step and to find remaining usability problems that were not picked up by the heuristic evaluation.

There are two major reasons for alternating between heuristic evaluation and user testing as suggested here. First, a heuristic evaluation pass can eliminate a number of usability problems without the need to "waste users," who sometimes can be difficult to find and schedule in large numbers. Second, these two categories of usability assessment methods have been shown to find fairly distinct sets of usability problems; therefore, they supplement each other rather than lead to repetitive findings (Desurvire et al. 1992; Jeffries et al. 1991; Karat et al. 1992).

As another example, consider a video telephone system for interconnecting offices (Cool et al. 1992). Such a system has the potential for changing the way people work and interact, but these changes will become clear only after an extended usage period. Also, as with many computer-supported cooperative work applications, video telephones require a critical mass of users for the test to be realistic: If most of the people you want to call do not have a video connection, you will not rely on the system. Thus, on the one hand field testing is necessary to learn about changes in the users' long-term behavior, but on the other hand such studies will be very expensive. Therefore, one will want to supplement them with heuristic evaluation and laboratory-based user testing so that the larger field population does not have to suffer from glaring usability problems that could have been found much more cheaply. Iterative design of such a system will be a combination of a few, longer-lasting "outer iterations" with field testing and a larger number of more rapid "inner iterations" that are used to polish the interface before it is released to the field users.

2.5   Getting Good Evaluators

As always in computing (Egan 1988), there are major individual differences between the performance of evaluators in heuristic evaluation. In eight case studies, the Q_3/Q_1 ratio between the number of usability problems found by the top and bottom quartile (best 25 percent versus worst 25 percent) of the evaluators ranged from 1.4 to 2.2 with a mean of 1.7. These numbers represent cases where evaluators with essentially the same background and qualifications were compared. Thus, there are major benefits to be gained if one could identify people who are good at doing heuristic evaluation as the evaluators. In one case study (Nielsen and Molich 1990), 34 evaluators with the same background evaluated two different user interfaces, and the correlation between the number of usability problems found by individual evaluators in the two systems was $r = .57$. This definitely indicates better than random consistency in the evaluators' ability to find usability problems ($p < .01$), but at the same time also indicates substantial unexplained variability in performance from one evaluation to the next. Even though it might be possible to establish a group of "good" evaluators over time by selecting people who exhibit good performance in several evaluations, it will likely be a slow process and will sacrifice performance on the first several evaluation studies.

In a case study (Nielsen 1992a), the same user interface was subjected to heuristic evaluation by three groups of evaluators: usability "novices" with knowledge about computers in general but no special usability expertise; "single experts" who were usability specialists but not specialized in the domain of the interface; and "double experts" with expertise in both usability in general and the kind of interface being evaluated. The performance of the novice evaluators was fairly poor, with each of them finding an average of 22 percent of the usability problems in the interface. The single experts found 41 percent of the problems each, making them 1.8 times as good as the novices, and the double experts found 60 percent each, making them 2.7 times as good as the novices and 1.5 times as good as the single experts. These results show that there are systematic group differences in evaluator performance in addition to the individual differences. Even though heuristic evaluation can be performed by people with little or no usability expertise (which is an advantage from a discount usability engineering perspective), it is preferable to use usability specialists as the evaluators; optimal performance requires double specialists.

Users as Evaluators

In addition to developers, usability specialists, and "double experts," a fourth category of possible evaluators might be actual end users. One might argue that the users are the ultimate domain experts and thus might contribute some of the same insights as the "double experts." Even so, I do not recommend performing heuristic evaluations with users as evaluators because of their poor conceptual understanding of usability and computer principles.

True, users know their work, but it is a very common experience in usability engineering that they do not know how their *future* work might be changed by new computer systems.

To the extent that one has access to real users during product development it is likely to generate substantially better insights to let them act as *users* and have them try out the user interface as part of a user test where they perform real tasks with the system. Instead of asking users whether they think that a certain part of an interface design is easy to understand, one can directly observe whether they are able to understand it when they encounter the dialogue element in the context of a real task. This latter kind of empirical data is likely to have significantly higher validity than the users' opinions. Similarly, one can certainly ask users for suggestions on how to change or improve an interface, but since users are not designers one should treat these suggestions as a source of further inspiration and not as the ultimate truth about how to improve the interface.

Educational Use of Heuristic Evaluation

One of the ways of getting better evaluators is to have the evaluators do many heuristic evaluations and have them compare lists. The first few times people serve as evaluators in a heuristic evaluation, they will often end up finding comparatively few usability problems; but a discussion of the many additional problems found by their colleagues can be an effective learning experience (see Kahn and Prail, Chapter 6). Thus, heuristic evaluation can be used in a bootstrapping fashion to serve as its own educational method. In addition to teaching the heuristic evaluation itself, having people perform heuristic evaluations also involves other instructional opportunities since the discussion of usability problems is the main way to make abstract usability principles concrete (Nielsen and Molich 1989).

Heuristic evaluation can also be used to improve the teaching of user interface design. In one project I was involved with, we wanted to teach graphical user interface design to developers who were very experienced in the design of character-based user interfaces (Nielsen et al. 1992). Design exercises served as a major element in the course, since design is much easier to learn by doing than by listening to lectures. We were able to provide the course participants with very rapid feedback on their designs by having two usability specialists perform heuristic evaluations on the designs during the coffee breaks following the design sessions. Admittedly, two evaluators are less than normally recommended, but the evaluators gained a status of at least double experts with respect to the exercise designs throughout the series of courses. Also, for instructional purposes it was not necessary to find all usability problems in the designs since there was not enough time in the course schedule to discuss more than a few aspects of each design. The important contribution to the course from the heuristic evaluations was in providing immediate feedback to the course participants; they did not have to rely on the traditional very slow feedback provided days or weeks after the completion of an assignment.

2.6   Conclusions

Heuristic evaluation is a basic usability engineering method that is very easy to use. The present description of heuristic evaluation includes several aspects of heuristic evaluation that may seem slightly complicated at first, such as the use of severity ratings or the evaluation of domain-specific interfaces. In fact, even these extensions to the method are quite easy. But most importantly, it is possible to start using heuristic evaluation without these elements. The basic components of heuristic evaluation are those described in Section 2.1:

- Have evaluators go through the interface twice; once to focus on its flow and once to focus on its individual dialogue elements.

- Ask the evaluators to inspect the interface with respect to whether it complies with a short list of basic usability heuristics and your general knowledge of usability principles.

- Combine the findings from about three to five evaluators and have them work independently of each other.

After the individual evaluations, you can have the evaluators meet for a debriefing session. You can also consider collecting severity ratings to help prioritize the fixing of the usability problems you will have found.

In any case, heuristic evaluation can only find usability problems in your interface if you in fact *use* the method. Reading about it is only the first step. Practical experience with using the method not only will improve whatever product you use it on, but will also make you better at using the method which, in turn, will benefit future projects.

Acknowledgments

Much of the work described in this chapter was done while the author was with Bellcore and on the faculty of the Technical University of Denmark. Gay Norwood contributed substantially to the case study of the Integrating System discussed in Section 2.2. Much of the author's early work on heuristic evaluation was done in collaboration with Rolf Molich. The author would also like to thank Tom Landauer for helpful comments on earlier versions of this manuscript.

Chapter 3

The Pluralistic Usability Walkthrough: Coordinated Empathies

Randolph G. Bias
IBM Corporation

When the first product designer first asked, aloud or subvocally, "How will my users use my [say] stone implement?" the usability walkthrough was born.

Sometime later, two or more early human factors professionals gathered to review a product design for its projected usability and the usability walkthrough became a more structured and accepted inspection method. In recent years, professionals at IBM-Austin, driven by a desire for testing efficiency, have extended the traditional usability walkthrough. Primarily, we have included three types of participants in the same walkthrough—actual users, product developers, and usability experts. This pluralistic usability walkthrough has yielded not only increased efficiency, but also increased utility, in that we have obtained new and valuable results, not typically gleaned from traditional usability walkthroughs.

This chapter describes the pluralistic usability walkthrough, including enough detail to allow the usability professional to conduct one confidently. The method's benefits and limitations are highlighted. And, in the absence of a crisp, a priori, theoretical motivation for the new approach, some of the recent empirical literature on participatory design, group dynamics, and the integration of evaluation and design are reviewed, to retrofit a theoretical explanation for the serendipitous findings. In the process, I will address this inspection method's objectives, accessibility, and effectiveness, as other contributors to this volume have done, to assist the interested reader in deciding when best to employ this method.

A particular view of usability inspections that will be addressed here is the notion of inspector empathy. Several recent researchers and practitioners have stated or implied that the more empathic an inspector can be, in a particular situation, the more effective the inspection. I will offer the interpretation that the value of the pluralistic usability walkthrough is based on the breadth of the collective empathies of the varied participants.

3.1 A Little Historical Context

Walkthroughs afford the human factors practitioner usability data on tasks for which no user interface simulation or prototype is available. Walkthroughs (exactly or nearly synonymous with "storyboarding" or "table-topping") provide a flexible technique for systematically reviewing the viability of a user interface and its flow. The flexibility of this method is illustrated by its varied uses, such as in verifying requirements (Andriole 1987), identifying design process problems (Golembiewski 1987), designing computer-based instruction (Morrison and Ross 1988), and evaluating the correctness of computer program solutions (McGinnis and Sass 1988).

It would make an elegant story to be able to say that there was a neat and distinct theoretical basis for our first use of the pluralistic usability walkthrough. In fact, we simply had little time in one particular product development cycle, but still wanted to obtain usability data from two different populations: end users and usability professionals. So the two populations were combined in one walkthrough. Additionally, since there were no supporting publications available, we wanted the developers present to serve as "living publications," to answer any questions that arose during the testing.

3.2 The Pluralistic Usability Walkthrough

The pluralistic usability walkthrough shares some characteristics with traditional walkthroughs (see Bias 1991) and with cognitive walkthroughs (see Wharton et al., Chapter 5), but there are some defining characteristics.

Defining Characteristics

There are five defining characteristics of the pluralistic usability walkthrough as it was conducted at IBM. First, as stated, the primary modification made to the familiar usability walkthrough was to include three types of participants in the same walkthrough: Representative users, product developers, and human factors professionals.

The second defining characteristic, shared with traditional walkthoughs, is that hard-copy panels (screens) are presented in the same order in which they would appear online. That is, a scenario is defined, entailing one linear path through a series of user interface panels. During the walkthrough, the participants confront the panels just as they would during the successful conduct of the specified task online, as currently designed, only in hard copy. (See Karat and Bennett 1991b, for more on " . . . the use of scenarios as one representation technique useful in focusing design discussions.")

Third, participants are all asked to assume the role of the user, whatever user population is being tested at the time. Thus, the developers and the usability professionals are supposed to try to put themselves in the place of the users when making written responses.

Fourth, the participants write down on each hard-copy panel the action they would take in pursuing the designated task online, before any discussion. Participants are asked to write their responses in as much detail as possible, down to the keystroke (or other input action) level. So, instead of "I would choose the fourth item on the list," the participant is encouraged to write "Press the down arrow key three times, then press 'Enter.'" These written responses produce some quantitative data on user actions that can be of certain value. Arguably, this aspect moves the method out of the realm of "inspections" and into the realm of "empirical user feedback." Too, though, these pluralistic usability walkthroughs could be considered simply multiple, parallel user inspections. This inspection/user testing discussion is continued in the later section entitled "Choosing to conduct a pluralistic usability walkthrough."

Only after all participants have written the actions they would take when confronting the panel in question does the discussion begin. This is the fifth definitional characteristic of pluralistic usability walkthroughs: The representative users speak first, in discussing each panel. Only when their comments (or, more accurately, their first round of comments) are exhausted do the usability experts and the product developers offer their opinions.

Materials

Participants are given written instructions and ground rules at the beginning of the walkthrough. The ground rules ask all participants to assume the role of the user (whichever user class is being tested), to write on the panels the actions they would take in pursuing the task at hand, to write any additional comments, not to flip ahead to other panels until told to, and to hold discussion on each panel until the walkthrough administrator calls for it.

A hard copy of the task scenario is given to each participant. That is, for each task covered in the walkthrough, a scenario is defined, complete with data to be manipulated. Then the panels are put together in a package, with one panel per page. Each subject receives a package, enabling him or her to write a response (i.e., the action to take on that panel in performing the stated task) directly on the page. The task descriptions are short, directive statements of each task. They include any data the subjects might need (e.g., assumed system parameters).

Accompanying Information

Since the usability walkthrough is usually conducted early in the development cycle, accompanying information (publications, online documentation, or online help panels) sometimes is not available. To maximize the representativeness of the inspection environment to the real-world setting, and thus the generalizability of the inspection results, two things have been tried. We sometimes simulate the accompanying information to the best of our ability, just for the purposes of the walkthrough. Alternately, and more frequently, product designers and developers have been present to serve as the "living publications." Anytime a participant has a question that he or she would turn to the accompanying information with, that question can be asked aloud, and the "living publications" answer aloud.

Selecting Subjects

As in any good end-user usability assessment, we consult our product audience descriptions, then find participants who are representative of our projected user population. In the pluralistic walkthroughs, we also solicit the participation of key product developers: architects, designers, coders, and writers. Predictably, this has proven to be a win-win situation. These product experts support the walkthrough as "living publications," and they gain first-hand knowledge of the representative subjects' reaction to our emerging product. Further, some collaborative, on-the-fly redesign is a welcome and common benefit of this methodology; having the product experts present facilitates good design and shared ownership.

Human factors professionals play an important role as walkthrough administrators. In addition to offering superior usability intuitions, they can help express the representative subjects' comments as cogent suggestions that will help guide the developers toward a particular usability improvement. Additionally, the human factors professional serves as an advocate for the user and must be wary to prevent the product experts from "explaining away" the concerns that the users have brought to the surface.

Procedure

The walkthrough is a group activity. First, participants are presented with the instructions and the ground rules, and the task description and scenario package. Next, a product expert (usually a designer) has been employed to offer a brief overview of key product concepts or interface features. This overview is intended to simulate any prerequisite written overview that would accompany the ultimate product and ensure that participants have any knowledge the ultimate product users are assumed to have.

Next, participants are asked to write on the hard copy of the first panel the actions they would take in attempting the specified task. After all participants have written their independent responses, the walkthrough administrator announces the "right" answer. (There will be more discussion about "right" responses in Section 3.3 on page 69) Next, the representative subjects verbalize their responses and discuss potential usability problems, while the product experts remain quiet and the human factors professionals simply facilitate the discussion among the users. This way, of course, the information gathered on the problems the representative subjects perceive is not influenced by the product experts. Of course, the representative users may be less willing to make critical comments due to the developers' presence. Thus, it is imperative that the developers assume an attitude of welcoming comments that are all intended to help maximize the usability of their product. Here, the usability engineer who is moderating can set this tone at the beginning of the walkthough and should alert the developers in advance of the importance of this attitude.

Once the discussion winds down, the product experts are invited to join in, often with explanations of why the design was the way it was. It is important, both for the continued candid responses of the representative subjects and for the continued working relationships with the product developers, to prepare the developers in advance for this as well. They should be told that they need to be thick-skinned and that all of the representative subjects' comments need to be treated with respect. This does not mean that every single subject comment must spawn a redesign. But developer defensiveness will tend to inhibit the representative users on subsequent panels. (See Wharton et al. 1992, for more on the moderator as "social-emotional leader.")

While we don't always take the time to derive a solution to every identified usability problem during the walkthrough itself, the presence of the various types of participants creates a potential for synergy that often leads to creative, collaborative solutions. Thus, we explicitly "keep a user-centered perspective while simultaneously considering the engineering constraints of practical system design" (Karat and Bennett 1991b, p. 92).

After each task, the participants are given a brief questionnaire regarding the usability of the interface they've just inspected. Sometimes an additional questionnaire is administered at the end of the day.

3.3 Limitations

Pluralistic usability walkthroughs, while affording an early, systematic look at an emerging user interface, have some limitations. First, the walkthrough must progress as slowly as the slowest person on each panel. The walkthrough is a group exercise; therefore, in order to discuss a screen as a group, we must wait for all participants to have decided on and written down their responses on that screen. This can mean that the participants don't gain a good grasp of the flow of the interface.

Second, in the walkthrough we can't simulate all the possible actions on hard copy; we select one viable path of interest through the interface. This precludes the participants from browsing and exploring, behaviors users often like to exhibit that can lead to additional learning about the user interface (cf., Carroll and Mack 1984).

Third, and relatedly, when there are multiple correct paths, participants who picked one that wasn't selected by the walkthrough administrator must "reset" and continue down the selected path. In the "Procedure" section it was stated that the administrator would announce the "right" action after each participant had written down a response. There is always more than one possible response on a screen that is acceptable (if only the selection of "Help," in addition to any action moving forward in the conduct of the task). It is certainly feasible that multiple paths could be examined, with the group taking one path, then being brought back to that point in the interface, and a new packet handed out to cover the other branch. But "knowing how way leads on to way" (Frost 1930), we have not ever tried to implement this logistically challenging procedure.

The same sort of reset is required by users who chose a "wrong" action, as well. Wharton et al. (Chapter 5) identify the same sort of need to "proceed to the next step, as if the correct action had been performed," in cognitive walkthroughs.

These limitations don't obviate the findings of a pluralistic usability walkthrough; they simply call for careful interpretation thereof. And, it is important, when deciding to employ such a walkthrough, to recognize what types of findings to expect. Some data, such as the data on the usability of a particular user interface panel, will be reliable and much like those gleaned from end-user testing of any sort. Other data, such as data on the user interface flow and navigation throughout the interface, must be accepted more guardedly, due to the single-path limitation. Yet other findings, such as task completion times, are unlikely to be of any value at all.

3.4   Benefits

Countering the limitations are several benefits that combine to make the pluralistic usability walkthrough a potentially valuable tool in the usability engineer's tool chest. Most obviously, such a walkthrough can provide early performance and satisfaction data from users when a user interface prototype is not available. Second, even if a prototype is available, the walkthrough can be the ultimate in rapid test-redesign-retest usability engineering, with the just-derived new designs being discussed and evaluated in the walkthrough itself. This is related to a third benefit: Synergistic redesign "on-the-fly." It is our experience that human beings, be they product designers or product users, hate to criticize without offering some potential improvement. Again, the moderator must keep the discussion moving and avoid the urge to solve, to the satisfaction of everyone in the room, every potential usability problem that arises. But the discussion of some of the identified problems will spawn neat, elegant, quick, usable, creative, corporate solutions.

Fourth, relatedly and empirically, we get results that we often don't get in on-line testing. The aforementioned redesigns provide one clear example. Another, and unexpected, type of result comes under the heading of "I got it right, but . . . ." Participant responses that were correct, but were made with uncertainty, have an opportunity to be discussed in this format. This may be true also in thinking-aloud tests, but some user testing can go along smoothly never noting such "lucky" correct answers.

Yet another rich vein is the synching up of the interface and the supporting publications. During the discussion, or even before when the participants may ask the "living publications" questions, we identify clear requirements for the accompanying documentation. Traditional, single-subject thinking-aloud studies may also reveal similar sorts of findings, but the group walkthrough affords us quick corroboration of the requirement ("Yeah, I was going to ask that too."). Plus, the subject working alone in a laboratory observation room may be more likely to quietly struggle to an answer, not hearing others validate the same concerns. (Though Hackman and Biers 1992, suggest that verbalization training can overcome the unnaturalness of thinking-out-loud to oneself.) Now, it is perhaps equally likely that the subject working alone in a lab cell may be more apt to speak up, as the walkthrough participant has a roomful of people who potentially will find a comment laughable. (See Desurvire, Chapter 7, for more discussion of the accuracy of judgments in groups and individually.) Two points need be made here. First, this demonstrates again the important job of the moderator in setting the tone of the walkthrough. (I realize this is a point made before, but it bears repeating.) Much like in a brainstorming session, in the walkthrough, when it comes to accepting comments from the users, "all critical judgments are suspended" (Hellriegel and Slocum 1992, p. 233); the developers must not be allowed to demean or minimize other participants' comments. Second, remember that the pluralistic usability walkthrough is not offered as a usability inspection panacea; a variety of methods will likely need to be employed in the complete program of usability engineering.

A fifth benefit of pluralistic usability walkthroughs is the immediate feedback and the increased buy-in achieved by having the developers present to hear the concerns of the representative users. Only told about users' problems, developers, with understandable ownership of the current design, can attribute the problems to other causes (e.g., inappropriately chosen or stupid subjects). And while observing user testing live or on videotape can help developers have more empathy for the plight of the user first confronting the favored (by the developer) user interface, actually interacting with the users, and observing and hearing their frustration at some unexpected usability glitch, can be very motivating for the developers. Mack and Montaniz (Chapter 12) have also "found that scenario-driven walkthroughs . . . are an important way to convey results."

Finally, if time and money are concerns, pluralistic usability walkthroughs should be considered. It is a fairly easy matter to put together the materials for a walkthrough (assuming a design exists) in a day or two. (This assumes the use of designers as living publications.) The most time-consuming aspect of the preparation is usually identifying and inviting the participants and tracking the RSVPs. Also, the cost-benefit analysis (see Bias and Mayhew 1994) is likely to be very positive, given that, in the lowest-tech version, photocopying expenses and your time will be the only costs.

3.5   Theoretical Post Mortem

So, in retrospect, why have we found pluralistic usability walkthroughs so useful—not only efficient, but also yielding data that might not be obtained in online testing? First, the focus on practice in the absence of theory is not new in the realm of human-computer interface (cf., Carroll and Kellogg 1989). But, to answer the question further, let's look at four relevant, convergent thrusts in software usability.

Early and Iterative Testing of Emerging Software User Interfaces

It is a truism, now, that early usability evaluations, and an iterative design/test/redesign/retest cycle are valuable components of a successful usability engineering program. The pluralistic usability walkthrough affords such early testing and, as stated, real-time group consideration of some redesigns.

Participatory Design

For at least a decade usability engineers have touted the involvement of "typical users" in the design of products (cf., Gould and Lewis 1983). The pluralistic usability walkthrough specifically brings users to the evaluation and design table with the product developers.

Group Process: Coordinated Empathies

"We think that one important factor in generating inspection results is the extent to which inspectors can draw on their own experiences as users and as problem experiencers" (Mack and Montaniz, Chapter 12). In the *CHI'92* Usability Inspections Workshop, "we agreed that a major factor is indeed the extent to which inspectors themselves have experienced these usability problems or observed others having them" (Mack and Nielsen 1993). Wixon et al. (Chapter 4) discuss bringing real users into design meetings when " . . . an understanding of the users' work . . . may or may not have been present in development or the usability team."

Thus, the inspectors' capacity for empathy is an important determinant in the success of the inspection. This is not the first use of the concept of empathy in relation to the quality of interface evaluations. Grudin, for example, recognized the value of tapping the intuitions of the users themselves: "Some engineers lack empathy or sympathy for inexperienced or nontechnical computer users" (1991, p. 157).

In the pluralistic usability walkthrough, the empathies of the various participants in product design can be tested and honed. With such a walkthrough, not only will the developers *not* be dependent on their own empathies for the users, but also those empathies will be heightened, as they listen to the types of problems the users identify with the emerging interfaces examined. Thus, the developers will be better prepared to create more usable interfaces in the future, before (or, in very constrained development environments, in lieu of) additional usability evaluations involving other users.

Wharton et al. (Chapter 5) address the potential for an "us versus them" attitude between designers and usability evaluators. Participating together in the pluralistic usability walkthrough can go a long way toward eliminating such barriers. The developers see the usability engineers working toward improved products and they hear the recommended improvements first-hand. And the usability engineers, who rarely suffer from too much sympathy for the software development process, will usually learn the motivations for particular design points.

Evaluation/Design Integration

Pluralistic usability walkthroughs address directly Brooks' and Wixon's question regarding the "utility [of inspections] with respect to influencing design change" (Mack and Nielsen 1993). Brooks (Chapter 10) has experienced that " . . . an expert interface evaluation is regarded as opinion." There is no better way to increase "the credibility and confidence developers have in inspection predictions and interpretations" (Mack and Nielsen 1993) than to have them take part in those inspections.

This point enjoyed perhaps a stronger consensus than any other in the Usability Inspection Workshop. In this volume, Karat (Chapter 3) and Desurvire (Chapter 7) both tout "seeing is believing," when it comes to developers and usability inspection results. And Wixon et al. (Chapter 4) talk of how, in their interdisciplinary design teams, the developers " . . . found an atmosphere of collaboration."

3.6   Choosing to Conduct a Pluralistic
Usability Walkthrough

Objectives/Accessibility/Effectiveness

The primary objective of a pluralistic usability walkthrough, like that of all usability inspections, is to help create maximally usable human-computer interfaces. This type of group activity has the additional objective of increasing developers' sensitivity to users' concerns, that is, increasing their empathy.

Might a software developer *not* trained in usability engineering conduct a pluralistic usability walkthrough with no usability professionals present? It is conceivable (though, of course, this would be a reduced-function pluralistic usability walkthrough, with only two types of participants), just as developers can perform cognitive walkthroughs (see Jeffries et al. 1991). But the developer who served as moderator would have to be vigilant to esteem the input of the representative users and *not* to allow any user concerns to be "explained away."

Others (e.g., Karat et al. 1992) have explicitly tested the effectiveness of usability walkthroughs. The pluralistic usability walkthrough has proven very effective as it offers a combination of heuristic evaluation and group process. As Mack and Nielsen (1993) pointed out, " . . . the difference between empirical tests with real users, and usability inspections with non-specialists is very small. Usability inspections look a lot like 'small-N' formative evaluation." Later, Mack and Montaniz (Chapter 12) will discuss further the advantages of group walkthroughs, including "more coverage of issues, from multiple perspectives, conducted more efficiently."

Validity/Severity/Generality

While I have not collected any data on the validity of the results of our pluralistic usability walkthroughs, there are various reasons to think they are valid. Studies have demonstrated the general value of group evaluations (e.g., Hackman and Biers 1992), and of walkthroughs (e.g., Karat, Chapter 8). And the combined sensitivities of the various participant types would seem to serve only to enhance the validity of the consensus findings.

As for the issue of severity of problems, we have tended to conduct pluralistic usability walkthroughs early enough in the product development cycle to have not worried about problem severity; if a problem is identified and agreed to be a problem, it gets fixed.

The one-linear-path constraint is nettlesome for today's object-oriented interfaces, which tend to provide the user with more flexibility in pursuing a task. One of the editors of this book has pointed out that "This technique may be most appropriate for the evaluation of traditional character-based, full-screen interfaces that are clearly divided into distinct screens for each of the users' sub-tasks" (Nielsen 1993a), and I agree. Nielsen also suggests that the technique could be used for a one-at-a-time look at dialog boxes or other GUI windows.

Parallel Use of Online Prototypes

All of the foregoing chapter has assumed a paper-based walkthrough with no online prototype available. In fact, we have used an available, generic (i.e., perhaps not showing the particular scenario in question, but representing the general interface style) prototype in a pluralistic usability walkthrough to demonstrate some aspects of the interface that are not easily shown on hard copy (e.g., color, cursor movement). Furthermore, given the benefits ascribed to this type of walkthrough, some of which may be unique among inspection methods, it makes sense to consider a pluralistic usability walkthrough of an extant online prototype or even working code. This could be as a complement to online user testing, or even a replacement if time was particularly tight.

This notion of group testing of online interfaces calls to mind the groupware-based requirements gathering (cf., Bias et al. 1993). With the technology such as decision support centers available, facilitating the display of user interfaces and the collection of individual reactions to it, it is a logical step to employ such groupware in usability walkthroughs. Thus, the combined benefits of individual usability testing and the synergistic group process could be derived.

3.7   Conclusions

Acknowledge, if you will, that "User interface design has become a multidisciplinary activity [and] . . . successful design requires coordination among these disciplines" (Grudin and Poltrock 1989). And recognize that "The participatory character of software design and development, involving HCI professionals, software engineers, and even users (as workers or customers) has emerged as an important theme in HCI research and practice" (Mack 1992a). Then it is easy to recognize, retrospectively, why the pluralistic usability walkthrough, with its focus on representative users, its bringing together users and developers, and its early applicability in the product development cycle, has yielded valuable results.

The pluralistic usability walkthrough is one method to consider to help avoid creating Stone-Age user interfaces.

Acknowledgments

I would like to recognize Ruven Brooks, Doug Gillan, John Karat, Clayton Lewis, and Jakob Nielsen for their selfless and knowledgeable responses to my many questions. I would also like to acknowledge three other groups of people: IBM colleagues who have helped me conduct pluralistic usability walkthroughs—Georgia Gibson, Rick Ragan, and Cindy Roosken; many thick-skinned and open-minded product developers who participated; and yet more representative users who were willing to participate and speak up.

Chapter 4

Inspections and Design Reviews: Framework, History, and Reflection

Dennis Wixon
Digital Equipment Corporation

Sandra Jones
Boston College

Linda Tse
Independent Consultant

George Casaday
Digital Equipment Corporation

In this chapter we propose a general framework for user interface inspections. This framework reflects the evolution of inspections of commercial products at Digital Equipment Corporation over the last few years. These inspections are reviewed and the types of problems and responses of inspection clients (development groups) are presented. Finally, inspections and their framework are discussed in relation to other methods and research possibilities.

History

At Digital we have been doing design reviews and inspections since 1987. A number of techniques evolved in response to

- The requests of development organizations

- The goals of the organization doing inspections

Over time, we recognized a need to create an overall framework for inspections and to review our past inspection work in relation to this framework. Three motivations sparked this attempt at systematization: advance of a framework for inspections, the practical use of inspections to improve products, and the developing literature on inspections.

4.1   Framework

Advancement of Practice

We needed a vantage point from which to review our efforts to date. The development of any methodology requires a systematic framework for consideration, evaluation, and evolution. Examples from other domains illustrate the importance of such a framework. The evolution of scientific thought clearly benefited from a reflective framework (Kuhn 1962). Only recently have such systematic approaches been developed in usability space (cf. Mayhew 1992; Wolf and Rhyne 1987; Nielsen 1992a). In addition, it has been suggested (Heidegger 1962) that any such work begins with an implicit perspective and framework and that, to the extent that the framework can be made explicit, all participants benefit (Schön 1983).

Practical Use

In addition to the advancement of inspection practice in general, development of a framework had clear benefits in our day-to-day work. First, without a systematic framework we could only train new inspectors by apprenticeship—a lengthy and risky process. Second, we believed that construction of a framework based on reflection from practice would provide clues for increasing our effectiveness with our client groups.

Developing Literature

Finally, as we were beginning to practice design reviews and inspections in a more systematic and disciplined way, a literature was beginning to develop (Jeffries et al. 1991; Nielsen and Molich 1990; Lewis et al. 1990). To fully benefit from this work, we needed to clarify, document, and systematize the methods we had used on a heretofore somewhat ad-hoc and unreflective basis.

The following section presents the general framework for inspections.

4.2   Framework for Inspections

To represent this framework, we use a metaphor—the lens of inspection. At the root of the metaphor is the idea that inspections are a way to view a user interface just as a lens is a way to view an object. One adjusts a lens to bring some things into sharp focus while others fade from view. Thus, at the outside of the lens are the "controls" where we "adjust" the focus depending on what we are looking for. For example, heuristic inspections bring usability into focus from the perspective of clear and straightforward usability heuristics. Other aspects, such as critical factors for market acceptance (cf. Brooks, Chapter 10) or performance by users, fade from view. Returning to the metaphoric image, the mechanisms of the lens are designed to support this overall focusing process. Thus, mechanisms or process of inspections should be developed and evaluated by considering the purpose of the inspection. We don't use a microscope to see stars. Similarly, we might not expect to "see" performance or customer acceptance problems with an inspection. Finally, in the center of our lens is the object to be viewed. In this case we are looking at aspects of a user interface. These concepts are depicted in Figure 4.1 and discussed in more detail in the subsequent text.

Goals

At the outside of a lens are the controls which are manipulated by an operator to achieve certain goals. Similarly in the development process, inspections may be considered to have two general categories of goals. The traditional goal of inspections, and the focus of most of the current research on inspections, is the improvement of the interface for the system being inspected. Questions within this category include the best method for inspections (e.g. Nielsen 1992a), and the cost-benefit of inspections (Karat et al. 1992). A second category of goals relates to the effects of inspections beyond their contribution to a particular interface. Goals within this category would include education of the development teams in user interface

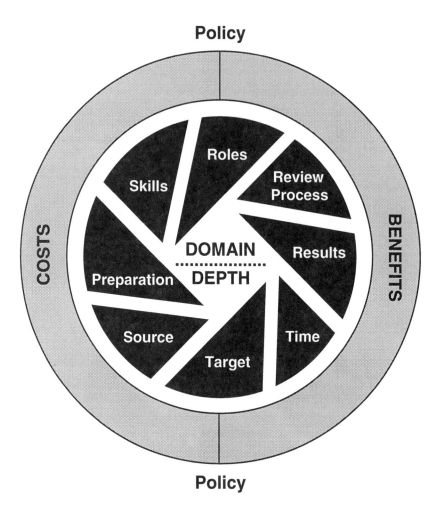

Figure 4.1 *The lens of inspection.*

design principles, integration of inspection methods into a general development process, development of new inspection methods, and the relative merits of inspection in comparison to other usability methods.

Focus

At the center of the lens is the object of concern. For usability inspections this object can be considered in terms of domain and depth.

Domain. Domain refers to those aspects of the interface which affect the quality of that interface in users' eyes. While the various domains of an interface clearly interact in nontrivial ways to produce an overall impression of the quality and usability of a product, they can be separated for the sake of clarity and convenience.

Inspections which have been done at Digital have covered a wide range of domains: adherence to guidelines, general usability, graphic design, and task relationship. Guideline inspections review an interface with respect to its conformance to guidelines such as OSF/Motif[1] (Open Software Foundation 1992), IBM CUA[2] (IBM 1991), or Microsoft Windows[3] (Microsoft 1992). General usability inspections cover those subsets of issues that all users would find problematic: for example, inconsistency in the use of key bindings, failure to provide feedback, lack of undo capability, and others. Nielsen's 10 principles (Nielsen 1993a; Nielsen and Molich 1990) for heuristic reviews cover such general usability concerns (see Karat et al. 1992, for a different set of principles). Graphic design relates to the look of the interface. While some aspects of the look are covered by guidelines, such as the OSF/Motif 3-D look, there is considerable latitude within that framework to produce visually pleasing and clear interfaces or crude and confusing ones. Task relationship refers to the adequacy of the software to support work products, the use of familiar terminology, and the extent to which the software follows the natural flow of work. These would be conducted by a potential user of the product.

In addition, one could extend the domain concept to other aspects which contribute to the overall success of a product. For example, if the user interface design was done first, programmers could inspect the interface to assess how easy it would be to implement. (Such an approach has the interesting characteristic of putting user interface design ahead of system design, and thus moving it to the front of the design cycle.) Another interesting prospect would be to have marketing experts evaluate an interface's marketability. The concept of setting a domain for an inspection both systematizes the current inspection work and suggests new directions for inspections.

---

[1] OSF/Motif, OSF, and the Open Software Foundation are trademarks of the Open Software Foundation Inc.

[2] IBM and CUA are trademarks of IBM Corporation.

[3] Microsoft is a registered trademark, and Windows is a trademark of Microsoft Corporation.

Depth. Depth refers to exhaustiveness with which one covers a specific domain and/or comprehensiveness with which a proposed design is reviewed. For example, with respect to a set of guidelines one could choose to cover a subset or to be exhaustive and cover all aspects of the user interface which relate to the entire set of guidelines. Specifically, any inspection could cover a subset of the entire interface, such as the main window and the most frequently used dialog boxes, or it could be more exhaustive.

Consideration of domain and depth help to make the goals of the inspection process clear. Such clarification sets the participants' expectations appropriately. In addition, clarifying both the domain and depth of an inspection determine the overall structure and process of the inspection.

Structure and Process

The structure and process for an inspection include all those considerations and steps that lead up to an inspection, what is done at the inspection itself, and what follows the inspection. Structure and process include: the roles of participants, skills and authority of the inspectors and participants, preparation for the inspection, execution of the inspection, what to inspect, the inspection product, the response, and the assessment.

Roles and Skills. In our experience the minimum set of roles represented at an inspection include: member(s) of the development team, inspection facilitator, and various inspection experts (graphics designer, usability engineer, task expert, etc.) depending on the domain which is chosen. Clearly, roles of participants in the inspection are coincident with their skills. For example, a task expert would not be qualified to review the graphic design of an interface. These roles should be clearly defined as part of an overall inspection process. Clarifying roles has contributed to the effectiveness of the inspection (see the discussion which follows).

Roles also need to be considered for the development team. Some types of inspections (see later discussion) require that the development team send members who are empowered to make commitments with respect to the user interface. If no one is willing to make such commitments, then this type of inspection should not be held.

Consideration of roles also clarifies the question often asked in the research literature—how much experience or training is needed for an effective inspection? When different roles are considered, the question becomes, what is the experience or training needed to fulfill a given role?

The roles that participants assume during an inspection can depend on the makeup of the inspection team. For example, when users of the product were present during inspections, roles tended to be more clearly defined. Human factors experts took on the role of UI experts, developers took the role of exploring possibilities given the current tool set, and the users took on the role of task experts. These inspections were more effective than those conducted without users and led us to incorporate the idea of roles in the framework for inspection.

Resources and Process

Preparation. Inspections don't just happen. They need to be planned. Within the aforementioned framework just outlined, the domain and depth need to be identified. Such identification helps clarify expectations and provides a background for deciding if the inspection is the right method and, more generally, if the inspection is worth doing. For example, if a development group is unclear about who will use the product and what their work is, then other methods may be more useful. Conversely, if the development is virtually complete and the development group is searching for a "blessing" from the usability experts, then the inspection may not be worth the time.

Resolving the domain and the depth of inspection allows one to plan for the preparation and inspection time, people needed, and the preparatory steps, (e.g., access to software or specification).

Preparation also allows the inspection team and the development team to jointly determine the goals of the inspection, the time to be taken, the specific schedule, the roles and skills needed, the process to be followed, the source and target, the response, and the assessment.

Review Process. Review process refers to how the inspection will be carried out. Inspections can be done individually or in groups. They can be accompanied by written reports or simply take place. The process can be more or less structured. However, inspectors may not accept a process which is too tightly structured.

Source and Target. A domain for an inspection has two elements: the source for the evaluation and the target to be evaluated. In effect, the source and target are what are "focused on through the lens." For example, for guideline inspections the source is the guidelines document and the target is the application interface (or its specification). For a usability inspection the source can be a set of heuristics or an interface standard (see the section on OSF/Motif Inspections) and the target a section of the user interface, a design for a section of the user interface, or even a flowchart for the system organization (Desurvire et al. 1992). For inspections with other foci, the source and target are less clear. Heuristics for graphic design are less well known and accepted. In some cases the source document was created for the inspection.

Results. The results of an inspection are like the "snapshot taken through the lens," that is the permanent record of the inspection. These results can take many forms: for example, a set of recommendations produced in the form of a document or an annotated interface. Another acceptable form is an audio or video tape of the inspection meeting. Experience suggests that it is important to document the inspection with a written report. Such a report produces a sense of closure and clarity with respect to user interface issues. When recommendations are not documented, some development teams have ignored suggestions and claimed to have had their designs "approved." Documenting the recommendations clearly avoids such misunderstandings.

Response. Response is the negotiated agreements for mutual follow-up after the inspection. This can take the form of a follow-up meeting to review the inspection results to clarify which changes the development group will be making and which will not be addressed. In addition, the reasons for making or not making a change can be clarified. Such a review can identify high priority areas to address in the overall development process. For example, if development groups routinely agree with the suggestions made in the inspection, but cannot implement them due to resource constraints, then it becomes clear that more general issues need to be addressed.

Assessment. Assessment is the broader process of evaluating the effectiveness of inspections. Most of the literature has assessed inspections in comparison with other usability methods in terms of their cost and benefit (Karat et al. 1992; Desurvire et al. 1992; Jeffries et al. 1991). Such work assumes that the goals of inspections are the same as those of the other methods. Alternatively, we could assume that usability tests and assessments do not have the same goals, and therefore, need not be compared. Some of the findings in the literature lend support to such a viewpoint. For example, (Jeffries et al. 1991) found that testing uncovered problems that the inspections would never have seen. Similarly, many users are not sophisticated enough with respect to graphic design to be of much value in evaluating a design. However, the overall quality of the graphic design may affect the overall impression about the software.

Within a noncomparative framework, usability inspections are evaluated relative to the goals set for them rather than in contrast with another technique.

4.3   History of Inspections and Design Reviews

XUI[4] Inspections

Background: XUI was Digital's first corporate-wide effort to construct a direct manipulation interface for workstations (for more detail, see Good 1988, 1989a). It was the largest software effort that Digital had ever undertaken, involving hundreds of engineers throughout the USA and Europe. Several methods were used to improve the usability of the XUI family of applications. These included:

- Writing a style guide
- Holding a trade fair
- Consulting directly with individual projects
- Using electronic conferencing
- Conducting focused empirical testing
- Inspecting user interfaces

Goals: There were three major goals for XUI design reviews:

1. To improve the user interfaces of all the XUI applications being developed

---

[4] XUI is a registered trademark of Digital Equipment Corporation.

2. To educate the engineering community about the XUI style in particular and direct manipulation interfaces in general
3. To use our UI design expertise efficiently

Method: Four to five usability engineers and four to five members of the development team gathered in one room where the developers demonstrated the interface as it ran on a workstation. The format was unstructured. There was no commitment to provide a complete review of the interface design or to uncover the bulk of interface problems. Often the products were at an early stage of development when user interface design and functionality were incomplete. We usually asked the developers what they wanted to show us. The developers usually demonstrated only small parts of the interface before questions and comments arose. The reviews generally lasted one to two hours.

Results: Usability concerns and strengths were uncovered quickly. Frequently the issues uncovered were general; for example, poorly chosen menu-item names or disorganized dialog boxes. Thus, review of a small part of the user interface often had implications for the overall design of the system.

The response of design teams was generally positive. They had expected to be treated critically by the usability engineers, but instead found an atmosphere of collaboration. Beyond the general demeanor of the review team, a number of factors contributed to this positive atmosphere:

1. Usability engineers avoided a policing role in the design of the interface (thus they did not present themselves as an obstacle).
2. Recommendations were clearly stated (consider making change X to dialog box Y).
3. Rationales were stated.
4. Positive aspects of the interface were pointed out.

Using a team of UI designers had mixed results. On the positive side, different people brought different experiences and concerns to a given design. The UI team shared a common vision of what a successful design should be. However, during the early stages, the XUI design "guidelines" were still evolving, and suggestions from the usability engineers were sometimes contradictory. The team agreed not to air design debates during inspections.

There were other limitations to the overall process. There was no systematic follow-up; we were never sure of what ultimately was changed in the user interface. In many cases, no task focus was present. Often design decisions required an understanding of the users' work. Such understanding may or may not have been present in the development group or in the inspection team. In a few cases, we brought real users into the design meetings. Doing so was very productive because they could address these work-related issues directly (in Chapter 3 Bias gives this three-part pluralism a much more complete treatment).

OSF/Motif Inspections

Background: With the formation of the Open Software Foundation (OSF) and the adoption of an industry-wide standard for workstation interfaces, it became necessary to migrate the XUI applications to Motif. By now most development teams were experienced in user interface design, having made the transition from a character cell environment to a graphical user interface in XUI. At the same time they were unfamiliar with the OSF/Motif style and with a 3-D look and feel, and they felt they needed someone to aid them in making the transition. This process was simplified by the fact that Digital had developed the basic OSF/Motif tool kit and that many underlying aspects of XUI were incorporated into the OSF/Motif standard.

Goals: The goal of these reviews was compliance with the OSF/Motif design guidelines. A secondary goal was to educate the development team about Motif.

Method: In comparison with the XUI design reviews, these inspections included a different mix of people. Often a single UI expert would work with a whole design team. Applications at various stages of completion were actively demonstrated by the UI expert who followed a definite sequence, paralleling the sequence of items that users would see as they perused the interface. There was no attempt to incorporate user scenarios into these reviews. Such an approach exposes the breadth of the interface without requiring an in-depth knowledge of the users' tasks. It assumes that users scan a dialog box from upper left to lower right, much as they would read a text. (Not knowing the users' task limits the focus of these inspections; it would be wrong to claim that the user interface reflected the natural work flow since that was not part of the focus.) Coverage of the guidelines varied. Reviewers felt that with practice it was possible to actively consider about 30 to 70 percent of the guidelines when doing the review (not including specific key and mouse bindings).

Results: Deviations from the OSF/Motif standards were uncovered in these reviews. These ranged from a simple violation of conventions, like the placement of menu items, to more subtle design flaws, such as the failure to use tab groups in dialog boxes. While it was not a goal, some of these meetings yielded suggested changes to the OSF/Motif UI standard. In addition to issues related to OSF/Motif, these reviews often uncovered violations of generally recognized principles of good design. For example, OSF/Motif provides a mechanism for moving the cursor systematically through dialog boxes using the tab group function. A review of the use of the tab group function would expose dialog boxes which were haphazardly arranged. Review of such dialog boxes provided the context to discuss the layout of the dialog box and its relation to work flow.

A systematic effort was made to transfer the experience from these design reviews directly to the development groups. For example, the reviewers developed check lists to remind themselves of guidelines; these eventually evolved into the OSF level 1 checklist. This highlights an aspect of inspections which has received little or no attention; that is, these inspections may lead to the development of specific design tools which can then be used by people with less design sophistication. In this specific case, the effectiveness of such a list has not been assessed. Experienced reviewers felt that the checklist was good for simple problems, but that more complex issues require dialog with an experienced designer. Thus, the checklist serves as an effective training tool and winnows out the simple issues, saving the professional designers time.

As with XUI, there was no regular follow-up to ensure that designs were compliant. However, the OSF offers a voluntary certification program that provides official certification to compliant applications.

Test Flights

Background: Unlike the XUI or the OSF/Motif design reviews, test flights were not developed in conjunction with the construction of a user interface standard. Instead, they were developed by consultants working on a contract basis inside Digital.

Goals: There were two major goals of the test flights. First they were aimed to highlight how the interface is communicated to a new user. Second, they were designed to give the usability consultant an overview of the system under development. An overall goal was to improve the interface.

Method: During test flights, the UI professional sat with the design team and interacted with the interface. The interface need not have been completely implemented, since the development team could describe portions of the interface which were not yet implemented or too unreliable to try. Generally, the review of the interface was completed in one hour. The development team guided the UI professional through the application, but the interface consultant worked the controls. The development team was requested not to explain the rationale behind their design. The UI consultant reported expectations, surprises, and what the interface communicated; criticisms were avoided. The discussions were tape recorded on audio tape for later review by the UI designer and the development team.

Results: These reviews met their goals. For the most part they resulted in user interface changes and an increased understanding of what the user interface is communicating to novice users. They also set the stage for future work on the user interface by the design consultant.

Consistency Inspections

Background: Increasingly, software products are becoming more integrated. Spreadsheets offer database, graphical, page layout, and sophisticated programming functionality. Development systems integrate compilers, editors, debuggers, code generators, project management, and front-end design into unified packages. This integration increases the demand for consistency among components. The challenge in producing a consistent interface is greater because the relevant work domain is expanded. In this context it became clear that generic interface standards, such as OSF/Motif, were not sufficient.

Goals: The aim of these reviews was to produce the maximum degree of consistency among all the components of a system within the time constraints of the development schedule.

Methods: First, a team of representatives was formed from each of the component's development teams. They were empowered to make decisions for their component at the review meeting. The UI expert reviewed all the elements and produced a document which described the current interfaces. A one-half day to full-day meeting was organized in a room that provided for projection of a computer screen. The document describing the interface was distributed to all who attended the meeting. Step by step, elements of the interface were reviewed and inconsistencies were examined and resolved. Unanimous agreement among the representatives of the affected components was required for a change to be adopted. Items which could not be resolved quickly were tabled. Agreements and change orders were noted in a consistency document that was being revised during the meeting. Thus, a clear set of decisions was produced in the meeting. Inconsistencies which could not be addressed in the near future were noted for future discussion. In addition, inconsistencies for which there was no simple remedy were noted for further design work.

Results: In relation to their specific goals, these meetings have been quite successful. A typical meeting has uncovered dozens of inconsistencies and produced a specific list of changes. The development of a document in the meeting contributed to a sense of closure. In some cases schedule changes, personnel changes, and project redirections have intervened to alter the timetable for user interface changes, but the suggestions are not lost and are eventually addressed. (Such changes may require additional work on the part of the user interface consultants.)

General Design Inspections

Background: In reviewing our past work, we decided to address some of the limitations of past design reviews. Specifically, we expanded the focus of the reviews beyond conformance to a standard of consistency. We began to develop an approach to preparation and follow-up. Thus, all those who request reviews are asked to prepare a list of questions for the review to address. We record the review meeting and produce a written summary for the team, giving them a record of the output. We also have begun to systematically track and document the impact of these reviews. We are currently surveying the teams we have worked with.

Goals: The general goal of improving the interface was the same. A secondary goal was to extend the scope of the review to additional contributors, such as graphic and information designers.

Methods: The development team presents the UI design including a general overview, and/or specific design questions. The presentation is usually a working demonstration, although some groups present specifications with mock-up screens and features at a very early stage of development. These reviews are unstructured and last two hours. A coordinator handles all set-up and logistical details and provides tape recordings and written summaries of recommendations. The participants include user interface designers, experts in particular style guides (such as OSF/Motif), and information/documentation providers. The meetings are tape recorded and transcribed. From the transcription, a list of recommendations is developed by the coordinator and sent to the development team.

Results: Since general design inspections have been conducted most recently (1990–1992) and because of our increased interest in studying the impact of inspections more systematically, we reviewed the impact of inspections in two major ways. First, we classified the types of issues which the inspections uncovered. Second, we surveyed the development teams that participated in inspections with respect to their reaction to them.

Issues uncovered: These results represent the inspections for eight products, including: system and networking tools, development environments, database query tools, and desktop management tools. The recommendations made during these reviews were classified into the following 16 categories:

1. **Improve feedback** included 23 specific types of problems such as: provide watch cursors, highlight targets for "dropping" objects, dim disabled buttons, label input fields, and others.

2. **Conform to a specific standard** included 15 specific types of problems, such as contents of menus, labels for buttons, and others.

3. **Conform to common UI conventions** included 15 specific types of problems, such as grouping like menu items, creating windows at a minimum size, and others.

4. **Improve aesthetics** included five specific types of problems, such as make buttons a uniform size, and others.

5. **Provide expected functionality** included six types, such as providing common sorting orders for file lists, and others.

6. **Preserve user work** included five types of problems, such as saving queries, providing a save state as part of customization, and others.

7. **Support work flow** included four items such as: group together menu items that are related to a specific task, reorder the dialog boxes, and others.

8. **Set proper defaults** included two specific types: reset the default size of the windows (since users were consistently resizing it), and set defaults to match novice preferences.

9. **Improve documentation** included three specific types of problems: documenting the underlying widget used, providing a journal capture file, and adding material to help.

10. **Prevent errors** included removing disabled choices from pop-up menus and asking for confirmation on destructive actions.

11. **Change for internationalization** included three items (e.g., left justify the text in labels).

12. **Allow to reverse action** included providing specific reversal functions (hide all-unhide all), and providing reset for multiple setting.

13. **Minimize memory requirements** included scrollable message areas and preserving a list of commands.

14. **Involve users in design** was recommended when it was clear that the development group had no direct contact with potential users of the application. (This suggestion points to the much larger issue of user involvement in the design process and participatory design [Greenbaum and Kyng 1991]. This recommendation was made when the inspectors would offer some alternatives to the current design and state that the choice depended on how users structured their work. They would then ask the design team if they knew how users structured their work. In most cases the design team was unsure and this led to the recommendation that they at least talk to some real users.)

15. **Eliminate unnecessary action** meant don't make users press a toggle button to type into a field.

16. **Be consistent** was just that. (Note: many of the suggestions in the categories above served to increase the consistency within an application; however, if a suggestion was related to a more specific class, it was placed in that class.)

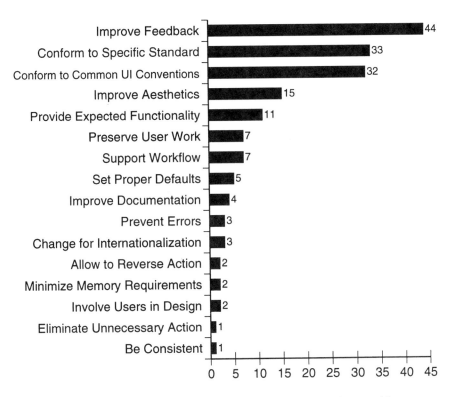

Figure 4.2 *Number of times various categories of usability problems were found.*

Two user interface designers classified the 172 recommendations into this category system. The reliability of classification was 95 percent; disagreements were resolved by discussion. The results are depicted in Figure 4.2.

The relative frequency of the various categories of recommendations reflects both the state of the applications reviewed and the implicit principles being used by the reviewers. By making the principles explicit in heuristic reviews Nielsen is able to more systematically assess the reliability and the effectiveness of various principles (Nielsen 1992a).

Response of client groups: One area not systematically addressed by the current literature is the reaction of client groups to inspections. For these inspections we surveyed the development groups with respect to the prepa-

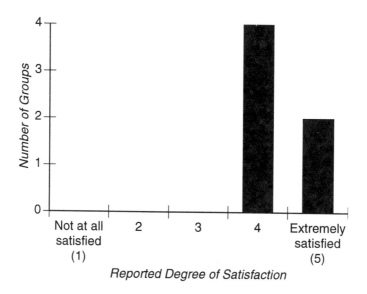

Figure 4.3 *Histogram showing the degree tc which the development groups were satisfied with the overall inspection process.*

ration for the inspection, the inspection process itself, and results of inspections. The survey was directed toward both measuring the effectiveness of the inspection process and improving its effectiveness.

As can be seen in Figure 4.3, the development groups were relatively satisfied with the overall inspection process.

All the groups said that they would recommend this process to other development groups. Open-ended questions confirmed these generally positive ratings:

> In fact, it exceeded my expectations. I was very impressed with both the number of people present and the level of expertise.

> We had Tom, Linda, and Dennis to do the review and their combined interests and areas of specialty were a great combination.

In response to the question, "What did you like best about the design review" groups reported:

Getting concrete suggestions and feedback on not only the overall UI, but also on specific screens/windows/dialogs and some leads on additional style information.

Without your visit, we could only surmise that we are on the right track— you added the needed objectivity.

Immediate feedback from knowledgeable people about our UI.

The insights into UI design, what works, what doesn't work, and *why* (their emphasis).

The group's understanding of the Motif guidelines.

A high level of design support, which included immediate feedback and suggestions for alternate design resources.

These findings suggest that conducting the inspections in a team setting contributes to both the effectiveness of and the positive response to the process.

In addition, we asked development groups about the effectiveness of the suggestions made. Again ratings were generally positive, as shown in Figure 4.4.

Groups reported making between 3 and 25 immediate changes to their product as a result of the design review. At least one group reported making about 50 percent of the recommended changes during the course of development. The case in which the fewest changes were made was somewhat deviant since the product being reviewed was bought from an outside vendor, and thus the "client" for the review merely passed the results on to a third party. In general, the most important reason for not making changes was lack of resources/time. This result suggests that conducting inspections earlier would have been more effective. Overall, development teams felt that the recommendations which came from the meetings were useful.

In response to the open-ended question "what they had done," development groups reported a number of interesting actions (some of which we did not anticipate):

We developed a small style guide that augments the Motif and DECwindows style guides and had each developer of a component adhere to that guidance. We also did establish some new

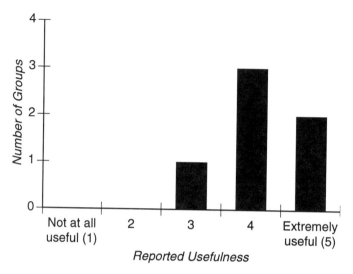

Figure 4.4 *The development groups' ratings of the usefulness of the suggestions made as a result of the inspections.*

tools to aid in resource consistency across all the components . . . .

We kept an online list of tasks . . . . We are able to use about 50 percent of your specific suggestions.

We used the review recommendations as one of the list of things to do before going to external field test. Some of them will be implemented immediately and some will be deferred until the next release due to schedule restrictions.

We did the design review early enough to incorporate the changes in the first version.

We changed our UI significantly to give products a sense of familiness.

While development teams were generally positive about design reviews, they did have a number of specific suggestions for improvements:

Involve as many of the engineers from the design team as possible.

They (the UI designers) should review the product ahead of

time.

Feedback was (too) unstructured.

A planned follow-up session would be very valuable; we could implement different solutions and see which were preferred.

We have such limited involvement with the UI design group, I think our product would benefit from more interaction.

The review should not be the first contact with the UI design group.

The time constraints.

Too crowded, too rushed. . .

There is no common interest beyond the review. There was no interest shown in seeing the products after the review. . .

Not enough "how-to" examples/discussion. I would have liked to have seen one UI screen redesigned on a white board, with discussion about user/software function impacts.

The clients' suggestions reflect a desire for an overall process for inspections which would be more integrated into the overall development process and would provide them with more contact with the usability professionals. Integration into an overall development process would probably make any usability method more effective. In contrast, inspections were developed in part to "spread" the expertise of the user interface designers across as many teams as possible and reduce the time spent by usability engineers with individual design teams. Requests for additional contacts are unlikely to be met unless resources increase or new processes are created.

Summary of General Design Inspections

In general, client groups have positive impressions of inspections, find the recommendations from them useful, and make a substantial number of the recommended changes to the final product. These results are particularly positive since the products inspected were at a late stage in development. Some of the outcomes were particularly encouraging, such as the development of their own style guide by one group. At the same time the client groups made a number of suggestions for the improvement of inspections. They wanted more preparation, more follow-up, and in general more exposure to the usability professionals.

4.4   Reflections

Overall Process

From a business perspective, the relative cost and benefit of inspections are important considerations. Most research has dealt with these issues from the perspective of the usability consultant. However, that is a fairly limited perspective when considering the commercial success of a product (Brooks, Chapter 10). Part of a broader perspective would look not only at costs of the inspection process, but also at the costs of addressing the issues raised by the inspection. Effort may vary dramatically and bear little relation to customer benefit (Wixon and Jones 1991). However, in general the earlier issues are uncovered, the lower the cost to address them (Pressman 1992). Hence (Desurvire et al. 1991, 1992; Nielsen and Molich 1991), techniques for extending inspections beyond user interfaces into work flow show particular promise. A cost analysis also needs to consider delays in product shipment which may occur as a result of addressing usability issues. For example Conklin (1991) estimates that a one quarter delay in shipping a product may result in a loss of 50 percent of the potential revenue for a product. (Of the cases covered here, we are aware of no delays in shipment as a result of addressing the issues raised.)

In terms of the framework outlined earlier, effort and impact clearly relate to what is inspected and the focus of the inspection. At different points in the development cycle, different documents or artifacts could be inspected. Different types of documents, (e.g., requirements, high-level design, interface design), are produced at different stages of development. Management could require that specific documents and artifacts be inspected at particular points in the development cycle. In that context, inspections become part of the general process of development.

Blatt and Knutson (Chapter 14) suggest an alternative framework of embedding the knowledge on which inspections are based in a development tool. This approach has many benefits and some risks. However, in contrast to the present approach which separates user interface specialists from the development team, the source of inspections would be embedded in a tool which would become part of the daily design process.

Relativity of Inspections

It seems that in evaluating the effectiveness of a method, one needs to consider the goals of the method.

Some goals are common to all inspection techniques we have used and are relevant to assessing any usability method. For example, the objective of improving the user interface by eliminating user problems extends to the vast majority of methods. However, a consistent goal of the inspections we conducted was teaching aspects of design to the development team and increasing the team's awareness of user interface issues. The specific focus of that teaching may differ. In some cases teams were introduced to a standard (e.g., OSF/Motif) or an entire approach to interface design (direct manipulation). Evaluation against such a broad goal is difficult and was not attempted. Such a training goal is rarely considered in user interface testing.

In contrast with the current research (Nielsen and Molich 1990; Karat et al. 1992; Nielsen 1992a), the goal of uncovering most of the usability problems was not the primary consideration in these design reviews (see previous discussion on focus). We never assumed that these limited reviews could uncover all the user interface issues. In fact we explicitly limited the depth and domain of many of the reviews.

When comparing inspection to other methods, both depth and focus concerns apply. Any alternative method should have the same focus as the inspection. In other words the alternative method should have the same domain of concern and the depth of review as the inspection technique. These "focus" distinctions can be applied to other usability methods. Usability testing can focus on short, well-defined test situations or take a more longitudinal approach. Before comparing methods, questions of domain should be broadly framed to be sure that we are not confounding method and focus.

Contrast with Other Methods

The inspection method can be contrasted with methods with which we have direct experience: usability engineering (Whiteside 1986; Whiteside et al. 1988; Nielsen 1993a) and contextual design (Holtzblatt and Jones 1990; Wixon et al. 1990).

There are two rationales for comparing and contrasting these (and other methods). First, we believe it is incumbent on the user interface design community in general to provide a general theoretical framework within which methods can be organized. This is part and parcel of the effort involved in building any new science. In fact, the systematizing of a methodology and the development of a framework of theory is at least one of the defining characteristics of science per se. Second, we believe that comparing and contrasting these methods will help provide a basis for managers and usability professionals to make informed decisions. Much of the work in the area of inspections has had this focus (Nielsen 1992a; Jeffries et. al. 1991; Karat et.al. 1992). One aim of this chapter is to "step back" from the direct measurement of effectiveness of methods and gain some perspective by raising some broader issues (see also, Bias, Chapter 3; Blatt and Knutson, Chapter 14; Brooks, Chapter 10).

Usability Engineering—A Laboratory Method

Usability engineering (Good et al. 1986) applies the principles of engineering to user interface design. It stresses operational definitions of usability embodied in a metric and relies on development teams specifying planned levels of usability to be achieved. By doing so it creates a favorable climate for usability testing in which development teams have specified the testing metric and the goals prior to the test. Using these methods, it is common to achieve a measurable 30 percent increase in the usability of products and to have between 80 to 90 percent of the usability problems raised addressed.

Given that usability engineering generates performance data, its results are readily extrapolated to cost-benefit analysis. However, as with any usability testing method, the extrapolation of the results of any usability engineering test depends on the representativeness of the test task, the representativeness of the test participants, and the representativeness of the general test environment.

In contrast with inspections, usability testing produces "objective" behavioral data. However, it is entirely possible that the data from an inspection may be more relevant than a usability test to a product's success. For example, corporations may set as the criterion for purchase of a product that it conforms to the OSF/Motif standard. Products which do not conform to the OSF/Motif standard will not be considered. In that case, an inspection focused on Motif compliance would be more relevant to marketplace success than a usability test.

In a larger sense, much of the effectiveness of usability engineering is based on the active participation of the development group in the specification of the usability goals and metrics. In a similar way much of the success of inspections could depend on the overall process in which the inspection is embedded.

Field Research

In comparison with laboratory methods, field methods such as contextual inquiry/design are aimed much less at evaluation and much more at the discovery of the structure and process of user work (Good 1989b). To put it somewhat dramatically, these methods consider "real users" doing "real tasks." As such, their input is most effective at the early stages of design and has the broadest design implications. Issues of representativeness of task and relevance of metrics do not arise. However, the representativeness of the participants is still an issue and the structuring of data becomes more challenging. When combined with other methods in a receptive development environment, contextual inquiry has been shown to have a positive impact on product acceptance and revenue (Wixon and Jones 1991).

These field research techniques differ fundamentally from more evaluative techniques in that they are "proactive" in the design process. That is, these techniques are used to shape the thinking of a product development team before any design exists (Good 1992). In contrast, evaluation techniques such as inspections "react" to an existing design and thus are aimed at "improving" rather than "creating." (Actually, field research techniques can also be used after a product is shipped. In this context they are useful for design input into the next version and for evaluation of the effectiveness of the design methods used in product development.)

At the same time, inspections may not be focused on evaluating the effectiveness of the user interface with respect to customer work or acceptance. They may instead focus on a number of other important aspects of interface design, such as compliance with a standard, good graphic design, consistency of look and feel, or conformance with simple usability heuristics. As such they may uncover limitations which user testing or field research methods would miss.

Research Directions

The research on usability inspections has been extremely active, very rigorous, and highly relevant to the practitioner. In particular, its focus on cost benefits and improvement of the technique has been noteworthy. The excellent track record of the current research notwithstanding, consideration of some questions would substantially broaden the scope of the current research. In particular, researchers could focus on the effects of inspections in relation to marketplace acceptance. Any data which would relate inspections to speed of marketplace acceptance would be most interesting. (A 10 percent increase in market acceptance corresponds roughly to coming to market three months early [Conklin 1991].) Moving inspections forward in the product development cycle and extending them to high-level design (such as work flow) also seems a promising area. Research on the effect of aspects of the overall development process into which inspections are embedded may be another fruitful area. Perhaps, the most effective studies will be longitudinal case studies in which the effectiveness of a number of methods are evaluated in relation to a total lifecycle.

Finally, it would seem that some theoretical work on a new approach to application development is needed (cf. Ehn 1988; Gould et al. 1991). Currently, usability is seen as an addition to the overall development process. Hence we understand the interest in reducing its cost and demonstrating its benefit. However, user interfaces now constitute between 37 percent and 50 percent of the engineering effort of a system, depending on phase of the project (Myers and Rosson 1992). Thus, the time may have come to consider an approach to developing systems that makes user interface design an integral component of the overall process.

Acknowledgments

Thanks to Tom Spine for supplying technical background. Pam Keenan developed the concept and the graphic for the lens of inspection. Thanks to Anne Duncan, Mary Beth Raven, John Bennett, and to our fellow authors for critical reviews.

The views expressed in this chapter are those of the authors and do not necessarily reflect those of Digital Equipment Corporation.

Chapter 5

The Cognitive Walkthrough Method: A Practitioner's Guide

Cathleen Wharton

John Rieman

Clayton Lewis

Peter Polson

University of Colorado at Boulder

The cognitive walkthrough (Lewis et al. 1990; Polson et al. 1992a) is a usability inspection method that focuses on evaluating a design for ease of learning, particularly by exploration. This focus is motivated by the observation that many users prefer to learn software by exploration (Carroll and Rosson 1987; Fischer 1991). Instead of investing time for comprehensive formal training when a software package is first acquired, users prefer to learn about its functionality while they work at their usual tasks, acquiring knowledge of how to use new features only when their work actually requires them. This incremental approach to learning ensures that the cost of learning a new feature is in part determined by the feature's immediate benefit to the user.

The target audience for this chapter is practicing software developers. The goals of the chapter are: to provide a detailed description of how to actually do a cognitive walkthrough, to show how the cognitive walkthrough fits into the development process, and to summarize experiences and evaluations of the method. Readers primarily interested in the details of the theoretical rationale underlying the walkthrough are referred to Polson et al. (1992a).

1. Define inputs to the walkthrough
   Identification of the users
   Sample tasks for evaluation
   Action sequences for completing the tasks
   Description or implementation of the interface
2. Convene the analysts
3. Walk through the action sequences for each task
   Tell a credible story, considering . . .
   Will the user try to achieve right effect?
   Will the user notice that the correct action is available?
   Will the user associate the correct action with the effect that user is trying to achieve?
   If the correct action is performed, will the user see that progress is being made toward solution of the task?
4. Record Critical Information
   User knowledge requirements
   Assumptions about the user population
   Notes about side issues and design changes
   The credible success story
5. Revise the interface to fix the problems

Table 5.1 *Overview of the cognitive walkthrough process.*

5.1   Overview

Brief Description of the Walkthrough Process

The cognitive walkthrough has the same basic organization and rationale as other types of design walkthroughs, such as requirements walkthroughs and code walkthroughs (Yourdon 1989). It is a review process in which the author of one aspect of a design presents a proposed design to a group of peers. The peers then evaluate the solution using criteria appropriate to the design issues.

In the cognitive walkthrough, the reviewers evaluate a proposed interface in the context of one or more specific user tasks. The input to a walkthrough session includes an interface's detailed design description (perhaps in the form of a paper mock-up or a working prototype), a task scenario, explicit assumptions about the user population and the context of use, and a sequence of actions that a user should successfully perform to complete the designated task. An overview of the process is presented in Table 5.1.

During the walkthrough process the group considers, in sequence, each of the user actions needed to accomplish the task. For each action, the analysts try to tell a story about a typical user's interaction with the interface. They ask what the user would be trying to do at this point and what actions the interface makes available. If the interface design is a good one, the user's intentions should cause that person to select the appropriate action. Following the action, the interface should present clear feedback indicating that progress is being made toward completing the task.

Scope and Limitations of Method

Cognitive walkthroughs focus on just one attribute of usability, ease of learning. Theories of skill acquisition (e.g., Anderson 1987) predict that facilitating learning by exploration will facilitate skill acquisition. Other attributes of usability like functionality and ease of use are correlated with ease of learning. For example, if an application's functionality is a poor match to a user's needs, and the user is required to perform arcane sequences of actions to complete tasks, then that system will be difficult to learn to use.

Use of the cognitive walkthrough as the only method for evaluating an interface would push design trade-offs in an interface in the direction of ease of learning. For example, the walkthrough process would give a negative evaluation to features intended to enhance productivity if these features make it harder to decide how to perform a task.

Cognitive walkthroughs evaluate each step necessary to perform a task, attempting to uncover design errors that would interfere with learning by exploration. The method finds mismatches between users' and designers' conceptualization of a task, poor choices of wording for menu titles and button labels, and inadequate feedback about the consequences of an action. The procedure uncovers implicit or explicit assumptions made by developers about users' knowledge of the task and the interface conventions. The evaluation procedure takes the form of a series of questions asked about each step in the task that are derived from a theory of learning by exploration (Polson et al. 1992a).

Later on in this chapter, we review some comparisons and evaluations of the cognitive walkthrough method as related to alternative methods (Cuomo and Bowen 1992; Desurvire et al. 1992; Karat et al. 1992; Wharton et al. 1992; Jeffries et al. 1991). (See also Mack and Montaniz, Chapter 12; Kahn and

Prail, Chapter 6; Karat, Chapter 8; Desurvire, Chapter 7; and Bias, Chapter 3 for related discussions.) These studies show that the method is narrowly focused. We argue that this is a trade-off. In the interest of acquiring a great deal of information about ease of learning, the method sacrifices obtaining valid information about other important usability attributes such as global consistency or the relative ease with which a user might be able to make catastrophic errors. All methods have their own strengths and weaknesses, and several methods will need to be used by the developer/evaluator to ensure good interface coverage. The methods presented in this volume complement each other and collectively serve to provide a reasonable suite of usability inspection tools.

5.2   Detailed Description of the Walkthrough Procedure

The cognitive walkthrough analysis has two phases: a preparatory phase and an analysis phase. In the preparatory phase, the analysts agree on the input conditions for the walkthrough: the tasks, action sequences for each task, user population, and the interface that will be subjected to analysis. The main analytical work takes place during the second phase, during which the analysts work through each action of every task being analyzed. The details of both phases, in particular the recording requirements, depend heavily on how the walkthrough is to be used within the evaluators' own development process.

How the Walkthrough Fits into the Development Process

Formally, the cognitive walkthrough is a usability inspection method to evaluate a design for ease of learning by exploration. It can be performed after specification of a relatively detailed design of the user interface, which occurs after requirements analysis and definition of functionality of an application. A walkthrough can also be performed on a paper simulation of the interface, or on a minimal prototype constructed with HyperCard, Visual Basic, Toolbook, or other similar tool, or on a full functioning prototype of the design.

The walkthrough can be an individual or group process. For a group evaluation, the designer presents the design to a group of peers, typically after an intermediate milestone such as prototype creation, and then uses the feedback to modify or strengthen the next revision. The peers may include other designers, software engineers, and representatives from other organizational units such as marketing, documentation, and training development organizations. Additionally, in attendance may be an interface evaluation specialist. Each member of the evaluation team has a specified role: One person should assume the role of recorder or scribe, another act as facilitator, and the rest contribute various kinds of expertise, such as knowledge of the potential market, user needs analyses, and so forth. Everyone is generally responsible for carrying out the evaluation.

An individual may also use the cognitive walkthrough to evaluate a personal design. Since the walkthrough is based on an explicit model of the process of learning by exploration, developers participating in their own (or other group) walkthroughs also have the opportunity to internalize knowledge of the processes associated with the underlying theoretical model. This knowledge can then influence the later design decisions that a developer makes when designing new or follow-on products. Thus, the evaluation processes can be used at the earliest phases of the design cycle by individual designers, developers, or groups of designers.

The cognitive walkthrough can have a beneficial impact on all phases of the design and development process. Marketing studies and related inputs to a requirements analysis can be influenced by the resulting interface evaluation. Too, the selection and evaluation of core user tasks will be of use when benchmark tasks are later selected, tested, and advertised.

Defining the Inputs to the Walkthrough

Before the walkthrough analysis begins, four areas must be agreed upon.

Who will be the users of the system? This may be a simple, general description, such as, "people who use existing ATM machines." But the walkthrough may be more revealing if the description includes specific background experience or technical knowledge that could influence users as they attempt to deal with a new interface. For example, users might be "Macintosh users who have worked with MacPaint." The users' knowledge of the task and of the interface should both be considered.

What task (or tasks) will be analyzed? The walkthrough involves detailed analyses of a suite of tasks. It is possible to do an analysis of all important tasks for a system with simple functionality, such as a basic voice mail system or other consumer-oriented, walk-up-and-use applications. Too, for existing systems, a single task may be evaluated, such as one that has proven problematic in a previous release. In general, for systems of any complexity, the analyses should be limited to a reasonable but representative collection of benchmark tasks.

A critical question is how to select these representative tasks. Task selection should be based on the results of marketing studies, needs analyses, concept testing, and requirements analyses. Some benchmark tasks should be sampled from the core functionality of the application, that is, the basic operations that the system is intended to support. In addition, some tasks should be included that require combinations of these basic functions.

The benchmark tasks should be made as concrete and realistic as possible. The task descriptions must include the necessary context, such as the contents of databases that users are expected to be using. This context should reflect typical conditions under which the systems will be applied. For example, in a database retrieval task, the sample database should be large or small with respect to the expected use of the system. More discussion regarding these and other related recommendations for task selection, complexity, variants, identical subtasks, task/application boundaries, and overall interface coverage can be found in Wharton et al. (1992).

What is the correct action sequence for each task and how is it described? For each task, there must be a description of how the user is expected to view the task before learning the interface. There must also be a description of the sequence of actions that should accomplish the task with the current definition of the interface. These actions may be simple movements, such as, "press the RETURN key" or "Move cursor to 'File' menu." Or, they may be sequences of several simple actions that a typical user could execute as a block such as, "login to the system" for experienced UNIX users, or "Select 'Save' from 'File' menu for experienced Macintosh users. The decision as to what level of action granularity is appropriate depends primarily on the level of expertise of the expected users. One rough guideline is that the actions should be described at the same level as a successful prompt or effective tutorial. Another guideline is that reasonable collections of similar keystrokes, such as those used to input a filename, be considered as a single action (Wharton et al. 1992).

How is the interface defined? The definition of the interface must describe the prompts preceding every action required to accomplish the tasks being analyzed, as well as the reactions of the interface to each of these actions. If the interface has been implemented, all information is available from the implementation. Earlier in the development process, the evaluation can be performed with a paper description of the interface. However, some important features of the system will be difficult to appraise, such as response time, color distinctions, timing of a speech interface, and physical interactions.

For a paper description, the level of detail in defining the interface will depend on the expertise that the anticipated users have with existing systems. For example, in preparing to analyze a Macintosh application intended for experienced Mac users, there would be no need to provide a detailed description of the appearance of the standard Mac menus; a simple listing of their contents would suffice.

Walking Through the Actions

The analysis phase of the walkthrough consists of examining each action in the solution path and attempting to tell a credible story as to why the expected users would choose that action. Credible stories are based on assumptions about the user's background knowledge and goals, and on an understanding of the problem-solving process that enables a user to guess the correct action. (Note that in earlier versions of the method, as discussed further on page 127, there was not the explicit use of credible and failure stories as are presented in this version.)

The problem-solving process is described by Polson and Lewis' CE+ theory of exploratory learning (Polson and Lewis 1990). In brief, that problem-solving process holds that users: (1) start with a rough description of the task they want to accomplish, (2) explore the interface and select actions they think will accomplish the task (or some part of it), (3) observe the interface reactions to see if their actions had the desired effect, and (4) determine what action to take next.

The theory also notes some specific heuristics that users apply when making their decisions. In particular, users often follow a "label-following" strategy, which leads them to select an action if the label for that action matches the task description (Engelbeck 1986). For instance, a user with the task of "print a document" might select an action with the label "print" or "document" (or a printer or document icon).

The critical features of the interface, then, are those that provide links between the user's task description and the correct action, and those that provide feedback indicating that the previous action advanced the user's progress. As the walkthrough proceeds, the analysts apply this theory as they tell and evaluate their story of why a user will choose the correct action at each step. In particular, the analysts ask the following four questions:

- Will the users try to achieve the right effect? (For example, maybe their task is to print a document, but the first thing they have to do is select a printer. Will they know that they should be trying to get a printer selected?)

- Will the user notice that the correct action is available? (If the action is to select from a visible menu, there is no problem. But if it's to triple-click the printer icon, the user may never think of it.)

- Will the user associate the correct action with the effect trying to be achieved? (If there's a menu item that says, "select printer," things will go smoothly; not so if the menu says "SysP.")

- If the correct action is performed, will the user see that progress is being made toward solution of the task? (If after selecting the printer a dialog box states that the "Printer is Laser in Room 105," great. The worst case is *no* feedback.)

These questions are loose guidelines, the meaning of which will be clear in the context of examples (success and failure stories) provided later in the chapter. However, it should be emphasized that the four questions are not absolute requirements. They are criteria that the analysts should consider in attempting to produce a credible story of the interaction.

Capturing Critical Information during the Evaluation

While performing the evaluation, it is important to capture information in a means that will allow the group to perform the evaluation most efficiently and effectively. A variety of recording means have been designed for and used during this process, most of which have been used with earlier versions of the method. For example, the evaluation session can be recorded on videotape (Rowley and Rhoades 1992), electronically (Rieman et al. 1991), using group visible materials such as flip charts or overheads (Wharton et al. 1992), and paper-based forms (Wharton 1992; Wharton et al. 1992; Lewis et al. 1991a).

For group evaluations it is strongly suggested that group visible materials be used. Where convenient, capture the entire evaluation process, including evaluator comments, on videotape. The videotape can serve as a record for going back and verifying or retracing comments or decisions. The group visible materials serve to capture and summarize all decisions and key information for the group.

There are several types of information that are useful to capture using group-visible means during the evaluation process. Most useful are user knowledge requirements, assumptions about the user population, notes about side issues and design changes, and the credible success story developed during the walkthrough. We suggest the use of three displays to capture all of this information. In particular, we suggest using one display (e.g., flip chart or overhead) for recording the key points of the group story, one display for cataloging all information about each class of user, and one display for capturing notes about side issues and design changes. The information about users may also be combined with the group story, with the relevant user information appropriately marked or singled out.

When recording the group story, we suggest capturing key points like those given in the next section. For user information we suggest capturing the following information for each class of user:

- What the user must know prior to performing the task
- What the user should learn while performing the task

For the side issues and design changes that are discussed during the evaluation process, we suggest making notes about the specific issue with enough appropriate context to reconstruct and address the issue more fully at a later time. For example, suppose during the evaluation of a particular action it is found that a menu item has a misspelling. We would record the particular menu that has the misspelling so that the problem can easily be located and corrected later. Videotapes of the evaluation can also be of use here. Examples of some information the group might record are given in the next section.

Success and Failure Stories

Recall that the analysis phase of the walkthrough consists of examining each user action and crafting a credible story as to why the expected users would choose that action based on assumptions about each user's background knowledge and goals, and on an understanding of the problem-solving process that enables a user to guess the correct action. To give a better idea of the kinds of stories the analysts derive during a walkthrough, we present several examples of credible success stories—stories that describe an interface working as it should—as well as stories that describe clear failures of interfaces.

Examples of Credible Success Stories

Success Story 1: An experienced Macintosh user begins a task by double-clicking an application's icon to start it.

Defense of Credibility:

- User is trying to start the application because the user knows you have to start an application to use it.
- User knows that double-clicking is possible from experience.
- User knows double-clicking is the action to use from experience.
- Changes to the display and menu bar signal start of the application.

Note that the first three parts of this story would not work for a person new to computers, and the second and third would not work for people without Mac experience.

Success Story 2: An experienced Macintosh user pulls down the GRAPH menu in preparing a graph in a presentation graphics package.

Defense of Credibility:

- User is trying to prepare a graph because that is the overall task.
- User knows to pull down this menu because the title GRAPH is clearly related to what is being attempted.

- User knows that pulling down the menu is possible, and that that is the action to take if the label looks good, by experience with the Mac.
- User knows things are going OK when a palette of graph types appears on the pull-down menu.

Success Story 3: A bank customer is using a phone-in system to transfer funds between accounts. The system says "enter your customer ID number" and the customer keys it in.

Defense of Credibility:
- User is trying to enter the number because the system said to do it.
- User uses the touch-tone buttons because they are visible and there is no other available facility for entering the number.
- User knows customer ID number because the user memorized it when the bank assigned it. (Note: this part of the story stretches credibility!)
- User thinks things are going OK when system goes on to play an audio menu of services.

Common Features of Success
With these examples in mind, we can revisit the four points that the analysts consider at each step and note some further details for each.

Users May Know <u>What Effect To Achieve</u>:
- Because it is part of their original task, or
- Because they have experience using a system, or
- Because the system tells them to do it

Users May Know <u>An Action Is Available</u>:
- By experience, or
- By seeing some device (like a button) or
- By seeing a representation of an action (like a menu entry)

Users May Know <u>An Action Is Appropriate</u> For The Effect They Are Trying To Achieve:
- By experience, or
- Because the interface provides a prompt or label that connects the action to what they are trying to do, or

- Because all other actions look wrong

Users May Know Things Are Going OK After An Action:

- By experience, or
- By recognizing a connection between a system response and what they were trying to do

Several of these points emphasize the importance of knowing how the user would describe the task. When the system uses the same terminology (or graphics) as the user, the user will pick the correct actions. This is the "label-following" strategy. Feedback will also be meaningful when it is expressed in the user's vocabulary. When unusual terms are used by the system, the user will find it difficult to succeed without additional knowledge.

Examples of Failure Stories—When No Credible Story Can Be Told
Success stories require success under all four of the analysts' criteria, while failure stories typically fail under a single criterion. With this in mind, we organize the examples of failure according to the criterion under which they fail. Note that each of these examples is based on user testing or field data.

Criterion: Will the User Be Trying To Achieve The Right Effect?

- *Example 1:* In an early office system it was necessary to clear a field on a menu by pressing a special key before typing into the field.

- *Failure story:* Users probably did not realize they needed to clear the field (so they never looked for the control).

Criterion: Will the User Know That the Correct Action Is Available?

- *Example 1:* In a particular graphing program, changing font and other characteristics of the graph title is achieved by double-clicking on the title to open a dialog box.

- *Failure story:* Users often do not consider double-clicking in this task context.

Command-oriented systems often have failures under this criterion. Users often know what effect they want to achieve (e.g., find the size of a file or create a new directory), but they don't know—and can't find—the name of the command.

Criterion: Will the User Know That The Correct Action Will Achieve The Desired Effect?

Example 1: In an early office system it was necessary to access key operations, like printing, from a special menu that was only accessible after a special key, labelled REQ, had been pressed.

Failure story: Users did not know what the special key REQ was used for, nor did they realize that they needed to press this key to access the requisite menu.

Example 2: In a word processor there are two menus. One menu is called FORMAT and the other is called FONT. Type styles are part of the FORMAT menu.

Failure story: Users do not know which menu to select if they want to put something in italics.

Example 3: In a telephone-based environment, an audio prompt may tell the user to "press the pound sign" on a phone keypad.

Failure story: Users often do not realize that the symbol "#" on the keypad is the pound sign.

Criterion: If The Correct Action Is Taken, Will The User See That Things Are Going OK?

Example 1: In an early office system you were required to sign off the system from a menu. After a user signed off, a sign-on menu appeared.

Failure story: Users didn't always realize that they had successfully signed off. Instead, some users would automatically fill in the sign-on menu again and get caught in a loop.

Example 2: In an early office system no feedback was presented to the user when a document was printed unless explicitly requested by the user.

Failure story: Learners didn't always realize that they had been successful. In this case, some learners repeatedly printed documents.

Some Other Problems to Watch For

- *Time outs:* Some systems, especially phone-based ones, give users only a certain amount of time to take action. Try to determine if the time allowed is adequate.

- *Physically difficult actions:* Holding down keys simultaneously, especially when they have to be pressed or released in a certain order, is hard. So is selecting small targets with a mouse, touching a screen, or the like.

- *Dropped terminator actions:* Users sometimes forget actions that signal completion of some part of a task, like pressing the pound sign after entering an ID number or a semicolon after a statement in a programming language. This may be because the completion is already apparent to the user. This may occur even though the user knows perfectly well that the action is required and even though they do it correctly most of the time.

In addition to these specific areas, the analysts need to be suspicious of supposedly credible stories that depend on users' knowledge of system terminology, or "commonly used" interaction methods, or complex plans.

5.3   Detailed Example

In this section we present a detailed example of a short walkthrough. The task is to forward calls on a campus phone system. We note that the walkthrough treats this system as a walk-up-and-use application, which may not have been the designer's intent. Nonetheless, our experience is that at least some users find themselves in the position of needing to use the system without training.

The Walkthrough: Preparatory Phase

Users: The larger class of users includes all staff and faculty on the university's campus, plus their guests and other visitors. It is expected that anyone needing to make a phone call has previously used either a touch-tone or rotary dial telephone. For the evaluation that follows we assume that our user is one of the university's professors. The professor has used the phone system several times to place outgoing and receive incoming calls. The professor further knows that you can program your phone to do assorted tasks such as forwarding your calls.

Task: I want my phone calls to be forwarded to my associate's office. My associate's number is 492–1234.

Action sequence: The seven required actions for accomplishing this task and the associated system responses on the phone system are as follows:

1. Pick up the receiver.
    Phone: `dial tone`
2. Press #2 (Command to cancel forwarding).
    Phone: `bip bip bip`
3. Hang up the receiver.
4. Pick up the receiver.
    Phone: `dial tone`
5. Press *2 (Command to forward calls).
    Phone: `dial tone`
6. Press 21234.
    Phone: `bip bip bip`
7. Hang up the receiver.

Interface: The phone is a standard size, touch-tone phone located on the professor's desk. There is a template that overlays the telephone's keypad (we assume it has not been mislaid) that includes the following material:

FWD *2
CNCL #2
SEND ALL *3
CNCL #2

The Walkthrough: Step-by-Step Analysis Phase

We now use the walkthrough process to work through the interaction and appraise each step:

1. Pick up the receiver.
    Phone: `dial tone`
    Success story:

    > This seems OK based on prior experience with phones. But note that there are now phones that you "program" without picking

them up!

2. Press #2 (Command to cancel forwarding).

   Phone: `bip bip bip`

   Failure story:

   - *Criterion:* Will The User Be Trying To Achieve The Right Effect?

     Big trouble is the result here. Why would the user be trying to cancel forwarding? They just have to know.

   - *Criterion:* Will The User Know That The Correct Action Will Achieve The Desired Effect?

     Even if the users know to cancel forwarding, they might not recognize CNCL on the template and they might think the required action is pressing just the number "2", not "# 2." Also they might try to press these buttons together (simultaneously) rather than in order (sequentially).

   - *Criterion:* If The Correct Action Is Taken, Will the User See That Things Are Going OK?

     Furthermore, how do users know they've succeeded? After experience they will recognize the `bips` as a confirmation, but will they at first?

3. Hang up the receiver.

   Failure story:

   - *Criterion:* Will The User Be Trying To Achieve The Right Effect?

     More big trouble results. Even if you know you have to cancel forwarding, why should you have to hang up before reestablishing it? This action has a system-oriented effect that the user will have no reason to try to achieve.

4. Pick up the receiver.

   Phone: `dial tone`

   Success story:

     This seems OK based on experience (but remember that not all phones require this now).

5. Press *2 (Command to forward calls).

Phone: `dial tone`

Failure story:

- *Criterion:* Will The User Know That The Correct Action Will Achieve The Desired Effect?

  Here the issue is deciding between *2 and *3. The description on the template is of little help: Some people won't recognize FWD, and SEND ALL will look good even if they do.

  Also, there's the small aforementioned worry about whether "*" should be pressed simultaneously or as part of a sequence.

- *Criterion:* If The Correct Action Is Taken, Will the User See That Things Are Going OK?

  Also, the feedback may be problematic: It suggests that you can dial something, but it is also unchanged from what you heard before taking this action.

6. Press 21234.

Phone: `bip bip bip`

Failure story:

- *Criterion:* Will The User Be Trying To Achieve The Right Effect?

  How does the user know to enter the number now? Maybe it's not an unreasonable guess, but the dial tone doesn't constitute much guidance because it only suggests that the phone is active.

- *Criterion:* Will The User Know That The Correct Action Will Achieve The Desired Effect?

  Also, there is a likelihood of error in not working out the *form* of the number that is needed. That is the user must understand that it is sufficient and correct to enter "21234" and that the entire number sequence of "4921234" is not needed.

- *Criterion:* If The Correct Action Is Taken, Will the User See That Things Are Going OK?

  As mentioned previously, the bips may not mean much to someone starting out.

7. Hang up the receiver.

Success story:

Seems OK based on prior experience with phones.

Fixes for Problems Discovered in the Example

The focus of the walkthrough is on spotting problems in an interface, but it also provides an explanation of those problems; that explanation can be useful in developing fixes. In the phone example, the biggest problem is the unexpected requirement to cancel forwarding. This might be fixed in one of two ways:

1. Eliminate the unexpected requirement.
2. Make it expected by providing a prompt.

Compare the two solutions. The first solution, eliminating the requirement, is obviously better. It eliminates a number of secondary problems, including the unexpected need to hang up. However, such a solution might be infeasible for some underlying technical reason. The second solution—providing a prompt so the action is expected—has some problems. Adding a spoken, audio prompt is almost certainly impossible for the underlying system in this case, which seems to have only tones as output. This leaves making an addition to the template, which is not very attractive but better than nothing. One could add material at the bottom such as "To forward calls first dial #2 and hang up. Then dial *2 and the number."

The second problem in the phone interface is the confusability of FWD and SEND ALL. In fact, these two operations are related. FWD allows you to forward calls to a number that you key in; SEND ALL allows you to forward calls to a prespecified number, not keyed in at the time of forwarding. One solution to this problem might be to add template material that attempts to clarify the role of these two functions, although brief wording of the distinction would be difficult. Other possible solutions include:

- Eliminate SEND ALL as a feature. Is its convenience worth the confusion?
- Include the feature but don't document it on the template, making it a "power user" feature that is only documented in a corresponding user guide.

- With spoken prompts, the system could offer a choice within FWD of providing a destination number or accepting a default.
- The designers could try to think of new labels for one or both operations, such as FWD or FWD TO SECY.

Each of the suggested fixes came about due to the walkthrough process and the categorization of problems according to type of failure. General guidelines about resulting fixes by failure type are described next.

5.4   Staying on Track and General Fixes

Staying on Track

The previous example demonstrates that the analysis always *tracks the correct actions*. That is, even if there is a major problem with the interface and digressions in the discussion occur, the analysis merely notes the problem and then proceeds to the next step, as if the correct action had been performed.

If the problem suggests that the user would select the wrong action, then the analysis nonetheless considers how the user would react to feedback if the correct action had been taken. Further, the state of the interface at the beginning of each action is always assumed to be the correct, on-track state, never the state after an incorrect action was performed. It is as if the system and user had been reset to the proper state.

Following this principle may force the analysts to assume a "fix" that will make sense for the rest of walkthrough. For example, the analysts may assume that the user possessed the knowledge necessary to select the correct action. That same knowledge might be used to make sense of the feedback and might even be needed again to select the next action. For this reason, it is important to clearly indicate what the user knows a priori or learns during the course of the task.

General Considerations for Using Results to Fix Problems

In general, having identified successes or failures, what should the analysts and the design team do? We noted that failures are typically associated with one of the four criteria of the walkthrough analysis; the "fixes" to avoid or repair failures can be similarly organized. Consider each of the criteria:

1. *Will the user be trying to achieve the right effect?* If the interface fails on this point—that is, if the user is not trying to do the right thing—there are at least three approaches to a fix: (1) the action might be eliminated, either taken over by the system or combined with some other action; (2) a prompt might be provided to tell the user which action must be performed; or (3) some other part of the task might be changed so the user will understand the need for the action, perhaps because it is now consistent with another part of the action sequence.

2. *Will the user know that the correct action is available?* If the user has the right goals but doesn't know the action is available in the interface, the solution is to assign the action to a more obvious control. This typically requires a menu or prompt, rather than an unprompted keystroke; or it might involve assigning the action to a hidden but more easily discoverable control, such as a submenu, or a single keystroke instead of a simultaneous key combination.

3. *Will the user know that the correct action will achieve the desired effect?* To correct failures under this criterion, the designer needs to know the users and have a good idea of how they will describe their tasks. With this information, the designer can provide labels and descriptions for actions that will include words that users are likely to use in describing their tasks. It may also be necessary to reword the labels of other controls that users might select in preference to the correct one.

4. *If the correct action is taken, will the user see that things are going OK?* Clearly, in most situations any feedback is better than none—and feedback that indicates *what* happened is better than feedback that just indicates that *something* happened. Further, feedback will be most effective when it uses terms (or graphics) that relate to the user's description for the task. Note that in simple situations, the interface may forego feedback per se in favor of prompting for the logical next action.

As a general approach, dealing with problems by *eliminating actions* is likely to be more effective than trying to fix up prompts and feedback. Where the interface shows several problems that indicate a mismatch to the user's conception of the task, the designer should look for chances to fix those problems by a *global reorganization* rather than focusing only on local improvements.

5.5 Evolution of the Walkthrough Method

The cognitive walkthrough is based on a theory of learning by exploration (Polson and Lewis 1990; Polson et al. 1992a) and on modern research in problem solving (Anderson 1987; Greeno and Simon 1988). The method has evolved rapidly from the original version described in Lewis et al. (1990) being shaped in part by evaluation experiments in our own and other investigators' laboratories (Jeffries et al. 1991) and Lewis and Polson's experiences in attempting to teach the method in day-long tutorials at CHI'91 and CHI'92. This section briefly describes the underlying theoretical model and summarizes our experience with and evolution of the cognitive walkthrough method. We also discuss criticisms of the method and its current status.

In summary, potential users of the cognitive walkthrough method must understand that it is focused very explicitly on one aspect of usability, ease of learning. It attempts to provide a detailed, step-by-step evaluation of the user's interaction with an interface in the process of carrying out a specific task. Both the narrow focus on a single aspect of usability and the fact that the method provides a quite detailed evaluation of ease of learning are sources of the method's strengths and weaknesses.

Underlying Theory

Modern theories of skill acquisition (Anderson 1987, 1993; Newell 1990) assume that problem-solving processes are used to discover correct actions and that the learning mechanisms store representations of correct actions with the users' current goals and task contexts. Versions of this general model have been used to account for skill acquisition in a large number of domains ranging from high school geometry (Anderson et al. 1985) to human-computer interaction (Kieras and Polson 1985; Polson and Lewis 1990). Such models predict that teachers and designers can facilitate the skill acquisition process by facilitating the problem-solving processes (Anderson et al.

1984; Anderson et al. 1989; Anderson et al. 1990; Anderson et al. 1992). The cognitive walkthrough attempts to provide guidance to developers to enable them to design interfaces that facilitate problem-solving processes that users employ to discover an action sequence necessary to perform a task.

The model of problem-solving underlying the cognitive walkthrough is based on laboratory research on problem-solving done in the 1960s through the early 1980s demonstrating that people with limited experience in a domain employ variates of means-ends analysis (Newell and Simon 1972) in a very large number of situations (Greeno and Simon 1988; Polson and Lewis 1990). Means-ends analysis is a problem-solving heuristic that selects the next action by choosing the action that will reduce the most important difference between the current state and the goal.

The walkthrough process hand-simulates the user's problem-solving processes: formulating a current goal, selecting a next action, and modifying the goal based upon the consequences of the action. The key idea is that correct actions are chosen based on their perceived similarity or relevance to the user's current goal. The sophistication and robustness of such a problem-solving process is dependent upon the users' knowledge of both the task and the interface based on their training and experience. The next action is selected based upon the users' representations of their current goal and available actions, also determined by training and experience.

Users with very limited backgrounds are almost completely dependent upon the label-following strategy (Polson and Lewis 1990). Such individuals will have simple and very concrete representations of a task and its goal structure. They have little or no knowledge of the consequences of actions, so they have a strong tendency to select menu items or other actions based on how well the labels of those actions match one or more components of their current goal.

Sophisticated users have knowledge of how to decompose a task into a collection of subtasks in order to organize the task in the fashion that permits effective use of a relevant application. They will also have extensive knowledge of possible actions and the actual consequences of those actions. However, the same basic principles apply. These users select actions that are relevant or similar to a current goal. However, the evaluation of similarity is driven by much more sophisticated knowledge of the task and the interface.

A cognitive walkthrough is a set of reasonable speculations about a user's background knowledge and state of mind while carrying out a task. This is one of its major strengths. The designer is forced to consider in some detail the kind of background knowledge a user must have and what sort of mental gyrations a user must go through to complete a task successfully. We feel that the method encourages a designer to directly confront the assumptions that are implicitly or explicitly incorporated into an interface about the user's task representation and background knowledge.

History—Current View

The history of our work with the cognitive walkthrough is the story of our attempts to achieve a balance between two conflicting goals: On the one hand, the procedure should be concise and simple so it can be used efficiently. On the other, it should provide guidance to analysts with no background in cognitive psychology and little experience in interface evaluation, leading them to examine an interface in detail and identify subtle problems that they would otherwise miss.

Our first version of the walkthrough used a single-page form, containing a series of brief questions which the authors of the method expected to be sufficiently instructive and complete (Lewis et al. 1990). But the single-page form failed when we tested its use with untrained analysts, including students in a user-interface design class and designers in industry. The most critical shortcoming of the form was its terminology, which implicitly assumed some background in cognitive science. Analysts without this background had trouble distinguishing "goals" from "actions," a distinction that is critical to the method's success. They also failed to identify some of the problems that we thought were obvious, often because questions that should have pointed to those problems were subsumed within broader general questions.

Our response to these difficulties was to develop the second version of the method, which was much more formal and far more complex. We expanded the form, breaking some of the questions into subparts, and supplied detailed instructions for each question (Lewis et al. 1991a; Polson et al. 1992a; Wharton 1992). This version required designers to perform an extremely detailed analysis of the problem-solving process, including providing an explicit description of a user's current goal structure, a detailed analysis of how the user would select an action based on this goal structure, and a description of how feedback and a user's interpretation of that feedback would modify the goal structure appropriately facilitating selection of the next correct action.

This was the version Lewis and Polson taught at a CHI tutorial in New Orleans in 1991. Generation and manipulation of detailed goal structures turns out to be an art that is difficult even for someone with an extensive background in cognitive science. In other words, there were serious usability problems with this version of the method. To address some of these problems, particularly the requisite cognitive science background, one of us (CW) also experimented with a richer structure for training, question presentation, and recording of results (Jeffries et al. 1991). This approach included the use of a trained facilitator or "champion" to guide a group of designers in performing the walkthrough. It also recorded the results of the process as several separate documents, most importantly a knowledge analysis and a series of problem reports, which were designed to be immediately usable in the next phase of the design process (Wharton 1992).

A side-effect of all these changes was to make the walkthrough process more tedious and time-consuming, which many analysts reported as a major short-coming (Jeffries et al. 1991; Wharton et al. 1992). One attempt to rectify this problem was the "automated" walkthrough, an Apple HyperCard stack that prompted for each question of the walkthrough and provided space for recording the analysts' evaluations, which could then be printed in summary form (Rieman et al. 1991). The automated system included a "help" screen for each question; it automatically disabled certain questions when they weren't relevant; and it allowed other questions to be manually disabled for an entire session (e.g., questions about time-outs in a system where none will occur).

Most of the published evaluation studies have examined variants of this second, more detailed, version of the method (Jeffries et al. 1991; Wharton et al. 1992; Desurvire et al. 1992; Cuomo and Bowen 1992). Discussion of some of these evaluation studies is presented later in this section.

Even with the aid of the automated system, however, many analysts found this version of the walkthrough to be inordinately time-consuming (Desurvire et al. 1992). In recognition of that difficulty, a third version of the walkthrough method was developed. This is the version that is presented in this chapter.

This current version represents a revised emphasis on our original goals for the procedure: This version de-emphasizes explicit consideration of the user's goal structure. The designer is now asked to try to motivate a user's choice of a correct action in the sense of motivation that one would expect to underlie the actions of characters in a novel or murder mystery. The designer is asked to tell a "credible story" that motivates the selection of the next correct action. We conjecture that designers will be able to tap the large amount of tacit knowledge that human beings have about individual's goals and the motivation of action.

In part, our conjecture is based on Lewis and Polson's experience with this new version of the method at their tutorial at CHI'92. The response received was dramatically different from the CHI'91 experience and quite favorable. Students using the simplified version of the method successfully completed several problems provided by Lewis and Polson during the practical portion of the tutorial. Working in groups of four to five, students rapidly and efficiently worked through the training problems, uncovering the difficulties that we had incorporated into the problems as well as having additional insights.

Another one of us (JR) has also used this version of the method with other students in a course on user interfaces. Results have been mixed in that students do not always make effective use of the success and failure criteria, but certainly they are much more favorable when compared to experiences with past versions. We note, however, that these acclamations are not the product of a formal evaluation study, but rather anecdotal reports of user experiences. We do not yet have any empirical data validating the new version of the method.

While we still believe that the process can now be used quite effectively by designers, we recognize that this can only happen if the designers are also given more training in cognitive theory than they would implicitly receive from the simple forms and brief instructions of our original attempts. Such training may come through a short class, such as the tutorials we have given at the CHI conference or it may be provided through the "champion" approach, where a member of the analysis group is familiar with the method and with basic cognitive psychology. A good starting point is the overview of psychological theory (presented by Wharton and Lewis in Chapter 13), which points out some of the theoretical aspects that are relevant to software design. A critical part of the training is to present examples of interfaces that fail or succeed, analyzed in terms of the underlying theory. We have included one such set of examples in this chapter.

Since we now recommend that analysts understand the theory that underlies the walkthrough, in this latest version we have shifted our attention away from the details of the questions and the forms on which the walkthrough's results are recorded. The questions should focus on the basic cycle of goal formation, action selection, and response evaluation, but the details of what to examine within each phase may vary from interface to interface. Equally important, what is recorded as the analysis proceeds should also be tailored to the needs of the design process in which the walkthrough is embedded.

To summarize, we originally conceived of the walkthrough as a simple question-and-answer process that designers could use effectively with little understanding of cognitive theory, much the way a person can fill in an income tax form with no deep understanding of tax law and policy. We now believe that a basic understanding of the cognitive theory is essential, and that given that understanding, designers can structure the walkthrough process to best fit the needs of their individual situations.

Criticisms Addressed and Current Appraisal

A variety of criticisms have been levied against the cognitive walkthrough. Most of these criticisms have been based on the second version of the method; we believe we have addressed nearly all of them in our third version of the method. The criticisms have fallen into two general classes. The first is the type of usability problem found. The second is how the method fits to the development process. We will address concerns in each of these categories by discussing the method's strengths and weaknesses.

Types of Usability Problems Identified

A number of people have identified concerns regarding the types of usability problems that the walkthrough identifies (Jeffries et al. 1991; Cuomo and Bowen 1992; Wharton et al. 1992). Issues that have been raised include usability problem severity, content, scope, and total numbers. We address each of these.

Severity

By problem severity two things are meant: How much the problem impedes user progress and how much the problem is in need of repair. Using such definitions, the Jeffries et al. study (1991) compared four usability evaluation methods: a variant of heuristic evaluation, standard usability testing, guideline application, and the cognitive walkthrough. In absolute severity ratings, for the first type of severity mentioned above, the walkthrough had the lowest mean at 3.44 on a 9-point scale (where 1 is trivial and 9 is critical). Usability testing had the highest with a mean of 4.15. But when compared to the other methods the difference was significantly less: Heuristic evaluation had a mean value of 3.59 and guidelines had a mean value of 3.61, reducing the mean difference between the methods to only 0.17. We (like Jeffries et al. 1991) believe that these results, particularly for usability testing, in part reflect the biased phrasing used to identify the problems: Biased phrases such as "users had trouble. . ." occurred with the usability testing problems whereas the others used personal references or more neutral language.

Additionally, when comparing the ratios of all usability problems found, of most severe to least severe, they found that guidelines and the walkthrough were quite similar, identifying roughly an equal number of each. The heuristic evaluation performed more poorly, identifying nearly twice as many problems of lesser severity than it did of those that were more severe, and usability testing found almost exclusively problems that were considered to be most severe. Such results are not surprising to us, reflecting what we believe to be the underlying approach of each method. (cf. the results obtained by Desurvire et al. 1992.)

Each method promotes a different style of analysis. The guidelines, usability testing, and walkthrough methods each suggest specific issues to be examined: The "path" of analysis required (i.e., examine *only* a suite of user tasks or apply specific guidelines) is expectedly quite narrow and deviations from the path are not rewarded because you still need to complete other required analyses. Conversely, heuristic evaluation promotes the notion of straying off a rigid path of analysis: The evaluator can look at any given part of an interface in any order and manner chosen. The reward for the heuristic evaluator is based on the breadth of an analysis, not a narrow one. For the walkthrough, this narrowness is in part due to the focus on user actions. Usability testing may be even more restricted.

Content

Both Jeffries et al. (1991) and Cuomo and Bowen (1992) have raised concerns about the content of the usability problems. Jeffries et al. (1991) performed two related types of content analyses: consistency and recurrence. Cuomo and Bowen (1992) examined problem content in light of the seven stages of user activity in both action execution and evaluation as defined by Norman (1986) and according to functional areas as defined by Smith and Mosier (1986). We will address each of these.

The walkthrough did not rate as well on recurring and general problems as the other methods. Consistency is a measure of how well problems indicate that one part of the interface is in conflict with another. Usability testing was found to be the method which addressed consistency problems the least, while all others were comparable. These results again mirror the narrow versus broad path of analysis used by each method.

A recurring problem is one that continually interferes with the interaction, as opposed to only interfering the first time. The walkthrough and heuristic evaluation were lower (by 20 percent) than the guidelines and usability testing methods. We believe this result mirrors the underlying learning principle of both methods. The walkthrough method assumes that users learn as they go along and also that the evaluation will "stay on track." Thus, the evaluation results will reflect these assumptions. Presumably this happens, too, in heuristic evaluations, but not in the other methods.

Norman's (1986) seven stages of user activities are: (1) establish the goal, (2) form the intention, (3) specify the action sequence, (4) execute the action, (5) perceive the system state, (6) interpret the state, and (7) evaluate the state with respect to goals and intentions. In a study by Cuomo and Bowen (1992) comparing three evaluation techniques—cognitive walkthroughs, guidelines for designing user interface software, and heuristic evaluation—problems found by each method were categorized into one of the last six stages of user activity in an attempt to learn the types of problems each evaluation technique addresses. As would be expected, the walkthrough predominantly addressed problems in stage 3 with which the method (particularly the second version) is most concerned. It also did comparable to the other methods in stage 2, although all methods were considered weak in this stage. The latter stages of user activities (4-7) we believe are now addressed better by this latest version of the walkthrough method. More generally, those problems identified across all stages by the walkthrough rarely overlapped with any of the other methods of guidelines and heuristic evaluation, finding unique types of problems.

Examination of the results that categorized problems by functional area indicates similar results to the stages of user activity. Of the four functional areas of (1) data entry, (2) data display, (3) sequence control, and (4) user guidance, the walkthrough performed better on those areas more closely aligned with the earlier listed execution stages of user activities. That is, there were more problems in the data entry and sequence control areas, than in the data display and user guidance areas. Again, we believe that the second version of the method masked the role that feedback plays in a user's inter-action because of its focus on goals. Our new version has now brought both of these concerns to a more level playing field.

Follow-up work done by Cuomo (personal communication, October 1992) indicates that the walkthrough, when compared to guidelines and heuristic evaluation, actually is a better predictor of problems when considering the above stages of user activity. In detail, Cuomo and Bowen performed a usability test and the results were then compared to the previously identified problem types. For each of the predicted problem types, evidence that the problem affected user performance was sought. Across all stages of user activity, of the 51 problem types identified by guidelines, only 11 problem types (22 percent) actually appeared to cause at least one noticeable user diffi-culty. Of the 35 problem types predicted by heuristic evaluation, 16 (46 percent) caused users difficulty and of the 24 problem types predicted by the walkthrough, 14 (58 percent) problems affected users. The cognitive walkthrough performed the best in terms of predicting problems which actually affected users' performance.

Scope

Two concerns have been brought up regarding the scope of the those problems identified by the walkthrough method. In particular, Jeffries et al. (1991) found that walkthroughs identified more specific problems than general problems. This is related to the point made by Wharton et al. (1992) regarding no high-level treatment of user tasks. Because the walkthrough is task-based and consequently follows a narrow path of analysis, there is no high-level treatment of user tasks nor are corresponding global interface problems identified. By a high-level task treatment it is meant that there is no way to determine whether a given task evaluates well as a whole (since only the actions are examined) or whether the interface as a whole matches well to a user's conceptual needs. A general flaw is one that affects several parts of the interface and not simply a single part. We believe this to be an expected trade-off. If more tasks are evaluated or more partial solution paths can be evaluated, the number of general problems would be expected to increase.

Total Number of Problems

As for the sheer number of problems identified by a particular method, this is still an open question. Jeffries et al. (1991) indicates that heuristic evaluation will yield more problems, with all other methods yielding fewer problems but equivalent numbers. However, Cuomo and Bowen (1992) found that guidelines may yield the most problems with the walkthrough yielding the second highest number, due to the method's narrowness. Heuristic evaluation then follows third. These studies have conflicting results because of the differing applications of such techniques. In these studies the number of evaluators, the differing man-hours or training and availability, and experience with the overall task and environment, were quite varied. For example, in the Cuomo and Bowen study, Smith and Mosier's (1986) guidelines differ not only in number—944 compared to 62—for those used by Jeffries et al. (1991), but also in content. Consequently, no general conclusions can be drawn at this time. However, we note a few points about the walkthrough method and the larger results generally.

Although we only have a couple of studies to draw on, there seems to be a "magic" number of roughly 28 to 43 identified problems (let's say 35 ± 7) that applies to both studies for each method group. For these two studies, we list the mean results in order of Jeffries et al. (1991) first, followed by Cuomo and Bowen (1992) second. A single heuristic evaluator (which could be considered as a single group) yielded 30.25 and 28.5 problems per evaluator.

The walkthrough yielded 35 and 43 problems. Guidelines yielded 35 and 113 problems. And usability testing yielded 32 problems in the first study. Exclusive of the results for guidelines (which cannot be compared directly because different guidelines were used), the walkthrough appears to yield roughly the same number of problems as the other methods, and in some cases slightly more. Thus, the method competes well with all other methods using this criterion.

Finally, it is important to note that when discussing comparative studies such as these, many other factors will influence the results. For instance, these include the number of inherent problems in the interface, the number of tasks used for the evaluation, the reality of the databases, the skill of the evaluators, evaluator familiarity with the tasks, and the style of interface (e.g., there are fewer guidelines for direct manipulation style interfaces).

Fit to the Development Process
Concerns have also been raised about how well the walkthrough fits into the development process (Jeffries et al. 1991; Wharton et al. 1992). With one exception, we believe that we have remedied all of these process concerns. Many of these concerns have already been addressed in some detail throughout this chapter, thus we only highlight them here, as necessary.

Bookkeeping
In addition to recording information about the walkthrough proper, we also recommend capturing information regarding any side issues for later discussion and about the success or failure story being told, particularly as it applies to users. We further suggest using group-visible materials and video-taping where convenient. (For details see page 112.)

Cumulative Evaluation Time
The amount of time it takes to perform a walkthrough in general will be longer than other methods because more detailed analyses are undertaken. The second version of the method required much more time due to the extensive bookkeeping requirements. Looser applications of the second version by one of us (CW) and our experiences with this current version have reduced the amount of time substantially, by a factor of between 2 to 4.

Group Process Concerns

Wharton et al. (1992) made several suggestions for ensuring a good group walkthrough. Further experimentation with the method in group settings by one of us (CW) and refinements made to our latest version have verified that by following many of the Wharton et al. (1992) suggestions, the evaluation will be much more successful and be rated more favorably. One issue not noted, however, is the need for a good facilitator. We cannot emphasize enough that the facilitator needs to be aware of and to manage expected group dynamics and discussions so that time is not wasted during the process.

Task Selection

Task selection is a critical component of the process. For an evaluation to be most informative, tasks should be selected by adhering to those guidelines given in the section starting on page 109. Working closely with marketing folks and others concerned about the product to derive well thought out benchmark tests serves the evaluation well. Task selection more generally is an area of research for the HCI community.

Requisite Knowledge for the Evaluators

As has been noted by various critics of the method, there still appears to be a need for at least one evaluator to have some basic understanding of cognitive science for a most effective application of the method. Currently there appears to be no easy way around this. However, the walkthrough method is not alone in this requirement. Like the walkthrough, other methods have been applied successfully by the typical software developer, but better results are yielded when someone has knowledge of cognitive science (Nielsen 1992a; Desurvire et al. 1992).

Current Appraisal

The adjustments and refinements that we have made to the method since its inception in 1990 have been many. We have responded to the number of criticisms made about earlier versions of the method. The result has been the new version of the method presented in this chapter. We believe that this new version of the method remedies as many of the concerns raised about best fitting the method to the development process, as is possible. As our comments indicate, the walkthrough is quite effective at the job it is designed to do. It is not a panacea, nor the ultimate method. There are trade-offs when one method is selected in place of another, as others' results have shown. Again, we suggest the use of multiple inspection methods for a thorough evaluation.

Offshoots and Other Uses

The cognitive walkthrough is aimed at the analysis of highly prompted interfaces. The questions posed by the method direct the analyst to examine the interplay between the user's intentions and the cues and feedback provided by the interface. But the underlying logic of the cognitive walkthrough can be applied in situations in which there is little or no prompting, and users must reason their way through a problem without help from an interface. The essence of the cognitive walkthrough is the description and evaluation of a hypothetical process— a conjecture about the steps the user will take in determining the correct actions in a problem situation. In the cognitive walkthrough we assume that these steps are largely guided by the interface. But nothing prevents us from imagining what steps might be taken in the absence of such guidance. We have seen and continue to see opportunities to apply and adapt the method in other situations.

Programming Walkthroughs

The programming walkthrough (Bell et al. 1994) applies this same idea to evaluating the design of programming languages. A typical programming environment provides no prompting and no immediate feedback for most actions: The programmer writes whatever code desired, and gets only delayed, collective feedback on the effect of all this code taken together. (So-called structure editors provide some immediate feedback as code is written, but only on the syntactic legality of the code.) The cognitive walkthrough as such cannot be applied in this situation. But it still makes sense to imagine the decisions faced by a programmer in writing a program in a language and to critique the language if some of these decisions appear to be difficult.

The programming walkthrough shares with the cognitive walkthrough a dependence on specific tasks. The analyst must have one or more specific problems for which programs might be written and examines the process of solving these. The whole process is subject to comment, including any needed reframing of the problem to make it amenable to solution, preliminary decisions about how to break the problem up into parts, and any other problem-solving steps, even those that may not depend on the details of the language. As with the cognitive walkthrough the analysis aims to point out places where the process is likely to break down; that is, where the programmer is likely to make a wrong move.

Because of the lack of cues from the environment, programming requires a good deal of knowledge to choose the right steps. The programming walkthrough produces an inventory of the knowledge required for the steps in the tasks that it examines. For example, if successful use of a language requires the programmer to define certain basic data structures before writing the code for operations on these structures, then the programmer has to know this. If the design is to succeed, this piece of knowledge and other necessary knowledge, must be conveyed to the programmer in some way. If this is not feasible or desirable, then the language design must be changed to eliminate the need for this knowledge. This inventory of necessary knowledge (called "guiding knowledge") is a useful by-product of the programming walkthrough method.

The programming walkthrough has been used in a number of language design projects (Bell et al. 1994). But the idea is not limited in its application to programming languages as such. Any tool can be examined in this way, since the key idea of the analysis is simply to describe and critique a plausible sequence of steps leading from a problem to a solution using the tool. The idea has been applied to a geographic information system, which combines highly prompted interfaces for some functions with programming-language-like unprompted support for other functions. We have applied the method informally to the analysis of algorithm animations, by asking how observations users might make in viewing an animation would or would not aid them in answering specific test questions later (Stasko, Badre, and Lewis 1993).

Designers' Self-Criticism and Design Rationale

In our earlier discussion we focused on the use of the cognitive walkthrough by a group of people, all serving as analysts for a particular design. Another approach is to have a separate group of analysts critique the design of another group. This division of labor between design and evaluation is traditional, but we think it can have undesirable effects. Having a separate evaluation group is costly in staff and in communication. Further, and sometimes more important, it can lead to an "*us* versus *them*" attitude, on both sides, in which the designers view the evaluators as kibitzers who do not contribute real work but slow down those who do, and the evaluators see the designers as not sensitive to the demands of usability. If designers know they must satisfy usability evaluators, rather than their own values, they may avoid taking any responsibility for usability beyond what is forced on them, instead of seeing usability as just another aspect of design for which they are professionally accountable and in which they should take pride.

In principle, at least, we think the cognitive walkthrough could ease this situation. Designers themselves might use the method and thereby gain some ability to assess the usability of their own designs. The logistical simplicity of the method is an advantage here; anyone can do a walkthrough by themselves, any time. It is not necessary to always perform group walkthroughs.

We have successfully used the programming walkthrough in this way in our own design work on various versions of the ChemTrains graphical programming language (Bell et al. 1994). Besides being a general aid to design, we found the walkthroughs also useful in producing design rationale; that is, the reasons for design decisions, as described in Lewis et al. (1991b). We found that choosing and analyzing specific problems, as demanded by cognitive or programming walkthroughs, is a good way to see and keep track of the strengths and weaknesses of alternative designs.

5.6   Value of the Walkthrough in Design

The cognitive walkthrough method promises to be a valuable addition to the designer's suite of tools. The new version of the method is flexible enough to fit into any given software development process. The method identifies problems with a design early in the process and, by describing the reasons for those problems, it suggests design changes early on. Testing the interface with actual users, by comparison, can only be performed after a prototype of the system is available; it generally yields less obvious insight into the reasons for the problems it discovers. The walkthrough can also be used to identify questions that can be answered by specific, focused user testing, such as questions about user terminology or task description.

Experience with an earlier version of the walkthrough has shown that it can be applied effectively by software engineers, although best results are obtained where one of the analysts has some background in cognitive psychology (Jeffries et al. 1991; Wharton et al. 1992). Our experiences with the newest version of the method are similarly positive. However, like other methods, the walkthrough is not designed to discover every problem with an interface. The method's developers suggest that it is best used along with other methods that designers may find effective in answering different questions about the interface.

Acknowledgments

We thank all participants in the CHI'92 Usability Inspection Methods Workshop for their comments and helpful discussions. We also thank the following people for their helpful discussions and detailed comments on earlier drafts of this paper: Randolph Bias, Louis Blatt, Donna Cuomo, Heather Desurvire, Barbara Diekmann, George Engelbeck, Bob Mack, and Dennis Wixon.

| Chapter 6 | *Formal Usability Inspections* |

Michael J. Kahn

Amanda Prail

Hewlett-Packard Corporation

The *formal usability inspection* method represents a conscious evolution from prior usability inspection and engineering inspection (Kepner-Tregoe 1982; Fagan 1976) methods. It was designed to help engineers, who serve as inspectors, to review a product and find a large number of valid usability defects. The method specifies a formal process for detecting and describing defects, clearly defined participant responsibilities, and a six-step logistical framework that defines the method as a schedulable "event" within the usability lifecycle. While the method was designed to help inspectors detect and log a large number of defects, it was also designed to use their time efficiently.

The first section of this chapter presents a description of formal usability inspections to provide the reader with the information needed to apply the method. The second section communicates ideas that underlie the design of the method and helps the reader determine whether it is appropriate for use within a particular environment.

A glossary of terms is provided at the end of the chapter.

6.1   A Description of the Method

Method Overview

A formal usability inspection is a review of users' potential task performance with a product. It is completed by the product owner (i.e., the engineer who is designing the product) and a team of peers, looking for defects. A formal usability inspection has the following characteristics:

- A defect detection and description process: To detect defects, inspectors always use user profiles and step through task scenarios. While stepping these hypothetical users through tasks, inspectors apply a task performance model and heuristics. Then, inspectors describe these defects in a user-centered manner as suggested by the task performance model and heuristics.

- An inspection team: Inspectors represent various areas of knowledge, including, as appropriate: software, hardware, documentation, support, and human factors engineering. The method also defines the responsibilities that inspection team members have to the inspection process (i.e., a moderator, owner, inspectors, and a scribe).

- A structure within the usability lifecycle: Defect detection is framed within a structure of six logistical steps. These steps provide an effective and efficient process and link the inspection into the usability lifecycle.

The rest of this section discusses these characteristics in greater detail.

Defect Detection and Description Process

A usability defect is defined as a product characteristic that makes it difficult or unpleasant for users to accomplish tasks supported by the product. While participating in many design discussions, informal reviews, and traditional inspections, it became apparent that most product development team members do not spontaneously notice usability defects during these activities. It was necessary to provide some structure to the design review process to increase engineer recognition of defects.

Label	System Administrator
Education	Computer Science degree or system administrator courses
Experience	Minimum of 6 months as a system administrator on an HP-UX system, including system setup and installing peripherals. May not have trouble-shooting experience

Table 6.1 *An example user profile.*

In cases where team members detected usability defects, these defects were often described in a form that did not aid finding the best solution. It was necessary to provide a form for the description of defects, so that users' problems could be more effectively communicated and, therefore, more effectively solved.

To inspect a product, inspectors are given an inspection packet (a collection of papers) which includes tools to help them step through the users' tasks, know where to look for defects, and know what types of defects to look for. (Note that best results are obtained when potential participants are given a one-day class, prior to taking part in their first inspection.)

Stepping Through the Tasks

The inspection packet contains, but is not limited to, a product description, user profiles, and task scenarios.

The product description usually consists of screen drawings and explanatory text, but could consist of storyboards or a prototype. Each user profile includes, at a minimum, the profile label, user education, and user experience (see Table 6.1). Note that the *experience* field, in Table 6.1, focuses on aspects of user experience that are relevant to the inspection of a trouble-shooting product.

Each task scenario includes, at a minimum, the user's goal expressed in user terms, the starting point in terms of the task situation and the product state, and any intermediary situations that the user will encounter (see Table 6.2). Task scenarios typically do not provide a list of task steps since, as part of the inspection, the inspectors will have to figure out how to perform the task.

Label	Task Scenario #1
User Goal	User wants to know if the computer is set up correctly and is ready for general use
Starting Point	User has taken the Model 807 out of the box, cabled all hardware components, and performed software configuration
Intermediary Situation	The LAN card is not working

Table 6.2 *An example task scenario.*

There are reasons for requiring the use of specific user profiles and task scenarios. Specific user profiles are provided to help inspectors understand users' perspectives and the knowledge brought and not brought to the task, and also to impress upon the inspectors that users are not the same as they are. Inspectors are asked to complete specific task scenarios, so that they complete pieces of "real" work, just like future product users. If inspectors work at an abstract level, they will overlook decisions that users will have to make.

In order to minimize inspection time-costs, inspectors might be given only one user profile and a small number of task scenarios. Usually the user profile that represents the greatest usability risk is that of the least sophisticated user type who will use the product. The tasks to be inspected should include tasks frequently performed by the user as well as tasks that are suspected to have a high cost of error. A more complete inspection would include a greater number of user profiles and task scenarios.

During the inspection, an inspector takes the role of a specific user and works through the task steps associated with a particular scenario. If there are a number of user profiles and task scenarios, this process may be repeated for each appropriate user-profile/task-scenario combination. If an inspector gets confused or cannot complete any task, the inspector has identified a defect.

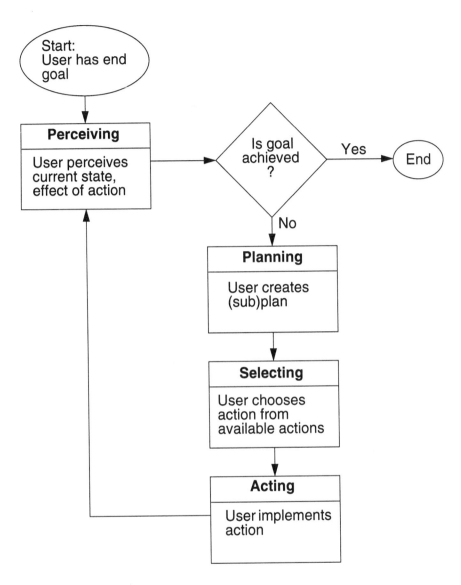

Figure 6.1 *Inspectors apply a task performance model.*

Where to Look

A tool called the *task performance model* (Figure 6.1) is provided to help inspectors learn where, in the user's task flow, to look for defects. The task performance model consists of a flowchart that provides an abstract description of human task performance. It contains four key phases (i.e., perceiving, planning, selecting, acting) of task performance, the first three of which are mental. As inspectors step through the tasks, they apply the model to define the cognitive or mental phases that need to be successfully carried out by the users.

While we do not expect inspectors to become experts in cognitive psychology, we do want them to be aware that a large percentage of task performance takes place invisibly within users' heads and that inspectors should be looking for what could go wrong with completion of these invisible phases. We also want inspectors to incorporate user profiles in order to determine how these users will see the task.

The following example shows how the model is applied: A user starts with an *end goal*, which is the result to be achieved by doing the task. In our example task scenario, the user's end goal is to determine if the system was set up correctly. During *perceiving*, the individual checks available cues and decides the system is providing no information on this question. During *planning*, the user creates a plan which consists of the interface-specific steps to be completed to achieve the goal. Planning will often include creating a mental model (i.e., a picture or script in the user's head which organizes system concepts), or importing a mental model from past experience, and then applying that model to determine one or more task steps. During *selecting*, the user decides which of the available actions to perform. During *acting*, the user attempts to implement that choice. Re-entering the *perceiving* phase, the user searches available feedback cues to determine if the action has been implemented and had the desired effect.

Each of the four perceptual phases is associated with a short set of questions. Inspectors can ask themselves these questions to help discover defects.

It is valuable for human factors engineers and other interested engineers to know about the task performance model and questions. Yet, training and application of the task performance model and questions need to be scaled to the appropriate levels.

All inspectors should be trained in, or exposed to, the task performance model. It is conceivable that inspectors would apply the task performance model with a *checklist approach* or with a *priming* approach.

Perceiving	Does the user see the information he or she needs? Can the user determine if the end goal has been achieved? What problem could the user have identifying: • The current product state? • If the action chosen was actually performed? • If the action chosen was correct? • An error state? • Appropriate error recovery actions?
Planning	What plan or model is the user likely to have based on prior experience with similar tasks? How does the user phrase the goal? What support does the user have for selecting/creating the right plan? Does the required product goal map to the user's goal or does the user have to translate the user goal into a product goal?
Selecting	What problems could the user have identifying available actions? Are there competing actions that the user could select in error? What cues have been provided to help the user select the right action?
Acting	What problems could the user have when trying to physically perform the selected action? What accidental actions could occur? Is the action something the user could do—or should the product do it? How much time does the action take, including waiting time, and it that reasonable?

Table 6.3 *Task performance questions.*

• Checklist approach: At each task step, the inspector applies each appropriate phase of the task performance model and, optionally, each appropriate task performance question.

- Priming approach: The inspector examines the task performance model and, optionally, the task performance questions, prior to stepping through the tasks in order to become sensitized or reacquainted with issues. While stepping through tasks, the inspector considers these elements in parallel.

It seems that the checklist approach would find more defects but, for most inspections, would be too time-consuming and tedious. Therefore, the priming approach is applied. The task performance model is taught to inspectors during the *Formal Inspections Training* class that is provided in advance of the actual inspection. Then, at the start of the inspection, the inspectors reacquaint themselves with the task performance model in order to sensitize themselves to what they already know. Inspectors might apply the task performance model in a checklist manner for a limited number of task steps.

At the current time, we think that many engineers will find that the task performance questions (see Table 6.3) provide too much examination of human cognitive processes. Therefore, the task performance questions should be taught only to human factors engineers and other interested engineers. To further reduce complexity, the task performance questions should not be included for application during the actual inspection (i.e., should not be included in the inspection packet).

What to Look For

This section provides a discussion of heuristics. While the task performance model is designed to help inspectors understand the places where they should look for defects, heuristics (also known as usability principles) represent a set of things to look for. Any observed instance of noncompliance with a heuristic is known to be a defect.

There are a number of sets of heuristics that have been compiled and application of any good list would be suitable for a formal usability inspection. Nielsen, in Chapter 2 of this book, provides a list of 10 generic heuristics that is both brief and comprehensive (see page 29). Nielsen (1992d, 1993a) also suggests that, for any design effort, it might be appropriate to use multiple heuristic lists. For example, one list might be generically applicable, while a second is tailored to the specific design project. We will provide additional discussion of heuristics to suggest the use of a larger generic set of heuristics and to demonstrate the relation of heuristics to user profiles and to the task performance model.

It is conceivable that inspectors would apply heuristics with a checklist approach or with a priming approach (just as was the case with the task performance model). As before, we believe that inspectors will want to save time by applying a priming approach. We provide a larger than usual set of generic heuristics (Table 6.4), with the belief that more sophisticated inspectors can use this list to remind themselves of a greater number of usability principles and, thereby, detect more defects.

The list is organized (i.e., chunked) into two types of heuristics. *Task-based* heuristics are used to assess efficiency of screen navigation and task flow, and do not require specific knowledge of user profiles. *User-based* heuristics require specific knowledge of target users. This distinction between task-based and user-based heuristics is provided to highlight the value of user profiles; if we do not know about our users, it is not possible to apply user-based heuristics in an effective manner.

It was stated earlier that the task performance model tells inspectors where they should look, whereas heuristics represent things to look for. This relationship is made apparent by comparing the heuristics (Table 6.4) to the task performance questions (Table 6.3). Heuristics can easily be rephrased and substituted for these earlier questions. Some of the heuristics map to only one task performance phase, while others map to a number of task performance phases.

How to Log Defects

It has been our experience that inspectors often describe defects vaguely (e.g., "I don't like the word choice for the menu item *Broadcast*") or as solutions (e.g., "We should change the word *Broadcast* to the words *Broadcast Command*"). It is important that inspectors describe defects in a user-centered format. In this way, the inspector comes to fully understand the user's problem and is able to communicate the problem, so that other inspectors will share the same understanding of the problem. (Shared understanding of the defect will be important later, when the group identifies solutions.)

Task-Based Heuristics	*User-Based Heuristics*
Minimize actions to accomplish tasks	Provide a mental model that capitalizes on pre-established mental models
Support the natural task flow	
Don't ask users to do what a machine can do better	Use a simple and natural dialog
	Speak the user's language
Provide defaults	Be consistent
Provide shortcuts	Provide an intuitive visual layout
Provide undo, redo, pause, resume	Make items distinct from one another
Make it very difficult to destroy work	
	Make functionality obvious and accessible
Make sure errors can be corrected with very little rework	
	Provide good help
Don't waste the user's time	Provide for multiple skill and use levels
Provide clearly marked exits	
	Allow user customization
	Put the user in control of the task and interface
	Provide feedback—minimize uncertainty
	Minimize memory load and mental processing
	Minimize modes
	Design for user error
	Protect the user from the details of the implementation

Table 6.4 *Task-based and User-based Heuristics (paraphrased from Shneiderman 1987; Nielsen and Molich 1990; and other sources).*

To describe defects in a user-centered format, the inspector can make use of the task performance model and heuristics. For example, by applying the task performance model, the inspector might write, "The goal in the user's terms

Knowledge Area	Description
Design Engineer(s)	Software or hardware engineer(s) who have been involved in the product development. Know the product and are skilled at generating solutions. High-level designers add value.
Peer Engineer	An engineer from an existing or related product serves as a knowledgeable reviewer who is not biased by knowledge of the evolution of the product. This engineer also adds value by catching cross-product inconsistencies.
Documentation Engineer	Person who has written or will write the documentation for the product.
Human Factors Engineer	Person with experience interacting with users, detecting defects, and generating solutions.
Support Engineer	Experience with similar products and resulting problems in the field.

Table 6.5 *Team members should represent most of these knowledge areas.*

is to send a command to a remote system. When the user sees the menu item *Broadcast*, the user may think this only allows broadcasting a message (the user's colloquial use of the word), but does not allow sending a command."

The Inspection Team

An inspection team usually includes between four and eight engineers. This number is effective since it allows access to appropriate skill areas. Team size should be limited, since each incremental inspector, on average, finds a smaller number of "new" (i.e., nonredundant) defects (e.g., Nielsen and Landauer 1993).

Knowledge and Experience of Team Members
Team members should represent various areas of knowledge in order to maximize the number and breadth (i.e., number of types) of defects found (see Table 6.5).

Responsibility	Description	Number
Moderator	Manages the process. Collects and distributes the materials to support the inspection. Schedules and facilitates meetings and coordinates Follow-Up. The moderator is recruited from outside the immediate project team.	1
Owner(s)	Generator or representative of design to be inspected (e.g., software engineer for screen interface, documentation engineer for manual). Understands each defect. Contributes to design solutions. Addresses defects when updating the product.	1*
Inspectors	Find and report defects. Contribute to design solutions. The moderator and owner can also serve as inspectors.	3–5
Scribe	Publicly records all defects and issues during the meetings. Scribe responsibilities can be dedicated to one inspector or rotated among inspectors.	1

Table 6.6 *Each team member has specific responsibilities during the inspection process.*
* A project team might send many owners or one "proxy" owner. If numerous project teams contributed to a larger interface, each team might send one proxy owner.

Clearly, the more exposure engineers have had to usability (e.g., user needs analysis, usability inspections, user tests, customer feedback), the more they will be able to anticipate defects. Yet, it is good to include less knowledgeable engineers so that these individuals can receive usability training.

Team Member Responsibilities

It has been stated that team members are selected to represent areas of knowledge. However, after they are selected, they are then given responsibilities as shown in Table 6.6, which define how they will contribute to the inspection.

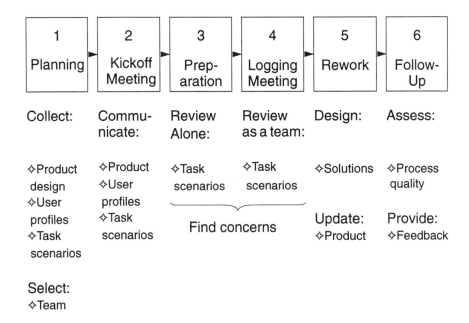

Figure 6.2 *There are six logistical steps in a formal usability inspection.*

Six Logistical Steps

A formal usability inspection is completed in six logistical steps (see Figure 6.2). These logistical steps ensure that the defect detection and description process, which was described earlier, is completed in an efficient and effective manner, and is linked to the more global user-centered lifecycle.

Step 1: Planning

The moderator and owner work together to ensure that the appropriate engineers are involved and that these engineers will have access to the information they will need to inspect users' tasks in an effective and efficient manner. To achieve these goals, they:

1. Define the Inspection Objectives—What they want to achieve.
2. Choose team members—Moderator, owner, inspectors, scribe.
3. Create the Inspection Packet (a collection of papers that inspectors will use, see Figure 6.3) which includes:
   - Inspection Instructions—Description of how to use the components of the inspection packet to look for defects.

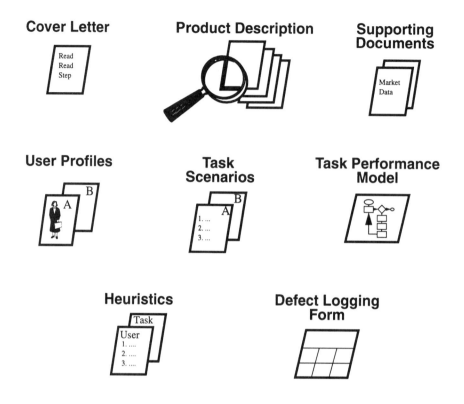

Figure 6.3 *A graphical representation of an inspection packet.*

- Product Description—Explanation of the product; e.g., a prototype, screen dumps and text, storyboards.
- Supporting Documents—Background information needed by inspectors; e.g., user demographics, standards, data on related products.
- User Profiles—One succinct description for each user type.
- Task Scenarios—Succinct description for each user task. (Instructions might include which user profiles are relevant to which scenarios.)
- Task Performance Model—An abstract model which summarizes the task flow. (Task Performance Questions are not included in order to reduce complexity.)
- Heuristics—Global principles which relate common usability defects.
- Defect Logging Form—Form used by inspectors to record defects.

- Logistics—Schedule and location of meetings.

Generally, task scenarios and user profiles are available from earlier user needs analysis or are prepared by the engineer on the team who represents usability.

Step 2: Kickoff Meeting

During the kickoff meeting, the team comes together for the first time. The moderator and owner give the inspectors the inspection packet and discuss its contents. The moderator discusses how inspectors should look for defects by applying user profiles, task scenarios, the task performance model, and heuristics. The moderator also emphasizes that the inspection represents a time that has been set aside for the inspectors to find and keep finding usability defects.

Step 3: Preparation

During preparation, the inspectors work alone. First, each inspector should become familiar with the contents of the inspection packet. Then, the inspector takes the role of a specific user and works through the task steps to complete a particular scenario. At any task step where the inspector cannot perform the task without confusion, a usability defect is logged. The inspector also applies the task performance model and the heuristics to detect defects. Defects are described in a user-centered manner. (Methods for detecting and describing defects were discussed at length earlier in this chapter.) This defect detection process is repeated for each appropriate user-profile/task-scenario combination.

For each defect, the inspector records the task number, the location of the defect, and a description of the defect (see Table 6.7). Defect location information might be recorded as follows:

- For a GUI, provide the window name and field name.
- For a command line, provide the command name and option name.
- For a document, include page and line number.

During defect logging, the inspector may choose to record a solution, but this is optional. *Severity* and *Fix Date* fields are provided for future use and generally would not be used during defect logging.

#	Location	Description	Se-verity	Solution	Fix Date
1	Window: *Realm* Menu item: *Broadcast*	The goal in the user's terms is to send a command to a remote system. When the user sees the menu item *Broadcast*, the user may think this allows broadcasting a message, but does not allow sending a command.		Change to *Broadcast Command*	

Table 6.7 *Inspectors log defects on defect logging forms. (Only one defect is logged in this example.)*

If the product or product description is not complete, and inspectors could not be expected to determine task steps on their own, it might be appropriate to ask inspectors to read the inspection packet, but not step through task scenarios until Step 4.

Step 4: Logging Meeting

After the inspectors have prepared on their own, they come together to aggregate their defects and to find more defects. In the logging meeting, the moderator steps through the user-profile/task-scenario combinations. The moderator paces the inspectors through each task scenario with questions such as, "What does the user do next?" and "Will the user have any trouble here?"

At each task step, the inspectors report any defects that they logged during preparation. As the correct sequence of task steps is revealed, an inspector may realize that, during the preparation, he completed the task incorrectly. At this time, the inspector would report this error as a defect. The synergy of the meeting will help inspectors find new defects which are also reported.

The moderator manages the meeting so that it is user/task focused, efficient, and constructive. At times, the moderator will help inspectors describe defects in a user-centered manner. The owner's role is to act as an inspector (optional) and to understand each defect reported. The scribe logs defects publicly (e.g., using an overhead projector), so that inspectors can see what is being logged.

Solutions may, optionally, be noted during this meeting, but brainstorming or discussion of solutions should be terminated, or inspectors tend to bog down in lengthy discussions. We have found that the inspection process is more efficient and constructive when logging defects are separated from brainstorming solutions. At the end of the meeting, each inspector may be given a copy of the list of defects.

A great benefit of this meeting is that inspectors learn how to find defects from each other. For example, a less experienced inspector may have found few defects during preparation. During logging, this inspector sees how the team applies the user profiles, task scenarios, task performance model, and heuristics to identify usability defects that he missed. From this experience, the inspector learns how to apply user-centered design to detect usability defects.

Step 5: Rework

During this step, solutions are found and implemented. This can be quite straightforward if there is only one design team and it is early in the design lifecycle. Otherwise, the moderator and owner, and others as appropriate, may group defects or provide severity ratings. Often, the owner will recognize that the solution to a defect will require a product change that is outside the owner's area of responsibility (e.g., another engineer is responsible for that piece of code). In this case, the owner will identify a *defect owner* to be responsible for this defect. For each defect, the owner or appropriate defect owner assesses whether to verify the defect (agree it is, in fact, a problem).

As necessary, the inspectors (and/or other appropriate engineers) meet and brainstorm or identify solutions. The owner and defect owners then select and implement solutions. The moderator provides feedback to the inspectors.

In some cases, the moderator examines the product or contacts engineers to ensure that solutions are being implemented. In less formal cases, monitoring may be turned over to a product team member.

Phase	Moderator	Owner	3 Inspectors	Total
1. Planning	12	4	0	16
2. Kickoff Meeting	1	1	3	5
3. Preparation	4	4	12	20
4. Logging Meeting	4	4	12	20
5. Rework	8	4	12	24
6. Follow-Up	4	2	3	9
Total	33	19	42	94

Table 6.8 *Example budget in staff hours.*
Note that since there are three inspectors, each hour of inspector time has been multiplied by three. Also, only four hours have been listed for the owner to work with the inspection team to create solutions. Additional solution generation and implementation time is not provided in this example, but must be preallocated.

Step 6: Follow-Up

Once the rework is done, the moderator collects, assesses, and releases data about the inspection process. Different inspection teams assess data at varying levels of detail. Most teams are interested in the number of verified defects found per total hours invested (a measure of efficiency) and the ratio of verified defects to verified defects fixed (a measure of effectiveness).

Follow-up data are sent to the team and management (optional) and the inspection is considered complete.

Implementation Issues

Budgeting and Scheduling

In the Hewlett-Packard engineering environment, it is necessary to provide engineering teams with a budget and schedule, often months in advance, so that engineer time can be allocated. An example budget and schedule are provided in Table 6.8 and Figure 6.4. (Actual budgets and schedules will vary with a number of factors.)

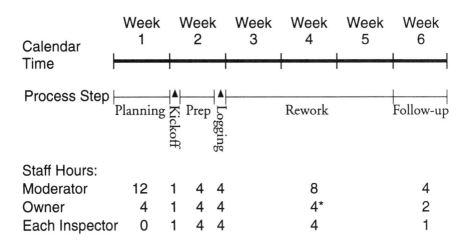

Figure 6.4 *Example schedule for a formal inspection. Note that staff time for the inspectors is given per person. Also note that four hours are allocated for the owner to work with the inspection team to create solutions in the "rework" step. Additional solution generation and implementation time is not provided in this example, but must be preallocated.*

Benefits

Completing a formal usability inspection provides a number of benefits.

Product-specific business benefits are:

- The design team has a list of defects and implemented solutions. The product is more usable.
- User testing will be more effective and efficient since users will encounter fewer problems.
- The design team has achieved a milestone in the user-centered lifecycle. In this way, the design team communicates to management that they are applying user-centered design.
- The design team has user profiles and task scenarios. These can be reused during future inspections and user testing.

Engineer training benefits are:

- Engineers are exposed to user-centered design which should cause them to create better designs in the future.

- Peer engineers are exposed to projects and design solutions other than their own. This increases the size of the "design solution library" that is available to these engineers.

- Participants are familiar with the project and can support the team in other ways in the future.

Formality and Time Costs

As with any inspection method, the greatest cost of using formal usability inspections is the cost of the team members' time. At first glance, it might appear that completing these steps will require a great deal of team member time. In fact, the method was designed in response to numerous usability and engineering inspection experiences in order to improve the *efficiency* as well as the *effectiveness* of the team members.

Formal usability inspections provide a clear "agenda" for each process or meeting. Therefore, team members know the exact set of things they must do to effectively find usability defects. Inspectors do not waste time trying to figure out what to do, nor do they do less or more than what is minimally necessary to be effective. The formality that formal usability inspections add is analogous to increasing meeting formality by providing an agenda. Preparing an agenda takes time, but in the long run, it increases meeting effectiveness and efficiency.

6.2   A Design History of Formal Usability Inspections

This section will communicate ideas that underlie the design of the formal usability inspection method that may help the reader determine whether this method is appropriate for use within a particular environment. A design method, like a user interface, must be consciously developed to meet the needs of its users. How this method was designed to meet the needs of Hewlett-Packard engineers will be discussed. We also present prior engineering and usability inspection methods which were considered, and method design heuristics we developed and applied.

User	Goals	Needs
Human factors engineer	Early impact Impact more teams	Off-load work Streamline work
Design engineer	Usable designs	Minimum time Maximum involvement User-centered knowledge
Documentation engineer	User-centered involvement	User-centered knowledge

Table 6.9 *Hewlett-Packard users of formal usability inspections.*

A User Needs Assessment of the Hewlett-Packard Design Environment

Suppose we were conducting user testing of a product and users consistently stated that they would not want to use the product. We would likely conclude that there is something wrong with the product, not that there is something wrong with the users. (Of course, to the extent that users did not understand our product or its benefits, we might have to educate them.)

It is clear that a design method, like a computer product, has a user interface and users (in this case, engineers) who interact with the interface. We knew that our usability inspection method would be rejected if it did not provide sufficient usability. Therefore, it seemed reasonable to start by assessing our users and their goals and needs. As you can see, we human factors engineers must sometimes take our own medicine.

In Hewlett-Packard's Computer Systems Organization, the most important users of a usability inspection method are human factors engineers, design engineers, and documentation engineers (see Table 6.9). User needs analyses conducted within different organizations may reveal different user types, goals, and needs. Therefore, other usability inspection methods or a modified version of formal usability inspections might be appropriate.

Human Factors Engineer

For human factors engineers, one goal was to provide usability feedback to design teams earlier in the design lifecycle. We were completing user testing on nearly completed products and, therefore, giving usability feedback to engineers late in the design process. Their responses indicated that they would have been more receptive to our recommendations if we had made them earlier. Also, earlier feedback would have introduced the design team to the idea of designing for usability while there was still time for iterative usability design efforts.

Our second goal was to impact a greater number of products. The problem was that we had a small number of human factors engineers, but a great number of projects. To put a finer point on our bandwidth limit, Nielsen (1993a) reports that most projects do not have enough usability staff, with a median of 1.5 usability engineer years per project. Our human factors group usually allocated two to three engineer months per project, and still not all projects were being impacted. Clearly, we needed to streamline our methods to enable us to join a project team, impact large usability increases in a minimal time, and then move to the next project team.

Design Engineer

A second user type is the hardware or software engineer. For the most part, design engineers want to create usable designs. Unfortunately, the competitiveness of the computer marketplace requires that products be designed and coded very quickly. The daily experience of each individual design engineer is that of working madly to meet an impending deadline. They will not let us help them achieve their usability goal, unless we find a design method that respects their time limit.

The design engineers also have ultimate responsibility for the interface and want maximum involvement in what *their* interface looks like and why it looks like that. Maximum involvement is necessary for two reasons. First, since the design engineers have been heavily involved in creating the interface, their human nature demands that they invite, and are involved in developing, feedback. Second, since they are responsible for the product, they need to fully understand the reasons why changes are necessary. A human factors engineer cannot simply hand a design engineer a list of unsolicited design solutions and expect these solutions to be implemented. We have a bit of problem here. The design engineer will allocate minimal time, yet wants maximum involvement. Clearly, we need a method that limits design engineer involvement to the key points of providing information and making decisions.

Another limit of design engineers is that they are generally lacking in user-centered knowledge. That is, they are still designing features and then linking them together, rather than applying knowledge of users and their tasks.

Documentation Engineer

A third type of engineer is a documentation engineer. At Hewlett-Packard, these engineers have traditional documentation responsibilities, but are also charged to increase the usability of the hardware/software product. (Organizationally speaking, there are approximately 10 documentation engineers to each human factors engineer.) The limiter is that these engineers have not had formal user-centered training and, like the design engineers, do not truly understand user-centered design. In summary, these engineers have the goal of increasing their usability involvement, but must become more fluent in user-centered design to be effective.

Prior Methods

When choosing or developing a product, one certainly wants to assess the products that exist. Before developing the current version of formal usability inspections, we considered four candidate design review methods:

- Kepner-Tregoe Potential Problem Analysis
- Formal Inspection
- Heuristic Evaluation
- Cognitive Walkthrough

Each of these methods had been experimented with to a lesser or greater extent within the Hewlett-Packard environment. What we learned from these experiments led to a generic set of methodology design heuristics.

Kepner-Tregoe Potential Problem Analysis

This is a generic method for protecting a plan from things that could go wrong (Kepner-Tregoe 1982). Since the sequence of steps a user applies to accomplish a task can be seen as a plan, it seemed appropriate to apply this method to inspect the user's required plan.

This method included creating task scenarios, documenting the steps to achieve each scenario, and then a team meeting. During the meeting, team members would brainstorm the problems that could interfere with correct performance of each step and find solutions to these problems.

As preparation, engineers were often given a quick seminar in user interface design (analogous to handing out heuristics), so that they would know what to look for.

We liked the idea of working in a step-by-step manner and continually asking, "What could go wrong here?" We also liked the approach to assessing the importance of potential problems, standard forms to log the problems, succinct documentation to describe the method, and the division of solutions into preventive and contingent solutions.

Problems with the method were that it was not widely known or understood within Hewlett-Packard, so it had to be justified and explained prior to its use (this problem was organizational and not inherent to the method). The meetings took a long time, since problems were being identified in real time and solutions were discussed as problems were identified. The method also required strong human factors leadership to help identify problems. Finally, there was no clear path for getting the method accepted as an R&D method that allowed human factors participation, rather than a human factors method that allowed R&D participation.

Formal Inspection
Hewlett-Packard began using formal inspections as defined by Fagan (1976) in the late 1970s, with design teams adapting the process to meet their needs. In 1989, Hewlett-Packard updated the inspection method based on contributions by many authors, including Gilb (1988). Currently, at Hewlett-Packard, there are over 300 trained moderators and the method has been used by teams in numerous software divisions.

Formal inspection requires inspectors to proceed line-by-line through a specific document to identify any potential problems (code, usability, or other) represented by the contents of the single line. We liked the team member responsibilities (e.g., moderator) and the six process steps. We also wanted to leverage the acceptance that the formal inspection method had gained. Yet, the approach of reviewing product descriptions in a line-by-line manner did not support the identification of user problems. If an engineer did not have usability expertise, it was too great a leap to go from viewing a part of a user-interface (e.g., the description of a field) to noting a problem that a user would have while completing a task.

Heuristic Evaluation

Nielsen's work with heuristic evaluations confirmed that we were on the right track in trying to create a design inspection method that could be made available to engineering teams.

The evidence that non-human factors engineers can find problems when armed with heuristics (Nielsen and Molich 1990) was valuable support for having engineers take an active role in problem detection. Research supported a team approach by indicating that each additional inspector will, on average, provide an increment to the number of defects detected (Nielsen and Molich 1990). Off-line problem identification in addition to online brainstorming seemed useful for a usability inspection method.

Heuristic evaluation was designed to provide a bare minimum approach in order to maximize engineer efficiency and acceptance. For our needs, what seemed to be missing from this bare bones approach was the formal inclusion of user and task information. What was also missing, due to the lack of formality, was the sense of the evaluation as an event in a user-centered design lifecycle.

Cognitive Walkthrough

The cognitive walkthrough method (Polson et al. 1992a) provides a way to apply cognitive theory to rigorously study users' mental processing during task completion. This approach has intuitive appeal to individuals with an understanding of cognitive theory, since it enables them to detect usability defects by applying knowledge of human cognition. Also, since many heuristics can be derived from cognitive theory, it seems that cognitive theory is actually the source basis for looking for and predicting potential defects, whereas heuristics are summaries of past findings. Finally, non-human factors engineers have applied this method to find concerns (Jeffries et al. 1991).

Our concerns with the cognitive walkthrough method were that the concepts and terminology of cognitive theory were foreign to nonhuman factors engineers. These engineers encountered difficulties in decomposing tasks into appropriate components and understanding how to use the forms associated with the method. Engineers also found it tedious to follow the procedure (Wharton et al. 1992).

Methodology Design Heuristics

On the basis of the user needs analysis, assessment of prior inspection methods, and ongoing experience with other usability methods, we developed a set of heuristics that we believe should be used in the design of an inspection method, as well as any other usability method, for the Hewlett-Packard environment. (Whereas a *design heuristic* is used to assess the design of a user interface, a *methodology design heuristic* is used to assess the design of a methodology.)

- *Minimize time cost to engineers who are on the critical path*

  Some engineers (often software and hardware engineers) are on the critical path of the product design process. Methods will be more successful if they minimize the time investment of these individuals.

- *Maximize involvement of engineers who will implement changes*

  It is the engineers' responsibility and human nature to want maximum involvement in inspecting the interface that they created. These engineers must be allowed maximal involvement in defect detection and solution generation.

- *Create a method that is an "event" in the usability lifecycle*

  Hewlett-Packard uses a formal lifecycle, which incorporates checkpoints and deliverables. Therefore, usability methods should have steps, roles, and deliverables that are identifiable and well labeled. These methods can be scheduled as an event in the lifecycle; managers and engineers will know, in advance, what is expected of them and at what times. After completing the steps, they can report having achieved a known milestone within the product lifecycle.

- *Team-based approach*

  A team-based approach, where engineers work together, is important for many reasons. First, it allows that appropriate knowledge areas are available for finding defects and, later, implementing solutions. Second, it is necessary that teams be able to proceed without a human factors engineer. Use of a cross-functional team (led by a trained moderator) lessens the risk that less-expert inspectors will miss defects. However, when a human factors engineer is available, this engineer can be easily incorporated into the process.

The team approach has the added advantage of being inherently rewarding to team members. It provides a social activity, which facilitates implementation of solutions and future usability efforts. It also fits the Hewlett-Packard culture which emphasizes team play.

- *Adapt existing methods—help do what is done better*

  Each organization has certain design methods that design engineers accept as valuable. To introduce a new method and get it accepted, one must go through a time-consuming effort of managing organizational change. Therefore, if possible, the designer of a usability method should modify already accepted engineering methods, rather than introducing completely new methods. In this way, the method designer will not need to "sell" the engineers on a new method, but only to show how an accepted method can be modified to enable finding of usability defects. The benefit to design engineers is that they can apply their own accepted engineering methods to find usability defects, rather than having to learn a foreign process.

- *Leverage the language and structure of well-established methods solving similar problems*

  When possible, usability methods should mimic the mental model, structure, and language of methods that are known to the design engineers. In this way, engineer learning time is decreased. For example, when modifying an existing engineering method, try to capture usability concepts in terms that are accessible to the design engineers.

- *Task orientation*

  A traditional, product-centered approach applies features as the building blocks of design, whereas a user-centered approach applies user tasks as the building blocks of design. This difference is fundamental and all usability methods should include task scenarios at their core. That is, it would not be appropriate to do a usability inspection in a screen-by-screen manner, examining each field for what could go wrong, since this would not resemble the user's experience of doing the task. Instead, the engineers should work in a task step-by-step manner and examine each task step for what could go wrong.

  In our experience (no controlled studies), this task-oriented approach enables engineers to find a greater number of defects. More importantly, this approach trains engineers to think in a task-centered manner. By applying user profiles and task scenarios in combination with a task performance model and heuristics, engineers can practice thinking in a task-centered manner and, at the same time, receive clues about which user defects to look for. Engineers will achieve success with this task orientation and begin the process of revising their mental models.

- *Clear potential integration with other parts of the usability engineering lifecycle*

Each design method is a component of the entire lifecycle, just as each subtask is a subcomponent of an entire task. Each method should indicate the inputs it requires from methods which are completed earlier in the lifecycle and the outputs which should be provided for methods which will be completed later.

For example, user and task information are necessary inputs to a formal usability inspection; these user profiles and task scenarios should be available from an earlier user needs analysis. If engineers are forced to invent profiles and scenarios on-the-fly, rather than relying on actual customer data, this lack of customer data becomes glaring. It is more likely that the team will collect customer data the next time.

Measures of Success

The formal usability inspection method represents a deliberate evolution from prior methods. Its current form has been derived from a combination of characterized user needs, experience with prior methods, and compliance with methodology design heuristics.

Some potential measures of success for a usability method include:

- Is a meaningful number (or ratio) of potential defects found?
- Are defects valid (i.e., users would have had problems)?
- Are quality solutions found?[1]
- Do engineers perceive enough value in the method to warrant participation?
- Do engineers enjoy using the method? (This represents an emotional component.)
- Do engineers become more effective designers for taking part?

---

[1] Contributed by Dennis Wixon during a verbal discussion.

To date, due to business pressures, we have not completed controlled studies to assess whether our products are more usable as a result of formal usability inspections. However, we have gathered anecdotal evidence that addresses some of the measures and leads us to believe that we are on the right track:

- Formal usability inspections are finding large numbers of defects. Engineers are verifying these defects and implementing fixes.

- There is a growing demand for training in the method, for both participants and for moderators.

- Engineers who have been through an inspection are requesting inspections for other products. This suggests that they are satisfied that the method works and provides good return on investment.

- User tests performed on products that have first been through usability inspections are finding far fewer defects than tests performed on products that have not been inspected.

Acknowledgments

Thanks to Rose Marchetti, who has been a major contributor to formal usability inspections. Portions of this chapter are based on material originally published in "Usability inspections—their potential contribution" by A. Prail and M. J. Kahn, in *Proceedings of the Human Factors Society 37th Annual Meeting*. 304–308. Santa Monica, CA: Human Factors and Ergonomics Society, 1993.

Appendix: Glossary

The terms provided in this glossary represent a specialized vocabulary that leverages engineers' understanding of terms used in Hewlett-Packard's Formal Inspection method.

Defect: A characteristic of a product that makes it difficult or unpleasant for users to achieve their goals.

Defect Detection Tools: Tools to help inspectors find defects. Tools include: the task performance model and heuristics.

Follow-Up: The sixth (last) step of the inspection process. Data are collected and distributed, and the inspection is closed.

Formal Usability Inspection: A formal review of the tasks that users will complete when using a product.

Heuristics: A relatively small number of concepts that inspectors apply to help find usability defects. Also called *Usability Principles.*

Inspection Instructions: A memo to inspectors describing how to inspect the product. Provided by the moderator during the kickoff meeting.

Inspection Objective: A statement specifying what the owner is trying to accomplish with the inspection.

Inspection Packet: A set of papers that provides the information that inspectors will need to inspect the product. Provided by the moderator during the kickoff meeting.

Inspectors: The participants in the inspection process who are responsible for finding and reporting defects. Likely to include design, documentation, support, and human factors engineers.

Kickoff Meeting: The second step of the inspection process. In this meeting, the inspection team is given the information they need to review the product and participate in the inspection.

Logging Meeting: The fourth step of the inspection process. Inspectors step through task scenarios as a group and identify usability defects.

Moderator: The participant in the inspection process who is responsible for managing the process.

Owner: The participant in the inspection process who is responsible for representing and then upgrading the product being inspected. There may be more than one owner.

Planning: The first step in the inspection process. During this step, the team is selected and inspection packet is prepared.

Preparation: The third step of the inspection process. During this step, inspectors become familiar with the product and work independently to detect and log defects.

Product Description: Something (e.g., screen dumps and text) that explains or displays what the product will look like.

Rework: The fifth step of the inspection process. During this step, solutions are selected and implemented.

Scribe: The participant in the inspection process who is responsible for recording all defects during the Logging and Solution Meetings. This role can be rotated during the meetings.

Solution Meeting: An optional part of the rework step of the inspection process. Inspectors brainstorm solutions to defects.

Supporting Documents: Information used to provide background information to the inspectors so they can find more defects. May include user demographics or information on similar or related products.

Task Performance Model: A flowchart model consisting of boxes connected by arrows which provides a simplified version of the steps a user goes through to complete a task or task step.

Task Performance Questions: Questions that inspectors apply to help find usability defects. A subset of the task performance questions would be asked at each phase of the task performance model.

Task Scenario: A succinct story describing a user's goal, start point, and intermediary factors that relate to product use. Any inspection is apt to make use of a number of task scenarios.

User Profile: A succinct description of a type of user who will use the product. Likely to include user education and knowledge. Most often, more than one user profile will be used during a usability inspection.

Verified Defect: A defect that the owner verifies (identifies) as a real problem.

Chapter 7

Faster, Cheaper!! Are Usability Inspection Methods as Effective as Empirical Testing?

Heather W. Desurvire
Citibank[1]

7.1 Introduction

Why Is It Important to Compare Usability Inspection Methods to Empirical Testing?

Human-computer interaction professionals seek faster and cheaper software evaluation methods because traditional laboratory evaluation methods are often expensive and therefore often not applied. In lieu of laboratory testing, a best guess approach is often used. The best guess may or may not be accurate, however. Because of this situation, several researchers have developed new evaluation techniques called usability inspection methods that have the promise to offer usability related information about the user interfaces in a manner that is faster and cheaper than if obtained from a laboratory evaluation. The most popular of these methods include heuristic evaluation (Nielsen and Molich 1990), cognitive walkthrough (Lewis, Polson, Rieman, and Wharton 1990), cooperative evaluation (Wright and Monk 1991a), and ergonomic criteria (Bastien and Scapin 1991).

---

[1] The work reported in this chapter was performed while the author was with NYNEX Science and Technology, Inc., and does not necessarily represent the position of Citibank.

These methods, each in its own way, have promised to provide data that could be used when laboratory testing is not possible or in conjunction with the laboratory. Perhaps these methods provide different and potentially useful information that the laboratory testing did not provide. With all the enthusiasm that has surrounded these new methods, there is the implication that these methods could replace empirical testing. The purpose of this chapter is to argue that this is a false assumption. For a further discussion of this issue, see Jeffries and Desurvire (1992). There is economic value in replacing empirical evaluation with inspection methods, although research is just beginning to examine the trade-offs.

Usability inspections uncover different problems which are sometimes not as complete as empirical testing or represent a different set of problems (Karat et al. 1992; Karat, Chapter 8; Jeffries et al. 1991; Desurvire et al. 1991, 1992), but they do have benefits to offer. The users of these evaluation techniques should be made aware of what the cost and benefits are. There are classes of problems that cannot be discovered via inspection methods, other than empirical. For example, in a study discussed later on in this chapter, human factors experts using heuristic evaluation, found only 29 percent of the most serious problems. That means that 71 percent of the most serious problems were not found.

The power of "seeing is believing" creates a bias for software developers towards empirical testing. In earlier studies (Desurvire et al. 1991, 1992), software developers had difficulty believing certain problems until they saw the users have these problems on videotape. However, empirical methods can be expensive; therefore, if the reliability and validity of inspection methods can be shown, perhaps developers and others will believe what they "hear."

A few studies have been conducted to learn about the validity and reliability of these methods. In this chapter, two such studies will be explained (Desurvire et al. 1991; Desurvire et al. 1992). Other studies of these issues include, Jeffries et al. (1991), and the others by Karat et al. (1992), Karat (1990a), Brooks (Chapter 10), and Mack and Montaniz (Chapter 12). There is an important distinction between these comparative studies. Jeffries et al. (1991) and Karat et al. (1992) compared inspection methods and laboratory data as equals, whereas the Desurvire et al. studies utilized laboratory testing as a benchmark to compare the fitness of the inspection methods (see also Mack and Montaniz, Chapter 12).

Desurvire et al. (1991), looked at laboratory experiment data that recorded users' task completion and error-free rates in completing a number of typical user tasks. Heuristic evaluations were performed by human factors experts, people who had actually used the system, and by nonexperts. (Also, "best-guess" predictions were made by the experts as to what percentage of the users could complete the task and what percentage would perform each task error-free.) All evaluators studied a telephone-based system prototype in the form of a paper flowchart diagram. The second comparison study by Desurvire et al. (1992) looked at laboratory experiment data that recorded task completion data, error rates, attitude of the user when making an error, and severity of the error. This data was also predicted by human factors experts, where experts, nonexperts, and system developers studied each user task via a paper flowchart diagram, utilizing the heuristic evaluation or the cognitive walkthrough method.

7.2 Issues and Mechanics of Comparing Usability Inspection Methods

What Is to Be Considered When Comparing Methods?

Benchmarks

A first consideration for undertaking a comparison study was what to compare the evaluation results against. Data and predictions of problems that may occur can be collected from the evaluators but a way is needed to find if these predictions were realized. One such way was a laboratory experiment. The best benchmark would be data from actual users and the system. The closest one can get to that is in the field. Next best to the field would be the laboratory.[2]

Problem Severity

The severity of a problem occurring is also an important ingredient in learning how good a usability inspection method is. If a method finds more problems than those found in the laboratory, but they were all minor problems, the method should be considered not very useful. Therefore, it is

---

[2] We intend to perform a field trial to compare with the laboratory data.

vital to record the severity of problems. In the Desurvire et al. studies, a 3-point scale for measuring severity was utilized. The scale started with a problem that caused minor annoyance or confusion, then a problem that caused an error, and finally a user problem that caused a task failure.

User Attitude

Many times, users will make an error and still be quite content and not frustrated with the system. On the other hand, users may make minor errors, yet become so frustrated with the system that they no longer want to deal with it. User attitude was measured by the experimenter. When the user made an error, the experimenter judged and noted the user's attitude. The attitude was measured on a scale where a low score meant that the user was still content with the system and a high score meant that the user was extremely frustrated with the system.

System Format

Defining what form the system will take is necessary as well. In the laboratory, a real system or prototype is usually utilized. It would be interesting to learn if the inspections methods, whether prototypes, or even paper flowchart diagrams of the system, can also be used effectively for evaluation. This would be a faster and cheaper method of evaluation, since a prototype takes more resources to create and often is close to the final stage of development. Other methods that seek to reduce this expense of building a prototype are those such as PICTIVE (Muller et al. 1993). If paper-flows are used instead, changes to the system can occur without as great of an overhead. Specifications were especially suited for telephone-based interfaces, since they are not seen but only heard. It was for these reasons that paper specifications were utilized. Using paper specifications for screen-based interfaces may not show the same results.

Evaluators

Originally, usability inspection methods were developed to utilize evaluators other than human factors experts, such as system developers (Wright and Monk 1991a; Polson et al. 1992a), and possibly nonexperts. Whether the system developers and nonexperts were actually effective as evaluators was the main question. It is because of this question that it is important to study what the difference between evaluators' evaluations are. Perhaps system developers will focus on aspects of the user interface that an expert would not.

An important goal of inspections is to influence the decision-makers; that is, the people who have the power to change the user interface. These people may be managers, marketers, and system developers. Perhaps these decision-makers could be trained to be effective evaluators. Wright and Monk (1991b) developed cooperative evaluation, a thinking-aloud method where system developers were the actual experimenters. Not only did they observe the user behavior, but they also actually took responsibility for running the experiment. This clearly motivated them to make user interface changes based on several observations of users.

One of the strengths of laboratory testing is that the user errors can be typically recorded on videotape. Usability inspection methods are unlike thinking-aloud methods in that the "seeing is believing" aspect is gone (because users are not observed). Therefore, when using inspection methods, if the system developers are a part of the process and given effective evaluation tools to accurately predict user errors, they would be both potentially proficient evaluators and would have the power to change the interface. This may be true for other decision-makers who would be considered nonexperts, but still have the power to make sure the user interface was improved.

Design and Evaluation Objectives

Important aspects of designing an evaluation of a user interface include defining what the goals are, determining what aspects of the interface will be studied, and knowing who the expected end users of the system will be. Will they be novice users who will remain so due to low usage; will they be novices who become expert users, or will they be expert users where the turnover is high so that the system must be easy to learn? In other words, is the main goal ease of use or ease of learning? Whether one or both of these goals, for example, is important will affect what questions will be asked in an evaluation. Whiteside et al. (1988) advocate explicit, measurable usability objectives and specific criteria that need to be met to achieve these objectives.

How the goals are defined affects the nature of an evaluation. At times, this could limit the problems that will occur. If the evaluation is task-based, then not all occurrences of user-interaction will occur. If the evaluation allows the user to interact with the system at will, then problems related to specific tasks may be missed. This observation may also apply to inspection methods, where the evaluator must somehow learn about the interface and explore possible user's interactions with it in order to predict what problems will occur. When evaluations are performed, it is important to determine what the least amount of data is lost, whether via task-based scenarios, free-flow interactions, or any other form. When an evaluation method is chosen, it is important to consider which method will produce the most design-relevant information: evaluations structured by representative end user tasks or an evaluator's free-form interaction with the system or prototype.

Many times, when beginning with a first design of an interface, usability specialists have no idea what problems are likely to occur with the interface. Sometimes it is only through a first iteration of an experiment that we are better able to define what we actually are looking for. A pilot study often serves to better define what your hypotheses are. It is also through serendipity that unanticipated problems occur. These are most likely to occur in the first iterations of an experiment. It is for this type of reason that experiments are expensive. In an experiment I performed at Bell Communications Research, a catastrophic error occurred amongst users 95 percent of the time (Desurvire 1989). Perhaps these problems can be discovered with inspection methods that are less costly and the more expensive experiments can be used when the problem space has been better defined. (See Karat 1990b for a thorough discussion on the cost-benefits of inspection methods versus experimental methods.)

A meta issue in defining goals is whether the user interface is intended to have good usability standards, like those defined by Smith and Mosier (1986), or is it more important that it be useful. Usefulness should begin with the design of the system and the original purpose for its development. Usefulness can be defined as facilitating the user's work task. Knowledge of the task is necessary. Usability is defined as having good human factor standards. It is the former goal that is more difficult to find and perhaps beyond the scope of usability inspection methods, but it should be mentioned. It would be interesting to learn if the usability inspection methods address the issues of usefulness. Perhaps new inspection methods will be developed just for this purpose.

Group versus Individual Evaluations

A choice can be made whether to perform inspections with evaluators working as teams or as individuals. There are benefits to evaluating as a group. This is due to an enhancing effect on task performance when people work in groups (Hackman and Morris 1975; Karat et al. 1992). This follows the old adage of "two heads are better than one." But does this apply to usability inspections? The evidence from Karat et al. (1992) is that problems reported by groups are more accurate because group members tend to police the false positives. With a larger group of people, the results tend to be more accurate. That is, the errors that are predicted by the evaluators tend to be ones that actually occur and not ones that cannot possibly. A potential disadvantage, however, is that individual evaluations give the evaluators more time to think and examine their own ideas, which might otherwise become diluted or not as focused upon in a group. This is an important consideration when performing usability inspection evaluations. Perhaps one inspection method is more effective when performed as a group than with individual evaluators.

7.3   Comparing Empirical Data with Usability Inspection Methods

It is with these considerations that colleagues and I embarked on two studies that intended to compare the effectiveness of the evaluation methods. We were able to consider some issues discussed in the previous section, but not all. The comparative studies discussed by Karat, Jeffries, and Mack and Montaniz, in this volume (Chapters 8, 11, and 12), looked at different issues, and complement what we found here.

Comparing Laboratory Testing Data with Heuristic Evaluators Who Are Users, Experts, and Nonexperts of the User Interface

Study Setup

The first study (Desurvire et al. 1991) sought to look at how predictive heuristic evaluations were of laboratory performance. There were three different groups of evaluators. The first group were end users of the real system, which was a telephone-based interface. These users were given a set of nine tasks to perform on the system and then were asked to evaluate the system. The second group were usability and interface experts who were asked to perform evaluations on a set of flowchart diagrams of the system. Experts were human factors experts with at least a master's degree in psychology and had at least three years of human factors work experience.

Method	R^2	F	$p<$
Users' heuristic evaluation	.56	8.83	.05
Experts' heuristic evaluation	.59	10.28	.05
Nonexperts' heuristic evaluation	.20	1.71	n.s.
Experts' "best guess"	.59	10.25	.05

Table 7.1 *Heuristic evaluation and "best guess" ratings when predicting laboratory task completion rates.*

They were given the same set of nine tasks and were asked to evaluate the system based on a description of the expected set of potential users. The third group of evaluators were not experts in usability and interface design.

A laboratory experiment was also conducted, where the users performed the same set of tasks given to the evaluators. This group served as a control to the three experimental groups. Laboratory data collected included task completion rates and error-free rates of task completion. The experimental groups were trained in the heuristic evaluation method whereby they were all given a lecture on the 10 usability guidelines. [3] The experts were asked, in addition to predicting task completion rates using heuristic evaluation, to also make their "best guess" predictions of the rate of users who would complete each task.

Results

Problems identified by the expert and end-user groups performing heuristic evaluations were predictive of both observed laboratory performance measures, task completion rates and error-free rates, as the upper parts of Table 7.1 and Table 7.2 show. Similarly, the experts' "best guess" predictions were significantly predictive of laboratory performance as the last lines of Table 7.1 and Table 7.2 show. On the other hand, the nonexperts' evaluations were not predictive of laboratory performance.

---

[3] Originated from Smith and Mosier's (1986) 60 guidelines, 9 of 10 were also used by Nielsen and Molich (1990).

Method	R^2	F	$p<$
Users' heuristic evaluation	.62	32.33	.001
Experts' heuristic evaluation	.61	10.79	.01
Nonexperts' heuristic evaluation	.16	1.33	n.s.
Experts' "best guess"	.79	24.60	.005

Table 7.2 *Heuristic evaluation and "best guess" ratings when predicting error-free rates.*

In the laboratory testing data we found user errors that violated 6 of the 10 heuristic evaluation guidelines, whereas in the heuristic evaluation data for all experimental groups we found that problem reports violated only one guideline.

Nonexpert evaluations were not predictive of performance. On the other hand, experts' and users' heuristic evaluation ratings were predictive of laboratory performance. The experts' "best guess" predictions of the laboratory data were about as good as their heuristic ratings. Heuristic ratings by experts using paper-flow diagrams and users using a live prototype for evaluation, support the idea that heuristic evaluations are useful in evaluation. They were predictive of laboratory data. One caveat is that there is still data missing from these evaluations that one gets from laboratory experimental data (these heuristic evaluations did not facilitate finding solutions to usability problems). This is perhaps because this experiment recorded evaluations on a 10-point rating scale. Since the user experimental group had the advantage of using a live prototype of the system and the experts had only the use of studying the paper specifications, perhaps the experts would have performed even better if they had had the same advantage as the users. The results of this experiment indicate that perhaps the heuristic evaluations could be used early on in the first few iterations of the design cycle.

The results from this study also indicated the need for a more thorough examination of method, evaluator, and data that could be gained from the methods, and data that would be lost if a laboratory experiment was not performed.

Comparing Laboratory Testing Data with Evaluators Who Are Experts, Nonexperts, and System Developers of the System, Using the Cognitive Walkthrough and Heuristic Evaluation Methods

Study Setup

In this study, we decided to ask evaluators to write down problems they identified in the interface, instead of using a questionnaire format to collect data. We also contrasted group versus individual evaluations. Finally, heuristic evaluations and the cognitive walkthrough method were contrasted between all groups of evaluators. In addition to the usability experts and nonexperts, we wanted to also test the evaluations by the system's developers, whom we were fortunate to have access to. We were interested as well in collecting problem severity information and user attitude data from both the laboratory and the evaluation groups. The study was set up as task-based, since there were only six basic tasks the user could perform on the system, unlike a system such as a screen-based word processor. The evaluators were given paper specifications of the system in order to assess the effectiveness of low-fidelity prototypes in usability inspections.

To summarize, this study compared heuristic evaluation and the cognitive walkthrough methods to laboratory testing results on a telephone-based interface. Three evaluator groups were used: experts, nonexperts, and the system's original software developers. Each evaluator group had three members. The contrast between group versus individual evaluations was implemented by having the heuristic evaluators perform evaluations individually, then each report the entire evaluation to the group. As a group they were asked to refute or support the other member's evaluations. At this time, they were allowed to change their evaluations by adding or deleting any predictions of errors. The cognitive walkthrough group performed evaluations as a group, since it is quite a time-consuming process.[4] As evaluations were performed in groups of three, a majority rule was applied for naming problems.

The laboratory data was collected from observing and videotaping 18 potential end users of the system, who performed six tasks representative of the system's usage. The experimenter collected data on task completion, error

---

[4] The time-consuming aspect of the cognitive walkthrough is being addressed in this volume by the original authors (Chapter 5).

data, time to complete the task, and evaluated the error severity based on observation of the user. The experimenter also categorized the end user's attitude when one of the users made an error. Both severity and attitude scores were rated on a 3-point scale. The Problem Severity Code (PSC) was as follows: 1 = minor annoyance or confusion; 2 = problem caused error; 3 = caused task failure. Users' attitude was categorized on the following Problem Attitude Scale (PAS): 1 = content with the system; 2 = frustrated with the system; 3 = exasperated with the system. The evaluator groups were asked to record what problems they predicted the users would have, then rate the problem according to the PSC and PAS scales. The laboratory and the evaluation group data were compared to learn what data was inaccurate, predictive of, and beyond the laboratory data collected.

For the heuristic evaluation, the 10 heuristics (adapted from Nielsen and Molich 1990), were placed in the evaluation room so that they would be visible throughout the prototype evaluation.

- Speak User's Language
- Minimize Memory Load
- Be Consistent
- Provide Feedback
- Provide Clearly Marked Exits
- Good Error Messages
- Prevent Errors
- Provide Shortcuts
- User Does Not Need Documentation[5]

After the evaluations, an experimenter classified each problem by what heuristic was violated. These were later checked by another experimenter for inter-rater reliability.

"Best guess" predictions were also taken, similar to the first study, by all evaluator groups (i.e., experts, nonexperts, and system developers).

---

[5] This last guideline differs from Nielsen and Molich (1990).

Method	Evaluators	Problems That Did Occur	Potential Problems	Improve-ments
Lab	Observed with users	25	29	31
Heuristic Evaluation	Experts	44%	31%	77%
	Software developers	16%	24%	3%
	Nonexperts	8%	3%	6%
Cognitive Walkthrough	Experts	28%	31%	16%
	Software developers	16%	21%	3%
	Nonexperts	8%	7%	6%

Table 7.3 *The top line in this table indicates the number of usability problems and interface improvement ideas that were observed during user testing in the laboratory. The remaining part of the table shows the percentage of these problems and improvement ideas found by evaluators using either heuristic evaluation or cognitive walkthrough.*

The cognitive walkthrough evaluators performed evaluations as groups using an automated version of the cognitive walkthrough (ACW), developed by Rieman et al. (1991). The ACW facilitated the use of the cognitive walkthrough by generating the correct questions, then calculating the results of the evaluation.

Results

Evaluation Method versus Laboratory

The evaluator groups in both methods described specific problems they predicted the users would have in the laboratory. These problems were then compared to the laboratory problems to assess similarity. Table 7.3 compares the problems that occurred in the lab with the end users to the predictions. The Potential Problem column expresses the problems that did not occur in the lab—perhaps due to the task sets not covering certain aspects of the interface—but could potentially occur. The Improvements column of the table represents the number of solutions an evaluator suggested to an

		Problem Severity Code (PSC)		
Method	Evaluators	Minor Annoyance/ Confusion	Problem Caused Error	Problem Caused Task Failure
Lab	Observed with users	5	3	17
Heuristic Evaluation	Experts	80%	67%	29%
	Software developers	40%	0%	12%
	Nonexperts	20%	0%	6%
Cognitive Walkthrough	Experts	40%	67%	18%
	Software developers	0%	0%	12%
	Nonexperts	20%	0%	6%

Table 7.4 *The top line in this table indicates the number of usability problems in three severity categories that was observed during user testing in the laboratory. The remaining part of the table shows the percentage of the problems in each of the three categories found by evaluators using either heuristic evaluation or cognitive walkthrough.*

interface problem. This represents information gained from the inspection methods, not from laboratory testing. We eliminated those issues named as potential problems that could not occur and improvements that were not feasible. For this reason, the totals do not add up to 100 percent.

The expert evaluators using the heuristic evaluation method found the highest percentage of problems that also occurred in the end-user evaluation (44 percent). Experts using the cognitive walkthrough predicted 28 percent of the problems identified in the end-user evaluation. Software developers in using both methods predicted the least end-user problems, 16 percent, and 16 percent for heuristic evaluators using heuristic evaluation and the cognitive walkthrough respectively.

Nonexperts in the heuristic evaluation condition listed some problems with the interface that were just not possible to occur, based on the design of the system as presented. A majority of the total number of problems named in

Method	*Task Completion Rate*
Actually observed in the lab	92%
Experts' heuristic evaluation	83%
Software developers' heuristic evaluation	100%
Nonexperts' heuristic evaluation	100%

Table 7.5 *Observed and predicted task completion rates.*

the heuristic condition (55 percent), were those that could not occur in the system. When analyzing these named problems, it seems that there was a misinterpretation of the system. See Table 7.3 for details.

The evaluators also listed solutions to possible user errors. Improvements are based on an evaluators' assumption that they may avoid a user's potential problem or annoyance. For example, "prompt <x> is too condescending to the user." Of all the improvements named by all the groups, the experts using heuristic evaluation named the highest percentage at 77 percent. The other groups named even less (3 percent to 16 percent; see Table 7.3 for details).

As summarized in Table 7.4, experts were best at predicting the most severe errors or those likely to cause task failure, especially for the heuristic evaluation method, where they named 29 percent of those problems that occurred in the laboratory. Interestingly, experts in the heuristic condition also named 80 percent of those problems that caused minor annoyance or confusion. The training and experience of human factors experts seem to sensitize them so that they are better at predicting a user's minor problems with a system (see Table 7.4).

The experts, especially within the heuristic evaluation method, were best at predicting users' attitudes when they made an error. Interestingly, the experts predicted that two of the user errors would cause the users' attitude to be exasperated to such a degree that they wanted to "throw the system out the window."

Method	Evaluators	Error Rates
Lab	Observed with users	36%
Heuristic Evaluation	Experts	42%
	Software developers	31%
	Nonexperts	26%
Cognitive Walkthrough	Experts	94%
	Software developers	23%
	Nonexperts	69%

Table 7.6 *Observed and predicted error rates.*

"Best Guess" Predictions

Evaluations in the heuristic evaluation group included "best guess" predictions. The experts underestimated the task completion rates and the nonexperts and software developers overestimated slightly. All groups predicted these rates reasonably well, as Table 7.5 shows.

Error rates were collected from evaluators from both usability inspection methods. For the heuristic method, all evaluator groups were predictive of error rates, but for the cognitive walkthrough method, only the software developers predicted error rates (see Table 7.6).

The types of problems delineated by the evaluator groups were classified into five separate categories by my colleagues and myself. We felt that this could help us to better understand the unique contribution of each evaluator group and inspection method to the evaluation. The categories for the telephone-based interface were defined as follows:

- Keying
  A sample error would be:
  "Order of key presses was 3,1,2; should be 1,2,3"
- Time
  A sample error would be:
  "It took too long to hear the beep"

- Task

  A sample error would be:

  "If the user dials 2, the user will never hear the <x> option"

- System

  A sample error would be:

  "The user should be allowed to also input <x>, as a person may be inclined to, but the system won't allow it"

- Prompts

  A sample error would be:

  "The prompt should say 'thank you' "

Experts were the best in almost all the categories at predicting errors, especially in the heuristic evaluation method. The only category in which they were not the best was the system type errors, where the system developers were the best. It follows that since the system developers are attuned to system errors, they would be good at this; but they were actually the best, predicting 33 percent of all the system-related problems that occurred in the laboratory. Experts who used heuristic evaluation predicted 75 percent of the time-related errors. This was the best any of the evaluator groups did using either method. See Table 7.7 for details.

Each error recorded by the evaluators in the heuristic group was rated in terms of which of the 10 heuristics it violated. Experts found most errors classified as violating the heuristic, "provide feedback" (37 percent), while software developers found errors that violated "prevented errors" (43 percent), which is consistent with their concern for system errors. The nonexperts focused the majority of their predicted errors on violating "provide feedback" and "preventing errors," where 26 percent of their named errors were found in each of these heuristics. The heuristics associated with the highest percentage of problems in the laboratory test were "be consistent" (25 percent), and "provide feedback" (27 percent). Less dramatic were the heuristics "minimize memory load" and "prevent errors" which were violated 17 percent, and 11 percent, respectively.

Similar to Nielsen (1992a), we found that "good error messages" and "clearly marked exits" had the lowest occurrence of being violated. These seemed to be of less concern to the evaluators than the other heuristics. The heuristic "be consistent" was also violated in only 2 percent of all the named problems,

		Category of Problem				
	Evaluators	Key	Time	Task	System	Prompt
Lab	Observed in the Lab	5	4	35	3	6
Heuristic Evaluation	Experts	20%	75%	11%	33%	33%
	Software engineers	0%	25%	3%	33%	17%
	Nonexperts	20%	0%	6%	33%	0%
Cognitive Walkthrough	Experts	0%	50%	12%	0%	33%
	Software engineers	0%	25%	0%	33%	33%
	Nonexperts	0%	25%	3%	0%	0%

Table 7.7 *The top line in this table indicates the number of usability problems in six categories that were observed during user testing in the laboratory. The remaining part of the table shows the percentage of these problems that was found by evaluators using either heuristic evaluation or cognitive walkthrough.*

whereas it was violated by 25 percent of the problems found in the laboratory. It may be important when performing heuristic evaluations to especially emphasize heuristics that evaluators tend to name less.

Group Interaction versus Individual Performance by Evaluators

Do group interactions enhance the accuracy of the predictions or do they interfere? The evaluators in the heuristic condition first made their predictions individually. They were then asked, one at a time, to present their list of errors to the group. For each error, the group discussed whether it was a plausible prediction. All reported errors were discussed. Each evaluator presented new errors not originally thought of, followed by a discussion of whether a named error may not be plausible. At this point, all evaluators were given the opportunity to change any of the listed errors. They could add or delete any of their original errors from their lists. Nonexperts reduced their erroneous errors by 2 percent due to the group discussion. Experts did not name any erroneous errors, so they were not included in this analysis. There is some evidence of facilitation of productivity with the experts and nonexperts, where experts added 16 percent of their total number of listed errors after the discussion, and nonexperts added 15 percent. Interestingly, the software developers neither deleted any of their erroneous problems, nor added any new errors as a result of the group discussion.

Experts were the best at predicting errors observed in the laboratory, especially using the heuristic evaluation method. However, at best only 44 percent of the problems found in the laboratory were found by the expert evaluators. That is, 56 percent of the errors in the laboratory were not predicted by performing an heuristic evaluation. The cognitive walkthrough facilitated the software developers in their error-rate predictions, more so than the other two evaluator groups. "Best guess" predictions were predictive in all evaluator groups. This is contrary to the result found in Desurvire et al. (1991), where only the experts were predictive.

Heuristic evaluation facilitated the identification of improvements to the user interface, especially for the experts. This is due, perhaps, to the heuristics reminding the experts to analyze more aspects of the interface than the cognitive walkthrough. The cognitive walkthrough focused on very minute details of the interface. This tended to blur the meta issues of the interface. The cognitive walkthrough was also quite tedious to perform and the evaluators were easily bored. This most likely also reduced their focus and may have contributed to its not being as effective as the heuristic evaluation.

Experts were best at predicting laboratory errors of all levels of severity; that is, those that caused task failure, errors, and those that caused minor confusion or an annoyance. The experts were also best at predicting the users' attitude when they made an error in the laboratory.

7.4 Enhancing the Performance of Interface Evaluators Using Non-Empirical Usability Methods

In order to learn about enhancing the performance of evaluators, we developed a new method designed to enhance the performance of expert, system developer, and nonexpert evaluators. Results are compared with heuristic evaluation, cognitive walkthrough, and empirical usability studies (Desurvire and Thomas 1993).

For at least two decades, empirical laboratory usability evaluation of user interfaces has been the major methodology of choice to ensure usable systems. In many cases, such studies can be conducted in advance of actually building the system via prototyping, pencil and paper simulations, or "Wizard-of-Oz" studies (Thomas and Gould 1975; Thomas 1976). As businesses have had to face increasing competitive pressures, there has been a growing recognition of the necessity of more usable internal and commercial products. At the same time there is increasing pressure to make the process of ensuing usable products faster and cheaper. Major techniques aimed at achieving these goals include the use of guidelines (Smith and Mosier 1986), cognitive walkthroughs (Lewis et al. 1992), formal models (e.g., GOMS [Card et al. 1983]), and especially heuristic evaluation (Nielsen and Molich 1990).

While heuristic evaluation is especially promising, it is most effective when used by human factors experts (Desurvire et al. 1992; Karat et al. 1992), especially when multiple experts are used (Nielsen and Molich 1990). Evaluation performance is enhanced further when the experts are "double-experts," knowledgeable in both general human-computer interaction and in the specific type of interface being evaluated (Nielsen 1992a). Yet, the reality is that many development efforts do not have the right expertise to utilize any of the aforementioned techniques.

In order to address these concerns we have begun to develop a method for enhancing the performance of evaluators at finding some of the potential problems of a proposed interface.

An earlier study found that organizing information is useful for evaluators (Scapin 1990). Our approach is to augment the evaluator's existing knowledge through the use of a set of perspectives that stimulates the evaluator to think about usability more broadly.

Earlier studies also found that many of the interface "errors" found by nonexperts were "false positives"; that is, these user errors could not actually occur (Desurvire et al. 1991, 1992). We were also interested, therefore, in whether this new approach, Programmed Amplification of Valuable Experts (PAVE), would reduce the proportion of these false positives.

We decided to compare PAVE to previous results acquired from performing heuristic evaluation and cognitive walkthroughs. This earlier work was reported in Desurvire et al. (1991, 1992) comparing a number of usability methodologies for a proposed voice interface.

Setup

Three evaluators from each of three groups—human factors experts, nonexperts, and developers—were asked to study flowcharts of a voice interface, as was used in the earlier study (Desurvire et al. 1992). Each evaluator then was asked to study the interface several times; once from each of several quite different perspectives. These included: whatever knowledge the evaluator typically brought to bear, a human factors expert, a cognitive psychologist, a behaviorist, a Freudian, an anthropologist, a sociologist, a health advocate, a worried mother, and a spoiled child.

All evaluators received the same order of "perspectives," as aforementioned, starting with the most typical and professional, proceeding toward the broader and more unusual. After reading a short orientation toward each perspective, the evaluators looked at a flowchart for each of the same three tasks, noted probable user errors, and suggested improvements; they were instructed to not repeat the same comments from each successive perspective.

Results

Number of Problems

Experts, developers, and nonexperts using PAVE found additional problems unforeseen by any of the previous non-empirical usability methods.

Reliability

Nonexperts were still the most unreliable; 10 percent of their named problems could not occur. However, this is much better than the 55 percent false positives they named with heuristic evaluation (Desurvire et al. 1992).

Which Perspectives Enhance Evaluation?

Each of the 10 perspectives contributed some amount of help to the evaluation for predicting lab results, naming improvements, and problems that could potentially occur in the interface. Of the more unusual perspectives, the worried mother and the Freudian contributed substantially for predicting

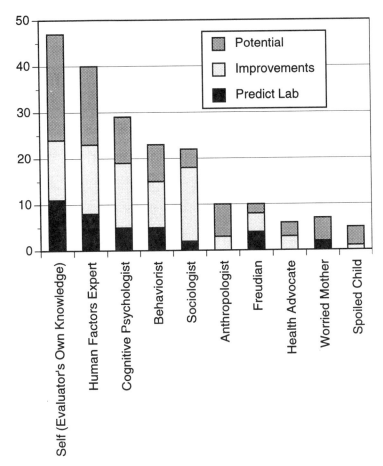

Figure 7.1 *Number of problems each PAVE perspective added to predicting lab problems, potential, and suggested improvements.*

laboratory results. For suggesting improvements, the sociologist was the most facilitative. For problems that could potentially occur in the field but did not due to the constraints of the task sets, the worried mother and the anthropologist contributed substantially (see Figure 7.1).

Predicting Laboratory Results

Expert evaluators using PAVE were fairly comparable to experts using the cognitive walkthrough method, but generally did somewhat worse than experts using heuristic evaluation. However, developers and nonexperts did

Method	Evaluators	Problems That Did Occur	Potential Problems	Improve-ments
PAVE	Experts	37%	27%	26
	Software developers	29%	33%	39
	Nonexperts	34%	40%	26
Heuristic Evaluation	Experts	44%	31%	24
	Software developers	16%	24%	1
	Nonexperts	8%	3%	2
Cognitive Walkthrough	Experts	28%	31%	5
	Software developers	16%	21%	1
	Nonexperts	8%	7%	2

Table 7.8 *The top line in this table indicates the number of usability problems and interface improvement ideas that were observed during user testing in the laboratory. The remaining part of the table shows the percentage of these problems and improvement ideas found by evaluators using either heuristic evaluation or cognitive walkthrough.*

better with PAVE in all categories than with either heuristic evaluation or cognitive walkthrough; in some categories, the improvement was quite substantial (see Table 7.8).

These preliminary results (with a small sample of subjects) suggest that the PAVE approach may offer substantial promise as a technique to enhance interface evaluations by nonexperts and developers in several dimensions, such as avoiding the flagging of false positives, finding real problems, and offering suggestions for improvements. A more detailed look at these results should enable us to improve PAVE itself prior to replication. The future deployment of this voice system in the field will also allow us to evaluate the effectiveness of PAVE in predicting difficulties observed in the real world, but not in the laboratory.

Conclusions from Studies

In summary, this study and the first study have shown that usability inspection methods can identify a number of interface problems and that these methods are especially beneficial when used by human factors experts. While the methods cannot replace expert knowledge and experience—nor can or should they eliminate laboratory experiments—they have potential to reduce the timing and cost of evaluation. At best, the alternative methods still fall short of the empirical experiments, where 56 percent of the problems found in the laboratory were missed by the best performing evaluator and method.

There is a difference in the type of evaluator and the quality of that person's evaluations. First, in both the Desurvire et al. studies (1991, 1992), nonexperts were unreliable in the prediction of laboratory results. That is, the problems they predicted when using heuristic evaluation could not occur in the system. Experts provide the "best" data, where their predicted problem sets cover a wider range of the user interface when using heuristic evaluation. They also had the best prediction of error rates, predicting the highest proportion of the most serious problems. They were best at predicting problems that frustrated users the most and provided the highest percentage of problems that were categorized as *improvements* to the user interface.

It seems from our studies that expert and nonexpert evaluators predicted a greater number of laboratory problems when they interacted with other members of their evaluator groups about these problems. System developers were not at all affected by this group interaction and their number of predicted problems was much lower than the other groups. There are differences between usability inspection methods and evaluator groups with respect to reliability and quality of results from the evaluations.

Usability inspection methods should not be used to replace traditional empirical testing because laboratory and field data are still the richest. After all, empirical results are used as the benchmark for comparing other evaluation methods. Inspection methods should only be used when they can provide the most benefit. When a company is lacking in funds, evaluation methods should be used as methods that are better than doing "nothing." Also, to reduce costs, time, and planning, usability inspection methods can be quite effective in the early stages of the development cycle (e.g., when one of two interfaces must be chosen). Also, flowcharts are an effective enough mechanism to convey the design for evaluation, at least for telephone-based interfaces. Their usage with usability inspection by evaluation reduces the number of problems of a user interface before the prototype has been built. One caveat is that evaluations should only be utilized by evaluator groups that have proved to provide reliable predictions.

The cognitive walkthrough is a good evaluation tool when one needs a very in-depth analysis of the task. For example, this can be true for systems that rely heavily on users performing a few key tasks. The cognitive walkthrough method will produce predicted problems that are germane to the task, but there will not be a plethora of information gained *beyond* the given tasks. On the other hand, when one uses the heuristic evaluation, one is gaining a lot of information about an interface beyond the scope of the tasks. This is facilitated by the list of heuristics. Empirical testing is a method that is expensive, time-consuming, takes a lot of planning, but is rich with real data. Empirical testing should be performed near the end of the development cycle, where only the most unpredictable problems will be discovered.

The usability inspection data that is provided by heuristic evaluation, and somewhat from cognitive walkthroughs, allow for more than predictions of problems found in empirical evaluations. They are also a forum for suggesting changes that are potential fixes to problems and for predicting problems that go beyond the scope of the empirically tested user's task set. We found this to be true in our study (Desurvire et al. 1992). From our experience with evaluators predicting problems beyond those found in the lab, it seems that heuristic evaluation would also provide a good forum for finding the good aspects of an interface. Here lies the strength of inspection methods as alternatives to laboratory testing.

More research of this type and that of Karat (Chapter 8) and Jeffries et al. (1991) is needed in order to understand better what, when, and how these usability inspection methods can be of greatest use.

Other Considerations Necessitate More Research

The studies performed by Desurvire et al., (1991, 1992), and those by Jeffries et al. (1991) and Karat (Chapter 8), cover various issues of usability inspection method efficacy. Still, there needs to be further research in a variety of areas in order to better recommend to practitioners of usability inspection methods various tools to conduct such evaluations. Ideally, a usability inspection method tool kit should be developed in which recommendations can be made concerning what method to choose; when in the design cycle to use it; who will conduct the evaluation; what type of specification format to evaluate; what type of user interface coverage to use; what type of information to expect; and how accurate all this data from the evaluations will be. Ideally, we are working towards this sort of tool kit.

First, though, more types of interfaces need to be evaluated with various inspection methods. Karat (1992) and Jeffries et al. (1991) compared screen-based interfaces. They asked evaluators to evaluate graphical user interfaces for actual running software. Desurvire et al. (1991, 1992) studied evaluators using paper flowcharts. It would be interesting to study evaluations of different interfaces using different formats of representing the interface, whether it be screen dumps, flowcharts, or an interactive prototype.

Guidelines on when in the design cycle an evaluation should be performed optimally, is also an area that has not yet been explored. Comparisons of evaluations should be made on what each inspection method contributes at different points in the design cycle, where differing goals are at play.

Whether all types of errors are found with the coverage of tasks utilized for the experiment is another area to be further explored. Perhaps having the evaluators explore the interface, rather than having the exploration be task-based, would be more effective using certain inspection methods with a certain type of interface.

In comparison studies, no one definition of severity is agreed upon (Jeffries, Chapter 11). No accepted definition of what constitutes an error is standardized either. Jeffries (Chapter 11) used three raters to indicate whether an error was in fact an error. Desurvire et al. (1991, 1992) used solely the judgment of the experimenter who was present at the experiment and who could use the videotapes to go back over an error if there was a problem. Researchers have various ideas and methods for scoring severity and what constitutes an error; this is largely based on the experts' experience and the interface they are working with. It would be useful if there was a standard by which all errors and levels of severity could be measured to allow comparisons between the results of different inspection methods.

The main advantage of laboratory and field testing is the realism of the tasks and users who perform those tasks. The results are going to be most representative of real users of a proposed system, especially from field studies. Usability inspection methods, however, do not address this realism. It is thus important to perform an empirical test later on in the development cycle, until more accurate and data-rich usability methods are developed. Methods other than empirical should be utilized earlier in the development cycle in order to "fix" problems that can be found and can be done so via flowcharts or a prototype.

Another area of interest with usability inspection methods is whether one method might actually extend the knowledge of a user-interface expert, and therefore improve the quality of subsequent inspection methods. It is actually the task of the inspection methods, to promote user-interface expertise; but whether this is enduring knowledge becomes the interesting question. One such study was performed to begin to learn about the enhancement of expert knowledge of non-human factors experts using various perspectives of knowledge from differing fields. While heuristic evaluation is especially promising, it is most effective when used by human factors experts (Desurvire et al. 1992; Karat et al. 1992), especially when multiple experts are used (Nielsen and Molich 1990). Similar results were found with the cognitive walkthrough, when experts were compared to system developers and nonexperts (Desurvire et al. 1992; Jeffries et al. 1991). Clearly, for these methods, human factors expertise is essential to carry out effective evaluations. Nonexperts have also been found to find "false-positive" errors, when performing heuristic evaluation (Desurvire et al. 1991). A new approach, PAVE (Programmed Amplification of Valuable Experts), was developed to encourage evaluators to consider alternative users, tasks, and contexts (Desurvire and Thomas 1993). PAVE was developed to encourage evaluators' existing knowledge through the use of a set of perspectives that stimulates the evaluator to think about usability more broadly. We developed these ideas by grouping them into a set of knowledgeable experts (perspectives) that would focus the evaluator on various aspects of the interface. For example, by using the perspective of sociology, we were interested in whether the evaluator might detect social issues that could arise from using a new interface. For example, if the interface was made easy enough for all members of a work group to use, as opposed to only a few, this might change the social hierarchy and motivations of work and success within the group.

This data will be interesting to compare to other usability inspection methods, such as heuristic evaluation (Nielsen, Chapter 2) and ergonomic criteria (Bastien and Scapin 1991).

Experimental data is a simulation of what a real user-computer interaction would be in real life. The laboratory is an attempt to capture, in a controlled fashion, the "real" world. In the comparison studies, to date, all comparisons have been with empirical data from the laboratory. Closer to the real world, than the laboratory, would be the field. The field is the real world; in fact, it is what the laboratory is emulating. It would be interesting to utilize the field as an ultimate benchmark of the inspection methods and as a benchmark of the laboratory which, interestingly, has been our only benchmark to date.

7.5   Call for Action

Usability methods that exist today are meant to deal primarily with the usability of a user interface. We have focused our efforts on applying good human factors standards and finding more cost-effective methods to attain good usability. As also mentioned earlier in this chapter, we need to focus not only on usability, but also on usefulness. Usability refers to how easy a system is to use, and usefulness is how well the system fits to the work tasks the user must perform (see Gould and Lewis 1983, for more discussion on this). Primary to a system's success is whether it can facilitate a users' job, task or life in some useful way. Is the task, for example, faster or simpler to perform due to the system than without it. Although this is often true, it is not always the case. Looking beyond the actual work task, perhaps the quality of life for a user is overlooked; it may deteriorate due to automation. There may be unintended consequences of the new system. For example, perhaps the user had to go upstairs to get a form signed by another work group. This afforded the user the opportunity to learn about company issues or talk about the weather or what others did over the weekend. This interaction connected the user to the company, creating good feelings and a positive outlook to the work day. If this process is automated, perhaps the user will not have the social contact anymore, and may become depressed and lonely as a result. This may result in lower productivity, higher absenteeism and, most importantly, an unhappy worker. More than how easy or frustrating a system is— that is its usability—is how the introduction of a system or technology into the workplace affects the quality of a user's life. Social, technical, or organization issues all pertain to usefulness, rather than usability. It is important too that new methods be developed to assess these types of issues. This is where human factors experts can have a great effect as well. There really exists no formal methods to address these issues. Task analyses deal with task-related inefficiencies, but do not deal with the more global issues of a user's job.

One task analysis in vogue, that does to some extent handle global, or rather organizational issues, is process modeling. One of many modeling processes uses the SPARKS[6] software that intends to look at organizational and global inefficiencies, but does not address the social issues, nor the true work context. Other process models include those such as GOMS (Card, Moran, and Newell 1983), and SOAR (Newell 1990). Process modeling attempts to model all the aspects of an organizational task. This process is limited, however, to only small processes of the work environment and is quite cumbersome to perform. It is also an expensive product and requires an expert who knows the software for modeling. It can take, at a minimum, six weeks for an expert to model a small working process. This is by no means cheap and fast; it is also not clear how effective this technique is, considering it does not incorporate quality of work-life issues. The process modeling is by no means the standard to compare all other techniques against, as is laboratory testing, but it would be most beneficial to the work lives of employees and to product success, if inspection methods that focused on usefulness could be developed.

Another component important to usability inspection methods is the concept of usefulness. Although this concept is beyond the scope of this chapter, it is an important concept to mention as "food for thought" for creation of future inspection methods. One way to describe the difference between usefulness and usability is that usability is focused more on the user and machine. Usefulness is more focused on interaction between the user and machine, as it facilitates the goals of the organization. These two concepts are not orthogonal; rather, they overlap. Usefulness is an important concept; future inspection methods should also direct their attention to it.

---

[6] SPARKS is a trademark of the Coopers and Lybrand corporation.

Another important question for inspection methods is how easily, and effectively the results can be communicated to the decision-makers of the product being worked on. Decisions about an interface can be made by different people: developers, managers, marketers, clients, and even human factors experts. Many times, if a decision-maker is not convinced of the importance of a change, then that needed change will not be made. Laboratory data, often accompanied by videotape, is an effective method for convincing decision-makers of the necessity for changing an aspect of an interface. Do the inspection methods have analogous information that is so convincing? That is why it is important that comparison studies be performed in order for the data to be convincing. Alternatively, belief in an inspection method should be tempered with how well it can really perform, as compared to traditional methods. Perhaps attempting to use and even design inspection methods with the decision-makers as the evaluators might be effective in having their agreement to make changes.

Finally, developing new methods that are intended to complement those that exist will add to the tool kit of usability inspection methods that now exists. Further research, such as that discussed in this chapter, should take place so that we can more accurately understand what specific methodological aspects are or are not improving these faster and cheaper methods.

Inspection methods have been compared to laboratory testing, and between themselves. Inspection methods have been found to be useful under certain conditions; for example, when they are used by experts of human factors knowledge. These methods have also been compared with laboratory testing, but not with real users in their real work environments who are performing real tasks. However, there is another, more important comparison: namely by predicting data in the field. Laboratory testing is just a simulation of reality. The next step would be to study the field, which is the closest non-obtrusive method an experimenter can get to real life human-computer interaction. These methods should be tested against field testing in order to see how well they compare to "real" life. It will be interesting to learn what the discrepancy is between laboratory testing data and field data. With these types of comparisons we can learn more about what we really gain and lose from using usability inspection methods.

Acknowledgments

I would like to thank, first, the co-authors of the two comparison studies discussed in this chapter, M. Atwood, J. Kondziela, and D. Lawrence. I am most appreciative to the editors of this book, J. Nielsen, and R. Mack for organizing the original Usability Inspection Methods Workshop at *CHI'92*, which inspired the creation of the this book. I would like to express my respect and appreciation to all the participants at the workshop for inspiring such good discussions on the topic of usability inspection methods. I am most appreciative to be among such bright, thought-provoking, and genuinely nice colleagues.

Chapter 8 — *A Comparison of User Interface Evaluation Methods*

Clare-Marie Karat
IBM Consulting Group

8.1 Introduction

Software development teams work within cost, schedule, personnel, and technological constraints. The managers of these organizations must make pragmatic decisions about the allocation of resources to groups. The goal of usability engineering is to make improvements in the utility and usability of products under development and thus increase the value of a product for a customer. In recent years, usability engineers have developed usability evaluation methods that address project management concerns regarding time, personnel, and financial resources for usability work and the economic benefits to be gained from its inclusion in current software development processes (Karat 1990a, 1990b, 1991, 1992, 1994). These methods have become increasingly incorporated into software development cycles.

A public domain usability engineering "tool kit" is currently composed of two types of techniques that practitioners rely on to evaluate representations of user interfaces: (1) empirical usability testing in laboratory or field settings; and (2) a variety of usability inspection methods. These latter methods have substantive differences and are comprised of pluralistic and usability walkthroughs, heuristic evaluations, cognitive walkthroughs, think-aloud evaluations, and scenario-based and guideline-based reviews (Bias 1991; Desurvire et al. 1991, 1992; Jeffries et al. 1991; Jørgensen 1990; Karat et al. 1992; Lewis et al. 1990; Nielsen 1989b, 1992a; Nielsen and Molich

1990; Wharton et al. 1992; Whitten 1990; Wixon et al., Chapter 4; Wright and Monk 1991a). Empirical usability testing and inspection methods differ in the experimental controls employed in the former method. The particular experimental controls employed may vary from one test to another. The controls are a set of variables and procedures which set the parameters for the social and physical environment in which the user will experience the system. These controls may relate to the information or resources a user has access to, the amount of time given to work on a problem, the type and format of questions asked during the testing session, the type of feedback provided to the user, and other variables and procedures. These experimental controls are executed by human factors engineers and other staff with the equivalent skills and competencies to conduct the usability tests with empirical rigor.

Human factors practitioners on development teams must make trade-offs regarding software-development schedule, human factors, and cost-benefit issues in selecting a usability engineering method to use in a particular development situation (Karat 1990b). These decisions involve whether to use empirical usability testing or inspection methods or both and the optimal points in the development process for them. Use of inspection methods has been encouraged by development cycle pressures and by the adoption of development goals of efficiency and user-centered design (Bias 1991; Bellotti 1988; Gould and Lewis 1985; Jørgensen 1990; Nielsen and Molich 1990, Wright and Monk 1991a). Initial data is available to assist in decisions in comparing the utility of inspection and empirical methods of usability assessment, and when and how they are most effective. Many questions remain to be addressed by future research.

8.2   Comparison of Usability Testing and Inspection Methods

The two types of usability evaluation techniques may be compared in terms of how they meet a usability engineer's and a software development team's concerns regarding a number of issues. This section compares the two methods on the following issues:

- Ability to address usability evaluation objectives
- Number and type of usability problems identified

- Reliability of the usability findings
- Human factors involvement
- Ability of a method to facilitate organizational acceptance of usability goals and activities
- Appropriateness of the method's use at different points in the development cycle
- Effectiveness of a method in generating usability recommendations for change
- Cost-effectiveness of the methods

The goal of this section is to raise questions for practitioners to consider when deciding whether and when to use usability testing, inspection methods, or both types of evaluation methods. Examples of current experience with the methods and research data are discussed. Recommendations are made to practitioners about how to proceed given the available data at this point in time.

Many different types of usability inspection methods are discussed in this section. The reader is referred to other chapters in this book and other articles for detailed descriptions of each of these methods. The goal of this section is to define some of the high-level distinctions between usability testing and inspection methods. In Section 8.3 on page 221 high-level distinctions among the different types of inspection methods are discussed.

Usability Evaluation Objectives

How do usability testing and inspection methods compare in their ability to address usability objectives for a software system under development?

There may be several objectives for any given usability evaluation. A usability evaluation may be completed to assess a system's ability to meet user performance and satisfaction objectives such as "95 percent of the users will be able to complete representative tasks on the system error-free by the third attempt," "80 percent of users will be able to complete tasks on the application without requiring assistance," "Users will be able to complete the X task in less than 10 minutes," or "90 percent of the users will be satisfied with the usability of the product." Current analysis shows that inspection methods are not able to address as wide a range of evaluation objectives as usability testing is able to. Bradford (Chapter 9) states that inspection methods are unable to provide an effective evaluation of a software interface design in its early stages. She states that in order to answer high-level evaluation questions about the usefulness and usability of an interface early in the software development cycle, practitioners may need to integrate results of user requirements definition, usability inspection methods, and user testing activities. Brooks (Chapter 10) concurs that inspection methods may not be effective at assessing the overall usability of the interface. Moreover, Brooks states that if the evaluation objective is to understand how an interface compares to several competitors, inspection methods do not provide the user trade-off matrix and the data on the value of various parts of the interface that user testing can elicit. If an evaluation objective is to obtain recommended changes from users about problems encountered during evaluation sessions, inspections that do not employ users as evaluators will not be able to deliver data directly on this issue. These evaluations will meet the needs of the project only to the extent that the stand-in for the user understands the user's key issues and relative trade-offs between them (Brooks, Chapter 10).

Nielsen (Chapter 2) states that a major difference between heuristic evaluations and user testing is the willingness to answer questions from the evaluators during the former sessions. The validity of this distinction depends on the evaluation objectives of a session. I have run usability tests which included assessment of a "hotline" service. Users called the "hotline" during the session when they wanted to ask questions and the hotline representative provided answers and tips related to the question asked.

Wixon et al. (Chapter 4) state that the evaluation objective of their usability inspections is not to uncover all user interface problems. They realize the importance of setting a clearly defined focus for the inspections. They explicitly use design reviews to educate design teams. They "close the loop" by looking at the response of the development teams to the reviews (e.g., do they make changes to products; how do they feel about the review process in general).

In using both usability testing and inspection methods in software development cycles, I have found that it is more difficult to obtain user performance data such as time-on-task, error-free task completion rates, and task completion rates with inspection as compared to testing methods. Karat et al. (1992) collected task completion data from walkthrough evaluators in an unobtrusive manner; but did not have a high degree of confidence in the validity of the data. Collection of time-on-task data and error-free task completion rate data was not deemed possible. Given the wider use of usability performance objectives in development and the need for competitive data, the difficulty in collecting relevant data in these areas is a limitation of some inspection methods.

In summary, practitioners need to clearly define the objectives of the usability evaluation and determine what method or methods are best suited to capturing the necessary data within the given development parameters. At the present time, it appears that usability testing is able to address a wider range of evaluation issues than inspection methods.

Usability Problems

How do the two families of methods (usability testing and usability inspection methods) compare in the number of usability problems identified in a user interface? Is one method better than the other in identifying serious problems? How many of the problems are found by both methods and how many are found solely by one method?

Recent studies provide some data on these issues. Jeffries et al. (1991) compared the effectiveness of usability testing, guideline, heuristic, and cognitive walkthrough (Lewis et al. 1990) methods in identifying user interface problems. The heuristic method diverged from the Nielsen and Molich (1990) method as it was completed by user interface specialists and did not include the use of written heuristics or guidelines. Prescribed task scenarios were employed in usability testing and cognitive walkthroughs. Results showed that the heuristic method identified the most usability problems and more of the serious problems, and did so at the lowest cost of the four techniques. Usability testing was generally the second-best method of the four in identifying problems. Usability testing found serious and recurring problems, but missed consistency problems. Guideline reviews identified recurring problems, but missed some severe problems. Cognitive walkthrough failed to identify general and recurring problems. The amount of overlap between the four methods in terms of usability problems identified was approximately 10 to 15 percent between any two methods (Jeffries, personal communication, 1991). Unfortunately, a methodological confound exists concerning these results. While the usability testing data was collected from each user across a few consecutive hours, the heuristic evaluation data was collected from heuristic evaluators who had two weeks to review and work with the system. The results are therefore open to alternative explanations of the data as the comparison of the methods was not conducted under equivalent conditions.

Desurvire et al. (1991) compared the effectiveness of empirical usability testing and heuristic evaluations in identifying violations of usability guidelines. The heuristic method they used was based on the method developed by Nielsen and Molich (1990), but differed from it in that evaluators rated guidelines on bipolar scales for each of a set of tasks. Laboratory testing identified violations of 6 of 10 relevant guidelines, while the combined results from the heuristic evaluations identified only one violation of a guideline. The heuristic ratings from user interface experts and empirical usability test participants were predictive of laboratory user performance data. Nonuser interface experts' ratings were not predictive of performance. Heuristic ratings were effective in identifying tasks where problems would occur, but not the specific user interface problems themselves. User interface experts' "best guess" predictions of user performance were comparable to their heuristic ratings.

Desurvire et al. (1992) compared the results of three different types of evaluators to laboratory testing results. The heuristic evaluation results predicted the laboratory testing results better than the cognitive walkthrough method; this result was due to the differential performance of the human factors experts who served as evaluators. Human factors experts predicted 44 percent of problems that occurred in the laboratory using heuristic evaluation and 28 percent of observed problems using the cognitive walkthrough method; they identified 31 percent of potential usability problems (problems not addressed by the particular tasks included in the study) using either method. System designers and nonexperts predicted from 8 to 16 percent of problems observed in the laboratory and 3 to 24 percent of potential problems identified. The study also found that experts were better than the other two groups at predicting more severe problems that would cause task failure, especially using the heuristic evaluation method. Nonetheless, the experts were able to predict at best 44 percent of the usability problems identified in the laboratory.

Karat et al. (1992) investigated the relative effectiveness of empirical usability testing and individual and team walkthrough methods in identifying usability problems in two GUI office systems. We extended work by Nielsen and Molich (1990) and Jeffries et al. (1991) to develop a usability walkthrough methodology to be used by individuals and teams. The usability walkthrough method included separate segments for (1) self-guided exploration of a GUI office system, and (2) use of prescribed scenarios. The procedure utilized a set of 12 usability guidelines. Walkthroughs were conducted individually by six evaluators in one condition and by six pairs of evaluators in another condition. The evaluators in the team condition conversed with each other about issues and problems during the sessions. The evaluators were responsible for documenting the usability problems they identified in the walkthroughs.

The empirical usability test method also had separate segments for (1) self-guided exploration of a GUI system, and (2) use of prescribed scenarios. The six users in the usability tests were asked to describe usability problems they encountered; problems were recorded by the human factors staff who were observing the sessions. Participants were randomly assigned to the usability walkthrough and testing sessions. As a group, the participants were primarily representative end users and developers of GUI systems, along with a few user interface specialists and software support staff.

The usability problems identified through use of the three methods were categorized using common metrics. Thus data could be compared across methods on dimensions including number and severity of usability problems identified in the interface. We completed each of the three methods (individual walkthrough, team walkthrough, and usability testing) on each of two competitive software systems (referred to as System 1 and System 2) to assess the reliability of the findings.

The findings were replicated across the two systems and showed that empirical usability testing identified the largest number of usability problem tokens (all problem instances), followed by team walkthrough, then individual walkthrough. The total number of usability problem tokens found by empirical testing was about four times the total number of problems identified by team walkthroughs, and about five times the total number found by individual walkthroughs. The difference in the distribution across the groups of the total number of tokens found was statistically significant for each system.

Empirical testing also identified the largest number of usability problem types (problem instances minus duplicates), followed by team and individual walkthroughs. For both systems, the total number of usability problem types found by empirical testing was about twice the total number found by the team walkthroughs, and three times the total number found by individual walkthroughs. Again, the difference in the distribution of the total number of problem types found in the three groups was statistically significant for each system.

For both systems, empirical testing identified the largest number of unique problem areas (e.g., problems areas identified by only one method). For both systems, two-thirds or more of these unique problem areas represented relatively severe usability problems in the user interfaces.

For both systems, about a third of the significant usability problems identified were common across all three methods (i.e., all three methods had identified a particular problem area). For System 1, 13 of the total number of 41 significant problem areas (32 percent of total) were common across the three techniques. For System 2, 10 of the 29 significant problem areas (35 percent of the total) were common across techniques. (For a more detailed discussion of the results, see Karat et al. 1992.)

Jeffries (1991) found much less overlap (10-15 percent) in usability problems found by any two of the methods in their study (Jeffries et al. 1991) than in ours. The higher degree of overlap in our study might be partially due to the fact that all methods used the same scenarios. These scenarios were rich and complex examples of typical work that end users need to perform and may have greatly aided in the evaluation of the systems by all methods. In contrast, the overlap in common problems found by the two methods in the Jeffries et al. (1991) study that used a common set of scenarios was no higher than that between the other methods tested in the study. This difference between the Karat et al. (1992) and Jeffries et al. (1991) studies may reflect fundamental differences in the two sets of scenarios used in the two studies.

In summary, the majority of the published studies to date suggest that usability testing identifies more usability problems than inspection methods do. The Karat et al. (1992) study shows that the usability problems that an inspection method missed were relatively severe problems. The low commonality in problems found between methods in the Karat et al. (1992)

and Jeffries et al. (1991) studies should caution human factors practitioners about the trade-offs they are making in employing one type of method rather than another or multiple methods. These methods are complementary and yield different results; they act as different types of filters in identifying usability problems.

A question remains about the degree to which the usability evaluation results reflect usability problems experienced by users in real-world settings. There is compelling anecdotal evidence regarding the high degree of similarity between the two. For example, Wasserman (1991) discusses a case study where usability problems found through usability evaluation were left unaddressed during development, and then resurfaced in the real world after product release. No formal studies in this area currently exist.

Reliability of Usability Findings

If the methods differ in their effectiveness in identifying usability problems in user interfaces, do these differences persist across different systems? Or is the effectiveness of an evaluation method system-dependent, based on the type of interface style and metaphor used in the interface?

The Jeffries et al. (1991) and Desurvire et al. (1991, 1992) studies each compared inspection and usability testing methods on only one interface. The Karat et al. (1992) study compared usability testing and inspection methods across two interfaces. The two systems selected for the study were commercially available GUI office environments with integrated text, spread-sheet, and graphics applications. The two systems (referred to as System 1 and System 2) differed substantially in the type of interface style and office metaphor presented. The results were generally replicated across the two GUI systems for both usability testing and inspection methods. The results covered usability problem identification, severity of problems identified, walkthrough method issues, and the cost-effectiveness data. It is not clear whether these patterns would be replicated on non-GUI systems; however, the sizable differences in the style and presentation of the two GUI systems in the study support the reliability of the results across these types of systems. Since the assessments were made using commercially available systems rather than paper-and-pencil drawings or prototypes, they may be seen as comparable to usability engineering work completed later in the development cycle and to competitive testing.

Human Factors Involvement

What amount of human factors involvement is necessary in the use of the two techniques? What issues arise in analyzing and interpreting data? How are data analyzed following an evaluation method, and who is responsible for completing the data summary?

Jeffries et al. (1991) had four human factors experts complete the heuristic evaluation individually across two weeks; the usability testing was conducted by two human factors practitioners who employed six users; the guidelines and cognitive walkthrough evaluations were each conducted by a team of three software engineers. The human factors time spent per evaluation session was:

- 4 hours per heuristic evaluation

- 33.2 hours per user in the usability testing

- unknown time per guideline review (the software development team spent 17 hours on the session; human factors time with them prior to the session is unknown)

- unknown time per cognitive walkthrough (the software team spent 27 hours on the session; human factors time with them prior to this is unknown)

After the sessions were completed, a team of seven usability engineers analyzed the data and assigned severity ratings to them. The amount of time spent on this activity is not provided. It is important to note that Jeffries (personal communication, 1991) said that data analysis and severity classification of usability problems was completed for the purposes of comparing methods in the study, but indicated that these steps are not normally completed when the methods are used in development at that particular computer company. Thus, analysis of the Jeffries et al. (1991) data regarding human factors involvement necessary for effective use of the usability testing and inspection methods is not possible at this time.

Desurvire et al. (1991, 1992) does not compare the amount of human factors resource necessary in using heuristic evaluation, cognitive walkthrough, and usability testing methods. Further analysis of these data is underway and cost-benefit data related to these studies may be available in the future.

Karat et al. (1992) did focus on the amount of human factors resource required to conduct usability testing and walkthrough evaluations. Some background on the procedures used in the different methods is necessary before discussing the results. Usability sessions for all methods each took about three hours. The first half of the usability sessions included an introduction by the usability engineer who administered the sessions and a self-guided exploration of the system by the participants. During the self-guided exploration, participants could go through online tutorials, read any of the hard-copy documentation shipped with the system, use and modify example documents created using the different applications and system functions, or create new application documents and experiment with system functions. In the second half of the sessions, participants worked through a set of nine typical tasks presented in random order and completed a debriefing questionnaire given by the administrator.

The empirical testing and walkthrough sessions differed in human factors involvement in the session and in how usability problems were documented. In empirical testing, two usability engineers administered each session in its entirety with an individual user. One person in the control studio interacted with users (who were in the usability studio and described usability problems they encountered during sessions), controlled the videotape equipment, and observed usability problems. The second person in the control studio logged user comments, usability problems, time-on-task, and task success or failure.

Usability staff involvement in the walkthrough sessions was limited to test the resource requirements of the method. One administrator was available on-call during the session in case of unexpected events. A few sample sessions were videotaped and observed by human factors staff; no session logging occurred. One administrator introduced the session and instructed walkthrough evaluators in the use of the guidelines for the usability walkthrough document and the usability problem description forms. The administrator emphasized in both individual and two-person team walkthrough conditions that the problem identification sheets were the deliverable for the session. In the team conditions, evaluators were given additional instructions to help each other by providing relevant information (Hackman and Morris 1975). They were told that if either one of the team members thought something was a usability problem, they should record it. A usability problem was defined as something that interfered with the user's ability to efficiently and effectively complete a task. Also, team walkthrough evaluators were instructed to take turns with the mouse and with recording usability problems so that each person had direct experience with the interface and with the usability problem description forms. Evaluators read the guidelines document and the administrator then left the studio. After the self-guided exploration phase, the administrator returned briefly to present the task scenarios and emphasize that it was more important to identify usability problems than to complete all the tasks.

Human factors time included preparation of all materials, administration of sessions, and data analysis. Total hours of human factors resource required was highest for usability testing. The hours of human factors resource required for each participant in the usability testing method was 21 per user. In the team walkthrough method it was 12.4 hours per walkthrough team; and in the individual walkthrough method it was 12.2 per walkthrough evaluator.

The lower amount of human factors time spent on the walkthrough methods had a negative impact on data interpretation and analysis work. In the comparisons we were able to make between the walkthrough and usability testing data, we found that the first issue we faced was one of data interpretation (Karat et al. 1992). In our walkthrough method, we focused on limiting the amount of human factors resource required to use the method, and thus did not have the human factors staff participate in or observe the walkthrough sessions. We worked with written descriptions of usability problems that the walkthrough evaluators completed during the session. The evaluators used different language than the human factors staff who analyzed the data. The lack of context presented difficulties in understanding and analyzing the problem statements. This difficulty in data interpretation was reflected in the lower inter-rater reliability scores for walkthrough data compared to usability test data, as categorized independently by human factors professionals not associated with the study.

We had no problems working with the severity ratings assigned to usability problems by the evaluators in our walkthroughs, and they were similar to severity ratings we assessed to like problems observed in usability test sessions. In our usability testing data, we captured much more data about parts of the interface the users had positive reactions to than we did in the walkthrough data. Data on positively viewed aspects of an interface can influence a variety of areas, including further interface design work, marketing, and education related to the product. Again, this shows an area where improvement in this walkthrough procedure is warranted.

In summary, in the Karat et al. (1992) study the amount of human factors involvement required to conduct the usability testing method was much higher than that required for the walkthrough method. The walkthrough data analysis and interpretation was much more difficult for the usability engineers than was the usability testing data analysis and interpretation due to the lack of context regarding the walkthrough data. The difficulty in walkthrough data interpretation was reflected in the lower inter-rater reliability scores for the walkthrough as compared to the usability testing data.

The Karat et al. (1992) study assumed that a development member with usability evaluation methods and data analysis skills is required to lead the usability work on a project. This person may coach others on the team in the performance of this work rather than directly performing the work. If the usability evaluation is not conducted with adequate skill, the resulting data may be of questionable value. The analysis of the resulting data also requires certain competencies. People with different backgrounds, skills, and roles in the organization will draw different conclusions about the necessity of product changes and the types of changes to be made to a product. I recommend that usability engineers or other staff with the required competencies at least coach the development team through the use of usability evaluation methods and the data analysis effort. The amount of human factors coaching or guidance will be greater for usability testing than for inspection methods.

Organizational Acceptance Issues

Is one method better than the other in facilitating developer "buy-in" in the usability goals and work related to the interface and an acceptance of usability data? How do the two methods compare in developer involvement in the evaluation sessions?

Brooks (Chapter 10) states that experience shows that management likes to make decisions based on quantitative data. Development managers want to allocate financial resource where there will be the most value to the user. Usability testing can provide data about the percentage of users experiencing a problem and the likely consequences for the product if released with this particular problem. Inspection methods may not be able to provide data that quantifies the financial magnitude of a usability problem. Brooks states that inspection evaluation data is regarded as opinion data and is weighed in against other opinions by hardware and software designers. Usability test data is viewed as facts, facts that tend to override an opinion by others. With usability test data, the organization spends less time in repetitive discussions and product managers believe they have a better basis on which to make decisions about resource allocation and other trade-offs.

It has been my experience in working with developers that the key factor in their acceptance of data from usability walkthroughs or testing is whether they had an opportunity to observe or take part in the usability sessions. There is a "seeing is believing" component at work, as well as an issue of their involvement in and commitment to the usability evaluation process. When I conduct usability testing, I have developers join me in the test studio and watch the sessions. During breaks we discuss possible solutions to identified problems. They are also given an opportunity to talk with the users during the debriefing sessions. As a result, programmers can become so motivated that they work to improve the prototype between user testing sessions to see if particular usability problems can be eradicated.

During many usability walkthroughs in development, developers and designers participate in the walkthrough, listening to the end users and watching their reactions. The developers and designers provide their own comments and work with others as a team to determine solutions to problems. They experience ownership in the process. Developers have responded very well to leading the group walkthrough sessions as well. Usability inspection methods also further the goal of user-centered design by providing many different members of the development team opportunities to become more involved in the usability of the interface (Bias 1991, Chapter 3; Karat et al. 1992).

As a social psychologist, I view management and product team acceptance of usability inspection or testing data as an organizational issue. An organization's structure and culture and coordination of the groups involved in a product development cycle can be employed to facilitate or hinder acceptance of usability data, regardless of whether it is based on inspection or testing methods. A key issue in terms of an organization accepting and using usability data to its advantage is the development team's perception of the value of the usability work on the interface. The perception of value may result from a myriad of sources and can be achieved using either type of usability evaluation method. Developer involvement in usability and "buy-in" in usability evaluations and iterative design is one path for creating perceived value. A review of the cost-benefit analysis of usability engineering on the project and discussions with customers about the value they place on usability are other ways to build perceived value.

Timing Issues

At what point in software development cycles is one method better suited than the other?

Jeffries (Chapter 11) states that usability inspection methods may be used early in the software development cycle to make design decisions that would be technically or politically infeasible later on when user testing was completed. She believes that the inspection methods she has used do not provide the high-level design guidance required. My experience has been that usability testing may be used much earlier than she considers (e.g., with low-fidelity prototypes or high-fidelity partial prototypes) and can provide high-level design guidance early in the development cycle. Karat et al. (1992), Desurvire et al. (1991), and Whitten (1990) have suggested that usability inspection methods may be well suited for evaluation activities early in the development cycle and when deciding among competing design solutions. They are methods of choice when resource is very limited (Nielsen 1989b). Whitten (1990) states that an ideal positioning of usability walkthroughs in a project development cycle may include an initial walkthrough during high-level design stage, a second walkthrough after low-level design, and then two iterations of usability testing. It is good to have a general plan for how one will position usability evaluations in a development project, but development cycles tend to include many unanticipated changes. I prefer to think of practitioners in development as having a "tool kit" of usability engineering methods (including various inspection methods as well as usability testing) that can be tailored to the requirements of the current project situation. Having the flexibility to choose among methods and knowledge of the trade-offs in the different methods should give practitioners a good opportunity for success.

Generation of Recommendations

How do usability testing and walkthrough methods compare in the generation of recommendations for change?

Some practitioners see identification of recommended changes to identified user problems as part of the objective of use of usability evaluation methods, others do not. For example, Bias (1991) and Karat (1992) think the generation of recommendations is a deliverable from both walkthroughs and user testing methods. Lewis et al. (1990) do not believe that recommendations are part of the cognitive walkthrough method. Some practitioners also use user testing or inspection methods to identify new or unaddressed user requirements for system interfaces.

Brooks (Chapter 10) states that BNR has found that inspection methods are not good at pointing out how the user makes trade-offs that impact the interface. On the other hand, user tests are excellent at pointing out these factors. She believes human factors experts are much better than the user at generating the solutions to usability problems given that they understand (from user testing) how the user makes trade-offs regarding factors involved in them.

Bradford (Chapter 9) and Jeffries (Chapter 11) both note the limitation of inspection methods (as compared to usability testing) in providing guidance or recommendations for high-level design issues.

Karat et al. (1992) state that the identification of usability problems is not an end in itself. Rather, it is a means towards eliminating problems and improving the interface. The part of the development process concerned with making recommendations for change based on the usability problems identified was not covered in the Karat et al. (1992) study. We believe that since we were working with a core set of scenarios developed in consultation with users, the problems identified during evaluation sessions were predictive of what would happen in real-world settings. We did find that the larger the number of problem tokens and types identified regarding a significant problem area of the interface, the richer the source of data was for forming recommendations to improve that portion of the interface. The data from Karat et al. (1992) showed that the empirical usability testing and team walkthrough conditions had the advantage over the individual walkthrough conditions in this area. The empirical test data contained four times as many problem tokens describing a significant problem area and providing context about it as compared to team walkthrough data, and team walkthroughs produced 33 to 50 percent more information as compared to individual walkthroughs.

Regarding the data providing a basis for suggested solutions to problems, one of the conclusions of our study was that we needed to improve our problem capturing and debriefing methods in order to obtain more walkthrough evaluator recommendations for changes to identified problems. We were able to obtain much more information about recommended changes to identified problems from users in our usability testing sessions as this aspect was more highly integrated into the process.

In summary, the available data show that current inspection methods do not generally facilitate the generation of recommendations for change as compared to usability testing.

Cost-Effectiveness

What is the relative cost-effectiveness of the two techniques in identifying the usability problems in an interface?

Many practitioners (e.g., Bias 1991; Brooks, Chapter 10; Karat 1993; Karat et al. 1992) perceive the cost-effectiveness of a method as the cost of an evaluation method and the return on investment that the evaluation method provides based on implemented changes. Brooks (Chapter 10) contrasts an inspection method that costs $2,000 to complete but misses a significant problem that is corrected later for $100,000 with a usability test costing $20,000 that corrects the problem prior to field release. Her research has shown that user tests are less expensive and provide a higher return on investment than inspection methods when viewed in terms of the development cycle. She argues that competitive usability evaluation data and strategic information make usability testing data more valuable to organizations as well.

Jeffries et al. (1991) calculate the cost-benefit of the four methods by dividing the time (person hours) spent on each method by the sum of severity scores assigned to problems identified by each method. The resulting ratio shows that heuristic evaluation was much more cost-beneficial than any of the three other methods. This analysis is incomplete in that it does not reflect the value of the changes that might have been made based on the results from each method.

The Karat et al. (1992) cost-effectiveness data show that empirical testing required the same or less time to identify each problem when compared to walkthroughs. The differences between these data and the cost-benefit data for usability test and heuristic methods in Jeffries et al. (1991) may be due to the differences in the walkthrough procedures utilized and in the type of data analysis performed in the two studies. If our walkthrough data had been analyzed in other ways or by different individuals (e.g., developers), the resource required might have varied significantly. However, the resource and skills applied to data analysis may be reflected in the quality of the analysis and the resulting changes to systems. Ultimately, the true cost-benefit of these methods will be realized through their ability to facilitate the achievement of usability objectives for systems in iterative development, and to provide measurable benefits that exceed the costs of their use (Karat 1990b, 1991, 1992, 1994).

The relative cost-effectiveness of usability testing and inspection methods, based on return on investment in implemented changes, is not clearly established at this time. Recent publications document large cost-benefit and return on investment results regarding investment in usability engineering (Karat 1990a, 1990b, 1991, 1992, 1994). While both methods are cost-effective, no studies to date have systematically compared the relative cost-effectiveness of inspections and usability testing.

Summary

Table 8.1 summarizes briefly the strengths and weaknesses of usability testing and inspection methods as related to issues discussed in this section.

Issue		*Usability Testing*	*Inspection Method*
Ability to address evaluation objectives		+	−
Number and type of usability problems identified		+	−
Reliability of usability findings		+	+
Human factors involvement	In conducting method	−	+
	Data analysis	+	−
Ability to facilitate organizational acceptance of usability goals and activities		+	+
Appropriateness of method's use at different points in development cycle	For numerous lower-level design trade-offs	−	+
	For high-level design guidance, full coverage of interface	+	−
Effectiveness of method in generating recommendations for change		+	−
Cost-effectiveness of method		+	+

Table 8.1 *Strengths and weaknesses of usability testing and inspection methods. Legend: + indicates a strength and − indicates a weakness.*

8.3 Trade-Offs Regarding Inspection Methods

Many different types of inspection methods exist; usability practitioners need to understand the trade-offs involved in the different methods. These methods may be compared according to the following set of possible differences inherent in their procedures:

- Method employs individuals or teams
- Evaluator expertise
- Prescribed tasks versus self-guided exploration
- Utility of guidelines
- Data collection and analysis
- Generation of recommendations
- Role of the debriefing session

This section raises questions for the practitioner to consider when tailoring an inspection method for use in a development situation. Available case study and research data related to the possible variants in methods are discussed.

Individuals versus Teams

Are inspection methods more effective when conducted individually or in teams?

Social psychology has documented that groups seldom perform up to the level of their best member (McGrath 1984). One exception in this area is that groups do offer the possibility of more accurate judgments than individuals, especially when working on complex tasks (McGrath 1984). The use of interaction-enhancing procedures may heighten group productivity as well (Hackman and Morris 1975).

Nielsen and Molich (1990), Nielsen (1992a), Jeffries et al. (1991), Desurvire et al. (1991) and others used individual evaluators in their methods. Bias (Chapter 3), Karat et al. (1992), Desurvire et al. (1992), Wixon et al. (Chapter 4), and Wright and Monk (1991a) employed teams of evaluators or group interaction during the inspection. If an objective in the use of a method is to determine solutions to complex usability problems, the team approach has an advantage over individual evaluators because of the wide range of skills and backgrounds necessary to identify and then resolve usability problems. The strength of group walkthroughs became apparent to me in practical application of these methods in the development process. The coordinated effort of the multidisciplinary perspectives and skills of the development team was required in one room at the same time in order to identify and understand usability problems and then determine appropriate solutions to them. Much additional time and effort would have been required to properly identify and solve these problems in other ways.

Bias (Chapter 3) describes a systematic group evaluation procedure called the pluralistic usability walkthrough that includes end user, architect, design, developer, publication writer, and human factors representatives who complete scenario-driven walkthroughs of software prototypes. Human factors staff lead the group sessions. The design-test-redesign cycle is reduced to minutes through the use of low-technology prototypes to illustrate alternative designs and through the presence and cooperation of individuals with the varied skills required to complete the work. This technique highlights the value of multidisciplinary activity in design (Grudin and Poltrock, 1889) and group problem solving (Hackman and Morris 1975), and the iterative design possible within tight time constraints. A question arises about the group facilitation skills and procedures required for human factors engineers to achieve high group productivity and accurate judgments in the walkthroughs (Hackman and Morris 1975; McGrath 1984).

Desurvire et al. (1992) compared the effectiveness of individuals completing usability inspections and group interaction and found some evidence for group facilitation of productivity. The experts added 16 percent, nonexperts added 15 percent, and software engineers added nothing to their final number of usability problems identified based on group discussion of problems found.

Karat et al. (1992) found that team walkthroughs achieve better results than individual walkthroughs in some areas. Teams found more problem tokens than did individual walkthrough evaluators for each system. For System 1, the average number of problems identified by the walkthrough teams was 19 while the average for individual walkthrough evaluators was 13. For System 2, these values were 18 for team and 11 for individual walkthroughs respectively. The fact that any differences emerged between the team and individual walkthroughs is encouraging. The brief period of the usability session, the lack of an established working relationship between team members, and the small size of the teams may have contributed to the small differences found. Many usability walkthroughs in product development are done by moderate-sized teams (e.g., 6-8 people) because of the wide range of skills and backgrounds necessary to identify and then resolve usability problems.

Therefore, due to practical and organizational considerations, team walkthroughs may be an area warranting future research. Work by Bias (1991, Chapter 3), Wixon et al. (Chapter 4), and Hackman and Morris (1975) may help identify ways to facilitate and enhance the performance of team walkthroughs.

Evaluator Expertise

Are members of development teams and representative end users effective evaluators in using inspection methods, or should the evaluators be exclusively human factors or user interface specialists?

The usability inspection methods developed and used by different practitioners and researchers vary regarding the criteria for evaluators who use the methods. Jeffries et al. (1991) employed user interface specialists in their heuristic evaluation procedure. Nielsen and Molich (1990) used participants in their heuristic evaluations who were not human factors experts; Nielsen (1992a) contrasted the effectiveness of novice evaluators (no usability expertise), regular specialists (usability experts), and double specialists (usability and domain expertise). Desurvire et al. (1991) compared the effectiveness of user interface experts and nonexperts, and Desurvire et al. (1992) compared the effectiveness of user interface experts, nonexperts, and software engineers. Lewis et al. (1990) stated that successful execution of the cognitive walkthrough methodology requires deep knowledge of the theory and that transfer of these skills to evaluators would require a suitable training program. Bias (1991, Chapter 3) included end users, developers, and human factors staff as evaluators in his pluralistic walkthrough method. Similarly, Wixon et al. (Chapter 4) employed a mix of development team members, inspection facilitators, and inspection experts. Karat et al. (1992) employed end users and developers of GUI systems, along with a few user interface specialists and software support staff as the walkthrough evaluators.

In terms of special strengths or weaknesses in the criteria for evaluators using these methods, Nielsen (1992a), Desurvire et al. (1991, 1992) and Jeffries et al. (1991) highlighted the effectiveness of user interface and domain expertise. If user interface expertise is available and time constraints are very tight, these methods show that use of experts or double experts is a real strength to draw on. However, if the goal is to have the development team become more user-centered in its development process, then the criteria for evaluators might be defined to include those on the development team and representative users to increase development team involvement in usability and increase focus on the end users. Karat et al. (1992) showed that evaluators who have relevant computer experience and represent a sample of end users and development team members can complete usability walkthroughs with relative success. A multitude of organizational, practical, and product development benefits are possible by involving more members of the development team in usability walkthroughs (Bias, Chapter 3; Gould and Lewis 1985; Jørgensen 1990; Nielsen 1989b).

Prescribed Tasks versus Self-Guided Exploration

In a usability inspection with prescribed tasks, evaluators step through a representation of a user interface (e.g., paper specification, prototype) or the actual system while performing representative end-user tasks. Other inspection procedures rely on self-guided exploration of the interface by evaluators who may or may not generate scenarios for that purpose. Do evaluators in inspections think that one approach is more useful than the other in identifying usability problems?

Jeffries et al. (1991) evaluated methods using prescribed tasks (e.g., cognitive walkthrough) and self-guided exploration (e.g., heuristic evaluation). Nielsen (Chapter 2) used self-guided exploration in his method and achieved good results with it. Karat et al. (1992) had the same evaluators try both approaches while completing a usability walkthrough and found that evaluators strongly preferred to use prescribed scenarios that had been defined in consultation with end users. The Karat et al. (1992) study began with human factors staff consulting with end users and developing a set of nine generic task scenarios to be used with both systems. These scenarios were representative of typical office tasks involving use of text, spreadsheet, and graphics applications, as well as the system environment. The tasks included a range of 1 to 13 subtasks and covered document creation, moving and copying within and between documents, linking and updating documents, drawing, printing, interface customization, finding and backing up documents, and use of system-provided and user-generated macros. During the debriefing, evaluators rated the relative usefulness of scenarios as compared to self-guided exploration in identifying usability problems in the systems. The evaluators used a 5-point scale where a score of 1 was the most positive response for use of scenarios. All walkthrough groups favored the use of scenarios over self-guided exploration; the average score across systems was 1.8.

It appears that both techniques are successful; relative strengths may depend on other objectives of the development process. For example, if the typical tasks of a new system are known and used as a set of core scenarios to drive development, it might be very reasonable to use these prescribed tasks to assess the quality of the interface in walkthroughs. However, at some point, self-guided exploration or further task-scenario development is probably necessary to ensure full coverage of the interface. Prescribed scenarios focus assessment on particular areas of the interface, and assessment of areas not covered by the scenarios is frequently left unaddressed.

Utility of Guidelines

What is the role of usability heuristics or guidelines in usability inspection methods? Are heuristics useful and necessary for experienced members of development teams?

Nielsen and Molich (1990), Jeffries et al. (1991), Desurvire et al. (1991), and Karat et al. (1992) all used guidelines in their inspection methods, while Bias (1991) did not. Evaluators in the Karat et al. (1992) study thought the guidelines were of limited value to them in conducting usability walkthroughs. In the beginning of the Karat et al. (1992) study, a two-page document of guidelines was developed for the evaluators in the walkthrough conditions. The document told evaluators their assignment was to identify usability problems with the interface initially by exploring the interface on their own and then by walking through typical tasks provided to them. A usability problem was defined as anything that interfered with a user's ability to efficiently and effectively complete tasks. Evaluators were asked to keep in mind the guidelines about what makes a system usable and to refer to them as necessary. The document provided brief definitions and task-oriented examples of 12 guidelines. These guidelines were compiled from heuristics used by Nielsen and Molich (1990), the ISO (International Standards Organization) working paper on general dialog principles (ISO 1990), and the IBM CUA user interface design principles (IBM 1991). The 12 usability guidelines included:

• Use a simple and natural dialog

- Provide an intuitive visual layout
- Speak the user's language
- Minimize the user's memory load
- Be consistent
- Provide feedback
- Provide clearly marked exits
- Provide shortcuts
- Provide good help
- Allow user customization
- Minimize the use and effects of modes
- Support input device continuity

During the debriefing sessions, evaluators were asked about the added value of using the guidelines during the walkthrough. A 5-point scale was again used and a score of 1 was the most positive response for guidelines. For both systems, the walkthrough evaluators thought the guidelines were of limited added value to them in identifying usability problems; the average score across systems was 3.9. The evaluators said that they thought the brief document was very effective in explaining and giving examples of the guidelines and that they would not change the format. They stated that because of their experience with GUI and other systems, they were already familiar with the guideline concepts, but that less experienced users would find it very useful.

These data are consistent with Desurvire et al. (1991) who found no difference between user interface experts' heuristic and "best guess" ratings. Guidelines may serve a useful purpose in promoting consensus about the usability goals for a development team and may be useful for less experienced evaluators during inspections. So again, the components of an inspection method may be used by practitioners to serve various objectives for an organization; the relevant objectives need to be taken into account in the selection of one method over another in a particular situation.

Data Collection and Analysis

Who should be responsible for collecting data during a usability inspection (the user evaluating it, the usability engineer or developer who coordinated the session)? And what type of data should be collected (data on usability problems as well as usability strengths of the interface)? Does a method treat all problems as being of equal severity or does it include a severity classification of usability problems?

Jeffries et al. (1991) completed data analysis and severity classification of usability problems for the purposes of comparing the methods in their study, but indicated that these steps are not normally completed when the methods are used in development (Jeffries 1991). Wixon et al. (Chapter 4) provide a written document summarizing the inspection findings and outlining recommendations for change as a standard practice when conducting inspections. When recommendations are not documented, development teams may ignore findings and suggestions and claim that their designs have been "approved."

Karat et al. (1992) set a standard for the walkthrough evaluators to use regarding what type of data would be collected. Then they had human factors staff complete the severity classification and summary as it is normally completed when the methods are used in the development cycle. The product manager is presented with a prioritized list of usability problems and recommended solutions in a results briefing. Negotiation then takes place about allocation of resource to the prioritized list of usability problems, starting with the most severe problems and working down the list as far as is possible given resource and time constraints. Depending on how the data is analyzed and by whom, different types of changes may be made to a product. The Karat et al. (1992) walkthrough method has a strength in having data analysis and problem severity classification as part of an inspection method that folds into a development process. While data collection and analysis were performed by human factors staff in the Karat et al. (1992) study, it seems quite feasible to work towards transferring the necessary skills to complete this work to other development team members through instruction and coaching by human factors staff.

Generation of Recommendations

Is development of recommendations for changes to the interface part of an inspection method? What are the advantages and disadvantages of including recommendations as part of the method?

Karat et al. (1992), Wixon et al. (Chapter 4), and Bias (Chapter 3) include identification of solutions as part of the process. Lewis et al. (1990) and Jeffries et al. (1991) have stated that identification of solutions to problems is not part of the cognitive walkthrough method. In practical application of usability inspection methods, I have found that it is a real strength of usability walkthroughs that recommended solutions are identified, proto-typed using low-fidelity methods, and then discussed in the walkthrough setting. Work by Bias (1991) supports this idea. In Karat et al. (1992) we found recommended solutions to be an area where the walkthrough method tested in our study needed to be refined to strengthen the value and usefulness of the method as a whole. The walkthrough data was classified using a generic model of usability problems that covered all interface features. The same model was used in classifying the usability testing data. The use of the model was combined with use of severity ratings so that it was apparent which features of the interface evoked the most severe problems. Data on the severity of usability problems associated with interface features and their role in completing typical tasks provided a useful assessment of the importance of interface features and guidance about where to allocate resource to improve critical parts of the interface. Identifying usability problems is not an end in itself. It is a means towards eliminating problems and improving an interface. We believed that we could improve the collection of user recommendations for changes by redesigning the debriefing section of the walkthrough method.

Role of the Debriefing Session

Is there value in having a debriefing session as part of an inspection method? If so, what are the roles of the people involved and the goals of the session?

Nielsen (Chapter 2) discusses the possibility of extending the heuristic evalu-ation method to conduct a debriefing session after the last evaluation session. Participants in the session would include the evaluators, members of the design team, and any observers of the evaluation sessions. This debriefing session would serve the purpose of discussing possible recommendations for changes to redesign usability problems identified during the sessions, as well as discussing positive aspects of the design.

Karat et al. (1992) discussed how to improve the debriefing session at the end of each usability walkthrough session. A debriefing session with walkthrough evaluators that included reviewing identified usability problems, capturing undocumented ones that evaluators mentioned in passing, collecting evaluator recommendations for change, and positive comments about the system under evaluation would improve walkthrough effectiveness. Users in the empirical testing sessions were given opportunities to provide both recommendations for changes to the usability problems they encountered and positive comments about the system; the walkthrough debriefing sessions could be expanded to capture evaluator recommendations and positive comments as well. The debriefing sessions might also be used to review identified usability problems. Walkthrough evaluators used different language than the staff who analyzed the problem reports. The data analysts' job of understanding these problem statements was made more difficult by a lack of context and lack of session observation. The difficulty experienced in interpreting walkthrough data was supported by the lower inter-rater reliability data reported for walkthroughs compared to usability tests. Moreover, from walkthrough sessions that human factors staff observed, it became evident that evaluators misattributed the sources of problems. Observations also showed that evaluators sometimes became so involved in the task scenarios that they forgot to document problems they encountered and identified. To overcome this demand characteristic of the walkthroughs emphasizing the importance of problem identification over task completion was emphasized, but it was not effective in some cases; further refinement of intervention strategies should be explored (Hackman and Morris 1975). The debriefing session could be used to understand the context of the usability problems and capture undocumented ones.

Summary

Table 8.2 summarizes this section by outlining the key questions to answer when tailoring an inspection method for use in a development situation. Recommendations are made based on current research and case study data.

8.4   Conclusion

Based on my knowledge of usability inspection methods, I recommend that users of the methodologies carefully define and consider their project objectives in selecting which method to use in a particular situation. There is a "tool kit" of usability evaluation methods available; users of these methods need to be able to select a method that meets their needs or tailor a method

Issue	*Recommendation*
Individual Versus Teams Complex judgment required?	Use a team

Evaluator Expertise
   Expertise available?
   Development team involvement goal, user-centered design?
	Use UI and domain experts
	Use representatives of development team and users

Prescribed Tasks Versus Self-exploration
   Typical tasks known?
   Full coverage of interface needed?
	
	Use prescribed tasks
	Use self-exploration

Utility of Guidelines
   Need to promote consensus about usability goals, bring along junior members on team?
   Experienced developers only?
	
	Use guidelines
	
	Little value in use of guidelines

Data Collection and Analysis
   Who responsible for data collection?
 	
   What data are collected?
 	
   All problems of equal severity?
	Usability engineers or they coach development team to do it
	Set a standard and communicate it
	
	Use severity classification scale to prioritize resource allocation

Generation of Recommendations	Include recommendations generation as part of inspection method

Role of Debriefing Session
   Discuss recommendations for change?
   Review identified problems?
   Capture undocumented problems?
   Collect recommendations for change?
   Collect positive comments about the system?
   Resolve interpretation issues?
	Include debriefing session with relevant components in inspection method

Table 8.2 *Summary of key issues and recommendations regarding inspection methods.*

to the requirements of their situation. The available data highlights the value of user interface and domain expertise in conducting usability inspections. Involving more members of the development team and representative end users in the usability evaluation of a system can reap numerous rewards for an organization. Personal experience in development suggests that team walkthroughs are an efficient and effective way to meet the objectives of identifying and resolving usability problems in complex interfaces. Team walkthroughs also require skilled group facilitators. Heuristics can be used to bring focus and consensus to the usability objectives for a project, while available research suggests they may be of limited added value to the effectiveness of the walkthroughs themselves. Use of prescribed scenarios or self-guided exploration may be determined based on characteristics of the evaluators and the project objectives. Consideration needs to be given to the way the data from the inspection methods will be collected, analyzed, and used in the development process. A debriefing tool may greatly improve the quality and completeness of usability inspection data.

Karat et al. (1992), Desurvire et al. (1991), and Whitten (1990) have suggested that usability inspection methods may be well suited for evaluation activities early in the development cycle and when deciding among competing design solutions. They are a method of choice when resource is very limited (Nielsen 1989b). Whitten (1990) states that an ideal positioning of usability walkthroughs in a project development cycle may include an initial walkthrough during the high-level design stage, a second walkthrough after low-level design, and then two iterations of usability testing. A general plan for how one will position usability evaluations in a development project is helpful, but development cycles tend to include many unanticipated changes. Having the flexibility to choose among methods and knowledge of the trade-offs in the different methods should give practitioners a good opportunity for success. Finally, I think there are organizational issues that factor heavily in the success of usability activities on a project and practitioners are advised to communicate with the organization about the value of usability.

Further research can help improve the understanding of the trade-offs being made in using one usability evaluation method rather than another. The modest degree of overlap in the usability problems found by the walkthrough methods and usability testing by Karat et al. (1992), and the even smaller degree of overlap in the problems identified by the methods used by Jeffries et al. (1991) raise serious questions about the trade-offs made in selecting one method rather than another or both. Usability evaluation methods act as different types of filters of user interaction with a computer system; this aspect of the methods needs to be better understood. It would be beneficial to better understand the added-value of components of the different techniques (e.g., prescribed scenarios versus self-guided exploration) through a more controlled analysis. Further study of team inspections is warranted. We do not understand all of the factors involved in evaluation methods, nor how to maximize their effectiveness. Improvements can be made in how data is collected, analyzed, and incorporated into the development process. The value of a debriefing tool in inspection methods has not been exploited to its full advantage. The available data can help practitioners be more effective in selecting or tailoring an appropriate usability evaluation method for a particular development situation, but many questions about usability evaluation methods remain to be addressed.

Chapter 9

Evaluating High-Level Design

Synergistic Use of Inspection and Usability

Methods for Evaluating Early Software Designs

Janice S. Bradford
Hewlett-Packard Laboratories

The focus of this chapter is on usability studies carried out in the early stages of software design. Traditionally, software implementation is carried much further than desired before usability evaluations are made because there are a lack of good methods that can be used on preliminary design ideas.

The goal is to provide early, accurate, low-cost information on the goodness of the high-level HCI design concepts and requisite functionality of a software system, by synergistically combining both usability inspection methods and methods involving the end user.

9.1   Importance and Role of Early Design Evaluations

The Need for Early Evaluation

Early feedback to the design process about the quality of the user interface[1] is critical to the ability to affect desired changes when they are still possible. Usability inspection methods are meant to be part of the software design process, an iterative cycle of design→evaluate→design, but are typically

---

[1] The user interface is defined as any part of the system that the user comes into contact with, either physically, perceptually, or conceptually.

carried out late in the design process. Design decisions made in early cycles, such as requisite functionality, choice of platform, and software architecture, can affect the usability of the system seen downstream in the later cycles. If effective evaluations are carried out upstream, in the early design cycles, then problems can be discovered before too much investment in the design has been made; they will be less costly to fix and therefore have an increased chance of being fixed.

Early evaluations can make designers aware that their sometimes seemingly unrelated design decisions about gross functionality, software architecture, control mechanisms, or data structures, for example, can have consequences to the system usability later in the design process. For example, a decision to limit the number of characters that a filename may have under the DOS operating system affects the user's ability to give meaningful names to files. It is now too costly to change DOS so that it accepts longer filenames, because of all the hardware and software that depend on these filename restrictions.

Currently, there is an absence of inspection methods that, on their own, will give an effective evaluation of a software interface design in its early stages. This is because the methods focus on the usability of interface implementation details which often haven't been worked out yet. There is a mismatch between the level of design detail of early designs assumed by the methods, and the level of design actually accomplished by the engineers.

In the early stages of product development, what are the developers worrying about? What kind of design decisions are being made? What type of impacts are being made on the user interface? What kind of methodology is wanted to evaluate them? In the early stages, software designers are working to solve design problems within many constraints: system performance, understanding and meeting user needs, adapting to the chosen hardware platform, software language requirements, working within a budget, and time and human resource limitations. They are defining the basic software architecture that will be used—the control mechanisms, data structures, and partitioning of major functionality.

Usually, at this stage explicit work on the user interface is either not done or is only roughly sketched and left undetailed; the embodiment of the user interface generally comes much later in the product development cycle. But at this early stage, many features of the user interface are being determined implicitly as the possible design space of the system is narrowed with each decision. We need to make the implicit impact of these design decisions on the user interface explicit so that by being clear they can be evaluated by the design team and adopted or rejected in an informed manner.

Since there usually is no detailed implementation of the user interface at this stage, the appropriate level of concern for HCI design is with the broader issues of *usefulness*, rather than *ease of use* usually associated with detailed implementation. At this stage "useful" is more important than "usable." This is especially true for systems that are implementing untested concepts such as the software system discussed in this chapter, rather than well-tested concepts such as a word processor. At this stage we want to test *is the concept right?* Then ask, *does the interface embody the concept well?*

Formalizing the Process of Design

What would we like in a tool for evaluating the high-level human-computer interaction concepts of early design ideas? We would like to rapidly turn around and evaluate preliminary design ideas. We would like to generate and compare alternative design ideas and be able to choose the best one. We want this process to be accurate and low-cost.

Also, if we had the ability to tie system design features to user requirements and needs (e.g., Carroll and Rosson 1991) this would allow the design team to identify those features or components of the system that would be most cost-effective to include in the software product. It would also allow analysis and gathering of concrete data tying user interface features to cost benefits.

Formalizing the design process makes it more predictable, repeatable, and cost-effective. If we developed a taxonomy and library of high-level human-computer interaction design features and understood the context they were useful in (e.g., design rationale discussed in MacLean et al. 1989, 1991), we would have the potential to reuse interface design components. When creating a new software system, we could first do an analysis of the user requirements of the new system, then look in our library for potential design solutions that have been used and analyzed for effectiveness in similar situations (e.g., Carroll et al. 1992).

Currently there are too few usability inspection methods accessible to the typical software developer in the early stages of system design. Most methods focus on the embodiment of the user interface design and ease of use issues, rather than the higher-level concerns at issue in the early design stages of whether this system is complete and will be useful for the user's task and make the user more productive. An attempt to use the cognitive walkthrough to gauge the goodness of design ideas represented in an early prototype of our system failed by focusing attention on the details of the system (Wharton et al. 1992) rather than the design concepts. Use of guidelines (e.g. Hewlett-Packard Company 1990) in walkthroughs require the software to be fairly developed before they can be applied, eliminating effective application to early design ideas. Heuristic evaluations and usability walkthroughs lack an underlying theory (such as the cognitive walkthrough has) or guiding principles (as software guidelines have), making the outcome too dependent on the previous experience and intuitions of the evaluators; and there is more room for disagreement between experts when evaluating multiple high-level designs in parallel or serially as will happen early in software development. In addition, when implementation details are not specified, as happens in early designs, evaluators will miss some problems because they infer the completed design differently than the developers intend on carrying it out; evaluators tend to give the developers benefit of the doubt (Jeffries, personal communication, Feb. 1992).

Usability inspections look only for problems; they don't tell what is good about the design, so that those features will be maintained or even strengthened as the design is completed. They also require that the design be fairly well along, making it difficult to rapidly evaluate and turn around early design ideas. Empirical, user-involved methods are very time-consuming and costly, making them prohibitive for most software development efforts. Most methods are not accessible to the design team (e.g., the cognitive walkthrough, Wharton et. al., Chapter 5) because they require skills typically not found on a software development team.

However, usability inspection methods have some features that make them desirable for evaluating early HCI design concepts. Results of user-involved studies can be difficult to interpret because the users are generally unable to separate evaluation of the implementation details of a prototype from evaluation of the concepts of the design the prototype represents. An inspection, done by the developers, has the advantage that the evaluators can focus attention on the concept of the design rather than the details of its implementation. Also, it can sometimes be difficult to determine the validity of the data collected during user-involved, self-reporting methods because users are unable to introspect accurately about certain aspects of their cognitive state and processes (Holleran 1991); usability inspection techniques have the potential to avoid these problems.

In the next section is a description of a program for integrating, early in the software development cycle, the gathering of user requirements, usability inspection methods, and end-user testing, for the purpose of making a high-level evaluation of the usefulness and usability of interface design concepts. Through the synergistic use of both inspection and user-involved techniques an evaluation program was developed that was used in the early design stage of a unique kind of CAD tool, the BCA+,[2] to evaluate the development teams' design ideas.

The BCA+ (see Figure 9.1) is a research prototype CAD tool; it is a unique system intended to be used by electrical engineers to design the construction parameters for a bare printed circuit board and to get feedback on the manufacturability of the design. For this evaluation program we had to both understand the context of use of the system and identify and make explicit those high-level design decisions that represent the core concepts of how the designers intend for the software system to meet the user's needs. Even though the BCA+ system looks fairly developed, the user interface shown in Figure 9.1—and other figures in this chapter—was created in a short period of time by use of an existing spreadsheet package and has incomplete functionality. It is the intention that the method for evaluation of the interface described in this chapter could be applied to rough interface designs sketched out on paper as well.

Summary

Early on, software engineers and their management need to evaluate the high-level explicit and implicit design decisions they have made in order to know that the design will be both useful and usable. Early evaluation of the concepts behind the key human-computer interaction and functionality of

---

[2] The Board Construction Advisor Plus (BCA+) is a research prototype CAD tool developed in Hewlett-Packard Laboratories.

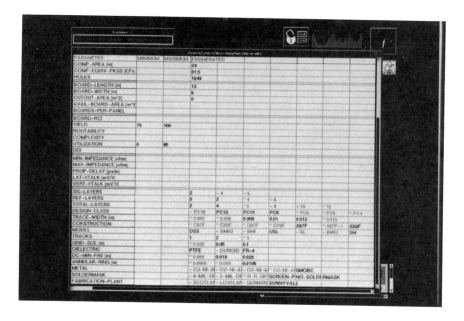

Figure 9.1 *The Board Construction Advisor Plus (BCA+) is a research prototype CAD tool intended to be used by electrical engineers to design the construction parameters for a bare printed circuit board and to get feedback on the manufacturability of the design. The parameters of the board design problem are listed in the left-hand column of the spreadsheet. The user constrains the possible values of the parameters by one of several means: entering a fixed or enumerated value; entering a range of values; or specifying members of a set of all possible values. When the board design has been constrained, the user requests that all designs that satisfy the problem be generated.*

the system has the potential to guide design—it will allow developers to avoid the "cut-and-try" approach. Effective, early testing of the design has the potential to reduce costs and improve software development products.

9.2   Building the Context for Evaluation

As usability professionals, we wanted to understand the task context and the criteria users would use to evaluate whether the software system met their needs. An understanding of the users, their work environment, and their tasks was the first step. This information helped guide system design, formed the basis for selecting evaluation methods, was written into scenarios illustrating core processes of the user's task, and was used to identify problems with the interface and compare results between evaluation methods.

Understand the Users and Their Tasks

The printed circuit board design task is complex, requiring the specification of many parameters and weighing trade-offs between a multitude of design choices affecting, among other things, cost, yield, and electrical performance. The task requires years to learn, is rich with contextual dependencies, and requires expertise in more than one domain. The required expertise is not readily available from a single resource and requires the knowledge and cooperation of many of the board designer's co-workers; domain expertise sometimes even crosses organizational boundaries. The purpose of the BCA+ is to provide the additional expertise the board designer will need.

Early on, multiple data collection methods were used to understand the user and gather high-level contextual information about the complexity of user work tasks through informal interviews, construction of annotated data-flow task diagrams, and collection of actual test cases.

The interviews were conducted with typical users and others that they interact and collaborate with in their work environment to accomplish their tasks. A data-flow diagram of the user's work task was constructed, then annotated with additional information to show, at a high level, the user task steps, information needed and produced at each step, ownership of the information, where information is obtained and stored, the goals of each step, and so forth (see Figure 9.2).

Finally, the four test cases studied were actual printed circuit board design problems the users had already solved. They were chosen to be representative of their typical work. The test cases were gathered in order to get examples of the contextual dependencies and constraints in the board design process related to the intrinsic problems of designing circuits as well as those related to organizational structure and other features of the work environment. Comparing the data gathered during the informal interviews to that gathered from the test cases shows that more concrete information about the complexities of the user's task was received from the test cases. By conducting the informal interviews first, enough knowledge of the user's task was gained to

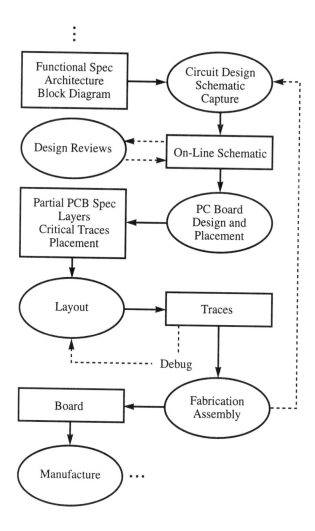

Figure 9.2 *The BCA+ users' task was represented in a annotated flow diagram. The rectangles in the diagram represent information products (e.g., circuit schematics) and physical products (e.g., the printed circuit board) that are generated during the task; the circles represent processes that occur during the task. Each element in the diagram is annotated (not shown here) with contextual information such as who performs the task, how long it takes, informal and formal procedures for accomplishing the task, what kind of problems commonly occur and how they are dealt with, among other things.*

- Compare and contrast the alternative design ideas.
- Introspect on the system design in the context of the user tasks and problem domain.
- Discuss the design with system designers.
- Examine the affordances of the artifacts of the interface style chosen.

Table 9.1 *Steps toward identifying high-level system design concepts.*

be able to intelligently select a small number of test cases for further study that would give a good coverage of typical board design problems the user faces.

We found that the BCA+ users will be infrequent users, reaching the point in the printed circuit board design process when they would use the BCA+ tool only once every one to three years. The BCA+ tool is more likely to be used by engineers that do not have a lot of the required expertise about board manufacturing. The typical user will understand the theory of circuit design and know what electrical specifications the board must meet, but achieving those specifications is a design problem. From this user profile, some domain expertise on the part of the user, but no expertise with the BCA+ system can be assumed.

Identify the High-Level HCI Design Concepts

After the informal user interviews were conducted, and in parallel with the collection of the test cases, the BCA+ developers generated system design ideas. From this, the key design concepts of how the user interacts with the system were developed and evaluated by the member on the design team assigned responsibility for usability (see Table 9.1). These concepts weren't always explicitly stated by the developers and were identified by comparison and contrast of different design possibilities, introspection on the design in the context of the user tasks previously identified, and looking at the affordances of the artifacts of the interface style chosen (e.g., the interaction style and properties of spreadsheets were examined since the spreadsheet is the primary artifact of the BCA+ interface).

Six key design concepts were identified in the BCA+ system. They are:

- Parametric Design
- Goal-Directed Design
- Constraints
- Trade-off Analysis
- Hierarchical Design
- Concurrent Engineering

These concepts are independent of the details of their particular implementation in the system. An example of one of the above design concepts is Trade-off Analysis:

> *The engineer will want to be able to make trade-offs between different possible board designs by comparing values of board fabrication parameters and metrics over those parameters. The engineer will know how to make complex trade-offs between the different values.*

This concept was identified by comparison of alternate design ideas generated by the system developers. In an earlier design idea, the BCA+ user would iteratively generate one possible board design at a time; in the current system the BCA+ user would generate many designs at once, all possible solutions to the problem. This many-at-once style versus iterative style has the quality of allowing comparison among the possible board designs, supporting the concept of trade-off analysis. Discussion with the BCA+ system developers indicated that their choice of the many-at-once style over the iterative style was for the purpose of supporting the concept of comparing possible board designs against each other. The design emerged out of an understanding that the user needed to compare designs; this evolved into trade-off analysis. In addition, looking at the primary artifact of the BCA+ interface, a spreadsheet, with its columnar format and ability to calculate and display numeric values of parameters and metrics, shows that the system affords comparison of board design solutions. All of these factors went into the development of the high-level design principle identified as trade-off analysis.

The BCA+ embodies the concept of trade-off analysis by providing the user a spreadsheet window showing multiple possible board designs, one per column (see Figure 9.3). The user may sort, subsort, and graph the designs by any of the numeric metric or parameter values (see Figure 9.4). The BCA+ provides the user the ability to look at many designs at once in order to

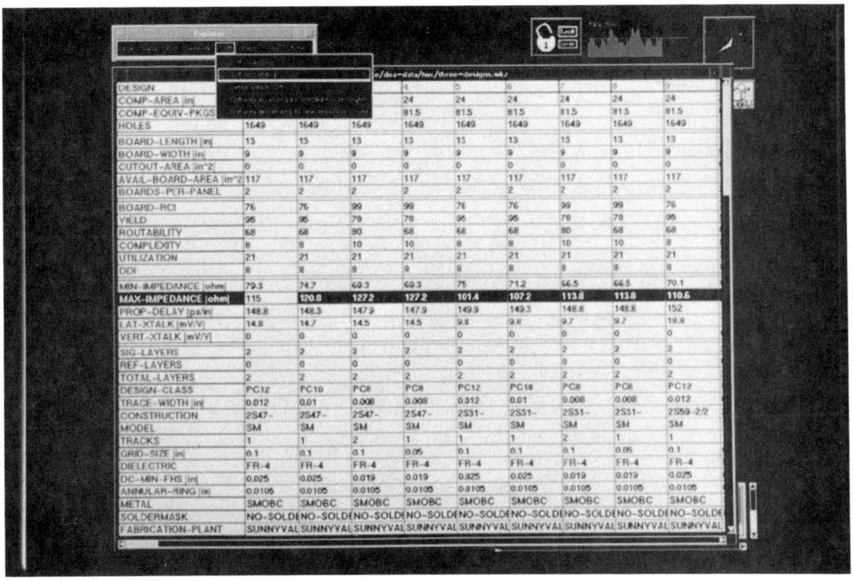

Figure 9.3 *The BCA+ shows all possible board designs that satisfy the constraints specified by the user. Each column in the spreadsheet is a board design. The user may sort the designs by any of the numerical parameter values.*

compare them and gives the user some basic tools to do a quantitative comparison of the board designs. But, the user must rely on personal knowledge of the domain of printed circuit board design to evaluate the values of the metrics and parameters and choose the best design.

We wished to evaluate both the concept of trade-off analysis and the method chosen to implement this concept in the BCA+ interface. The first focuses on whether it is a valid and important part of the user's task. The second gets at whether the particular embodiment in the BCA+—for example, sorting and graphing board design parameters—effectively supports trade-off analysis.

Once identified, these explicitly stated design concepts served as attributes of the total system design (cf. Carroll et al. 1992).

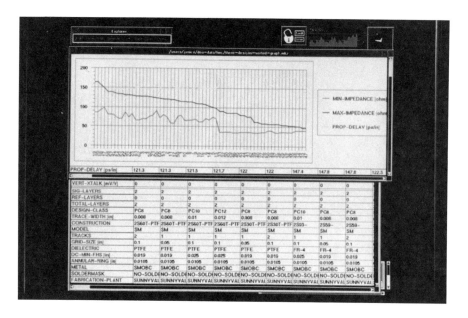

Figure 9.4 *The BCA+ user may graph the board designs by their numeric para-metric values. This is an aid to understanding which board design is the best solution to the design problem.*

Create Scenarios Illustrating Core Processes of the User Tasks

The information about the BCA+ user and the test cases were used to create scenarios. Each scenario is based on one of the four test cases gathered and describes a real printed circuit board design problem. Among other things, they illustrate the core processes of the user's work. The scenarios include the engineers' design goals; the functional, manufacturing, and cost constraints they were working under; problems they encountered along the way; the method and tools they used to accomplish the actual board design; and their final board design solution. An excerpt from one of the scenarios illustrating many of these components follows:

> The engineers are undecided as to whether they should use a larger board which has only four layers and get fewer boards per panel, or try using a smaller trace width with a four-layer board (this will increase board size only slightly but also increases the complexity so the board becomes harder

to route and manufacturing yield could decrease), or use a six-layer board and get more boards per panel. . .

9.3   Synergistic Use of Multiple Methods

Scenario-Based Evaluation Methods

The scenarios were used in a variety of usability tests, including both user-involved and inspection methods. Concept testing, informal design walkthroughs conducted by the development team, user-involved evaluation, and heuristic evaluation conducted by experts were used. It was found that each method had its strengths and weaknesses, but they informed each other in a synergistic way.

Concept Testing

The high-level contextual information contained in the scenarios was inspected for evidence of each of the BCA+ design concepts. This *concept testing* gave qualitative information about whether the key design concepts, such as the aforementioned trade-off analysis, had a place or need to exist in the BCA+ system. As the scenario excerpt in Section 9.2 shows, the BCA+ users do indeed perform trade-off analysis as part of their core work process, so including support for trade-off analysis in the high-level design of the BCA+ is valid.

The scenarios gave a good idea of the role and importance of each of the high-level design concepts in the user's work process. Two of the four test cases featured trade-off analysis prominently in the board designer's solution.

The concept testing gave a coarse analysis of whether the BCA+ system would support the user's need, but beyond that the details of the embodiment of the concept in the BCA+ was not examined at this stage. After concept testing, the question remaining to be answered for the trade-off analysis concept was whether displaying the parametric values of each board design, sorting, and graphing them would be adequate tools for the user to select the best board design.

Design Walkthroughs

Informal design walkthroughs were performed by the BCA+ development team, using the scenarios. The team first read the scenario, then as a group used the BCA+ system to solve the design problem, under the constraints described in the scenario. They relied on their knowledge of the typical user and the user's task, based on the informal interviews and the annotated data-flow task diagram, to evaluate the BCA+ interface and identify potential usability problems.

The scenarios provided the context for the software design team to exercise its ideas for the BCA+ system. The richness of the scenarios provided more than just raw "test data." The design team understood the users' goals, what domain expertise they were likely to have and what they weren't, what information would be readily available to the users in their workplace and what would not, what information the users would need to hand off to their co-workers, what other tools they would have available to help them, and the time constraints they would be working under.

The information in the scenario made some problems with the interface immediately apparent. For example, some fields in the spreadsheet had edits that would accept only integer data, when the actual board design data was decimal. By using the information in the scenario, the designers were able to generate new design ideas and extend the current design to handle these types of problems.

The scenario-based walkthroughs gave the BCA+ designers the opportunity to make explicit how they envisioned the use of the system and compare it to actual use. This allowed the designers to find those assumptions they had designed into the system that were and were not appropriate. For example, the designers assumed the BCA+ user would understand all the manufacturing terms displayed in the spreadsheet interface, but actual use showed that many of the terms were unfamiliar to users. When there was disagreement among the design team about whether the BCA+ user would have a problem with a particular feature, a note was made to explore this during the other evaluations made with the heuristic evaluators and with the actual users. This allowed some focusing of those further evaluations to get the most useful information for lower cost.

Of all the evaluation methods described here, this was the easiest to keep focused on the high-level design; low-level problems were only dealt with when they were very serious. The design team could easily separate those features of the interface that were not important to the embodiment of the concepts of the design, such as menu structure or types of buttons chosen.

Some questions remained unanswered because the scenarios can contain only so much data, the design team was over-invested in their design and missed some problems, and the uniqueness of the BCA+ user made it difficult to come to the correct conclusion about all design issues. Performing the evaluations, using the same scenarios, with the actual users, other domain experts, and heuristic evaluators overcame these limitations.

End Users

After the design team conducted the informal walkthroughs, the same was done with end users. These four users were the same ones that had solved the actual board design problems in the test cases that had been written up into the scenarios used throughout this evaluation. The users were given a brief description of the purpose of the BCA+ tool, and were asked to redesign the printed circuit board of the particular test case they worked on, this time using the BCA+ system. They were not given any information about what strategy to use with the system or any explanation of particular fields or terminology in the interface unless their progress was stuck. The users were asked to think out loud as they worked through their board design.

While working with the end users we saw the actual use of the system and found the strengths and weaknesses of the BCA+ design. Because we could tell which part of the board design process the user was in at any particular moment and what design concept applied, such as performing trade-off analysis, we were able to associate the strengths and weaknesses of particular features of the interface design to the support of the high-level design concepts of the BCA+ system.

There were many benefits to conducting the tests with actual end users. The questions raised during testing with the design team and the heuristic evaluators about whether a particular design feature would be a problem were answered, creating synergy between the methods. Also, the results of testing with end users impacted the actual design of the BCA+; the designers had a lot of confidence in these results. Finally, the tests with end users were better at indicating the importance of problems than the other methods, allowing the development team to determine the severity of problems.

Some drawbacks of the method were that the users weren't good at suggesting improvements to the system or solutions to interface problems. The heuristic evaluators and the BCA+ design team were a better resource for how to make changes to the system to overcome problems and limitations. Another drawback was that the end users did not want to separate the high-level concepts from the implementation they saw before them. They would often focus on menu structure or other low-level design issues, blocking the way to an understanding of the larger issues.

Domain Experts

The scenarios were also used with an independent domain expert, from the printed circuit board manufacturing domain. The expert was asked to read over the scenario, then look at the particular solution the engineer had chosen from those the BCA+ had presented as possible solutions, and the decisions the engineer had made along the way to the final board design.

This was important because the engineer is required to choose board designs based on how well they satisfy certain manufacturing requirements using domain expertise that the engineer is largely unfamiliar with. So, it was necessary to understand whether the BCA+ system would present the engineer with enough information to allow the correct decisions to be made.

From this we learned important information about errors the engineer had made while using the BCA+, that the engineer had not been aware of and would have remained undetected otherwise. In one case, the board design the engineer chose would not have satisfied all the manufacturing requirements for that board.

Heuristic Evaluators

The same scenarios were used with two heuristic evaluators (two scenarios per each evaluator). The evaluators were largely unaware of the engineering problem of printed circuit board design, but had heard about the BCA+ system and seen the interface before. The scenario was useful in giving some understanding of the domain knowledge required to operate the BCA+.

There were several advantages to using heuristic evaluators. About 50 percent of the problems found by the heuristic evaluators were high-level, so this method was fairly successful in finding problems relating to the design concepts. The heuristic evaluators were able to identify potential problem areas and specifically suggest areas to focus on with end-user testing. They helped to see previously identified problems in a different light and were very good at suggesting improvements to the design.

However, because of lack of familiarity with the users' task they had difficulty in determining the severity of problems. Also, the heuristic evaluators tended to give the user the benefit of the doubt too easily. They assumed that even though they themselves didn't have the domain knowledge, the user would; so, they missed some important problems due to their lack of familiarity with the end user.

Synergy between Methods

Each scenario-based evaluation method had its strengths and weaknesses. The weaknesses were compensated for by using the methods together. The software design team was good at separating the high-level design being tested from the implementation details that are less important in the early stages, and at elucidating the model of use designed into the system for comparison with actual use. The heuristic evaluators were good at making suggestions for improvements to the system. Since the BCA+ users' task is so complex and requires a great deal of domain knowledge to understand, performing evaluations with the end users was an important source of information on actual problems with the interface and their severity. The double check of the BCA+ user with the domain expert provided an independent check for errors in the engineer's work that would not have been detected otherwise. It was hard for the designers and heuristic evaluators to know the BCA+ user; likewise, it was difficult for the BCA+ user to suggest changes to the system. The synergy between these two groups was needed to have an effective evaluation.

The previously identified design concepts were assigned goodness (or badness) values by our evaluation method, giving direction to future design development. For example, we found that trade-off analysis was important to the user's task, and that the basic embodiment of the concept in the BCA+ interface was good; the users were able to accomplish their board design using the trade-off analysis features in the interface. Goal-directed design, another of the design concepts, is also important to the users' task, but the BCA+ users were not able to express their goals in the language of the system. Thus, the design concept is important, but not embodied well in the system. Another design concept, the use of constraints to limit the possible printed circuit board design space, is important to the operation of the BCA+ system in order to generate the possible board designs the user would choose from. But, it was not found to be represented in the users' task as they had been performing it, without the BCA+, and caused confusion when they had to deal with constraints in the interface. From these findings the evaluation method recommends maintaining the features of the BCA+ that support trade-off analysis, improving the features of the BCA+ that support goal-directed design, and making the constraint-driven part of the system invisible to the users and independent of their task.

9.4   The Power of Scenarios

The Inspection Method

Can we evaluate the high-level design concepts of a new software system? Yes, by identifying them, collecting high-level contextual information as scenarios, and evaluating the design in the context of the scenarios with the design team, real users, domain experts, and heuristic evaluators. In our study, the scenarios tied all these evaluations together. They proved to be very useful for many different techniques and were the common element throughout that allowed us to look at the same problem across all techniques.

The data on the users and their tasks, written up in the form of scenarios, was the foundation for all evaluations of the design of the BCA+. Additionally, this data allowed the developers to take the user perspective early in the design process by raising their level of awareness of the user's needs; the user-centered perspective was not lost among the other competing design interests outlined in Section 9.1. We used the knowledge of the user's tasks and environment to develop synergy between the evaluation methods and used it as a framework for comparing and interpreting results between the different methods previously described. This information allowed effective use of less expensive inspection methods for design evaluation.

Accessibility of Method

Even if a design team doesn't have access to all the aforementioned evaluators (e.g., heuristic evaluators), value will be gained by gathering the scenarios and working through them with the design team and a few end users. If the information gathered from the heuristic evaluators in this study is omitted, we still have a lot of useful information about the high-level design of the BCA+ gained from the concept testing, scenario-based walkthroughs by the design team, and scenario-based walkthroughs by end users.

9.5   Conclusion

The use of effective usability inspection methods early in software design has the potential to improve the software development lifecycle. It will be much easier to make design changes if the need for them is discovered early in development. There will be a lower investment required to test new ideas for software systems. If good, clear answers can be had early in the design cycle, then the intermediate stages of development (prototyping and evaluation) can proceed more rapidly to implementation.

The scenario-based evaluation method described in this chapter, which combines both user-involved and usability inspection methods, shows that we can identify strengths and weaknesses of early interface designs and attribute them to one or more design concepts. These design concepts act as a taxonomy of the system and framework for the evaluation.

Acknowledgments

The BCA+ prototype was developed in Hewlett-Packard Laboratories by Lee Barford, Norman Chang, Felix Frayman, Stan Jefferson, and Dan Kuokka. Dan Kuokka also participated in gathering information on the printed circuit board design process.

Thank you to Robin Jeffries and Cathleen Wharton for many valuable discussions about the evaluation method described in this chapter. Thank you to Bob Mack for comments on early versions of this chapter.

Chapter 10   *Adding Value to Usability Testing*

Patricia Brooks
BNR

10.1 Introduction

The information in this chapter is based primarily on experience in the product development area rather than on experimental data. Over the past nine years I have been involved in the development of many products at BNR, some that were tremendously successful and some that were not. We have learned which processes can help ensure successful products in the market; some of this learning will be described in this chapter.

The most critical phase of any evaluation is understanding who will use the data and what decisions they will make with the data. Once this is understood, an appropriate evaluation method can be chosen.

The first section of this chapter describes situations when inspection methods are an appropriate evaluation technique; the second section describes situations where inspection methods fall short of delivering the necessary information and user tests are more appropriate. The final section puts forth the hypothesis that user tests can also fall short of providing important information and that they need to evolve to meet the changing needs of the decision makers in today's more competitive global market.

10.2 When Inspection Methods Provide Value

The first step in the evaluation process is to understand what decisions will be made using the results from the study; from this the objectives of the study can be defined. Once the objectives have been defined, then an evaluation method can be chosen that will best meet the objectives. Inspection methods, user testing, or market testing may be the appropriate method, depending on the study objectives.

Inspection methods are appropriate to use when the objectives of the study are:

- To find some of the major problems in the interface before user testing or implementation of the product is undertaken. It is less expensive to identify and remove some of the major problems at this early stage of product development rather than at a later stage. Also, if modifications are made as a result of the inspection test, then the user test can verify whether the modifications were successful. The user test is then testing the solution rather than identifying the problem.

- To evaluate the usability of noncompetitive products. If a company is choosing between two text editing packages for *internal* use, as opposed to developing a product to sell, then inspection methods may provide enough information to make an effective purchase decision. However, if a product is being designed for sale in the competitive market then user testing is probably needed to (1) provide the type of data necessary to convince management that the product will be successful in the competitive market, and (2) ensure product success.

Sometimes products that will only be used within the company need to be tested with user testing because these products may be one of the reasons that the company has an edge over its competitors. For example, if insurance company A chooses a software package that allows it to fill out forms electronically on the road, whereas company B has to fill out forms manually, then company A may have a competitive edge over company B. It may be very important to choose the right software package; the decision may require user data rather than expert opinion. The bottom line is that the company needs to understand into which decisions the evaluation will feed, and then the appropriate method of testing can be determined.

- To verify that customer demands have been met. Sometimes customers articulate a demand, such as "make the interface more consistent" or "comply with Motif standards." In these situations experts are needed to verify compliance.

- To identify issues that need to be examined through user testing. Heuristic evaluation helps clarify usability issues so that the usability test can be designed to answer meaningful questions. Without this expert input the user tests risk bringing back data that cannot impact the design decisions.

- To evaluate design alternatives on dimensions that are less important to users.

There is never enough time in the product design cycle to test every element of the product. Even if there was enough time, it may not be wise from a strategic perspective to spend time and money to test every element. If the decisions that will be made are high risk, or involve factors that are very important to users, then user testing is the evaluation method of choice.

Inspection methods, on the other hand, are suitable for providing input to decisions on factors that are less important to users. We have found inspection methods to be particularly helpful for deciding between alternatives proposed by interface designers. Inspection methods can be used to compare the pros and cons of each alternative and provide some structure to the design process.

One should be aware that heuristic evaluations tend to generate a "large number of specific, one-time, and low-priority problems." In one heuristic evaluation 105 problems were identified, whereas cognitive walkthroughs and usability testing revealed 30 problems (Jeffries et al. 1991). It is not in a company's best interest to spend time and money fixing all 105 problems. Instead of fixing the low-priority problems, the company may be more successful and the users more satisfied, if the time is spent on activities that will have higher value to users.

In summary, inspection methods can be used effectively when the objectives of the study are to identify usability problems and choose from among the design alternatives in the early stages of the product development cycle. In their CHI'91 tutorial, Lewis and Polson (1991) stated that cognitive walkthroughs "can prepare the ground for prototyping and testing" but "they are not a replacement for user testing"; I agree with these statements. When the risk is low, and decisions are not being made on factors that are critical to the product success, then inspection methods are appropriate. There are, however, a range of issues in the design process that are difficult for an expert to address. The user is the best person to provide knowledge about important factors that impact the interface design and user data is necessary to understand what correlates with product success in the market.

10.3   Where and Why Inspection Methods Fall Short

Many decisions made by the product design team and management require more information than inspection methods can effectively provide. When the following types of information are needed, user testing, field trials, or other customized usability tests are more appropriate evaluation methods than inspection methods.

Predicting the Users' Trade-Off Matrix

Inspection methods are not as good as user testing for understanding the user trade-off matrix—which dimensions (e.g., speed or accuracy, categorizing options, or seeing all alternatives) are most important to users in their particular environment. It is easy for an expert to identify some potential usability problems. However, if you are to find a good solution to that problem you often need to know what dimensions/factors are important to the user. For example, consider that the display that labels function keys on a phone is limited to 40 characters. Users could be provided with five function keys, each labeled by an 8-character word, or there could be eight keys, labeled with 5-character words (see Figure 10.1).

The first interface has the benefit of having long, meaningful labels, but users cannot see all the available options at once. The second interface shows all the options, but some of the abbreviations will be hard to understand. For the user the trade-off is the length of labels versus the number of visible options. A heuristic evaluation can accurately point out that abbreviations are a problem, or that users would like to see all eight options at once.

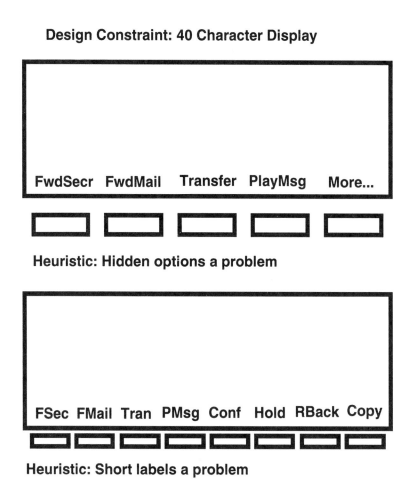

Design Constraint: 40 Character Display

FwdSecr   FwdMail   Transfer   PlayMsg   More...

Heuristic: Hidden options a problem

FSec FMail Tran PMsg Conf Hold RBack Copy

Heuristic: Short labels a problem

Figure 10.1 *Example of user trade-off between having all options present and having longer, meaningful labels. The issue of which factor is more important to users cannot be resolved from the basic heuristics.*

However, it is difficult for the expert to predict which dimension in the trade-off is more important given the user's environment. Would the user prefer seeing all the options or having long labels?

A human factors expert may have enough knowledge to apply known human factors principles, in order to see if the design comes into conflict with these, or have enough knowledge of the users' goals to be able to predict a probable error path. However, the heuristics of interface design are often interdependent and it is sometimes difficult to comply with one rule without breaking another. In these cases it is necessary to understand what the user is doing and the trade-off matrix. Inspection evaluations are not as good at providing this information as user testing.

Predicting the Acceptability of the Whole Interface

Inspection methods are excellent at finding potential problems, but it is much more difficult for the expert to provide an opinion about how users will react to the total interface. Will users perceive that the interface just does the job, or will the interface delight the user and actually provide the company with a competitive edge?

A demonstration of this limitation was given in a recent lab test. Using heuristic evaluation our expert predicted a number of usability problems; follow-up user testing confirmed these problems. However, what this heuristic evaluation did not predict was that the users built the wrong conceptual model of the interface because it was in conflict with a conceptual model users had already internalized from another product. In the end, the whole product was redesigned taking into account the competing conceptual model. Thus, in this case, the heuristic evaluation was not accurate in predicting that users would already carry a conflicting conceptual model and that the interface as a whole was not acceptable. If we had understood the customer better we may have been able to use an inspection method to identify this mismatch, but without this knowledge it was necessary to complete a user test.

Predicting How Acceptable the Interface Is Relative to Competitors' Interfaces

The inspection methods are very effective at pointing out many of the usability problems, but *finding usability problems is not enough any more*. A company wants to deliver a product that is not only usable, but one that is more usable than the competitors' products. If a competitor has a better interface, then our product may not be purchased, even if our product has no usability problems.

To prove the interface is competitive, testing needs to compare several interfaces. Testing a single product will not provide the necessary strategic information. If an expert can use an inspection method and state which interface is best and why it is better than a competitor's interface, then inspection methods can be used to provide this necessary information. But our experience indicates that inspection methods are not very good at predicting which of several interfaces will be the most usable. User tests are more accurate because they provide data on the underlying trade-off matrix and the value of the various attributes of the interface. This, rather than a list of problems, is what the design team needs to make the best interface and what management needs to make strategic decisions.

Predicting Trade-Offs with Other Aspects of the Product

The interface is one very important part of the total product. There are other parts that are also important—for example, functionality, image, size/weight, cost, and reliability. Sometimes recommendations for the design of an interface need to take account of the 'non-interface' product attributes. For example, say a new color portable computer is being evaluated using inspection methods. The expert might state that color should be used, rather than monochrome, because the color helps the user build a better conceptual model of the system. However, the addition of color will make the portable computer heavier, and more costly. Color is only beneficial to the user if the factor of ease of use is more important than the factors of ease of carrying or cost. Thus, the information the expert provided to the product design was of minimal value because the expert did not acknowledge or discuss the trade-offs in the larger design environment.

A reasonable counter argument is that the expert is a human factors expert and it is not up to that individual to understand factors like weight and cost. The human factors expert should only be making recommendations about the interface. However, the human factors expert must understand the needs of the people within the company to which the recommendations are delivered and must provide value to these people. Sometimes it may be necessary for the human factors experts to expand their knowledge to include an understanding of the "big picture" of product design if they are to provide value. This does not mean the expert needs to understand all the technical information in the other content areas; it means that the human factors person must be aware of the factors that are important in the other areas.

The human factors group may be the only group in the company that has expertise in the evaluation area, so it may be the ideal place to evaluate the trade-offs already discussed (i.e., ease of use versus heaviness and cost). It is possible that the best way for the group to add value to the design process is to expand its role and provide the capability to examine the larger trade-off matrix that includes factors outside of usability.

Predicting User Preferences

Many of the decisions about the design of a user interface are based on human factors principles; inspection methods are very helpful at pointing out places where one of these principles has been violated. However, there are many instances in design when the decision cannot be made on the basis of a human factors principle. Sometimes the decision is simply a matter of preference. For example, today telephones can capture the phone numbers of people who called while you were out and the list of unanswered calls can be shown on the phone's display. Do people have a conceptual model that the oldest call should be displayed first or the newest call displayed first? Do users want the newest call to be identified by the biggest sequence number or the smallest? We found that we could not answer these questions with expert evaluation; we had to bring in users to make sure that the list would operate the way they preferred.

The main point is that if there are many issues that the human factors literature does not cover, sometimes it is difficult for an expert to predict which implementation a user will prefer. For important preference decisions the user should be brought into the design process.

A note of caution: Users' short-term and long-term preferences may differ, and the user may tend to focus on the short-term preference during a test. The expert may need to point out the difference in perspective to the user and ask the user to comment again given the long-term perspective.

Predicting Differences in the Interface Trade-Off Matrix between Users, Choosers, and Distributors

Traditionally, usability testing, whether it is done using inspection methods or lab tests, is examining usability from the users' perspective. This makes sense, since it is the user that will ultimately spend the most time with the product.

However, there are other important people in the value chain. For a business product like a computer, distributors have to be convinced that the product will sell or they will not stock it. Also, most companies have someone who makes the decision about which computer will be purchased (this person is called the "chooser"); this person also needs to be convinced about the acceptability of the product. The distributor and the chooser often have a different trade-off matrix than the end user with respect to the interface. For example, the distributor and chooser may not want to stock or purchase computers that have mice: This would mean more inventory to stock and track and an extra piece part that may easily become lost or stolen. The distributor will only want the computer with the mouse if convinced that the ease-of-use for the end user is great enough to increase computer sales, thereby making up for the extra costs associated with carrying more inventory. To create the optimum product you need an interface that maximizes the trade-offs between these three different groups of people—distributors, choosers, and end users. In the past we have used two methods to ensure that the needs of all three groups in the value chain are considered:

1. Have choosers and distributors evaluate the product as part of the normal design and verification process. Their trade-off matrices can then be understood; it may then be possible to design an interface that meets the most important needs of all three people in the chain: the distributor, the chooser, and the end user.

2. Provide marketing/sales with data that clearly demonstrates the value the interface design has to the end user. The data can be used by sales to convince the distributor (who can then convince the chooser) that the appropriate trade-offs have been made.

In summary, you can increase product success if you consider usability from the perspective of all groups that have a vested interest in the product's interface—the distributor, chooser, and end user.

Predicting Usability in the Global Market

One of the major trends in the computing, telecommunications, and other industries is globalization. With increased R&D costs, and more competitors, it is necessary to look globally to find a market that is large enough to sustain company growth and R&D costs. Another change is that the nations themselves are becoming more multicultural. Many countries have more than one cultural group and more than one language.

Globalization presents a real challenge to usability testing because a product will have a wider variety of users using it than it did a decade ago. Many of the people using our products may speak English as a second language, so they may have a different understanding of the vocabulary in the interface. Also, the interface may need to be translated into a foreign language; this has implications for the design and usability of the product (Nielsen 1990e). We have found that people from other cultures have different expectations and different criteria about usability than our "native" users. For example, a usability test was done on 2-line phones using North American subjects. The evaluation indicated that if a person is on a call on Line 1, then a call coming in on the second line should have soft ringing. The phone was designed that way, then shipped to sell in Sweden. But Swedish users didn't even want to know that the second call existed. They wanted the second call put on autohold and, according to their custom, the person waiting would know that call would be answered next.

The multicultural world makes it less likely that inspection methods will produce an accurate evaluation of an interface. The inspection evaluator has a particular learning style, problem solving strategy, and experience that may not be representative of the potential users of the product. The validity of the inspection method could be improved by having experts from the different cultures evaluate the device or it may be necessary to have users from the various cultures test the product.

Closure to the Development Cycle

It is our experience that an expert interface evaluation is regarded as opinion. And there are other experts (e.g., hardware designers, software designers, marketing) who also have opinions about the direction the interface should take. The development cycle can go into endless loops while experts discuss their opinions. On the other hand, results from user tests are viewed as fact and these facts will tend to override an expert opinion. This results in closure on issues. User data typically brings closure to the issues being discussed in product development.

10.4   Evolution of User Testing

In the previous sections it has been argued that often inspection methods cannot provide the strategic information necessary to make the decisions to ensure a successful product. But today *traditional user testing also often falls short of providing the necessary information.* The fact that the market is more competitive and end users are more sophisticated means that managers need different kinds of information than they did a decade ago. The changing needs of businesses are changing what user testing needs to deliver. User testing needs to evolve to meet these changing needs.

Usability labs need to provide data that:

- Aids the development decisions being made by the product development team and management

- Indicate how acceptable the interface is: Will it delight users or cause returns

- Indicate how the interface will perform in the competitive global market

Following are some of the changes we implemented in our interface evaluation process to ensure that we were delivering the necessary information.

Customize the Test to Meet the Needs of the Design Teams and Management

Tests that are customized to meet the specific needs of the design teams and management (stakeholders) provide more actionable information than "cookbook" tests. The first step in designing a customized test is to ensure that the evaluator thoroughly understands the needs of all the stakeholders. This is often a difficult and time-consuming process, but it is an essential step in the evaluation procedure. We typically do this in face-to-face meetings between all stakeholders and the usability evaluator. One useful question to ask the stakeholders in these meetings is what decisions they are trying to make about the interface. The objectives of testing should then be documented by the evaluator and circulated to the stakeholders to ensure that everyone has the same understanding of the issues. After consensus on the issues has been reached the test can be designed. While designing the test, the evaluator should remember that the results should be actionable; that is, someone can make a decision and take action based on the results. The planning phase of the customized test takes longer than for a standardized test, but other phases of testing take about the same amount of time.

Following is an example where this process was followed and management was provided with actionable results:

1. Management and the design teams were probed and it was found that:

    • They wanted to have the best interface possible, given a product cost of $X.

    • To improve the interface the size of the display could be increased or an alternative input device could be provided, but product cost precluded doing both. Management needs to decide which way to spend research and development dollars.

2. The evaluator documented the objectives to be:

    • Determine whether a larger display or alternative of input device provides more benefit to the interface from the user's perspective.

    • Determine which combination of display size and input device provides the most acceptable performance over a wide range of users.

3. The following test was carried out:

    • Several prototypes were built that had different display sizes and different input devices.

    • Forty users completed a variety of tasks on the prototypes.

    • Users were asked to state their preference for display size and why.

    • Users were asked to state their preference for input device and why;

    • Each user completed tasks on two prototypes that had the characteristics of their preferred prototype: (A) a prototype with their preferred display size, and their second preferred input device, (B) a prototype with their preferred input device and their second preferred display size.

    • Users were asked which prototype they would prefer: A or B. If they preferred A, then display size was more important to them than input device. If they preferred B, the reverse was true.

4. Results indicated that for the types of tasks users completed:

    • Increasing the display size did not improve usability or acceptability.

- Users consistently chose the prototype with their preferred input device, rather than the one with the preferred display size, indicating the input device was a more important factor than display size.

- Speed was more important than accuracy or ease of learning for device choice.

5. Management was able to make decisions that led to high product acceptability based on the results from the test.

Do Comparative Testing

A good rule of thumb is to always test a new interface idea against another interface.

Managers need to know that an interface works well and that all the usability problems are gone; traditional usability testing provides this information. In addition, they need to know that the interface is easier to use than the one they sold last year or that it is better than the competitor's product that will be sold next year. To provide this information the interface being developed needs to be tested against other interfaces.

A new interface can be tested against:

- The interface it will replace in the market—A new interface needs to be better than the old one; otherwise, the research and development money is not justifiable.

- Another idea for a new interface—If you only test one new interface idea, you do not know whether it is better than a completely different idea. This is a variant of the parallel design method (Nielsen 1993a; Nielsen et al. 1993).

- A competitive interface or simulation of a competitive interface—Your company may have developed an interface that has no usability problems, but if it is not easier to use than the competitor's interface then the product may not be successful.

Often the product that will compete with your product is not being sold yet, but competitive comparisons are still possible. Competitors will often provide information about the characteristics of their future products long before product introduction; they may even show demonstrations of the future interface at trade shows or conferences. In addition, trends can be monitored by examining patent applications, FCC submissions, company technical journals, and other secondary source information. With this knowledge it is possible to predict what the next generation product interfaces could be like; then these future interfaces can be simulated, and compared to simulations of your company's future interface.

Some companies may feel that they cannot afford the time and money to predict the future direction of competitors' interfaces. As an alternative, these companies could generate ideas for two interfaces, simulate them, and test the relative usability of the two interfaces. If only one interface idea is generated and tested then all you can do is perfect that particular interface. You have no way of knowing whether it is better than an alternative idea for the interface. If two ideas are generated and tested, there is more information to judge whether the total interface idea is acceptable.

Design the Test so that You Understand Which Factors Are Important to Users and How These Factors Trade-Off

Earlier in the chapter the reasons why it is important to understand the user trade-off matrix were discussed. Following is an example of an experiment where the trade-off information was obtained. The objective of the experiment was to examine entry of alphabetic characters through a small keyboard and a telephone dialpad, and determine which method was more usable and acceptable. It was predicted that performance would be faster, more accurate, and easier to learn on the small keyboard; the experimental performance data confirmed this. However, the results also indicated that users preferred to enter characters on the harder-to-learn, less accurate, multistep procedure on the dialpad for two reasons: (1) the key size of the dialpad was bigger and users indicated that key size was a more important factor than speed, accuracy, or ease of learning for this type of task, (2) the keyboard was considered "overkill" for the task since the functionality was only needed for a small percentage of time that the telephone was in use. The evaluation provided information on the relative importance of factors to the users; this knowledge, rather than data on problems and performance, was used to make the final design decision.

In the evaluation the following types of questions can be asked to probe for the trade-off information:

• Which do you prefer and why?

- If you were purchasing a product like this, what characteristics would you make sure the product had?

Or to examine a specific trade-off (e.g., to determine if key size or "overkill" is a more important determinant of acceptability):

- Assume now that the key size on the keyboard is the same as key size on the dialpad, which product would you choose?

Given the trade-off information the designers may even be able to hypothesize a third alternative for alphabetic entry that could provide higher acceptability than the two methods that were originally tested.

Understanding the underlying factors that are important to users and how these factors trade-off makes it possible to implement the best design.

Examine the Interface Overall

Users in a usability test may indicate that they have problems with a procedure, or they may not like the way something works. It is advantageous to know whether the problem is large enough that it will impact the overall acceptability of the product. Questions like the following allow the severity of the problem to be estimated.

- If you owned this product, is there anything about the way it works that would make you want to return it? Why?
- Compare the way this product works with the way the product you own today works. Which do you prefer? Why?
- If you arrived at work tomorrow, and this product was on your desk, would you want to keep it? Why, or why not?

If a large enough percentage of users mention the same issue in response to these questions, then you know you have a problem that will affect overall product acceptability. The spontaneous complaint level in the lab that corresponds to returns in the field (or another objective measure) can be determined through correlation of lab tests, field tests, and market performance.

Correlate Field and Lab Information

Today the focus is on finding a means of prioritizing usability problems. For inspection methods Lewis et al. (1990) developed a scale to differentiate severity levels of usability problems ("0 = no users would have problems;

1 = few users would have problems; 2 = more than half of the users would have problems; 3 = most users would have problems"). The scale is a good starting point because it tries to relate the problems to the end-user experience and it provides a means of separating low priority and high priority problems. However, the scale is not correlated with the market complaint levels. What scale value means that the company should fix the problem? If a few users experience the problem does this translate into 0 percent, 5 percent, or 10 percent product returns in the market? Ideally one should know what each point on the scale means in terms of *market* complaint levels.

User tests have more validity in predicting market complaint levels than inspection methods because end users are providing the data. However, even *user tests need to be correlated against market data.* For example, one objective measure tracked in our user tests is the "percent of users that got a procedure right the first time they tried." If 80 percent of users in a lab test complete a procedure correctly the first time they try, is that performance good enough to ensure success in the market? What percentage is high enough to ensure the company will experience minimal product returns? We only know the answer if lab and market data are compared. Benchmarking will provide the researchers with the information they need so they know how to interpret future lab data and understand whether 80 percent is high enough or not.

The evaluation of the effectiveness of inspection and user tests has been limited and has not considered factors relevant to the success of commercial products. Usability testing needs to evolve so that the results are not just prioritized; the results need to predict market performance.

Cost Effective User Testing

It is often said that the major drawback of a user test is the cost; by comparison inspection methods are inexpensive. However, there are ways to decrease the cost of a user test. The most expensive part of the test is the labor of the evaluators. To cut down on this cost at BNR, we have done the following:

- Only one person actually views the test and *all data* is collected *live* by this person. The video tapes are not used as part of data analysis; they are just back-up. The person viewing the test needs to be highly skilled (usually has a minimum of an M.A. and three years working within the company).

- A flexible customized software package was developed so that quantitative and qualitative data could be captured quickly and accurately by one person. The software also does some preliminary analysis (e.g., average task times, frequencies of events such as errors, number of users that got task right the first time, users making comment X, users making preference Y) which decreases the cost associated with analysis.

- The cameras are operated remotely by the evaluator so a technician is not needed during testing.

The test may not pick up every single usability problem, but it captures the problems that would likely emerge in the market as problems—the ones that will likely be targeted in a design review as important to fix.

10.5 Summary

Inspection methods are effective evaluation tools when they are used to meet objectives such as minimizing problems before user testing is undertaken. However, the increasingly competitive market makes it essential that the user opinion is obtained in areas of high risk and areas that are critical to user acceptance. The changing business environment also makes it necessary to evolve user testing so that it can provide the necessary strategic information to the product design team and management.

Chapter 11 *Usability Problem Reports: Helping Evaluators Communicate Effectively with Developers*

Robin Jeffries
SunPro[1]

The goal of a usability inspection is to identify potential problems users will have with an application. A variety of methods can be used to predict usability weaknesses: heuristic evaluations (Nielsen, Chapter 2), cognitive walkthroughs (Wharton et al., Chapter 5), guideline checklists (Perlman 1989), formal usability inspections (Kahn and Prail, Chapter 6). The identified problems must be conveyed to the developers who will make modifications to improve the usability of the application. Some inspection methods attempt to eliminate that step by having the developers do their own evaluations. But there are many reasons for evaluations to be done by people not on the development team: lack of time, training, or inclination on the part of the developers, and the desire for the evaluation to be independent of the assumptions of the designers. In fact, the majority of usability inspections are done by someone other than the product's developers.

How can evaluators ensure that the usability problems they identify will be understood correctly and taken seriously by the developers? Misunderstood problem reports may be interpreted by developers as *false alarms*—requested changes that would have no positive impact on usability and might even

---

[1] This work was carried out while the author was at Hewlett-Packard Laboratories.

make the application less usable. The misunderstandings that lead to developers interpreting a problem as a false alarm can come from either side: evaluators—who typically study an application for only a few days or even hours—may not grasp all the factors that led to a particular choice and that have an impact on its usability, while developers may not have a rich enough understanding of users and the ways they will be misdirected by an interface feature. When usability problem reports are subject to interpretation as false alarms, there is a dual cost—the cost of making changes that do not improve the usability of the product and the even more serious cost of developers coming to treat all problem reports as "mere opinions," which will be taken seriously if they concur with the developer's biases and ignored if they do not.

In order to determine how significant a problem false alarm reports are in usability evaluations, I examined a large collection of usability problem reports written from the perspective of several methodologies (Jeffries et al. 1991). This chapter will explore the potential for these reports to be interpreted as false alarms. This leads to recommendations of ways that evaluators can change their evaluation approach and their communication style to minimize both misunderstandings of the product's usability constraints and failures to communicate usability concerns to developers.

11.1   The Data Set

In Jeffries et al. (1991), four usability evaluation techniques (heuristic evaluation, cognitive walkthroughs, usability guidelines, and usability testing) were compared on the same product. The evaluations were done under conditions that were as realistic as we could manage. The heuristic evaluations were done independently by four usability specialists; the cognitive walkthrough and guidelines evaluations were done by teams of three software engineers; and the usability test was the actual product usability test. Each evaluator/evaluation team filled out a report form for every usability problem identified, giving a short description of the problem. This provided a large pool of problem reports found by a variety of inspection techniques as well as by usability testing.

Both cognitive walkthroughs and guidelines are intended to be done by the developers themselves; however, in this experiment the evaluators were chosen to be similar in backgrounds to the developers, but were not the actual developers. Hence, they did not have the detailed knowledge of the design constraints and the trade-offs that determined the current user interface to the product. Thus, all the problem reports in the data set were done by nondeveloper evaluators; we cannot comfortably generalize to situations where developers do their own evaluations. In addition, the product being evaluated was a full functionality, near-final version. Very different issues might have come up had an early prototype been evaluated.

The report forms were more informal than typical written reports that usability specialists provide. They were more like the notes which evaluators might take during their assessment of an application. Since we did not ask the evaluators to convert these note-like reports into formal narratives, we cannot be certain that the wording of the reports we were given is the form in which the recommendations would have been fed back to developers. On the other hand, these reports are very similar in style and wording to actual usability assessments we have seen and written.

The product being evaluated was a pre-release version of a graphical desktop for UNIX. It covered a wide range of functionality—file management, setting of defaults (colors, mouse behavior, fonts, screen savers, etc.), mail, printing, and screen management. A total of 230 problems were reported (including duplicates, but not including the problems found via the usability test). The problems reported ranged from the very minor, such as a typo in the documentation, to the catastrophic. For example, it was possible with this version for a user to get into a state where it was impossible to log back in to the computer. This could only be repaired by a system administrator.

11.2 Looking for False Alarms

We first attempted to predict the fraction of problem reports that were potentially *false alarms*—problem reports that did not identify actual usability problems in the application. The best way to determine the impact or lack of impact of a potential problem would be to gather field data on the problems experienced by users in real work situations. This option was not available to us. The next best alternative would be to compare the inspection reports to usability testing data. We do have problem reports from a usability test of the application; however, that test was focused on novice users in their first few hours of experience with the application. Many of the problems reported by our evaluators would not be likely to occur during such a test (and did not occur). Thus, given the design of the specific usability test, the fact that a predicted problem did not occur is not particularly strong evidence that it constitutes a false alarm. Hence, we were forced to look for more indirect measures of whether a problem report was valid.

Our first approach was to have three experienced usability evaluators classify all 230 problems into two categories: *core problems*, described as reports that most usability specialists would agree were valid usability problems; and *taste problems*, defined as reports for which usability specialists might have diverging opinions about their validity. The taste problems are potential false alarms—at least some usability experts would claim that correcting the "problem" identified in such a report would have no positive impact on the usability of the application. Inter-rater agreement was very low on this: On the first pass, all three raters agreed on the classification of about two-thirds of the items. (In standard rating tasks, agreement of less than 80 percent is considered poor; the score here is particularly bad when you consider that the raters should have achieved between 25 percent and 50 percent agreement by chance—depending on the *a priori* probability of a false alarm.) Since the problem reports tended to be written in a rather telegraphic style, the raters worked together with the application in front of them to determine if the disagreements were due primarily to misunderstandings of what the evaluators had written. Resolving these misunderstandings did increase the agreement somewhat, but a much larger source of disagreement was differing standards of what constitutes a usability problem. From the sessions, it became clear that raters differed on a variety of values that influenced their judgments. For example, one rater weighed the problems of novice users most strongly, while another was willing to trade off novice problems, especially one-time problems, for greater efficiency for day-to-day users. The lack of inter-rater reliability demonstrated in a microcosm the problems that usability specialists and developers have in determining whether a reported problem will have an impact on usability.

Because of the variability of the ratings, reporting the numbers of false alarms based on those ratings would be meaningless. Instead, this chapter looks at the kinds of reports that were singled out by one or more raters as potential false alarms. There were a small number of reports that all raters agreed should not be counted against the program's usability. The first were problems that we could not reproduce; for example, that characters were not echoed when the evaluator typed in a text box, but the next time he tried the task, the characters were echoed. This might be a program bug or might have been evaluator error, but the evaluator was not able to provide enough additional information to enable us to reproduce the problem. The second set contained clear mistakes on the part of the evaluator. For example, one evaluator complained that the *File* menu in the File Manager does not have a *Copy* item, when there is such an item. When we pointed out the discrepancy to the evaluator, he could not account for why he had overlooked it (as opposed to other cases, discussed later, where the evaluator's failure to find available functionality was attributed to the way the feature was presented). There were 8 reports of the first type and 10 of the second, representing 8 percent of the data. In a nonexperimental situation, the evaluators would have made a second pass over their reports to check for these kinds of errors; we did not ask them to go through this checking step, so our data contain small numbers of items that most likely would have been filtered out in an actual usability evaluation. These clear cases of invalid reports were very easy for both the raters and the developers to identify.

11.3 Examples of Problem Reports

Instead of using the raters' assessments of validity of the problem reports, I will explore a set of example reports that demonstrate the kinds of issues that led various raters to question the validity of some recommendations. A small number of themes runs through these examples:

1. Evaluators often go immediately to solutions, without describing the problem that needs to be solved.
2. User interface design involves a large number of trade-offs among competing dimensions. It is easy for an evaluator to overlook some of the most critical but subtle dimensions that contribute to a situation.
3. When a problem is described at the wrong level of abstraction (e.g., a single example of a more general problem is focused on), the solution is likely to be too narrow and may make some parts of the interface worse.

Mistakes as Usability Problems

Many of the problems that, narrowly taken, represent cases of evaluator error, were not counted as such because they could be reinterpreted as examples of usability problems, where the mistake made by the evaluator might also be made by users. For example, one evaluator noted that the dialog box to modify the audio feedback level and duration provided no way to test the newly set values. That was not true—the new value is tested by clicking on the slider that sets the value. There is no label or other indication that the slider serves this dual purpose. If we interpret the report as "it is difficult to figure out how to test the audio values," this is a valid report.

There were more difficult cases in which the evaluator's specific report was invalid, but if taken at a more abstract level, was indicative of a valid problem. For example, several evaluators complained about the placement of items on menus. Each report singled out a different menu and/or item; for each complaint, one could come up with reasons that justified as well as challenged the item's current placement. However, for the menus taken as a group, it is likely that a better set of assignments of items to menus could have been found. No evaluator saw the big picture; rather they simply noted the specific menu item that made them notice that the organization of the menus was not coherent. It is seldom the case that one instance of a large category of decisions (in this case the placement of menu items) can be looked at outside of the context in which the full set of decisions was made. Of course, seeing the larger category of which the current problem represents an instance is often very difficult. For example, given an incongruent item on the File menu, is the relevant higher category all the menus for the given window or all the File menus across all the windows in the system?

Trade-Offs

Some problem reports espoused a strong preference for one possible resolution to a complex trade-off. The evaluators did not appear to recognize the fact that their solution optimized one dimension at the expense of others. One report noted that double-clicking on a directory icon in a File Manager window brought up a view of that directory in the same File Manager window, rather than spawning a new window. This is an option that can be modified by the (experienced) user and the nondefault option can be selected via the menu. Thus, the full range of functionality is available and there is provision for users who will prefer different default options. But the default has to be set one way or the other. While there are good arguments for both possible default settings, the problem report gives no justification for why the evaluator recommends the opposite default and, in fact, does not make it apparent that the evaluator recognizes the trade-off involved. This problem would be more likely to be seen as valid if the developer were confident that the recommender had taken all constraints into account.

Another type of trade-off has to do with whether the interface should be tuned to the needs of new or experienced users. One problem report noted that several similar widgets differed gratuitously in their text background colors. In actual fact, the differing background colors indicate two different types of interaction boxes—selection boxes and type-in boxes. The evaluator missed the distinction. Novices may well find the apparent inconsistency to be disconcerting, whereas more experienced users can use the color difference as an implicit cue to the semantics of the interactor. What is a reasonable cost for new users to pay if it increases the usability of the system over the long term? Does that trade-off change when both the cost to novices and the benefit to the experienced is relatively small, as in this case?

Evaluators often couched their concerns in terms of consistency, without appearing to recognize that consistency trades off with other desirable attributes of an interface. One consistency issue that was noticed by many evaluators has to do with two styles of dialog boxes that exist in this system. Some dialog boxes have buttons labeled *OK* and *Cancel*, while others have *Apply, Close,* and *Cancel.* The functionality of the *OK* button is to *Apply* the changes made and immediately *Close.* The alternate form separates those two actions at the cost of requiring two button presses to get the same result. The application developers have made judgments of when the task supported by the dialog box is likely to be a one-time change (e.g., change the audio feedback loudness) in which case the *OK* button set is used versus when users will want to make a series of actions using this dialog box (e.g., a text search dialog box), where the *Apply* button set is used. Evaluators who considered this to be a usability problem focused on the visual inconsistency of having two different button sets in very similar situations, rather than on the tasks that the dialog boxes were used for and whether the button choices were appropriate for that task.

The evaluators may be right, but the lack of explicit recognition of the trade-off makes it likely that the recommendation will be challenged. Furthermore, had the evaluators recognized the nature of the trade-off involved, they might have discovered a solution that satisfies both the constraints of visual consistency and task congruity.

Conflicting Recommendations

An interesting set of usability issues arises when different evaluators disagree in their recommendations. This would seem to be a clear indication of an issue that was a matter of individual taste, but the actual cases are not so clear cut. First, contradictory recommendations are relatively subtle in this data set. A clear case of a contradiction would be when one evaluator praises a feature and another condemns it. However, the evaluators did not consider it to be part of their task to comment on the user interface features they approved of, so we don't have examples of this. In general, contradictions come from different evaluators commenting on different parts of the application, where both recommendations can't be implemented simultaneously.

An example of a contradiction came from two evaluators commenting on scrollable lists used in different parts of the application. In one case, the list had scroll bars even when the number of items in the list was small enough to be presented all at one time. The evaluator considered the scroll bars to be a waste of valuable screen space. In the other case, a short list was shown without scroll bars (but the list would have acquired scroll bars had there been enough items to necessitate scrolling). This evaluator was concerned that if items were added to that list, the user would not be able to scroll to find off-screen items. The lack of feedback that this was a potentially scrollable list disturbed the evaluator.

These two evaluators are using different criteria for their recommendations (make functionality apparent versus don't waste screen space). From the problem reports and from examining the interface, there is no apparent justification for different solutions being used in the two cases. What would a developer getting both these recommendations do? Here the evaluators have been quite explicit in their recommendations and justifications. However, because they both seem to have missed the trade-off involved, there is no information to justify their choices in the trade-off space.

Another contradiction exposes a particularly complex issue. One evaluator complained that there were three different ways to move down the directory hierarchy to a child directory. (The three options are: double-clicking on the directory icon in the parent directory view, selecting the directory in the parent directory view and then choosing *Open* from the *Actions* menu, and choosing *Change To* from the *Directory* menu and typing in the full path name of the child directory.) The evaluator felt that providing multiple ways of doing the same thing simply confused users and that the developers should settle on a single method. Another developer noted that the *Directory* menu provided a menu item to move up the directory hierarchy, but not one to move down. The interface was criticized for its lack of consistency here. This would have been a fourth way of moving down the directory hierarchy. Are multiple ways of performing the same action good or bad? Nilsen et al. (1992) demonstrate that at least in some circumstances (spreadsheet applications), the existence of two ways of doing the same task can have a very high cognitive overhead, costing users seconds every time they have to choose between the two approaches. Yet many arguments can be made for providing multiple ways of accomplishing the same goal, especially in a navigation context (Nielsen 1990a). Most likely there are circumstances when the user interface is improved by providing multiple methods to achieve a given goal and others where users are slowed down by the choices; however, the current knowledge base of human computer interaction does not permit us to determine which applies in this situation (or even if it matters). One of these recommendations is most likely wrong, but without an intricate experimental design focused on exactly this question, we cannot determine which it is.

Another example of a trade-off that has no good resolution is a report that claimed that file copy operations involving unrelated directories were too cumbersome. In this case, the user must either open two file browsers and drag with the mouse the file to be copied (using the <shift> modifier to ensure that it is copied, not moved), or select the file to be copied and a menu option that requires that the full pathname of the destination directory be typed in. The operation is cumbersome, but there may not be a more straightforward approach to this situation that doesn't make more common operations awkward. What are the trade-offs between making common operations simple while making uncommon ones much more complex versus making the more common operations slightly more cumbersome in order to lower the complexity of the less common ones? How should this judgment be made? And what if the evaluator has overlooked a solution which lowers the complexity of all the operations in question?

Evaluator Biases

A final class of possibly invalid problem reports has to do with "religious" opinions of the evaluators. These might well indicate usability problems with the application, but they were stated as generalities that many usability experts would disagree with. These include: An evaluator who found the icons distracting and wasteful of screen space; another evaluator who felt that the graphical file manager was not as usable/useful as the normal UNIX directory facilities; and a report that suggested that animation be used to provide better understanding of the hierarchical file relationships. It is hard to imagine that these reports would be taken seriously by the developers they are fed back to, both because they provided no justification for the positions taken (especially important in these cases, where substantial changes in the interface would have been required) and because they challenged the core assumptions of the application. The style of reporting used in this experiment is definitely not adequate when an evaluator proposes a major redirection of the user interface. One might question whether usability is ever served by this kind of feedback late in the development process; wouldn't a more usable application result from improving the interaction within the current assumptions of the user model as compared to reimplementing a large fraction of the interface from scratch (with typically no time left in the schedule to fine tune that interface)?

11.4 Which Are the False Alarms?

The examples above demonstrate that there were many problem reports in this data set which, if taken at face value, might not have led developers' to make improvements in the usability of the application. Should these be considered false alarms or is there another lesson to be learned from these examples? In almost every case—the exceptions being the small numbers of nonreproducible problems and factual mistakes—the problem reported could be interpreted as an instance of a valid usability concern. In many cases the evaluator didn't have enough information to interpret the usability issue correctly (e.g., the evaluator who thought the problem was a lack of test functionality in the audio settings box, when the problem was that the test capability was hidden); other times the evaluator focused on a portion of the problem, when seeing the larger picture would lead to different solutions (e.g., problems with specific menu items, when the entire menu structure needed to be re-evaluated). In other cases multiple goals needed to be traded off one another; the evaluator either didn't recognize the competing goals that led to the implemented solution or didn't make clear to the developers why that solution was better when all relevant goals were taken into account.

If these data lead to the conclusion that virtually all usability problem reports, if correctly reinterpreted, identify valid usability issues, then what is the impact of so many reports that require this additional interpretation step? Developers are not likely to be willing or able to see the real usability problem in the flawed description of the issue. They will either fix the problem as described or ignore it, neither of which leads to the desired improvement in usability. Thus, if developers are to get maximally useful feedback from usability inspection reports, evaluators must find better ways to ensure that the problems and solutions they describe identify the true usability issue or trade-off that underlies the observation.

11.5 Better Problem Reports

Since the vast majority of the potential false alarms would be seen as valid problem reports had they been described differently, can some of the mistakes that evaluators made be categorized and can better ways be prescribed to give usability feedback? The preceding examples demonstrate a number of shortcomings in the way problem reports are written.

Many of the aspects of problem reports that keep them from being taken as valid could be minimized by a more careful attention to the information included in the problem report. Problem reports can be decomposed into four aspects: the problem, the justification for why the current situation is a usability problem, the proposed solution, and the justification for why the proposed solution is better. In virtually all reports some of the aspects are missing and others are merged. Our evaluators were not required to give justifications for their problem reports; they often did not or did so implicitly. Seldom did they give both kinds of justifications; the assumption seems to be that the negation of the problem justification is the solution justification and vice versa.

The most apparent confounding in the problem reports is that problems are often described in terms of their solutions. It is extremely rare for an evaluator to simply describe a problem, unless the problem is seen as not having an apparent solution (e.g., "copy action is very clumsy when directories are unrelated"). Sometimes the solution is implicit in the problem description (e.g., "no automatic completion of filenames provided," or "poor error message for. . ."), but the most common phrasing of a problem report uses the terms "should" or "should not". This was true for all the evaluation techniques and for both expert evaluators and engineer-evaluators.

Is this conflation of problem reports and solution reports a good thing? Describing the problem in terms of a solution is first of all a very natural approach. If users will have difficulty accomplishing the task of logging out because they can't figure out how to invoke the command, then saying "the logout button needs a better label" may seem to evaluators to be simply the description of the problem (after all, they didn't say what the label should be). However, there are several reasons why separating the problem from the solution and presenting both would improve the quality of problem reports. First, describing the problem forces the evaluator to focus on users and tasks and makes those aspects of the evaluation more salient to the developer who reads the recommendation. Second, making the problem description explicit facilitates providing some justification for the problem independent of the solution justification. If the problem description is task-oriented, the description may serve as its own justification. Third, if the solution proposed is infeasible for reasons unforeseen by the evaluator, the developer may be able to use the problem description to find a related solution that does meet the constraints of the situation. Finally, the intentional inclusion of a solution both provides specific guidance to the developer (e.g., saying that a label is poorly worded does not help the developer, whose expertise is not in label semantics, figure out how better to label a button) and helps the evaluator place the solution in the larger context. The latter may help the evaluator notice where the solution might lead to problems elsewhere in the interface (e.g., the new label might be confused with another button label on the screen).

It is also important to provide justification information. I suspect that evaluators failed to provide justification only in cases where they thought it was "obvious"; but what is obvious to a usability expert or to someone steeped in an evaluation methodology may not be obvious to the developer who has to implement the change. Furthermore, the developer needs to be sure that the evaluator has considered constraints that may be more apparent to someone who has worked through the design trade-offs or at least that the solution is consistent with those trade-offs. Making justifications explicit helps the developer determine whether the proposed solution meets the required criteria. Also, having an explicit justification decreases the likelihood that the change will be incorporated mechanically; the developer can understand what purpose the change serves and aspects of the change that were not described by the evaluator (e.g., what error message to return when the action cannot be carried out) are more likely to be done in a manner consistent with the usability concern. Whether independent justifications of the problem and the solution need to be provided is not clear—there were no cases where evaluators explicitly provided both (although the missing justification could usually be inferred and was the complement of the justification provided), so we do not have data that enables a comparison of explicit versus implicit justifications. There are times when the justification of one does not imply the other—for example, when a problem is caused by lack of consistency, the solution will generally be justified both on consistency grounds and with some other user interface principle. Evaluators need to consider both problem and solution justifications and make each one explicit when a single rationale doesn't cover both cases.

Some problem reports represent a situation where there is no perfect answer (e.g., the decision about whether to spawn a new window for a new directory or to reuse the current one). The developer has chosen a particular point in that space representing an understanding of the tasks and populations to be supported. If that decision is challenged, then the evaluator needs to show an understanding of the trade-off space, the tasks, and the population. In several cases in our data, evaluators appeared to be advocating certain solutions as universally correct, rather than as a local optimum in a trade-off space. It may be that they had carefully considered all the alternatives and had excellent justifications for the usability of their choice, but it was impossible to infer what those justifications were. Thus, an additional component that needs to be added to many problem reports is a discussion of the trade-off space and where the original solution and the proposed new solution sit in that space.

Laying out the dimensions being traded off and the justification for the selected solution helps in a variety of ways. It enables evaluators and developers to identify any differing assumptions, so that further discussion of the issue is more likely to be productive. It also makes the problem report still valuable if the recommended solution is not viable due to other constraints. The trade-off space where the modified solution must be found is the same with additional constraints imposed and the new solution's usability will be maximized if all the competing dimensions are taken into account. Finally, making assumptions explicit helps ensure that a consistent set of assumptions underlies the entire application, rather than trade-offs being based on differing values in different parts of the interface.

An additional piece of information that is very valuable to developers was an estimate of the severity of the problem being reported. At a coarse level severity is pretty obvious—the problem description most likely makes clear if work is lost or if users will not be able to accomplish their task. But the severity of more subtle problems may not be apparent to developers—for example, how often the problem will occur and whether it impacts most users or only a few users. Making an explicit severity assessment will help developers prioritize changes under typical time-constrained conditions. In the original experiment, evaluators used a numerical severity rating. We found that the relative severity ratings correlated well with independent severity ratings that were obtained. However, evaluators differed greatly in their absolute assessments of severity—some considered similar problems to be much more serious than others did. Prose descriptions of severity should help the calibration problem. Also, explicit consideration of severity helps the evaluators assess whether the proposed solution is consistent with the size of the problem it solves.

An area that is of special concern to developers is usability problem reports that require additional functionality to be added to the application. Responding to such concerns typically takes a large amount of resources, always an issue in deadline-driven situations. Furthermore, adding functionality in a piecemeal fashion ("why doesn't the application have feature x?") often leads to the sort of "overfeaturitis" that many applications suffer from today—complexity increases and usability suffers because of functionality that is used by a very small number of users. Requests to add functionality should require particularly strong justifications that the absence of this functionality impairs usability. It would be too strong, however, to demand that evaluators should never request that features be added. The request for a test capability in the audio dialog box is a good example of functionality that may be worth the development cost. A more complex example from this study is that the functionality of the file-finding dialog box was a small fraction of what is possible via the UNIX find command and the subset available was not coherent. One evaluator claimed that because it was so hard to recall whether a particular option was available in the graphical interface, most users experienced with UNIX would not use the graphical interface at all, but would do their file-finding via the command line. When missing functionality causes users to avoid that portion of the interface, the impact of the missing functionality can outweigh the cost of making a substantial change to the interface.

Couching usability problem reports at the appropriate level of abstraction greatly improves the likelihood that an appropriately general solution will be found. For example, it is seldom useful to object to the placement of a particular item on a menu—a careful look at the overall structure of the full set of menus (which is often a trade-off among competing desiderata) is likely to produce a different, and frequently better, recommendation. Another example is the partitioning of functionality across different tools; the decision of where to place particular actions needs to be worked out in the context of all the available functionality. Right now, finding the right level of abstraction is a skill that evaluators acquire with experience. Tools or procedures that teach this skill explicitly or that give evaluators ways of recognizing the appropriate abstraction level for a problem are needed. At this stage evaluators must make a concerted effort to ensure they are not focusing on a symptom of a problem rather than the problem itself.

The most problematic usability reports were the places where evaluators demonstrated their biases (e.g., "I don't like the use of icons for file management"). These reports are typically characterized by their sweeping generality and their lack of specific changes to be made to the user interface. Such reports were seen only in the data from heuristic evaluators, most likely because the constrained approaches used by the guidelines and cognitive walkthrough groups did not encourage reports of this type. If reports always describe a specific usability problem and/or give concrete recommendations for changes to be made to the user interface and additionally give objective justifications (e.g., usability principles), then these sorts of reports would be all but eliminated.

As the assessor of these reports, I often came to a different interpretation of a given usability issue than the individual evaluators did, simply because I was looking at the full collection of usability problems. It was much easier to identify trade-offs, see consistency problems, notice situations where the local improvement the evaluator focused on would be offset by negative impacts elsewhere in the application, and pick out contradictions. Adding an additional step to the evaluation process, where the full set of problems are considered together, is extremely valuable. This is generally a part of evaluations done by usability professionals, but techniques that gather independent evaluations often do not give this final aggregation step enough emphasis. It is particularly important that the final pass be done by someone trained in human computer interaction, even if the individual evaluations are done by developers. Evaluators couch even closely related problems in very different language, which makes it surprisingly difficult to identify related reports. In some of the examples described above, the problem reports being contrasted focus on very different parts of the system; there are no superficial clues that the same underlying problem is being discussed in the two reports. In fact, some of the contradictory reports were identified only after 10 or more passes through the data set.

11.6 Recommendations

The goal of usability evaluations is to provide useful feedback about needed usability improvements to the people implementing the application. Since developers' goals, understanding of user interaction principles, assumptions, and priorities are different from those of evaluators, it is important to provide needed information so that a developer can understand and carry out the intention of the proposed modification. What can evaluators do to ensure that their reports are appropriately understood by developers?

1. Provide a description of both the problem with the current interface and the proposed solution, but describe them separately. The description of the problem should be focused on the user and his task. It should also lay out the issues clearly enough so that the developer can test whether an alternate solution could solve the same problem.

2. Provide justifications for both the problem and the solution. Often one will be the complement of the other, so only one justification need be given; but give explicit consideration to the possibility of providing

independent justifications. One sort of justification that can be very useful is to reconstruct the justification the developer may have had for the original solution and demonstrate why other concerns override that reasoning.

3. Provide an assessment of the severity of the problem; this can help the developer prioritize the various changes to be made. The severity assessment should be prose, where the evaluator describes the nature and the extent to which the problem interferes with effective use of the application. This could also be combined with a numerical judgment, if there is a need to compare severities across problem reports. Developers should recognize that numerical judgments by different evaluators are not likely to be comparable.

4. Think about trade-offs explicitly. What will be improved by the change being recommended and what other aspects of the user interface may suffer? Most usability problems arise from situations where a trade-off among competing principles is desired. Making explicit what principles are being traded off and where the proposed solution is in that space will at least move the discussion to one of what types of users and tasks is the application intended for. Even if that question cannot be easily answered, the application can only be improved by explicitly considering these issues.

5. Consider carefully any solution that requires new functionality to be added to the application. If the functionality is more than trivial, this is a potential source of many problems—schedule difficulties, new usability problems from functionality that is less tested than other parts of the user interface, lack of consistency, excessive complexity, and so forth. At least flag the functionality being added and indicate how critical it is for the immediate release of the product. A typical product will undergo additional releases with enhanced functionality—if the functionality proposed is not essential to the core tasks the application supports, it might better be delayed to a later release.

6. Evaluators need to be aware of the biases they bring to the evaluation. Making the justifications for recommendations explicit should go a long way to eliminating problem reports that appear to be nothing more than the evaluators' preferences; but it is worth taking the time to explicitly examine reports to make sure that the recommendations are based on the needs of the intended user population and the tasks to be supported, not on the preferences of the evaluator.

1. Describe the problem and the solution separately.
2. Provide justifications for the problem and the solution.
3. Include an assessment of the severity of the problem.
4. Explicitly consider possible trade-offs.
5. Evaluate carefully any solution that requires new functionality to be added to the application.
6. Be aware of biases that you, the evaluator, bring to the evaluation.
7. Try to look at each problem from multiple levels of abstraction.
8. Examine the problem reports as a collection, replacing local optimizations and trade-offs with general solutions that fit the application as a whole.

Table 11.1 *Recommendations for improving problem reports.*

7. Examine each problem report to see if the problem and/or solution would be different if described at a different level of abstraction. If the problem refers to a specific menu or dialog box, is there a general issue that applies to all the menus or dialog boxes? If the problem is one of consistency, is there a broader notion of consistency that might lead to a different solution? If an alternate mechanism is being proposed, can the two mechanisms be seen as supporting differing user populations and is there a solution that works for both populations? Every usability problem can be described differently at the next higher level of abstraction. Find that description and see if it changes the proposed solution.

8. Make a final pass through the problem reports where the entire collection is examined as a whole. Many of the problematic reports discussed here represent local optimizations, for which different solutions were proposed when we considered the application as a whole. This final step, which needs to be done by a trained individual, can ensure that the individual problem reports are not based on misunderstandings of the application, that they don't contradict one another, that the full impact of any trade-offs is taken into account, and that the recommendations are applied broadly (e.g., to all scrolling lists, not just to the one the evaluator noticed).

These recommendations are summarized in Table 11.1.

The proposed changes certainly come at a cost, primarily in the increased time it takes for individual evaluators to write up their more extensive assessments and for the final aggregation step to be done. This cost will be substantial for any application of significant size. However, the cost of improving the quality of usability evaluations has to be compared to the cost

Evaluator 2: Difference between OK and Apply buttons, Cancel and Close.

Evaluator 3: Background menu says "apply"—inconsistent. There is no "OK" to accept the background as there is in color. You choose "close," which is counter-intuitive.

Figure 11.1 *Two examples of actual problem reports for the Apply/OK problem.*

of missing usability problems or of making changes that do not improve the usability of the application. If the improved reports lead to more modifications being made that have a positive impact on usability, both because the evaluators provide better assessments of the usability problems and their solutions, and because the developers have a better grasp of the problems with the current implementation, the additional hours will be well spent.

An Improved Problem Report

Let us look at an example problem report and consider how it would be improved if these recommendations were applied to it.

The problem of the Apply versus OK buttons in dialog boxes was noticed by several evaluators. Figure 11.1   shows two of their reports. Figure 11.2 demonstrates a possible way this could have been rewritten.

Obviously, the second version of the report is much longer, and the additional information can only help improve communication between evaluators and developers. The nature of the information is different—the problem is described at a different level of abstraction, with an explicit recognition of the trade-offs involved. A solution (actually, two) is proposed. Justifications are given for both problem and solution—justifications that take the trade-offs into account. Finally, the severity is discussed in a way that helps the developer understand the impact of what may appear to have been a relatively minor issue at initial assessment.

11.7 A Research Agenda

The origins of this chapter are in a research study of evaluation methodologies, but the focus has been on the pragmatics of making usability problem reports accurate and useful to developers. Bringing this full circle back to the

Problem: Some dialog boxes have the labels "Apply," "Close," and "Cancel," while others use "OK" and "Cancel." This will be confusing to users, who in both situations are looking to commit changes they have made. While the choice of a button set appears to be based on an analysis of the task being done—the Apply set seems to be used in cases where the user might want to try out several examples before dismissing the dialog box, whereas OK is used when a one-time operation is likely—new users may not be sensitive to those distinctions and may be confused when they encounter an Apply dialog box, which is the less common version.

Severity: Users will encounter this discrepancy regularly. Once (if) they infer a justification for it, the difference may not negatively impact them; but until they do, they will often be looking for a button label that is not present, which will slow them down each time they encounter a dialog box. It will have the biggest impact on new users, but many users may never infer the rationale that makes the different options less arbitrary.

Solution: Because the lack of consistency is so jarring and shows up in so many places, I would recommend using the same option in all cases—the Apply/Close/Cancel set, since it provides more flexibility to the user, albeit at the cost of an extra button press (but it saves having to invoke the dialog box a second time, which is a more complex operation).

An alternative solution that improves consistency somewhat while keeping the task-specific approaches would be to label the OK button as Apply+Close. That makes clear the relationship between the button sets, makes the labels more consistent, and still provides the task-specific functionality. New users will still find this jarring, but many more of them will be able to infer the relationship between the two button sets and be able to find the button they require (usually, the Apply button) based on its label.

Figure 11.2 *An improved problem report for the Apply/OK problem, using the recommendations in Table 11.1.*

research community, the same data provides important information for researchers of usability issues. Many of the potential false alarms exist because the field of human-computer interaction does not have answers to some basic and pervasive issues in usability. Application developers and practitioner usability specialists are unable to make accurate predictions of usability in many areas, because they don't have information about which of several principles dominates in a particular situation. Any collection of usability problems would expose a number of these issues. A variety of them have come up in the examples described in this chapter; they make an interesting agenda for user interface research. While all of the problems describe a usability issue for which additional empirical data would be useful, here are some issues that I perceive to be of widespread applicability and value:

1. *Consistency versus task congruity:* Often, to match the actions to the task demands, it is necessary to sacrifice consistency across operations. The example of the Apply versus OK buttons in dialog boxes in this interface lays out the two dimensions quite well and similar trade-offs occur in many applications. Under what circumstances should consistency be the overriding concern? When should task congruity dominate?

2. *Multiple navigation methods:* Are multiple methods for accomplishing a navigation task an asset or a liability to a user interface? What are the trade-offs between the cognitive overhead of selecting among methods and the availability of methods that are tuned to the specifics of the current goal? The example from this data set is the multiple ways of moving up and down the directory hierarchy.

3. *New versus experienced users:* When is it reasonable to expect new users to tolerate some confusing or hard-to-understand aspects of the interface in order to make things easier for more experienced users? The example here was a visual distinction between two types of interactors, which confused new users but provided useful information to proficient users.

4. *Undo versus reversible operations:* When is an undo operation needed and when is it sufficient to have reversible operations? One evaluator criticized the interface for not having an undo command in the File Manager; however, all the operations he wanted to make undoable could be reversed by carrying out the inverse operation (e.g., the inverse move, undelete). Is that an appropriate substitute for undo or is it important to have an operation that cancels the previous step without the user needing to work out what actions serve as the needed inverses?

Answers to any of the above questions would greatly advance our understanding of what makes a usable application and would do as much as the process recommendations in this chapter to improve the likelihood that a usability recommendation is a valid one. We need to move forward both in our theoretical understanding of the causes of poor usability and in the practical issues of communicating usability problems to developers.

Acknowledgments

I'd like to thank the people who read earlier versions of this chapter and who helped me understand many of the subtle issues surrounding false alarms: Janice Bradford, Bob Mack, Jim Miller, Jakob Nielsen, and Vicki O'Day.

Chapter 12 *Observing, Predicting, and Analyzing Usability Problems*

Robert Mack
IBM Watson Research Center, Hawthorne

Frank Montaniz
Rensselaer Polytechnic University

12.1 Introduction

Usability inspection methods refer to methods of evaluating software user interfaces using rules, guidelines, or heuristics, rather than acquiring (and analyzing) behavioral end-user feedback. Inspection-based evaluations can have more than one objective. However, this chapter focuses on usability inspection methods as a source of usability-related evaluative information about software. We will discuss this objective in terms of three issues, summarized in the following list, along with the conclusions we will develop for each issue in the remainder of this chapter:

- Inspection data can be regarded as a source of predictions about problems end users would have, under appropriate methods for acquiring and interpreting inspection data. As such, inspection-based predictions have similarities and differences with empirical usability problem data. It is useful to understand these comparisons, especially if we want to understand how well inspection data can predict usability problems derived from empirical evaluations (and perhaps substitute for them).

- Inspection data, treated as problem predictions, are generated by inspectors in the role of users experiencing problems themselves or in the role of simulating end users. Several factors contribute to the relative success of this simulation process. These factors also help us understand the relation between inspection data and usability problems.

- The utility of inspection data (especially as predictions) depends on larger user-centered design analysis process, in two senses: (1) this larger context motivates inspection methods, and (2) this larger context broadens the scope and methods for conducting inspection methods and analyzing inspection results.

These three topics frame a set of methodological issues that we believe will contribute to understanding the strengths and limitations of inspection methods. In particular, we want to understand how well inspection data can serve as a source of data pertaining to usability problems and ultimately as a source of insight into possible design solutions for usability-related problems. The plan of the chapter is to develop support for the aforementioned conclusions by analyzing the characteristics of usability problems derived from usability testing and from usability inspections, both obtained from studies in our laboratory.

The methodology issues involved with usability inspection are diverse and complex enough that would be useful to discuss our experience with and assumptions about usability evaluation methods. Accordingly, we begin with a brief discussion of the background for this technical discussion and the key assumptions being made.

12.2 Background

Our experience with usability inspections appears similar to that of other HCI professionals who have described the use of usability inspection methods or conducted research on such methods (based on the CHI 1992 workshop from which this book derives; see Mack and Nielsen 1993). In general, we contribute user-centered design expertise to research and development projects within IBM Research and in partnership with IBM Development labs. Behavioral data from empirical user evaluations plays an important role in our contribution as usability engineers to software development, but we have also found that *usability analysis* (for want of a better term) of software designs and design issues, broadly construed, pervades our activities. Usability analysis refers to a wide range of psychologically informed activities, from rendering informed opinions about interface and usability issues to more formal and systematic analyses of these issues. Usability analyses play a prominent role in user-centered design for several reasons.

First, gathering behavioral data is not always possible. Even when it is possible, it is time-consuming and difficult to obtain. Moreover, it is difficult to keep up with the volume of design questions that need to be answered. Nonetheless, we may need to offer opinions and technical judgments about various usability-related questions. Second, even where we can carry out empirical evaluations, usability analysis plays a role in setting up evaluations and interpreting results. While empirical evaluations always provide new and surprising insights into software usability (at any stage of implementation), it is also the case that we learn a lot simply designing a behavioral evaluation. For example, selecting and setting up scenarios and questionnaires already involves developing and applying intuitions about software quality. In our experience, testing per se is as much confirmatory and case-building as it is a way to discover facts about interface quality. Third, usability analysis plays a role in interpreting empirical results and developing a basis for solving design problems. We have found that scenario-driven walkthroughs, conducted with a design team and led by a usability specialist are an important way to convey results. Conducting these analyses in the context of a design team can give legitimacy to the results and help build an appreciation of usability and user issues. Walkthroughs also provide a framework in which many other usability issues and questions can be raised beyond those covered directly in testing. There are always more design questions than "data" that might address them. Specific empirical "facts" often need to be extrapolated, and used to support arguments for untested but analogous design questions.

Usability analysis is pervasive in usability engineering activities, even though it may not be recognized as an explicit methodology. The question is to what extent these usability-related analyses can be turned into a usability evaluation method and how the results of such a method compare to the results of more familiar empirical evaluation methods. In this regard, we credit Nielsen and colleagues (Nielsen and Molich 1990), and Lewis, Polson and colleagues (Lewis et al. 1992; Polson et al. 1992) with bringing focus on usability inspections as a relatively standalone usability evaluation method, albeit perhaps with different motivations and drawing on different psychological bases. That is, usability inspection methods can be seen as an attempt to derive evaluation methods from a wide-ranging set of more or less explicitly developed usability analysis techniques. Our interest in this specific question has also led us to conduct a study of a variation on cognitive walkthroughs, the details of which are reported elsewhere (Montaniz and Mack 1993b). Here we summarize the objectives, methodology, and results because our qualitative discussion in this chapter will be based largely on this study.

Summary of Usability Inspection Study

Interest in trying to adapt the cognitive walkthrough method was driven by experience with, and belief in, the utility of certain kinds of questions as a tool for encouraging reflection and analysis in design problem-solving situations (see colleagues Bennett 1984; Karat and Bennett 1991a, 1991b; also Mack 1992). We have found that conducting walkthroughs structured by user scenarios and driven by "cognitively-motivated" questions about how well what users see and do in interaction with a software interface matches expectations users might have for how to accomplish these goals.

This *process* of question-driven walkthroughs as we have practiced it in group design situations is quite different from the standalone method of Polson et al. (1992a, 1992b). Group design walkthroughs tend to be more wide-ranging and opportunistic in what is covered and how it is covered. For example, a walkthrough may actually stimulate a variety of software design activities, not exclusively involving user interface issues. Identifying potential user interface problems may be only one of several objectives for such design reviews (see Wixon et al., Chapter 4). However, we were interested in developing an even more focused and systematic approach, specifically aimed at uncovering potential usability problems. The cognitive walkthrough method seemed to be in the same spirit, albeit based on a theory of how computer novices learn to use software (Polson and Lewis 1990).

In brief, our study contrasted problems based on a conventional empirical end-user software evaluation, with problems derived from usability inspections obtained under four conditions. These conditions correspond to two groups of computer professionals differing in the degree of usability-related training and two inspection methods. Specifically, we compared professionals in IBM development and research with experience mainly in software human factors and usability engineering to professionals whose experience was mainly in software interface design and implementation. These two groups were asked to identify potential usability problems while completing a set of standard user tasks (or task scenarios) with a graphical user interface style computer environment. One half of each type of professional, usability versus software developer, was asked to identify problems with no specific

	Intuitive Walkthrough	*Cognitive Walkthrough*
Software Engineer, Designer	36% (22%)	36% (15%)
Software Human Factors, Usability	45% (18%)	42% (13%)
Total problem types across inspection conditions	60	
Total problem types for end-user evaluation	30	

Table 12.1 *Design and results of usability inspection study. Numbers for each condition are the percentage of inspection problem types for that condition that match the total number of problem types over all inspection conditions. Numbers in parentheses are percentage of inspection problems that match the 69 empirical user problem types.*

inspection guidelines beyond examples of usability problems and guidelines on writing "useful" problem descriptions. We called this the "intuitive walkthrough" condition. The other two professional groups were asked to identify problems using a modified cognitive walkthrough technique. The modifications involved fewer questions and less technical question forms, in our judgment, compared to the published versions of cognitive walkthroughs at that time (Lewis and Polson 1991). All inspectors were given additional guidelines for writing problem descriptions in behavioral terms (as will be explained in detail later), and were also given a software tool which guided them through the tasks and the inspection guidelines. To summarize, we had four groups of inspectors, five per group: usability specialists who inspected the software "intuitively" (without specialized inspection guidelines), non-usability specialists who conducted intuitive inspections, usability specialists who used the modified cognitive walkthrough technique, and nonusability specialists who used the walkthrough technique. The design and its results are summarized in Table 12.1. Select quantitative results will be discussed a little later.

In addition, we carried out a conventional usability evaluation of the same software in the laboratory, using the same user tasks. We tested five office temporaries from a temporary employment agency. Each had experience with GUI-style personal computer software, but no specific experience with the particular GUI "desktop" environment tested in this study. The office temporaries and all four groups of usability inspectors received the same introduction and practice with the software they were asked to use or inspect.

We identified 69 total problem types (not tokens) over the four usability inspection groups. How the problem types were identified will be discussed in detail in the next section. Table 12.1 summarizes the rate of problem identification for these four conditions. The first percentage in each cell is the percentage of the 69 total problem types identified across the four inspection groups. Overall, in the Intuitive Walkthrough condition usability specialists identified more of the 69 total inspection problem types identified than non-specialists, 45 compared to 36 percent, respectively. In the Cognitive Walkthrough condition, usability specialists identified more of the total 69 problem types than nonspecialists, 42 compared to 36 percent, respectively.

The rate of problem identification across inspection conditions is comparable to the overlap of inspection-based problem types with the end-user problem types, shown in Table 12.1. The table shows these numbers in parentheses, as percentages of the 60 end-user problem types we identified.

These four rates of problem detection, between 36 percent and 45 percent are well within the range of problem detection reported in the literature (Jeffries, Chapter 11; also Mack and Nielsen 1993). Lewis et al. (1990), for example, found that cognitive walkthroughs predicted 30 percent of 55 action choices that led to novice user errors. Nielsen and Molich (1990) trained groups of computer science students to use heuristics to evaluate three software systems. Problem reports were compared to the total number of problems identified by the authors and participants in the study. On average, participants identified 20 to 51 percent of the 34 to 54 known problems. A fourth group of software professionals inspected another system intuitively and, on average, identified 38 percent of 30 known problems. Wright and Monk (1991a, 1991b) found that teams of computer novices and software engineers were able to identify 30 percent of 29 known problems (an aggregation of problems identified by the authors and by the teams). Our results are in the same range as these comparisons. However, it is clear that the four inspection groups in our comparison and these other studies were only able to detect at best half the problems that end users experienced. To understand why these differences occur, we want to discuss in more depth the attributes of empirical usability problems and of inspection-derived predictions, based mainly on the study just summarized.

12.3 Observing and Analyzing Usability Problems

A user experiences a problem when that user cannot accomplish some task because of the software tool being used, or can only do so with more diffi-culty than is expected or is acceptable. We assume a user has some goal (based on some task) to accomplish and that this overall goal can be broken down into a sequence of subgoals and actions appropriate for achieving each one. To the extent that these tasks are well-understood and practiced, we can characterize the goal-directed behavior as a routine cognitive skill. To the extent that the tasks or software interface are novel, we can characterize the goal-directed behavior in problem-solving terms and in terms of learning. In these qualitative terms a problem arises when a mismatch occurs between the action a user carried out and the goal the user intended to accomplish. These actions, in turn, lead to unintended outcomes and more or less complex recovery actions.

In this section four sets of issues related to the analysis and reporting of usability problems will be discussed. Four types of qualitative analyses are summarized in Table 12.2. These are mainly qualitative, although these qualitative analyses can provide the basis for classifying and counting problems in quantitative analyses. The first is analyzing breakdowns in relating goals and actions. The second is characterizing the interface inter-action which causes or is associated with the problem. The third attempts to infer what causes the "wrong" action and to characterize aspects of possible problem-solving involved in recovering from wrong actions. The fourth develops problem reports to summarize these analyses, emphasizing interface design issues that may underlie user problems and suggestions on how to remedy those problems. We may also be interested in quantitative aspects of problems in the aggregate. For example, we may be interested in counting types of problems and in categorizing problems by the impact of problems

1.0 Qualitative analysis by breakdowns in goal-directed behavior
    1.1 Cannot find action
        1.1.1 system does not support goal
        1.1.2 system supports goal with action
    1.2 Chooses wrong action (goal is supported)
        1.2.1 intentional
        1.2.2 slip (intended correct action)
    1.3 Chooses correct action, in wrong context
        1.3.1 object (to be acted on) not selected
        1.3.2 prerequisite not fulfilled by some prior action
        1.3.3 system is in a state or mode that interferes with correct
            action
    1.4 Chooses correct action, noticeable effort
        1.4.1 to find action
        1.4.2 to execute
    1.5 Confused by consequence of action
        1.5.1 correct action, confusing outcome
        1.5.2 incorrect action, requires problem recovery
        1.5.3 problem tangles
2.0 Qualitative analysis by interface interactions
    2.1 objects and actions
    2.2 higher-level categorization of interface interactions
3.0 Inferring possible cause(s) of problem(s)
4.0 Problem reports
    4.1 design-relevant descriptions
    4.2 quantitative analysis of problems by severity

Table 12.2 *Empirical usability problems. Summary of analysis and reporting issues.*

on completing goals which are the user tasks. These quantitative aspects of problems can help focus resources on the most serious problems in a larger development context.

Examples of Usability Problems

These distinctions will be discussed in more depth in this section. First, we summarize selected problems based on the study of usability inspections we discussed in the previous section. The nine examples to be discussed are summarized in Table 12.3 through Table 12.5. The examples are based primarily on our observations of end users attempting to complete one of four tasks (user test scenarios) we gave in the study summarized in the preceding *Background* section. We will call this task "Copying a folder to diskette." The task consists of several subtasks in which users are asked to create a new folder, move several existing documents from multiple existing folders into the new folder, and then copy that folder into the diskette, as if backing it up. The problems summarized beginning in Table 12.3 are drawn from a set of 38 types (not tokens) of problems we inferred from five end users' attempts to complete this specific "copy folder to diskette" task scenario.

Breakdowns in Goal-Directed Behavior

User Cannot Find Action

This category (1.1 in Table 12.2) refers to cases where, at one extreme, users may fail to find an action for a goal because the goal is not supported by a software tool. In design terms, the tool "lacks the function needed to support the user's task." These problems are not so obvious in controlled laboratory evaluations where users are given tasks that can be accomplished by the software in question. Field studies of what users do (or fail to do) with computers are more likely to uncover missing functions. The usability evaluation we alluded to in the *Background* section did not provide an opportunity to discover such goal and action mismatches. In some cases, however, the system may indeed support the user's goal, but it may seem to a user that the goal is not supported in the sense that a user cannot find the action the system designer intended. In this case, users either reach an impasse (and look for assistance or documentation), or they may make a guess and try an incorrect action. We found only a very few cases in our usability study where users were unable to find a way to accomplish a (sub)goal given to them and were unable to proceed without assistance. Problem 1 in Table 12.3 comes close: Here, a user forgets how to create a new folder and spends time rediscovering how to do so.

Choosing Wrong Action Chosen (Goal is Supported)

This category (1.2 in Table 12.2) refers to cases where the user's task can be accomplished, but for some reason the user carries out the wrong action. The correct action may not be obvious to the user, but the user nonetheless makes a more or less well-motivated guess as to that action. In other cases, the user might have intended the correct action but simply "slipped up" and executed an incorrect action (see Table 12.2). These two subcategories of problems are by far the most common type of problem observed in controlled laboratory

Problem 1

Cannot find action

Task:

Copy folder to diskette. Subtask: Create new to-be-copied folder.

Action:

Select menu option to "Create new." (Object: folder.)

Description:

Seems to have forgotten correct menu option. EU1 "forgets" how to create a new folder (has done so in practice). Explores menu bar options before checking documentation and rediscovering how to do so.

Problem 2

Wrong action for goal

Task:

Copy folder to diskette. Subtask: Copy operation.

Action:

Select to-be-copied folder. Select menu bar pull-down option "copy to diskette." (Object: folder.)

Description:

Feedback problem, verifying copy action. EU2 tries Edit pull-down Copy/Paste options. Disk activity seems to suggest success (no other feedback noticed). Does nothing else to confirm. Starts next step. Task failure.

Problem 3

Correct action, wrong context

Task:

Copy folder to diskette. Subtask: Copy folder.

Action:

Select to-be-copied folder. Select menu bar pull-down option "copy to diskette." (Object: folder.)

Description:

Select menu action, no object selected. EU1(09) selects menu option without selecting folder. Menu option disabled. User tries "list view" of desktop objects. Opens (double-clicks) to-be-copied folder instead of selecting (clicking). Menu option still disabled. Requests assistance.

Table 12.3 *Usability problems 1-3, categorized by interface, interaction, and goal-action problems.*

evaluation. Of the 34 usability problems observed for this scenario, we classify roughly a third of them as involving "wrong actions for intended goal."

Problem 4

Wrong action for goal: Specifying device and filename for to-be-copied object.
Task:
Copy folder to diskette. Copy operation
Action:
Enter (type) device and filenames. (Object: Dialog window, entry fields.)
Description:
EU3, EU3, EU2, EU4 all enter incorrect device or filename or filename extension. Possible causes based on comments, actions include: DOS filename conventions are confusing. Default filename is confusing and leads to wrong device name, filename that is too long. Wrong filename extension.

Problem 5

Wrong action for goal: Specifying device and filename for to-be-copied object.
Task:
Copy folder to diskette. Subtask: Specify attributes of to-be-copied folder.
Action:
Enter DOS path and filename in dialog entry field. Default path and filename visible. (Object: Dialog window for entering copy attributes.)
Description:
(EU3 enters invalid filename, gets error message). Believes error means to-be-copied folder is empty. Repeats copying of to-be-stored items to folder to-be-copied to diskette (has two copies of everything now). EU3 spends time moving and sizing existing folders to find and (re) copy to-be-stored items.

Problem 6

Slip/Dexterity: Problem selecting with mouse.
Task:
Copy folder to diskette. Subtask: Select to-be-copied folder.
Action:
Click to-be-copied folder with mouse selection button. (Objects: icon, mouse pointer)
Description:
EU4, EU2, EU5, EU2, EU1 make multiple attempts to select document icons. Inadvertent clicking on desktop. Multiple clicks (select then deselect). Double-click and opening icon instead of single click (then close document window).

Table 12.4 *Usability problems 4-6, categorized by interface, interaction, and goal-action problems.*

Problems 1 through 5 (Table 12.3 and Table 12.4) are examples of incorrect actions that appear to be genuine mistakes (not slips). In problem 1, for example, the user looks for a "copy" action in a menu bar pull-down for the desktop. In fact the operation is called something else that does not involve the term "copy" and is not grouped with other actions that seem to pertain to editing. It takes some exploration of other menu bar pull-down options before the user decides to try the alternative action and initiates the sequence of steps necessary in this environment to "copy a folder" to a diskette. It seems reasonable to infer here that the system action needed to "copy the folder to a diskette" did not match how the user thought about copying. Indeed, there is an alternative, and possibly more obvious copy action that is used to copy folders from one part of the desktop to another or from one folder to another. In this sense, there is also an inconsistency. There is a rationale for the problematic "copy to diskette" action, but it was not obvious enough to our users; this could be due to the level of training we provided.

A subcategory of the problem category "choosing the wrong action" involves cases where users may know how to accomplish a task using a software tool, but make some relatively low-level misperception or mis-step. Norman's characterization of action *slips* seems like an appropriate interpretation of these problems (Norman 1983; see also Lewis and Norman 1986). The correct action is intended, but the wrong action is executed. In the graphical user interface (GUI) style software we have tended to evaluate, this category of problem arises most often in connection with using a mouse pointing device to select interface objects like icons, menu options, or direct manipulation controls to move and size windows, among other things.

We interpreted problems 7 through 9 (Table 12.5) as exemplifying slips involving use of the mouse to select icons, open icons into windows using double-click, or closing windows by double-clicking the window system menu. In all cases, the users attempted these actions repeatedly, either mispointing or, in the case of double-clicking, not making two clicks quickly enough for the system to interpret them as double-clicks.

Correct Action, Wrong Context

Actions can be correct for a goal, but carried out in the wrong context. Three cases are identified in problem category 1.3 (Table 12.2). First, a correct action may require some prerequisite action to be carried out or a condition to be in effect (perhaps the result of the prerequisite action). Problem 3 (in Table 12.3), for example, involved a user who selected a menu action without selecting an object (in this case, a folder) to which to apply the action. The object-action style of interaction for the software we evaluated requires, in general, that users select an object before applying an action to it. Second, a

Problem 7

Slip/Dexterity: Problem double-clicking.
Task:
Copy folder to diskette. Subtask: Close a folder.
Action:
Double-click mouse selection button on system menu. (Object: Window, system menu)
Description:
EU1, EU4 carry out multiple attempts to close window by double-clicking. Timing causes system menu pull-down to appear or pointer off system menu. Nuisance.

Problem 8

Slip/Dexterity: Inadvertently clicks scroll bar while sizing window border, scrolls window contents out of view.
Task:
Copy folder to diskette. Subtask: Find to-be-copied document in existing folder.
Action:
Open folder. Size folder window contents to bring document into view. (Scroll would bring document into view also.) (Object, icon in folder.)
Description:
EU2 inadvertently clicked scroll bar while sizing window, causing icons to scroll out of sight within window. Nuisance. User scrolled icons back into view.

Problem 9

Slip/Dexterity: Inadvertent multiple selection, drag multiple cascaded icons.
Task:
Copy folder to diskette. Subtask: Move to-be-copied document to folder.
Action:
Select document icon. Other document icons already selected. Multiple selected icons cascade at pointer. Drag/drop into folder (open in window) using drag button on mouse.(Objects: document icons.)
Description:
EU5 and EU1 select a to-be-copied folder icon. A document icon from a previous operation remains selected. Both selected icons are dragged together in cascade form and dropped into folder. User moves unwanted document back to source.

Table 12.5 *Usability problems 7-9, categorized by interface, interaction, and goal-action problems.*

correct action may be blocked by the consequence of some prior, and possibly incorrect action. An example not described in the tables, but we suspect quite familiar to readers, was a user who made an error entering information in a dialog window, which caused an error message to pop up. The user ignored the error message and tried to proceed with the re-entry of information in the original dialog window. The user was unable to do so, however, because the error message was a mode that had to be acknowledged.

Correct Action, Noticeable Effort

There are cases where a user carries out the correct action and obtains the intended result, but nonetheless, the effort involved is somehow noticeable. In several cases, users in our evaluation made comments about having to move windows out of the way in order to find things on the desktop. We did not record these episodes as problems, although problem 5 (in Table 12.4). includes an allusion to a user comment about window rearrangement. However, these episodes represent a category of experiences which, depending on users' expectations and tolerances, can influence overall satisfaction with a software system. This category of "effort problem" also can point to general user interface issues. Window management is a good example: Certainly issues related to electronic desktop management are taken seriously in the HCI research community (e.g., Card et al. 1991).

Consequences of Incorrect Actions

Problem Tangles

Executing the wrong action can create outcomes that may need to be undone in order to achieve the original goal intended. In several of the aforementioned problems, executing a "wrong" action relative to an intended goal resulted in some outcome that had to be undone before the user could try another, possibly correct, action. Problem 2 in Table 12.3 is an example. The user carried out the wrong action for "copying a folder to diskette" and failed to copy the folder. The folder was not copied, but the feedback that would indicate this failure was not obvious. Moreover the user interpreted unrelated disk activity as confirmation that the copy action worked and moved on to the next task. In this case, the user failed the task without assistance. In other cases, there may be no consequence of an incorrect action, beyond the failing to achieve the desired result; the user simply has to try the correct action again. Problems 7 through 9 beginning in Table 12.5 involve mouse selection slips; these are good examples of where the failure of an action was immediately obvious, no consequences required recovery, and it was straightforward to do the action again.

A third situation involving the consequences of incorrect actions (or problems executing correct actions) is where the outcome creates a further misunderstanding or problem. That is, there are situations where one problem can cause or contribute to another, producing what we have called "problem tangles" (Lewis and Mack 1982; Mack et al. 1983). We identified "problem tangles" in early work on how novices learn word processing. Problem tangles were not as salient in this study because we encouraged users to request assistance when they reached an impasse and because the tasks were relatively structured. However, any of these problems could initiate a sequence of further problems. Problems 3 and 5 give examples of what we would describe as problem tangles. In problem 3 a user makes multiple attempts to copy a folder to diskette. The first attempt fails because the user did not select the folder before selecting the correct menu option. Realizing this problem, the user tried to select the folder, but double-clicked instead and opened the folder. Selecting the correct menu option failed in this case because the folder was opened and was not in icon form. Eventually the user gave up and requested assistance. The user experienced several problems here, which we suspect created confusion about whether the menu action was actually correct. In problem 5, described earlier, a user failed to copy a folder to a diskette and did not know that the attempt had failed. Subsequent tasks that depended on the result of copying would fail unless the user was able to discover the original failure and correct it.

We believe, and have argued in the references cited earlier, that problem tangles are a very salient experience for users. From a psychological and usability engineering perspective these problems are difficult to interpret. Indeed, in the full problem corpus from which we drew the examples summarized in Table 12.3 through Table 12.5, we found several cases of tangles. However, we also went to some lengths to "untangle" them in the interests of categorizing and comparing problems across experimental conditions. Here we only note that problems do interact, and a problem of one type, such as a seemingly simple slip, may indeed trigger a sequence of interactions that result in a larger problem.

Qualitative Analysis of Interface Interactions

A second kind of qualitative analysis of problems is in terms of user interface objects and actions. That is, an attempt to identify what aspect of the interface caused or is implicated in a user problem. This description is important in a software development context for identifying problems with user interfaces and possible solutions for these problems. It is also a more objective characterization of user problems: Whatever the plausibility of interpretations we may develop to characterize a problem in terms of goal-directed behavior or to provide a possible explanation for why a problem occurs, we can in any case objectively observe and characterize what the user *does* in terms of interface actions and the objects acted on. In our analysis of the usability problems referred to in Table 12.3 through Table 12.5, we ultimately classified problems by the interface objects and actions involved, as best as we could infer these from the qualitative problem descriptions. As can be seen in these tables, each problem description has two-line descriptions, the first describing the object and action constituting an interface interaction, the second describing a categorization in terms of goal-action breakdowns.

Analyzing problems in terms of the interface object and action associated with them can also be done at more than one level of categorization. We may decide that the problem does not involve a specific interface interaction (or function), but a more general interface principle that applies to several interface techniques and the problems associated with them. The best example we have observed is illustrated in problem 4 (in Table 12.4). In this situation the user tries to select a menu pull-down option without selecting an object first. In fact, we observed several instances where users appear to select an action before specifying an object to which that applies. In each case, there may be a problem unique to the specific action involved (e.g., the specific menu pull-down option). However, we believe (and we have evidence from other studies; e.g., Mack 1991; Lewis et al. 1989) that there is a more general "cognitive" problem implicated here, whereby some users, in some cases, find it intuitive to try to select what they want to do before specifying what object they want to act on. Again, this suggests a higher-level problem, not necessarily with these specific actions, but with the more generic concept of object-action interaction.

The Causes of Problems

Most "cognitive problems" (not involving "slips") result from an interaction between the design of the interface and the expectations that users have about how the interface functions and appearance maps into actions achieving the task goals users have. For us, analyzing the causes of user problems means trying to understand in psychological terms how interface design elements contribute to goal-action mismatches. These mismatches can be characterized in many psychologically based terms. In general, looking for possible causes allows us to bring to bear plausible psychological perspectives that are useful for guiding design. For example, goal-action terminology is appealing because it leads to plausible inspection heuristics, as exemplified in the cognitive walkthrough method (Lewis et al. 1992). For example, one heuristic is to ask about what the interface interaction might suggest as an alternative to the "correct" action intended by the designer. Another is to ask how an outcome of an action might be misinterpreted by a user.

What makes the interpretation of problems especially challenging for analysts is the well-supported claim that users are *cognitively active* learners and users, capable of making inferences and stories about what is happening that can be quite at odds with the design intentions behind some interface interaction (Carroll and Rosson 1987). This general observation has been developed along several lines. For example, Carroll and colleagues (Carroll et al. 1987) among others (e.g., Douglas and Moran 1983), have argued that users learn computer skills by drawing on prior knowledge and that specific analogies play a large role in both successful learning and, on the negative side, in driving user problems based on misleading user expectations. The nature of these user interpretations in specific domains, notably word processing, has been analyzed by Carroll and Mack (1984), and in more general HCI contexts by Lewis and colleagues (Lewis and Norman 1986; Lewis 1988; Polson and Lewis 1990).

What makes inferring potential causes for problems at all plausible are situations where we have substantial context for inferring what users intend to do and where what they do is observable. This is the case where users are given specific tasks to carry out and where users provide complementary information about what they are thinking and doing (e.g., "think-aloud" comments).

Problem Analysis and Report

In our experience problem reports are a key way to communicate the results of usability evaluations to software developers. These reports consist of both qualitative and quantitative components and are often done in the larger group design context alluded to in the *Background* section. Qualitatively, we are interested in classifying and describing problems in terms that identify problematic interface design elements or issues, give insight into why the problem might have occurred, and what to do about it. As we suggested in the preceding section, we are especially interested in identifying the specific interface design elements with which we associated problems.

We are also typically interested in the quantitative analysis of problems by frequency of problem type and problem impact. Once we have categorized problems, for example, by what aspect of the interface appears to be implicated in the cause of the problem, it is possible to count instances of each category. Similarly, we can categorize the outcomes of problems by their impact on accomplishing tasks. For example, problems can cause users to lose data and fail to complete tasks without substantial assistance or they can simply cause users to become side-tracked and waste time. Standard schemes exist in most corporations for analyzing problem frequency and severity (Snyder 1991; Lewis et al. 1990). Quantitative analyses of this kind are valuable for making decisions about where to devote development resources to solving user problems. We will discuss the relevance of this analysis further in the section *Analyzing Usability Problems* (see Desurvire, Chapter 7; Karat, Chapter 8)

Discussion

The first two qualitative analysis schemes—one based on goal-directed behavior, the other on interface interactions, cast in terms of interface objects and actions—are different but also complementary. The goal-action descriptions make a set of second-level distinctions that can be useful in at least two ways for accurately characterizing what specifically is problematic about an interface interaction. First, it may be useful in characterizing an interface problem to identify more fine-grained design issues in goal-action terms. For example, it may be useful to distinguish problems with the feedback for an action from problems in understanding what prerequisite conditions need to be fulfilled. Second, it can be useful to understand the larger goal-action context in which an interface interaction occurs. The goals a user has may derive externally to the specific software interface, but they interact with the interface design and with task context. The effect of inconsistencies is a good example: We can identify inconsistencies in design (e.g., terminology of similar actions), but the potential impact of these inconsistencies also depends on opportunities for users to experience them which depend, in turn, on how the tasks users carry out might involve common interface elements.

The characterization of problems discussed in this section is well-established in cognitive science and in the domain of human-computer interaction (Kieras and Polson 1985; Lewis and Norman 1986; Norman, 1986; Norman 1988). Indeed, the analysis of problems in terms of goal-directed behavior is the theoretical basis for cognitive walkthroughs as developed by Lewis, Polson and colleagues (Lewis et al. 1992). We should emphasize that these analyses are interpretations we make as observers. We make no claim about how users experience problems. From the user's perspective, the characterizations we draw may or may not be relevant. This is especially true for problem tangles, where we suspect that users may end up completely misconstruing the reasons for their problems. Also, this scheme represents an idealization of problem behavior and problem analysis. The analysis scheme we outlined is perhaps most plausible in controlled laboratory situations where we have some control over what users are doing (because we ask them to complete task scenarios), and where we have converging evidence for interpretation, based on user comments (e.g., during debriefing or from encouraging think-aloud comments). In order of certainty, the analysis of problems by goal-directed behavior is least certain and the identification of interface interaction most certain. However, from a more practical usability engineering perspective, this circumstance probably does not matter. We are concerned about the more psychological analyses to the extent that they contribute to the larger objective of identifying and helping to resolve design problems. For example, characterizing an interface problem (e.g., with selecting icons) in additional terms as a "slip" or as an intentional misunderstanding of how to select can make a difference in how a problem is weighted or in how we try to solve this problem. We will return to this topic in Section 12.5 on page 336.

12.4 Inspection-Based Usability Problems

Having described distinctions that are useful for characterizing user problems as a trained observer, we can raise the following questions related to usability inspections:

- How are inspection and empirical problem descriptions similar or different?
- How can we account for the mismatches between predictions based on inspection methods (perhaps different methods) and empirical end-user problems?

The answer will be developed by analyzing inspection data gathered in our lab, both on its own terms, and then in the terms in which we analyzed empirical usability problem data in the preceding section. This analysis will provide the basis for the answer to the second question.

The answer to the first question is that it depends on who is doing the inspecting and especially on what inspection guidelines, training, and experience the evaluator has been given. That is, to some extent, we create the answer to the first question by our methodology. The methodological factors underlying the first question can define several inspection methods. In terms of inspection goals, the focus in this chapter in on inspections as possible predictors of usability-related problems and ultimately as a source of feedback about the usability of a software tool. Other inspection goals are certainly possible, as suggested in the *Introduction*. For example, we may not be interested in user problems per se, but in assessing conformity to a set of interface standards (Wixon et al., Chapter 4). Or we may want to develop design specification directly through user-centered walkthroughs (Bell et al. 1994; Karat and Bennett 1991a). We will discuss these possibilities further in the last section. In particular, observations about how inspections are carried out is influenced by our own background and approach to usability inspections, as we summarized these in the introduction to this chapter. To reiterate:

1. Inspectors were given relatively detailed task scenarios to use in exercising the software. Inspectors are users themselves in some sense, with extensive hands-on experience with an existing interface.
2. Inspectors were explicitly asked to look for usability-related problems.
3. Inspectors were given guidelines on and examples of how to describe problems they suspected would arise. For our part, we intended from the outset to try to analyze inspection data in terms similar to how we analyze empirical usability problem data.

Problem Report 1
Correct action. Feedback non-obvious. Effort to verify success.
Task:
Copy folder to diskette. Subtask: Copy action.
Action:
(Object: To-be-copied folder is selected. Diskette is inserted in drive.)
Select action labelled "copy folder to diskette" from (name of) action
bar pull-down menu. Focus on feedback of action.
Description:
CW14 Having found the "Bergman" disk, (I) inserted it in the disk drive and
located in the help menu the proper steps for copying the "Atlanta" folder to the
"Bergman" diskette. I proceeded to do so. When in the window where I typed
the filename "Atlanta" would be copied to, I hit return automatically and the
window closed. (There was) no feedback as to whether the folder was actually
copied. I spent several minutes trying to verify that. I finally found an option to
"copy folder from diskette" from the diskette in the drive and figured if copying
had been successful I would be able to retrieve it from the diskette, which I
could. Not a big problem, but disconcerting due to lack of closure.

Problem Report 2
Slip/Dexterity. Problem opening by double-clicking.
Task:
Copy folder to diskette. Subtask: Open to-be-copied folder.
Action:
(Object: folder) Double-click mouse selection button on to-be-copied folder.
Description:
CW2 In passing, I note a general problem with opening things: fast double-
click is occasionally not recognized, and must be repeated. This is usually just
annoying, but causes lost time and may be confusing to a novice user.

Table 12.6 *Usability inspection problem reports 1-2.*

4. In the case of the cognitive walkthrough inspectors, they were given a
   very structured inspection framework, supported by a heavily prompted
   software tool.

Clearly we tried to strongly influence how the inspectors used the software
to-be-evaluated and how they conducted inspections. Inducing inspectors to
develop interface evaluations in these terms is not simple. In pilot work three
characteristics of usability inspection descriptions emerged:

1. Problem descriptions tended to express likes or dislikes with respect to
   interface design, as opposed to descriptions of problems others might
   have.

Problem Report 3
Correct action, effort. Window management.
Task:
Copy folder to diskette. Subtask: Move document into to-be-copied folder.
Action:
(Object, folder.) Document is an icon, visible; receiving folder open, visible.
Drag and drop document icon into open receiving folder.
Description:
IW3 The open "Marketing" folder overlays the "Seattle" folder, and has to be moved before you can move a report from one to the other. This is more work, but how to do it should be obvious.

Problem Report 4
Wrong action: Alternative menu option.
Task:
Copy folder to diskette. Subtask: Copy operation.
Action:
(Object, folder.) Select menu option "copy to diskette."
Description:
IW4 Describes own problems finding correct menu option (despite prior practice), and "incorrect" options considered or attempted.

Table 12.7 *Usability inspection problem reports 3-4.*

2. Problem descriptions, when they were generated at all, tended to be non-specific in terms of the behavioral distinctions discussed in the first section.

3. Problem descriptions, when they were more specific, tended to be self-reports of inspector's own problems.

These characteristics were more pertinent for inspectors lacking experience and training in behavioral sciences, and human-computer interaction in particular. We had to go to some lengths in pilot work to encourage this group to think in terms of interaction problems and behavioral descriptions. Indeed, this was our motivation for a set of questions we asked inspector participants to answer in their inspection problem reports. These are called the *What (problem)? Why?* and *So What?* questions. These questions were aimed at encouraging inspectors to describe the problem potential users might have, infer why they might have it, and describe the possible consequence of the problem. These guidelines seemed to help, although we have not made formal empirical assessment of this claim (see Montaniz and Mack 1993b for more in-depth discussion of these guidelines).

Problem Report 5
Correct action, wrong context. Select action but not object.
Task:
Copy folder to diskette. Subtask: Select "Copy to diskette" menu option.
Action:
(Object, folder.) Select menu option "copy to diskette" (but target folder is not selected).
Description:
CW11 (Evaluator selects correct menu option "copy to diskette" but the intended folder is not selected. Realizes problem. Believes sometimes actions are disabled even when the object is selected. No prediction for others.)

Problem Report 6
Correct action. Effort.
Task:
Copy folder to diskette. Subtask: Find existing folder, open, containing documents to copy to target folder.
Action:
(Object, windows.) Move and size existing folder open in window, to see contents of another.
Description:
IW3 (Evaluator comments on having to move one window to work on another. Predicts this will be a nuisance to end users, but that it should be obvious how to do this.)

Table 12.8 *Usability inspection problem reports 5-6.*

Examples of Usability Inspection Reports

Tables 12.6 through 12.11 provide twelve examples of usability inspection problem reports which we will analyze in some detail in this section. Here is a brief introduction to these reports. Report 1 in Table 12.6 is a good starting point. This is a description of a problem from a software engineer in the intuitive walkthrough condition. The inspector is actually describing a personal problem with verifying that a copy operation actually occurred. The inspector refers to exploring a method to verify the outcome, in effect, creating an ad hoc scenario which was not part of the task that was given to usability inspectors and end users in the empirical evaluation connected with this study. The inspection report itself is classified in terms of the interface objects and actions involved and the goal-action breakdown we infer for the problem the inspector is describing.

Problem Report 7
Wrong action: Copy by drag/drop.
Correct method not consistent with interface style.
Task:
Copy folder to diskette. Subtask: Select "Copy to diskette" menu option.
Action:
(Object, folder.) (To-be-copied folder is selected. Diskette is inserted in drive.)
Select menu pull-down option "Copy folder to diskette"
Description:
CW12 The user will probably expect an icon on the desktop representing a
diskette that the user can drag the file to. Here, the user model is drag-and-
drop, and the system expects a "menubar" model (for lack of a better descrip-
tion). This will be a big problem for experienced GUI users.

Problem Report 8
Wrong action: Menu option, not direct manipulation. Past observation.
Task:
Copy folder to diskette. Subtask: Copy object to folder.
Action:
(Object, folder.) Drag folder from source folder, drop on destination.
Description:
CW12 (Predicts user may look for alternative to drag/drop method.
Comments: "Don't laugh. I've seen it.")

Table 12.9 *Usability inspection problem reports 7-8.*

Report 5 (Table 12.8) paraphrases an inspection report in which the
inspector himself once again experiences a problem directly, one that is quite
similar to that which end users experience: namely, trying to select a menu
action without first selecting an object (specifically a document icon) to
which the action applies. Recall that Problem 3 in Table 12.3 described an
instance of this problem type, observed in the end-user test. In the inspection
report, the inspector does not actually make an explicit prediction about the
possibility that end users would also experience the same problem.

Inspection report 9 (Table 12.10) provides an example of an inspector
describing a potential problem that involves extrapolating beyond the task
we gave either usability inspectors or end users. The inspector is creating a
new folder, a subtask of which involves selecting a folder template in a
window dialog in the form of a folder icon. This specific template is available

Problem Report 9

Correct action. Effort. Find template to create new folder

Task:

Copy folder to diskette. Subtask: Create to-be-copied folder

Action:

(Object: folder.) "Create new" dialog window is open. Select object type (folder) from list.

Description:

CW2 In general, if the icon to be copied is not visible in the "Create new" window, it may take the user a while to find it. Some users may not realize that the icons are scrollable, thus not realize that the icon that they are looking for is just not visible, versus nonexistent. In this case, it is not a problem, since "Folder" is the first icon in the window.

Problem Report 10

Wrong action. Dialog window organization confusing, may mislead

Task:

Copy folder to diskette. Subtask: Create to-be-copied folder

Action:

(Object, create new dialog window; specify copy object name.) ("Create new object" dialog window is open.) Enter title for new object (folder).

Description:

CW13 The visual layout is confusing, and suggests that there are other goals that the user may not have thought of. In other words, it would be better perhaps to have the title option appear only after the user has selected the folder icon. The user's goals are influenced by having so much stuff on the screen. The screen layout suggests goals that the user doesn't have. So what? So the interface is not intuitive. I think I have to perform two actions—type in title and select a template.

Table 12.10 *Usability inspection problem reports 9-10.*

without scrolling through a list of templates, but the inspector speculates on the likelihood that users would be able to find a template that was not in the visible subset.

Given these examples of inspection reports, let us analyze some key characteristics, in the course of which other inspection problems reports summarized in these tables will be discussed.

Problem Report 11
Correct action: Non-obvious feedback. Explores method to verify success.
Task:
Copy folder to diskette. Subtask: Copy action, feedback
Action:
(Object, folder.) Action "copy to diskette" completed. Dialog window for specifying operation closes.
Description:
CW15 Comments on lack of feedback for "copy to diskette" action. Believes users will want feedback. Explores method for doing this.

Problem Report 12
Wrong action. Move instead of copy. Control move/copy state of drag/drop
Task:
Copy folder to diskette. Subtask: Copy documents to target folder.
Action:
(Object, folder.) Drag document (icon) from existing folder to new folder, drop document in folder.
Description:
CW16 (Evaluator comments on differences in visual cues when drag is copy compared to when drag is move. Suggests end users might be confused and move when they wanted to copy, and vice versa. Also suggests possibility that when something is inadvertently moved, user might lose track of where the document was moved to.)

Table 12.11 *Usability inspection problem reports 11-12.*

Analysis of Inspection-Based Problems

Based on our analysis, five issues related to generating and interpreting inspection reports have been extracted. These are summarized in Table 12.12. Each will be discussed in the context of the example inspections introduced previously.

Inspection Context

The context of the inspection is central to interpreting what the report is about; it is a tacit component of the inspection report. What the inspection is about is given largely by the task itself; that is, what step of the task scenario the inspector is working on, and what aspect of the interface is referred to by the inspector or is inferable by an observer. It is analogous to the "interface element" content of usability problems. The explicit content of descriptions is entered into frames defined by the task step and, in the case of

1.0 Generating inspection reports
  1.1 Inspection context
    1.1.1 task steps
    1.1.2 logging tool
    1.1.3 guidelines
  1.2 Inspector notices something ("interface defect") that does not necessarily create problem for the inspector but was not expected or conflicts with some expectation
  1.3 Inspector elaborates on potential problem. Inspector:
    1.3.1 experiences problem directly, make self-report
    1.3.2 remembers having problem in the past in similar situation
    1.3.3 refers to having observed others having this problem
    1.3.4 simulates/explores interface, to generate a problem scenario; asks "what if" questions, answers by exploring interface and possibly generating ad hoc scenario.
2.0 Inspection report content. Inspector:
  2.1 appeals to some principle or guideline
  2.2 extrapolates own problem or something noticed to hypothetical end user, in
    2.2.1 general terms (e.g., "User would be confused by. . ." "...would not be obvious to novices that. . .").
    2.2.2 specific terms (i.e., frames problems in terms of specific behaviors, outcomes, possible causes of misunderstanding).

Table 12.12 *Inspection reports. Summary of analysis and reporting issues.*

walkthroughs, as a response to one of a set of specific walkthrough questions. In all conditions, reports were also made using a structured inspection tool (hardcopy form or online tool; see Lewis et al. 1992; or software tool Montaniz and Mack 1993a; Rieman et al. 1991). Inspection guidelines or heuristics are also part of the context and may be explicitly presented in the inspection tool.

Noticing Potential Problems
Issue 1.2 in Table 12.12 refers to whatever causes (or influences) an inspector to begin an inspection evaluation (in the context of working through the steps of a task, and given inspection guidelines and so on). One objective of inspection heuristics or guidelines is to stimulate inspectors to notice things about the software interface that might lead, on further reflection, to identifying a potential problem. The "label-following" heuristic in cognitive

walkthroughs is an example: Inspectors are asked to consider how a task (or subtask) goal description might seem to match, for a real user, the label of the interface action the designer intended for accomplishing that goal.

The examples presented in Tables 12.6 through 12.11 do suggest two other factors, apart from inspection guidelines that could induce someone to notice a potential problem and start an evaluation: The inspector experiences a problem directly or remembers an earlier case involving this kind of interface interaction.

Elaborating the Problem

Once a potential problem is suspected, the inspector must develop the specifics of the problem description. In cases where the inspector is effectively a user experiencing a problem, corresponding to issues 1.3.1 and 1.3.2 in Table 12.12, this amounts to reflecting on one's own experience; that is, self-report. The four inspection report examples in Table 12.6 and Table 12.7 describe problems inspectors experienced themselves.

Report 1 (Table 12.6), as discussed earlier, describes one inspector's difficulty verifying the success of the action "copy to diskette," without explicitly predicting that this will be a problem for end users. In fact, feedback for this operation was also a minor problem for end users. Report 3 paraphrases an inspector who had difficulty finding the correct menu option to "copy to diskette." Several inspectors predicted this would be a problem, although it was actually not a serious problem for actual end users we tested. Table 12.12 also suggests that remembering past problems, or recalled observations of others having problems in similar task situations is a factor in generating problem descriptions. Problem reports 7 and 8 are two examples involving the same inspector. This person is explicit about having tested end users with similar software tasks. Usability specialists have a potential advantage in drawing on this source of insight since they are trained and have experience doing usability evaluations. In fact, while we suspect that this is a generative source of problems, we found few explicit references by inspectors to their previous experience as users as the basis for predicting a problem in their role as an inspector.

The fourth factor (issue 1.3.4, Table 12.12) involves going beyond one's own experience and simulating a potential problem, perhaps by exploring a new, ad hoc scenario or scenario variation. Problem report 1 in Table 12.6 and the report examples in Table 12.8 describe cases where inspectors explored the software in order to develop a characterization of a potential user problem. In problem 1, the inspector wants feedback for the success of the "copy to diskette" operation and explores some methods for verifying the successful outcome. This involves adding to the task given the inspectors and the task given end users. Problem report 11 is a similar case involving verifying the outcome of this operation. In problem report 9 the inspector is selecting a template for creating new folders from a list of templates only a subset of which are visible in a list. The inspector notes that if the task given to the inspector (and end users) involved a new object template that was not immediately visible, then end users might have difficulty finding that template; that is, realizing that the list was scrollable. Problem report 10 begins with a characterization of the visual layout of a dialog window for creating new objects as confusing. The inspector suggests that end users may think they have to do more than they have to because of all the prompts and entry fields. This user was an inspector with usability experience in the cognitive walkthrough condition. The inspector's description uses goal-action terminology, which was encouraged by the inspection questions and the walkthrough logging tool.

To summarize, one important factor in generating inspection results is the extent to which inspectors can draw on their own experience as users and as problem experiencers. The extent to which inspectors are themselves cast in the role of users will depend on their experience with systems and tasks of the sort we ask them to evaluate. It will also depend on the extent to which the methodology gives users opportunities to explore the system and make mistakes. In both the Intuitive and Cognitive walkthrough conditions, interface inspectors were given explicit action sequences for the tasks we wanted them to use in evaluating the interface. However, in neither case were we willing to make inspectors follow the sequence in lockstep (and it might not have been possible to do so). The action descriptions were also specified at a certain level of detail where users had to fill in procedural details. In some cases, such as using a mouse to point and select, detailed instructions were not needed. In other cases, more detail might have been useful; lacking it, inspectors had the same opportunity to experience problematic aspects of doing the (sub)task as end users.

Simulating users' experiences and problems is another generative source of problem content, and requires extrapolating, to some extent beyond one's own experience. Encouraging this kind of qualitative simulation on the part of inspectors is a second important factor in generating useful problem descriptions. However, there is a trade-off to be made in encouraging simulation. On the one hand, we believe it is an important mechanism for generating problem reports. We would expect that training in software human factors and usability evaluation would improve the inspectors' ability to extrapolate their own or other's experience in this way. On the other hand, this process must be managed so that inspectors do not create evaluative situations that are incomparable to those with which we might want to compare problem descriptions. We will return to this issue in the section on Comparing Problems Based on Users and Inspections (page 325).

Inspection Problem Reports

Tables 12.6 through 12.11 provide examples of the verbatim inspection reports our inspectors generated, as they typed their comments in a software usability logger customized for cognitive walkthroughs (described in Montaniz and Mack 1993a). As suggested earlier, inspectors were encouraged to enter inspection reports that focused on predicting problems they thought other users (of a certain specified) skill level would have and to make explicit reference to the behavioral specifics of the problems they predicted. In fact, as the reader can judge, the inspection reports are relatively short and non-specific. Only occasionally did reports make explicit reference to the *What (Problem)? Why?* and *So What?* questions, or to the goal-action terminology encouraged by the cognitive walkthrough guidelines. Inspection report 10 in Table 12.11 is an example of where the latter are evident in the inspector's comments. Only occasionally did inspectors cast descriptions in terms of language of goals and actions for an inspector in the cognitive walkthrough condition. Nonbehaviorally trained inspectors told us in debriefing that the *What (problem)? So What?* and *Why?* questions were helpful, as were the cognitive walkthrough questions in "forcing" them to think about user actions and potential problems. The depth of behavioral framing is relatively slight on the part of either behaviorally trained or untrained inspectors. Of course, the surface form of the inspectors reports is not as important as the content. We conclude that it is simply difficult for inspectors to generate reports with this content and structure, at least given the level of training and experience with our walkthrough technique. The inspection reports we have discussed have been analyzed by the authors along the same lines as the end-user usability problems.

Factors Influencing Quality of Inspection Problem Reports

We can frame inspection goals and procedures in such a way that inspectors can generate problem predictions in a form that, with some additional inter-pretation, provides similar information as trained observers record about user problems in usability evaluations. On this analysis it also seems relatively clear how the two factors identified earlier—inspection method and inspector experience and training—could influence each of the inspection processes summarized in Table 12.12. Software usability specialists are more likely to be able to draw on the experience of observing and analyzing user problems and to have the experience with psychological analysis and description of problems and of usability issues in design.

Comparing Problems Based on Users and Inspections

The second question we set out to answer in this section is: How can we account for the mismatches between predications based on inspection methods and empirical end-user problems? As suggested in the *Background* section there have been few comparisons between relative effectiveness of usability problems identified from inspections and from empirical evalua-tions. These comparisons would require common scenarios and common problem analysis methods for empirical and inspection evaluations. We have gone to some lengths to describe our analysis methods, for the purpose of making such a comparison.

Our approach to comparing user problems and inspection-based problems has two parts. First, we identify the interface interaction referred to in the inspection problem report, using the object and action terms used in analyzing usability problems. This classification is no more or less difficult for us than for usability problems. We rely heavily on the task or scenario we ask inspectors to walk through and, of course, on the content of inspection reports. The inspection problem reports beginning in Table 12.6 use the same interface object and action terminology as in the end-user usability problem summaries beginning in Table 12.3. Second, we make assumptions about what constitutes a problem prediction. As suggested earlier, we basically consider an inspection description as "predictive" of a usability

Subtask and Interface Interaction	User Problem	Inspection prediction
Comparison 1: Copy old folder into new folder — Object: folder (icon). Action: copy by drag/drop	**Wrong action for goal. Slip/Dexterity:** EU4 Moves instead of copies. EU4 Then copies. Now has two copies of documents in folder. Corrects.	**Inspector as user having problem:** CW2 Selected wrong icon to copy, released vs. cancel (by ESC), deleted copy of icon.
	Wrong action for goal. Slip: EU4 Selects and copies wrong object. Repeats action.	**Inspector remembers related usability problems in others:** CW12 Predicts user may look for alternative to drag/drop. "Don't laugh, I've seen it."
	Wrong action for goal/lose track of goals: EU3 Moves instead of copies. Then copies. Using drag/drop. EU3 Explores and uses Edit...Copy/Paste commands for operation.	**Inspector simulates circumstances underlying possible problem:** CW16 Visual cues to distinguish move/copy. User might get confused (could want copy, but move) and lose track of where document was moved to.

Table 12.13 *Comparison 1 of user testing and inspection-based problem reports.*

problem if the both of these are roughly "about" the same interface interaction. This is a somewhat liberal judgment to make, rather than something we necessarily expect the inspector to explicitly declare for us. In some cases, the judgment of common attribution is plausible, while in other cases it is not. The difference is illustrated in Table 12.13 and Table 12.14 where we directly compare two usability problems and their corresponding inspection problem reports.

Subtask and Interface Interaction	User Problem	Inspection prediction
Comparison 2: Copy folder to diskette — Object, folder. Action, menu option "copy to diskette."	**Correct action, wrong context:** EU1 Correct action disabled because to-be-copied folder is open	**Inspector as user having problem:** CW11 selects menu action "copy folder to diskette," folder not selected
	Correct action, wrong context: EU4 Correct action disabled. Concludes this action must not be correct. Folder not selected. Selects and does action correctly.	
	Wrong action for goal/ Loses track of goals: EU5 Correctly copies folder to diskette but does not put to-be-stored documents into folder	

Table 12.14 *Comparison 2 of user testing and inspection-based problem reports.*

The first two comparisons provide two examples of "hits"; that is user problems that were anticipated by usability inspectors, at least in terms of our criteria for defining predictions. In comparison 1 two users had trouble controlling whether drag and drop of icons moved or copied those icons. End user EU4 experiences a problem tangle in trying to undo an inadvertent and extra copy. End user EU3 starts with the same problem, using drag and drop but inadvertently moves instead of copies; then, instead of drag and drop, decides to use a valid (but not specified) "Copy" menu option. We categorized the inspection reports as "predictive" of these problems. The cognitive walkthrough inspector CW12 predicts end user EU3 exactly and explicitly refers to prior experience observing users responding to this

	Problem Predicted	Problem **Not** Predicted
Problem Observed	10 (hits)	10 (misses)
Problem Not Observed	14 (false alarms)	N/A

Table 12.15 *Quantitative comparison of predicted and observed problems.*

problem in this way. Comparison 2, choosing a menu action to apply to an icon without selecting the icon first, has been discussed earlier. This comparison simply juxtaposes the end-user problem and the inspection problem report.

An analysis of end-user and inspection-based usability problems suggests that under the right circumstances there should be considerable overlap in problem descriptions as these two comparisons illustrate. First, inspectors are often essentially users themselves, at least in our approach where inspectors were not highly experienced with either the specific software under inspection or with the inspection technique. In this case, inspections are not unlike think-aloud protocols of users trying to accomplish tasks using a computer. Second, as pointed out earlier, the inspection method itself is intended to encourage inspectors to focus on problems and on a procedural or behavioral description of problems. In the case of cognitive walkthroughs, this encouragement was built into the walkthrough questions.

Set against these reasons why inspection-based problem descriptions seemingly should be predictive of end-user problems, is the empirical fact that predictions are not typically highly predictive of user problems, at least given the kind of analysis developed so far in this chapter. Table 12.15 summarizes the discrepancies quantitatively in terms of "hits," "misses," and "false alarms" for matching inspection-based problems (what we call predictions in the table), and the 34 observed end-user problems for the task scenario "copy folder to diskette" we have been discussing in depth.

Numbers correspond to matches for each cell with the 34 end-user problem types observed for the "Copy folder to diskette" scenario used in the walkthrough study. In this table we see that we can match inspection problem descriptions to about 30 percent of the 34 observed problems. Ten observed problems were not predicted ("misses" in the table) and 14 predicted problems were not observed ("false alarms" in the table). In this

1. End users and inspectors are doing different tasks. Example: Inspector may explore an *ad hoc* scenario outside the scope of end-user test scenario and generate problem based on this scenario.

2. Inspectors make inappropriate assumptions about users' skills or susceptibility to a potential interface problem.

3. Inspection guidelines or heuristic not sufficient to infer or stimulate noticing or generating potential problem. Example: Perceptual-motor slips are not likely to be noticed except where inspectors have additional guidelines or experience.

4. Inspectors may not apply inspection guidelines thoroughly enough. Inspector may not analyze consequences of incorrect actions.

Table 12.16 *Source of potential discrepancy between predictions and empirical problems.*

section we analyze this discrepancy in terms of four issues, summarized in Table 12.16, and illustrated qualitatively in four additional comparisons presented in Table 12.17 and Table 12.18.

In essence, the issues in Table 12.16 come down to (1) ensuring that the inspection and end-user test situations are really comparable (issue 1), and (2) questions about the effectiveness of inspectors and the inspection framework to generate insights into potential end-user problems (issues 2, 3, and 4 in the table). The former issue is a general requirement, applicable to assessing the comparability of any two sets of data. However, this requirement plays out in different and more specific terms when applied to the inspection generation and reporting issues we discussed in the preceding section.

The first source of discrepancy is where end users and inspectors are doing different things, even where the intent is to have both carry out the same nominal tasks. User problems or unanticipated concerns can drive users, in effect, into other scenarios that may be tangential to the main task of interest, but certainly are a source of additional problems. Conversely, end-user problems may result from actions that drive users into interface interactions that depart from the task given to inspectors. The same possibilities exist for inspectors as they work through task scenarios. Indeed, cognitive

Subtask and Interface Interaction	User Problem	Inspection prediction
Comparison 3: Create new folder. *Object, folder.* *Action, menu option "create new."* *Outcome, new icon on the desktop*		**Inspector as user having problem:** (Correct action. Confusing outcome): IW1 Reports auto-scrolling of desktop contents, making desktop objects disappear.
		Inspector simulating circumstances underlying potential problem: CW18 Comment that with busy workplace, user may not see new icon on workplace (plus three other inspectors).
Comparison 4: Create new folder. *Object, folder. Window dialog.* *Action, select menu option "create new."* *Entry fields for specifying attribute*		**Inspector simulating circumstances underlying potential problem:** IW20 Dialog window too busy. Not clear order in which to do things. CW13 Dialog has several options that might suggest new goals to user that are not necessary, leading to unnecessary actions to uncertainty (plus...four other inspectors).

Table 12.17 *Comparisons 3 and 4 of user testing and inspection-based problem reports.*

walkthrough instructions may actually discourage inspectors from deviating too far from a target scenario, in the interest precisely of not creating too

Subtask and Interface Interaction	User Problem	Inspection prediction
Comparison 5: Object, window. Action, close by double-click. Slip/Dexterity, problem double-clicking folder		EU1 and EU4 both have trouble closing folder. Double-clicking timing seems off, or pointer not on system menu icon.
Comparison 6: Object, icon. Action, locate in folder. Cannot find correct action	EU4 cannot find document icon in folder. Icons are scrolled out of view. Assistance: Use scroll.	
		IW1 comments that folder names are not connected to office them (looking for folder referred to in task). CW15 comments on lack of function for finding objects in the desktop.

Table 12.18 *Comparisons 5 and 6 of user testing and inspection-based problem reports.*

much diversity among inspectors (see Lewis et al. 1992).

There is some evidence that some discrepancies in predicting usability problems arise from end users and inspectors in effect doing different scenarios. In one instance (not shown in the comparison tables), an end user had difficulty finding a document icon on the desktop and changed the view from a spatial layout of icons to a list of text titles. In this context, the user had a minor problem selecting the document in the list view. However, this subgoal (i.e., select the object from a different representation of the objects) was not given to end users or inspectors in general. Conversely, inspection reports based on simulating or exploring task variations can generate ad hoc scenarios and problems based on them. Comparison 3 in Table 12.17 provides an example of a false alarm that suggests two things. The walkthrough participants are commenting on the potential for losing track of objects on the desktop. In fact, there were cases where end users had to move a window out of the way or resize a folder window to find an icon. We did not always count these actions as problems, but there are plausible conditions where our users could experience these situations as problematic. We could have populated the desktop and the folders with enough objects to make these "false alarms" very likely real problems. A final point is that regardless of whether end users have problems suggested by these inspection reports, the comments could seed quite useful design analyses of interface issues connected with managing and finding information in complex desktop environments.

The second source of potential discrepancy is possible mismatches in the conditions of testing end users and of generating problem reports. The extent to which end users have problems depends not only on the quality of the interface, but on the training and practice users have as part of the testing situation, and on the conditions under which users perform the test task. The other side of these testing conditions is how they translate into the assumptions inspectors make about the end users and how these assumptions influence generating inspection reports. Inspectors might predict different types of problems for end users whom they assumed were experienced, in contrast to those whom they assumed were relatively inexperienced. In fact, in the cognitive walkthrough conditions, we followed Lewis et al. (1992) in giving inspectors explicit instructions about the level of expertise of the end users whose problems they were to predict. It was not clear how effective these guidelines were.

Comparison 4 in Table 12.17 raises a different issue related to testing conditions. This comparison is one of several in which inspectors made predictions about the likelihood of end-user problems for relatively complex aspects of the interface. Comparison 4 refers to a subtask where users are asked to create a new folder. Part of this task is specifying attributes (e.g., a name) of this folder in a dialog window. Walkthrough participants judged this dialog to be complex and that end users would be confused and possibly invited to do things that were not "necessary." In fact, as comparison 4 shows, we did not record overt end-user problems (expressed in a wrong action or clear comment). Moreover, the task instructions given to end users were general and required end users to fill in details based on prior practice or inference. However, it may also be that what we asked end users to do was sufficiently focused, and the dialog sufficiently structured, that users had no problem carrying out this task. In this case, we could conclude that inspectors overestimated the complexity of the interface, at least for the task they were asked to evaluate. In this regard inspectors are quite different from end users. The latter are asked to accomplish tasks in which the software is intended to be in the background. The inspectors' task, however, is to take a critical perspective on the interface.

The third source of potential discrepancy is that the inspection guidelines (heuristics or walkthrough questions) may not be sufficient to stimulate inspectors to notice problems or generate problem descriptions. This may account in particular for "problem misses" where inspectors fail to predict problems that do occur. The perceptual-motor problems or slips described earlier are examples. These problems will be hard to predict, especially for an experienced user of GUI-style interfaces, except under special circumstances. Comparison 5 in Table 12.18 is an example. These circumstances include giving the inspector guidelines that specifically focus on such problems, or where the inspector experiences these problems directly, or where the inspector has some specific experience with problems of a particular type. With respect to the first circumstance, we might provide specific instructions that encourage a focus on action slips, if for example, the software involved a touch interface and some new pointing device. With respect to the second circumstance, where inspectors experience low-level slips themselves, we have already noted cases in the inspection data previously discussed. There were seven end-user problem types involving mis-selection and double-clicking, and only two inspection reports that referred to these end-user problems. Both inspection reports were also self-reports of inspectors having similar end-user problems (inspection problem report 2 in Table 12.6 in one example). The role of experience in this category of problem is also suggested by the authors' experiences as inspectors. While we did not include ourselves as participants in this study, we both carried out pilot inspections; we were aware of being sensitive to the possibilities of slips involving the mouse, largely due to our mutual experience evaluating interface methods involving touch interface methods for GUI-style interfaces (Mack and Montaniz 1990).

A fourth source of potential discrepancy may result from inspectors not applying inspection heuristics to sufficient depth. As noted earlier in describing pilot work, without specific guidelines, inspectors tended to describe interface preferences and not problems cast in language of goals, actions, and outcomes. Moreover, it is especially important to encourage inspectors to extrapolate beyond their own experience. Relying on self-reports of one's own problem experiences is a limited basis for predicting problems, especially where an inspector's experience differs from the hypothetical users about whom predictions are being made. In fact, in none of the comparisons beginning in Table 12.13 is there identification of key details of the corresponding end-user problems. Inspection reports might allude very generally to a precipitating event, but not develop the problem as a scenario in its own right. Comparison 1 in Table 12.13 is an example of a "hit" where the predictions nonetheless fail to describe the specifics of the user's problem. The essence of this problem is that the user confuses how to control move and copy for dragging and dropping icons and inadvertently moves when copy is intended.

Our liberal criterion for classifying an inspection report as a prediction militated against this source of potential discrepancy (i.e., we did not require an exact match in terms of our goal-action or interface object-action schemes). Comparison 6, however, is an example of an ambiguous miss. Here an end user has "lost track" of document icons in a folder. There are inspection comments, but they are so general as to stretch even our liberal criterion for classifying an inspection report as a prediction. The question posed with this example is, under what conditions would inspectors predict this problem? The user actually lost track of the icons as a side-effect of having inadvertently added icons to the folder and having a window too small to see them without resizing. In effect, we are asking inspectors to predict a "new scenario" (find a icon in a folder that an end user filled with items). To do this would require inspectors to explore the behavior of folders under conditions of drag and drop, and varied window sizes. This is not implausible and the interface issues are not at all exotic. But it would require more simulation and exploration than our inspectors were inclined to do (and encouraged to do).

Discussion

To summarize, the issues in Table 12.14 all point to general methodological considerations we would have when assessing the appropriateness of comparing data from more than one experimental study of any kind. Where the interest is in assessing the overlap of inspection-based problems and empirical end-user problems, we need to make sure that both groups have the opportunity to do comparable tasks. It is also necessary to consider how well the inspection procedure can stimulate an inspector to notice, analyze, and describe problems.

With respect to the mismatches between problem predictions and end-user problems, our analysis suggests plausible sources of discrepancy, as summarized in Table 12.16. Moreover, we suspect that formalizing the potential sources of discrepancy in this table would allow us to account for discrepancies in a more satisfying way. For example, if we set aside end-user problem types relating to "slips" (involving mouse selection, double-clicking, and so on), and "ad hoc scenarios," we find that the 22 combined misses and false positives in Table 12.15 are reduced to twelve misses or false positives that still need to be accounted for. Here we can only say that "simulating" a problem situation cannot bring into play all the contributing factors that cause real problems in users. There is a point where we may simply face the empirical fact of the relative effectiveness of inspection methods and the belief that with further research, we can improve inspection heuristics or guidelines and achieve higher levels of predictability (or validity) for problem predictions with respect to actual end-user problems.

The preceding analysis is intended to be taken largely on qualitative terms. The main point is that we can begin to account for mismatches in terms of a more detailed analysis of conditions under which user testing and interface inspections are carried out. From a practical perspective, however, we are really interested in two things: (1) Are inspections pointing us to the problems we should be trying to understand and solve, and (2) under what conditions do usability problem descriptions really have an impact on design and development? These questions bring us to the last topic of this chapter.

12.5 Analyzing Design Implications of Usability Problems

The third issue introduced at the beginning of this chapter (see Table 12.1) pertains to the utility of usability inspection results. We claim that:

- Usability inspection results are valuable mainly in the larger context of user-centered design activities.

- Usability inspection predictions and usability problems serve similar roles in the larger context of usability engineering.

Descriptions of problems, whatever their origin, give potential diagnostic clues to design problems. However, the diagnostic value derives from an interpretive process that draws on both the content of the problems and other factors. Here we discuss this interpretive process, the similarities and differences between empirical usability problems, the problems based on inspection predictions, and these other factors. As suggested earlier, group design reviews are how usability evaluation results and usability issues are typically worked into the software development process. Other chapters discuss group design in more depth, so our comments will be limited (Wixon et al., Chapter 4).

Group design walkthroughs are relatively common in software development, and specific methodologies have developed to guide them(e.g., Yourdon 1989). From a software engineering perspective these walkthroughs typically involve comparing designs and implementations against objectives and specifications. Design walkthroughs focused on usability issues are complementary to software engineering design walkthroughs, but also different. They are focused on assessing how well design and implementations meet usability objectives. Bennett and Whiteside, among others (Bennett 1984; Whiteside et al. 1988), have argued forcefully for inclusion of usability-related objectives, and the adoption of user-centered walkthrough methods (Karat and Bennett 1991a, 1991b). Group design reviews are an important context for conveying problem reports and working through the implications of usability problems, whether identified in testing or in usability inspections. Group walkthroughs provide a way to situate an already known problem or issue in the concrete context of the design. Walkthroughs provide a way to make the case for some usability problem by recreating the problem situation. In this respect they serve a role perhaps similar to the use of video presentation of user problems in driving home the seriousness and concreteness of a problem.

Analysis of usability problems can also play a role making trade-offs in allocating development resources or in meeting multiple, possibly conflicting, design goals. There is seldom only one solution to a problem and solving a problem has costs in a larger development context. For example, we may consider solving a problem by modifying the interface, elaborating on training or online help, or we may decide that the benefit of the tool outweighs the potential problems and user dissatisfaction. It may be more important to ship a product on schedule than to hold it up until usability problems are solved. This decision in turn may be influenced by the severity of problems (i.e., frequency and impact on users). These are decisions that must be made in the context of all development objectives and constraints, not just those pertaining to usability issues (Bennett 1984).

Walkthroughs carried out by a design team are a form of usability inspection, sharing important similarities to individual walkthroughs as we have conducted them. These walkthroughs can serve as a means for discovering problems in the first place. That is, a design team may discover problems by taking a usability-oriented walkthrough of a design (e.g., Karat and Bennett 1991a; Mack 1992). Group walkthroughs provide a framework for identifying design implications. Karat and Bennett (1991b) document an example of the method as part of a project that involved analyzing a CUA-related interface design issue (see IBM 1991). The role of walkthroughs in design is to support the generation of possible design solutions, "testing" of them against usability-related criteria, among others. This process is an interplay between general specifications and objectives played out against the specifics and concreteness of interface design, as it is expressed in the look and feel of the interface, the interface flow from one interaction task to another, and with respect to attributes like consistency across aspects of design. Group walkthroughs have advantages as inspection methods. Managed properly, group walkthroughs may allow more coverage of issues from multiple perspectives, conducted more efficiently in terms of time spent compared to insights and issues analyzed. Design and evaluation can be more closely integrated. These advantages may find their place in methodological variations of standalone inspection methods (see Bias, Chapter 3; Desurvire, Chapter 7; Karat, Chapter 8; Nielsen, Chapter 2).

12.6   General Discussion and Conclusions

This chapter assumes that a major objective of usability inspections is to generate descriptions of potential usability problems with an interface design. There are other objectives (see Wixon et al., Chapter 4)—indeed, in the immediately preceding section we discussed these objectives—and similarities between usability inspections as standalone evaluation methods and group design walkthroughs in the larger context of design and development. We claim that there are strong similarities between inspection data and empirical problem data in terms of how inspection data are generated, described, interpreted, and used in user-centered design reviews. Inspections can produce problem descriptions whose form and content are quite similar to that of end-user problems discovered in empirical usability evaluations. In some circumstances inspection data are essentially self-reports of inspectors experiencing and resolving problems. Discrepancies appear to result from differences in what end users do and experience compared to inspection evaluators. The inspection task may truncate the inspectors' interaction with the interface and hence the depth of problem and interface analysis the inspector engages in.

We have not discussed possible differences among inspection methods in terms of our preceding analysis—in particular, differences between heuristic evaluation and cognitive walkthroughs. Within the domain of inspection methods as standalone evaluative techniques, heuristic evaluations remain, in our opinion, the most efficient and effective method. The rationale for cognitive walkthroughs remains convincing, but these methods as recommended so far, and even our attempted simplification, are complex and require more practice and skill than heuristic evaluations. The technique is evolving, however, and this situation may change (see Wharton et al. 1992; Rowley and Rhoades 1992).

Finally, of course, the predictability of usability inspection data is not the only criteria to judge the effectiveness of problem descriptions based on inspections (or empirical usability evaluation, for that matter). These data are valuable in the larger software design process as sources of insight into design implications of usability problems. The group design process itself is a form of usability inspection. That is, there are similarities between standalone usability inspection methods and group design reviews.

Acknowledgments

This chapter is based on a presentation at the *CHI'92* Workshop on Usability Inspection methods (Mack and Nielsen 1993) where many of the ideas discussed were presented by the first author. We thank the other members of the workshop for their useful comments. We also thank the other contributors to this book, especially Dennis Wixon, Jakob Nielsen, Heather Desurvire, and Randolph Bias for their useful comments on earlier drafts of this chapter.

Chapter 13

The Role of Psychological Theory in Usability Inspection Methods

Cathleen Wharton

Clayton Lewis

University of Colorado at Boulder

Someone once told one of us that "the only good user is a dead user." At the other extreme one could say that "software can only be successful if extensive user testing and detailed analyses of a user's cognitive skills are undertaken prior to a product's release." But constraints in development practices, schedules, resources, and time-based competition in industry do not currently allow for such extensive usability work. This creates the context in which the first remark was formulated.

From a researcher's perspective the context of real usability work provides a challenge. How can the theoretical ideas of the researcher aid a practitioner who is always short of time and for whom usability is only one of many important design and development goals, not all of which can be met?

This chapter will consider what can be done to bring psychological theory to bear on actual design problems in real software development organizations. We begin with a very quick sketch of psychological theory in which aspects that are potentially relevant to software design will be pointed out. We then consider how these theoretical ideas might be applied in practical settings.

13.1 What Psychological Theory Has to Offer

Psychologists have established a number of important facts about the mental machinery of people which are pertinent to design problems. Psychological theory aims to connect these and other facts into a predictive and explanatory framework, in much the same way that a physical theory, like Newtonian mechanics, aims to predict and explain the behavior of physical systems. (What will happen when we let go of the neck of this balloon? Why?) To provide background for our subsequent discussion we list here some of the facts that a psychological theory might encompass, stressing those facts that we think designers need to apply.

Some things are easier to see or hear than others. Everybody knows this, but there are models that provide quantitative data on the effects of contrast, loudness, size, and like factors.

Some things don't look or sound the way you would think. For example, the same color looks very different against different backgrounds. This means that in using color to identify areas of a map which share some common feature, one may actually have to adjust the colors to get different patches that are supposed to be the same color look the same.

Only some of the contents of a complex display are likely to be seen. What is seen depends on size, color, organization, and movement as well as where the viewer is looking, what the user knows about the structure of the scene, and what the user is trying to do. As a simple example, suppose you have two sets of data displayed, each in a different color. To the user you have two groups of data; if the elements are in close proximity, this association will be even stronger (Tullis 1988).

Precise movements take longer than gross movements (Fitts and Posner 1967). For example, if an interface makes use of numerous buttons or sequences of button presses, the distance between buttons in the sequence and their size becomes an issue. There are good quantitative models which predict how long a movement of a given length and requiring a given precision will take.

Mental operations take time. It takes time to recall information from memory or to make a decision. It is possible to make reasonable quantitative estimates of the times involved, at least for fairly simple operations, and it is possible to break up complex operations into simple parts for purposes of estimation.

People can perform some mental and physical operations in parallel. People can operate a keyboard while talking or listening, for example. Quantitative models can be used here: Gray et al. (1992) made a very accurate analysis of the parallelism in the use of a telephone operator's workstation, for example.

People get faster the more often they perform a task. The Power Law of Practice (Newell and Rosenbloom 1981) states that the more frequently a task is performed, the quicker it will be accomplished. The rate of improvement is rapid at first, dropping off as the task becomes performed more often.

Novice users may perform tasks differently than expert users. There are individual differences in the way that knowledge is mentally represented between novices and experts. Such knowledge is a direct reflection of the way that a task is both understood and organized by people at different levels of expertise (Egan 1988).

It takes time to learn things well. If only a little time is available for learning, only a little bit of information can be learned well enough to be remembered even a short time later. It is possible to make quantitative estimates of the time required to learn a skill to a reasonable criterion, based on a decomposition of the skill into small parts (Kieras and Polson 1985).

Prior knowledge can be beneficial. Information related to prior knowledge is easier to learn and less likely to be forgotten than completely new information.

Recognition is easier than recall. Under usual conditions it is easier to recognize something when you see it or hear it than to recall it. This was one of the basic design principles of the Star design (Smith et al. 1982; Johnson et al. 1989) which triggered the decisive shift toward graphical interfaces, in which interaction is dominated by recognizing and selecting depictions of objects and actions rather than by recalling and typing names and commands.

People forget things, especially if they have not had ample time to rehearse the material, and if the material is not meaningfully related to things they already know. It is hard to keep arbitrary information in mind for even a short time while performing a task. So, for example, remembering and following advice from a help screen will be difficult; using the advice will be easy only if it can be kept visible while it is used.

Behavior is often guided by goals. People choose actions that they believe will accomplish their goals. If an action appears to lead away from a goal, they will not select it. A strategy called "label-following" is often seen: people pick actions whose labels are obviously related to their goals (Engelbeck 1986). For example, if people have the goal of archiving a file they will readily choose an action labelled *archive* and less readily one labelled *disk mainte-nance.*

Alternative methods can cause problems. Problems in which many alternative methods seem plausible are harder than problems for which only a few alter-natives seem plausible.

People try to assess progress. If they do not seem to be making progress towards a goal, people may abandon a task, seek to undo earlier actions, or find an alternative method. So enabling them to make an accurate assessment is important.

Other summaries of much of this material, and more, can be found in Card, Moran, and Newell's seminal book *The Psychology of Human-Computer Inter-action* (1983) and in Olson and Olson (1990).

This list is far from complete. For instance, we haven't included facts about interference, stimulus-response compatibility, and other useful ideas. But it will serve to indicate the sort of thing psychological theory might supply to designers.

13.2 How Might System Designers Become Aware of and Apply This Knowledge in Their Work?

Some possible answers to this question are considered in a hypothetical dialogue with a software developer.

This is all common sense, so there's no problem. This simply isn't true. Some of the subtle points, such as that the same color patch will look very different when presented against different backgrounds, are known by very few people. Beyond these, even some of the "obvious" points were not reflected in design until fairly recently and are probably not widely known even now. Take the superiority of recognition over recall: This entered design practice (and as we noted quickly became dominant) only circa 1980 (Smith et al. 1982). If it were common sense we would have seen designs reflecting this principle from the earliest days.

OK, this isn't all common sense but designers all know it by now. We doubt it. Our experience in discussing this material with designers is that few of them have encountered many of the concepts here, such as the role of goals in guiding behavior.

Well, they don't really know these things, but they act as if they do: Current design practice already reflects these insights, so designers who follow established style are doing OK. There is much truth in this claim. It is true that designers who adapt the features of successful applications are able to produce designs which on the average are far superior to those prevailing several years ago. But one still sees many design flaws resulting from conflict with these ideas. Sometimes this happens because designers do not follow a successful model; perhaps the model they are using has to be extended or adapted or maybe some of the principles can't be applied without considerable analysis.

Consider the importance of goals. Designs often fail because they (implicitly) assume that users have particular goals that they don't in fact have. For example, if one wants to forward calls on our university phones one must first adopt the goal of cancelling forwarding. This is a bad flaw, because nobody brings this goal with them until they learn they need it by painful experience. But a flaw like this, or the avoidance of it, isn't visible on the surface of an interface. One must carefully examine the action sequences required for various tasks to spot it.

I still don't think designers need to know any more about these things than they do now. They can fix these flaws by doing user testing of their designs or by getting more user input during design. These are both good things to do. We would never argue that ideas from cognitive theory can be more than a useful supplement to these approaches. But we do argue for that much: Relying only on testing and user interaction is a slow way home. If you start testing with a design with serious flaws, testing takes a long time to work them all out. This is true partly because problems can mask each other in testing: You may not be able to get data on problem B before you have fixed problem A, if problem A throws users off the track before they get to B.

You've sold me on the need to do something about getting these ideas into practice. I'll adopt a set of design guidelines right away. This approach will work for some of these principles but not for others. Consider the problem with our telephones discussed earlier. There's no simple guideline for avoiding this problem that can be applied to an interface just by looking at it. Some process in which the steps required to perform tasks with the interface are examined and critiqued is needed.

I can see that this problem is harder than I thought. Designers should build complete process models of what is needed to use their systems. Then they'll smoke out any problems that exist, no matter how far below the surface they are. This is a good idea. In some situations it can be done and provides very useful results. An excellent example is the work of Gray et al. (1992) in modelling the interface for a telephone operators' workstation, in which they were able to identify subtle but extremely important flaws in a new design.

But there are two common problems with building models. First, only some of the principles above are understood in enough detail to support accurate modelling. What is well understood tends to be the quantitative aspects of the principles: how long it takes to make a movement, for example. And even for these quantitative aspects only the behavior of highly skilled or highly constrained users can be modelled accurately.

A second problem is that building a complete process model is a major undertaking. It can approach or even exceed in effort the task of building the interface itself. Worse, before beginning to build a model one needs to invest considerable time in mastering the modelling framework and any tools that may be available to support it. In some situations, like that of Gray et al. (1992), where small changes in interface performance are worth a great deal, this investment may pay back handsomely. It may be that a sober analysis of the economics of usability, if we knew enough to make such a analysis, would show that the investment would be worthwhile in many common design situations. But it is clear that in most current design environments the payoff won't be recognized, even if it's there, and the investment just won't be made.

Let's forget about this problem. It's insoluble. Not so fast. We can envision a method for analyzing designs that does some of what building a model would do but at much less cost. For instance, in the cognitive walkthrough method, discussed in Wharton et al. (Chapter 5), a design evaluator builds and applies a simple process model in real time while examining an interface. Any problems encountered in doing this are noted as the evaluation proceeds. We consider this approach more fully in the next section.

You're right, I gave up too soon. And I can see other solutions, too: how about hiring some cognitive psychologists and getting them to look over my designs? They already know the theory. This isn't a bad idea. But there are some things to worry about. One is finding cognitive psychologists who know enough about user interfaces to be able to apply the principles. Another is the "kibitzer problem": It can cause trouble in your organization to have people whose only job is to criticize somebody else's work or even to make supposedly helpful and constructive suggestions about somebody else's work. Besides, it's expensive enough to have designers, let alone kibitzers.

I'll just have the psychologists do the design. Again, this is not a bad idea. But the supply of psychologists who can do the design is even smaller than for kibitzers. For example, in your organization they probably have to understand the X Window System to get started.

How about teaching some cognitive theory to computer people so they can do a good job on interface design? This is another good idea. We should do that, but we also need to do something in the meantime.

Can Theory be Reflected in Inspection Methods?

Having considered some general approaches to involving psychological theory in design, let us zero in on the specific idea of using inspection methods, including the cognitive walkthrough, as a way to bring theory into design. We'll do this by continuing our dialogue with the hypothetical software developer, but now presuming that the developer has attended a workshop at the CHI conference on inspection methods or has read the introductory chapters of this book.

I'm really taken with the idea of inspection methods. They are cost-effective and fast. And I can get my existing design personnel to use them. Actually the data are mixed on both of these points. Heuristic evaluations are fast (Molich and Nielsen 1990; Nielsen and Molich 1990), but cognitive walkthroughs (Lewis et al. 1990; Polson et al. 1992), at least using the original procedures, are not. And there's evidence that usability expertise helps when applying these methods (Jeffries et al. 1991; Wharton et al. 1992; Nielsen 1992a). It remains unclear whether these methods will be competitive with other approaches in an organization like yours with few experienced usability people. Anyway, why do you think other people in your organization will share your enthusiasm and be willing to put time into using these methods? That doesn't always happen in organizations we know about.

It seems to me that a method like the cognitive walkthrough will definitely be a step in the right direction for us, anyway, since we'll get the benefit of some psychological knowledge we now lack. We hope you are right. But it's unclear whether all of the ideas we hope to import from theory can really be brought in by an inspection method. Consider the ideas about perception and attention in the inventory of useful ideas at the beginning of this chapter. Both the cognitive walkthrough and heuristic evaluation allow for judgements about perception or attention to be made, but they do not help inexperienced people to make them. They don't, for example, provide people with facts about perception or attention that they may not already know.

Couldn't these methods be extended to provide more coverage? Perhaps. But can we do this while keeping the methods acceptably simple and fast, and without requiring extensive pretraining in the concepts involved? The beauty of the heuristic evaluation approach is its simplicity; we've seen that the original cognitive walkthrough was too complex and slow. Extending these methods won't be easy.

There may be problems, I agree, but this seems to be the most promising approach. Cognitive modelling is never going to be practical in my organization. You may be right. Remember, though, that for the right problem cognitive modelling is already very effective: If you are dealing with highly skilled users on an application with very high sensitivity to user performance, modelling will pay off. Beyond that, it may be possible to build cognitive models for *classes* of interfaces, as Peter Polson (personal communication, November 1992) has suggested. (Cf. heuristic estimation which estimates training times for classes of interfaces [Polson and Olson 1992; Polson et al. 1992b].) Then you and your people could pick up a generic model, do a little tailoring, and have a good model of your design. Or maybe some design questions could be settled by the model at the level of the whole class of interfaces, so that you wouldn't even need to tailor the model. To some extent this is already happening: There are good theoretical analyses of different menu selection mechanisms, for example, that could be applied by designers without requiring new modelling to be done.

But if this kind of thing is done couldn't the results be incorporated in inspection methods, in the form of questions to ask about the features of an interface? That's a good idea. It could lead to inspection methods specialized to interfaces of a given class. The first versions of the cognitive walkthrough suffered from not doing this: people evaluating a graphical user interface had to answer questions that were unlikely to be relevant except for telephone interfaces. Targeting inspection methods on particular classes of interfaces could be a way of extending inspection methods without making them too complicated, since the method that would be used in a given situation would include only a subset of all the possibly relevant issues. But then there's the problem of organizing a lot of different inspection methods for lots of specific settings.

My organization could do that for the kinds of interfaces we build. Maybe so.

Another advantage of inspection methods for us is that we can use them very early in design. We can't do that with user testing. That's another point that needs more exploration. You can do user testing very early if you use paper and pencil or quick and dirty screen mock-ups, but we don't have any comparison of inspection methods with this kind of early test.

A problem we are concerned about is getting fixes to the problems an inspection method turns up. In principle that is a big advantage to having a theoretical grounding for the inspection. The theory ought to tell you *why* something is a problem, not just that it *is* a problem. And knowing why something is a problem is a big step toward fixing it. For example, knowing that a color patch looks wrong *because* its appearance is influenced by the surrounding context is much more helpful than just knowing that it looks wrong. But we don't have data on how well this works in practice.

Conclusion

We conclude the above hypothetical discussion.

We are going to try inspection methods in my organization. We'll try to push the methods to connect more with psychological theory, by using methods that offer some "why" information as part of the evaluation. We'll share our contributions and also work with the research community, and our industry colleagues, to keep up the flow of ideas and data on these methods and how they compare with others. Sounds good to us.

Acknowledgments

We thank all participants in the CHI'92 Usability Inspection Methods Workshop for their comments and helpful discussions. We also thank the following people for their helpful discussions and detailed comments on earlier drafts of this chapter: Randolph Bias, Louis Blatt, Barbara Diekmann, George Engelbeck, Peter Polson, and John Rieman.

Chapter 14

Interface Design Guidance Systems

Louis A. Blatt

James F. Knutson

NCR Consulting Design Group

We define any system that supports a software developer or designer in creating user-system interfaces as an interface design guidance system (IDGS). This chapter describes the methods we used to determine what is needed for an effective and useful IDGS. The four phases of our research outline the IDGS investigation and prototype development to date. The first phase was to review the current research done that related to user interface design and evaluation as well as the tools currently used in software design and development. Based upon the results from this research and previous experiences with other similar concepts, we performed a requirements definition analysis to look at the use and representation of user interface design examples for software development. Phase three was a rapid proto-typing effort that resulted in the design and development of four different online IDGS application examples. Each embodied some of the require-ments discovered during the previous research phase. In the last phase the concept of an online IDGS was demonstrated to software developers during a focus group activity along with a prototype IDGS. Reactions, comments, and criticisms are listed and should be considered in future instantiations of any IDGS.

The advent and proliferation of standard environments (e.g., Microsoft® Windows™ and OSF Motif™), standards documents, guidelines, usability inspection methods and software tools have not solved the usability problems that retard a wider adoption of computer systems by the general population.

Design guideline documents, which are the most widely used type of IDGSs, suffer in that they do little to ensure compatibility between the user interface and the user's expectations (Potter et al. 1990), are not well suited for use during interface development (Tetzlaff and Schwartz 1991; Thovtrup and Nielsen 1991), are often too general (Chapanis and Budurka 1990), difficult to use (Eason 1983), and are often perceived as limiting creativity. Although there has been an increase in computer-aided software engineering (CASE) workbenches (see Vessey et al. 1992) and critiquing systems (Silverman 1992), such systems do not yet provide a complete tool set for ensuring that the interface allows users to perform the tasks in a way that is consistent with how they expect the tasks to be performed (cognitive compatibility). In addition, few of the current solutions provide the information in the form of examples, which has been shown to be especially desired by and useful for, software developers (Tetzlaff and Schwartz 1991; Barber et al. 1991).

Motivating the need for an IDGS is the underlying goal to make interfaces consistent with user's tasks and industry standards, which can lead to an easier to use and useful interface. Consistency within and between interfaces can provide benefits. For example, if a user selects a menu option labeled "print" to print a file in one application, there should be a significant performance benefit in using the command name consistently across other applications. The consistent use of interface features allows a positive transfer of knowledge between applications. This positive transfer permits people to learn applications with greater ease. This ease of learning can then translate into increased sales in that users may be more willing to purchase and learn new applications that look and behave in a manner similar to their current application. Temple, Barker, and Sloane (1990) found that Microsoft Windows users (a system generally acknowledged as having a relatively high level of interface consistency) were more productive, self-sufficient, and confident than users of a character-based interface. A more confident, self-sufficient user will be more apt to purchase, install, and learn a new application. This will result in increased system sales for companies that employ an effective IDGS.

In our view, an IDGS should support a broad spectrum of user-centered design activities. A tool to support the designer's task of maintaining interface consistency is important; however, an IDGS should also support the collection, representation, and analysis of data resulting from usability engineering activities. Examples include requirements definition analysis, task analysis, and the usability assessments found in this book.

14.1 Secondary Research

The first phase of our research was aimed at understanding the current state of interface design guidance. We reviewed current strategies used for design guidance in the software industry and analyzed their benefits and limitations. Companies currently obtain interface design guidance in various ways. However, each of the current methods fails to singularly provide sufficient support to help developers and designers make appropriate and timely decisions during the design process. Some current solutions to interface design support include the use of developer's personal experience, design guideline documents, and software tools. These are defined and reviewed in the following sections.

Developer's Experience: No Guidance

In some current situations the only support used is the designer's and developer's past experience. Often design decisions are based upon the look-and-feel of products that the developer or designer has experienced. The problem with this method alone is that it limits the possible design solutions that are considered and perpetuates any errors from past designs that may have not yet surfaced as errors. It also fosters the inappropriate use of previous design solutions. A successful design, using this method of support, is dependent upon the developers' and designers' memory, the breadth of their experience, and their ability to associate and accommodate a potential design solution with the problem at hand. More importantly, this method does not directly support the developer or designer to consider the end user's task in the design solution. Rather, many developers entertain the problem of design rationale by considering the widgets (e.g. scroll boxes, buttons, list boxes) that they have already created or are readily available, not what the users' task requires. In addition, except for the developer's memory, there is no system to save or retrieve relevant examples from previous projects or other developers.

Design Guideline Documents

Although we realize that standards, guidelines, style guides, and design rules are different, for simplicity we will call them "design guidelines" throughout the chapter. Some examples of design guidelines are the *IBM Common User Access (CUA) Advanced Interface Design Reference* (1991), the Microsoft's *The Windows Interface: An Application Design Guide* (1992), and the Smith and Mosier (1986) guidelines. One or more of these books often represents all of the design support a developer is given to design software. The documents represent, at varying levels of detail, recommendations for the design of an interface. Developers, designers, human factors professionals, and others rely on these relatively inexpensive design guidance systems to ensure interface consistency. Similar to using developer's or designer's past experience, this solution also suffers from depending too heavily upon the developer's or designer's ability to associate the guideline with the current design problem. Design guideline documents supply information needed to arrive at a solution, but they do not directly provide a solution in the form of usable code. Developers and designers need the code that will serve as the design solution, all referenced by specifying parameters about the proposed user, task, and environment.

Currently available document-based IDGSs have been criticized for doing little to ensure that the interface allows users to accomplish their goals in a way that fits their model of the task (Potter et al. 1990) which is sometimes called cognitive compatibility (Barnard et al. 1981). In addition, document-based IDGSs are characterized as not well suited for use during interface development (Tetzlaff and Schwartz 1991; Thovtrup and Nielsen 1991), too general (Chapanis and Budurka 1990), difficult to use (Eason 1983), and perceived as limiting creativity. Although they have gotten much better, it is still not clear whether they overcome these limitations. These issues are described more fully in the following sections.

Design Guideline Documents Often Do Little to Ensure Cognitive Compatibility

Two types of consistency are relevant to the design of an interface: look-and-feel (LAF) consistency and task consistency (cognitive compatibility). LAF consistency addresses inter-application consistency between two applications by the same end user, and intra-application consistency between dialogs within the same application, by standardizing certain visual, lexical, and behavioral characteristics of interfaces. LAF consistency ensures that certain features of one or more applications will look and behave in the same way. Guidelines like the IBM *CUA Advanced Interface Design Reference* (1991) and the Microsoft *Application Design Guide* (1992) are examples of documents that entertain LAF consistency. Most current guidelines support this type of design consistency. However, Grudin's (1989) observation that a LAF-consistent interface may still be difficult to use poses a more difficult problem. He continues saying that it is sometimes more important to be consistent with how the user expects the task to be performed (cognitive compatibility) than LAF consistent. Although adherence to guidelines is necessary to develop effective interfaces, compliance to stylistic issues alone is not sufficient. Potter et al. (1990) reported that an interface may have usability problems even when an interface standard is not violated. It is more important to understand how the users accomplish tasks and then design interfaces that are consistent with the user's models. This is achieved through the consideration of cognitive compatibility.

Cognitive compatibility refers to the extent to which the interface is congruent with how a user expects to accomplish a task. It includes the structure and content of the information, and the characteristics of the user, the user's knowledge, and the task to be performed (Barnard et al. 1981). Cognitive compatibility is typically more difficult to achieve than LAF consistency, but plays a large role in the initial usability and ability to learn to use an interface. It results from building an application that is compatible with a user's mental representation of how an interface should operate in order to enable a task to be performed. The well-defined methods used by human factors professionals can be used to ensure cognitive compatibility. These methods may include such methods as requirements analysis, task analysis, heuristic evaluation (Nielsen 1992a; Nielsen and Molich 1990; Nielsen, Chapter 2), usability walkthrough, and cognitive walkthrough (Lewis et al. 1990; Polson et al. 1992a; Wharton et al., Chapter 5) and other usability assessment techniques.

The *HUFIT Planning, Analysis, and Specification Toolset* by HUSAT (1990) is one of the few examples of a design guidance document that goes beyond LAF characteristics. This workbook allows a developer without human factors knowledge to derive an interface that is cognitively compatible. It does this by providing a description of how to identify the user, task, and environment characteristics for the proposed product as well as providing template documents for these activities. However, one of the reasons that this workbook falls short and has not been adopted in the mainstream of software development is because it does not make creating a user-centered interface any easier or faster than creating an interface the traditional way.

Design Guideline Documents Are not Well Suited for Use during Software Development

Ironically, design guideline documents, which are typically provided by human factors professionals seem not to have been designed with the developer's task in mind. Design guideline IDGSs such as the IBM *CUA Reference Guide* (1991), Microsoft *Application Design Guide* (1992), Smith and Mosier (1986), and other guidelines, are all designed in such a way as to be relatively context-free. By achieving the goal of allowing for context-free design guidance, a natural shortcoming results. In fact, it is entirely possible that many of the issues that are of particular interest to the developer will not be specifically entertained by these documents. The result of not being able to generalize the design information to the design issue at hand precludes developers from effectively using the design guideline. In addition, the fact that current systems are not online necessitates time-consuming search tasks when using the document. For example, the user must locate the book. In a developer's environment (which is often a cubicle cluttered with documents and other books) this is not as easy as it sounds. After having found the guideline book, the developer must then search for the relevant guideline. One attempt at solving this problem has been to put the guideline online (e.g., Microsoft Companion, Microsoft Visual Design Guide, Navitext, DRUID).

Although a serious limitation of paper-based design guidelines is that of the paper medium, putting a design guideline document online does not solve other limitations. Developers must still search for information about their design problems. Once found, the information is often incomplete, ambiguous, or too general. Even restructuring the information in the form of hypertext (Fox 1992) has not facilitated the adoption of such guidelines as Smith and Mosier (1986) in the software development community. As will be described later in this chapter, what the developer wants is interactive examples and code to the exact solution to the current problem. What the developer gets when using guideline documents is information which needs to be interpreted and then coded for their own solution, rather than a directly usable code solution.

An IDGS that can be used concurrently with the design process will make for greater integration of human factors issues into designs. This can be done through the application of methods such as requirements analysis, task analysis, heuristic evaluation (Nielsen 1992a; Nielsen and Molich 1990; Nielsen, Chapter 2), usability walkthrough, and cognitive walkthrough (Lewis et al. 1990; Polson et al. 1992a; Wharton et al., Chapter 5) and other usability assessment techniques. Human factors professionals usually publish the results of their work as internal reports and later in external publications. Although in most cases the authors of the documents have written the reports in the interest of software developers, it is not the developers who get to see them. There are many more people designing interfaces than people who belong to societies like the special interest group of the Association for Computing Machinery's (ACM) special interest group on Computer-Human Interaction (CHI), or the Human Factors and Ergonomics Society (HFES). Many people designing products have no idea of the extent of information available about interface design. These people are doing interface design and development without any guidance. The technical journals and company confidential reports are not accessible to the mainstream of software developers. Knowledge across the industry and even within companies related to user interface design rationale is rarely documented and thus continually lost. Even if the developers and designers see the results in journals, these are often not explained in a form that is easy to incorporate into their development process (Chapanis and Budurka 1990). Design rules and results of interface design studies, with real life examples should be published in a form that is included in an online product. This would provide not only access and the ability to search for specific topics, but also an up-to-date account of the state of software design, development, and assessment techniques.

Design Guideline Documents Are Too General

The literature suggests that current design guidelines are usually too general. Tetzlaff and Schwartz (1991) found that the list structure taken by most guidelines is an inappropriate representation: People work better from examples. Document-based guidance tools do not allow the developer or designer to explore the behavior of the application. The developer or designer is supposed to create an interface from a two-dimensional picture which provides little information about the actions resulting from interaction between the user and the interface. Moreover, by not having an effective means to retrieve the information, designers are likely to follow their intuition, and often miss important issues. Some literature has suggested that providing specific interactive guidelines may be more effective. Thovtrup and Nielsen (1991) report a study in which they required developers to use guidelines during the development of a product. When the study was completed, they asked the developers if the experiment matched their normal way of working. Some of the participants indicated that the experiment artificially induced guideline usage. One participant claimed that he had never used guidelines in real life; rather, he used examples of the interface environment. Through day to day interaction with developers, we can corroborate that this is a fairly common way for developers to make interface decisions. As human factors professionals we often hear, "well Excel did . . . ." or "the Print Manager handles that issue by . . . ." It would be beneficial and consistent with the way developers currently handle design problems, to provide them with specific interactive examples of design solutions that are retrieved based upon characteristics of the user, task, and environment rather than on the specific widget to be used.

Design Guideline Documents Are Difficult to Use

One method to make IDGSs easier to use is to evaluate them with real users. Current design guidelines require memorization and induction to be used effectively. De Suza and Bevan (1990) had three designers design an interface using a draft of a design guidelines document for designing menu interfaces. They reported that the designers violated 11 percent of the rules and had difficulties in interpreting 30 percent of the rules. The draft standard was improved after this experiment. The conclusion drawn from this experience is that any tool to support design should be evaluated and redesigned based on the results of that evaluation. More usable interfaces will only result when tools to support design and development are easy to use and useful.

Design Guideline Documents Are Perceived as Limiting Creativity

It is our experience that developers often claim interface design guidelines hamper creativity or flexibility. When developers design an interface object and arrive at an entirely new control that serves a useful purpose, no one should point at it and say, "that is not standard." An interface is only non-standard if the design deviation adds little for the user and is inconsistent with stated guidelines (Grudin 1989). For example, a pull-down menu that requires the user to press the right mouse button rather than the left in order to view the menu item is a mistake; not an act of creativity. When Microsoft used icons at the top of the screen which acted as menus, no one stated that they did not comply with the standard. The utility of providing the user easy access to commonly used functions was obvious.

Software-Based Tools

Another approach to aid software development has been the use of software tools. User interface management systems (UIMS), computer-aided software engineering (CASE) workbenches (see Vessey et al. 1992), expert critiquing systems (see Silverman 1992), system toolboxes, and off-the-shelf proto-typing tools are used in an effort to achieve productivity gains in implementation and effective interfaces from the user's point of view.

The main limitation of most of these tools is that they are usually developed to increase the efficiency of the developer rather than to develop excellent interfaces. The main objective of most of these tools is to support the implementation of interface objects and little support is given for considering how the interface will support the end user's tasks. Although still lacking in some areas, CASE workbenches and critics represent some important pieces which allow the designer to consider the end users' characteristics, tasks, and environment in the design of the interface. As the selection of online tools is changing as fast as code can be written, the following short review should be considered as only a brief look at some examples, rather than a comprehensive review of all of the current tools.

CASE workbenches have been heralded as "solutions to the software productivity problem" (Vessey et al. 1992). A CASE workbench is broadly defined as a software tool that provides automated assistance for software development, maintenance, or project management. Although future CASE systems may prove to be useful, current CASE tools have been shown to have little or no effect on productivity and a relatively weak effect on the quality of specification produced (Vessey et al. 1992). This may be the result of not supporting the designer or developer at the high level of abstraction needed. One system reported to provide this capability is ACE (Johnson et al. 1993). This tool reportedly allows the user to specify the interface at the semantic level and generates a user interface based upon this high-level specification, freeing the developer from worrying about the specific widgets and focusing more on the overall scheme of the interface. Although more high-level programming tools may prove to be fruitful, as yet even these systems do not typically ensure that the end user's specific task set will be considered in design. Perhaps what the developer requires is some sort of expert system or critic to provide feedback on design ideas.

Critics examine the developer's solution and provide feedback specific to what the developer did wrong. Commonly used examples of critics are the grammar and spell checkers found in most word processor applications. In addition to word processing applications, critics have been developed for many environments such as CAD design (Steele 1988), architectural design (Fischer et al. 1990), LISP tutors (Fischer 1987), and medical diagnosis (Langlotz and Shortliffe 1983). Silverman (1992) provides a limited review of critic systems that have been developed, discussing important issues in their implementation. Only a few online systems have been particularly concerned with usability issues, considering the user and the task environment. The work of Fischer and colleagues (see Rettig 1993, for an overview) considers not only the implementation of the objects, but also the aspects of the user and environment pertinent to the system being designed. These systems are also extendible to allow developed ideas to be integrated into the example base and provide design rationales as added guidance. One limitation of any critic is that it provides a post hoc analysis of the design. By its very nature, it requires something to critique.

Another interesting development is the system explained by Barnard (1991). Barnard describes a demonstrator expert system that provides context-sensitive descriptions of the interface, proposed users, and tasks that are supported, by considering the cognitive and perceptual limitations of the user as related to the task and system. Although this tool is consistent with user-centered design in that it considers the user, tasks, and environment before design starts, Barnard's tool only provides a piece of what a developer would need to facilitate software design.

Since these previously mentioned tools seem to be adopted in preference to human consultants and guideline documents, it is logical to conclude that for any IDGS to have an impact on software design, it must make user interface design and development easier and faster. Simply ensuring a higher quality interface is not enough incentive for the adoption of an IDGS, because the software development community is biased towards the production of the underlying code, often at the expense of the user interface.

Conclusions

Although design guidelines and software tools do add some benefit, they do not offer a complete solution to the design of usable and useful software. In light of the problems with the currently available design guidance systems, we must look for a better alternative. In addition, every company which develops user software has experience with interface design, but this experience is not shared or made accessible to interface developers or designers except in the form of the released product. Thus, the design rationale is not available. The information that experts use to design interfaces and perform usability assessments needs to be made accessible to the mainstream of software developers and designers. As Eason (1983) suggests, standards and guidelines as they exist will not help designers; they must take the form of tools to enable the designer to follow human factors design principles. A tool which resides on an individual's workstation has the potential of providing guidance during the concept stage of development. This information should be provided in a tool which works synergistically with the current methods of software development. In summary, for a tool to be useful in affecting interface design in a positive way and be adopted by the mainstream of software development, it must meet the following requirements. Under each requirement are specific implementations that could satisfy those requirements.

Requirements:

1. Ensure that the developed user interface is congruent with how end users perform tasks (cognitive compatibility) by supporting the use of well-defined human factors methods.

   - Provide support, training, and tools for requirements analysis, task analysis, heuristic evaluation, usability walkthrough, and cognitive walkthrough, and other usability assessment techniques.

   - Provide design rationale for design issues with examples of good and bad implementations.

2. An IDGS must be online and be designed to work with the accepted software development practices and tools.

- Provide interactive examples of user interface designs.
- Provide design advice tailored to the developer's current design problem.
- Provide the source code for user interface examples and a way to integrate it into the interface under development.

3. Make design and development easier and faster, while improving the quality of the resulting interface.
    - Provide interactive examples of user interface designs.
    - Provide design advice tailored to the developer's current design problem.
    - Provide the source code for user interface examples and a way to integrate it into the interface under development.

Our research and personal experience suggests that including examples in an IDGS seems to be particularly important. However, the question of how to represent the interface knowledge becomes an immediate problem when considering the issue of supplying user interface examples. In the next section, we discuss the next step to identify characteristics of a useful IDGS. This requirements analysis explored how developers and designers would use user interface examples as well as the most effective method of presenting those examples.

14.2 Requirements Analysis Research

One of the findings from phase one was that developers find examples helpful when designing user interfaces (Tetzlaff and Schwartz 1991; Barber et al. 1991). Tasks such as establishing goals for a new interface, finding clever ideas to include in the new product, determining how specific widgets operate in a particular environment, and providing guidance for the appropriate task based upon the use of existing interface widgets, can all be addressed with an IDGS that effectively integrates interface examples. Presenting examples in a way that permits the developer to extract the needed information easily and apply it to the interface being designed is extremely important. For example, our experience shows that many developers turn to existing software for examples of how to design an interface rather than design guidelines and examples they may contain. In turning to existing software for examples, the design rationale and version evolution behind these examples are not evident, so developers must rely upon their own experience and intuition. Developers often copy many examples wholesale, based upon the specific widget characteristics, so that both good and bad aspects are carried over into their designs. To address this issue, we conducted a requirements analysis study to determine how designers would use examples in designing interfaces and solving design problems. The goal was to establish user interface requirements for the representation of examples in an IDGS.

Method

Twenty participants in the study came from technology companies (e.g. Unisys, Siemens, NCR, Bell South) in the Atlanta, Georgia area and represented various vertical industries (retail, medical, academia, and telecommunications). They were recruited because of their expertise in user interface development, but had various job responsibilities (e.g. systems analysis, user interface design, and software engineering).

Information on how to represent examples in an IDGS was gathered from three sources: a background questionnaire, an interview (to determine the steps taken in designing an user interface), and a participatory design task.

The design task required each participant to design a screen for representing interface examples and relevant information as part of an IDGS. The task provided participants with suggestions about what types of information they could include in the interface, but they were not required to use any of these suggestions. Additionally, participants could add information they felt should be included. Once participants decided what information should be included, they were asked to design the interface. This step was modeled after the Plastic Interface for Collaborative Technology Initiatives through Video Exploration (PICTIVE) style of requirements analysis (Muller 1991). PICTIVE was developed to enhance user participation in the interface designing process. We used a PICTIVE approach since it permits participants to create an interface quickly and to arrange, rearrange, add, and delete the information in the interface. Since this research was so preliminary and many developers have different ways of thinking about interface design, we were concerned that a group situation may not allow individuals to represent their own ideas. To avoid some of these group dynamics, we did not use multiple participants at the same time.

The PICTIVE approach asks participants to design a system using information provided by the experimenter in conjunction with information suggested by the participant. PICTIVE represents the computer screen with a sheet of paper. The paper screen is videotaped while participants create their interface. Information is printed on Post-It™ notes and small pieces of plastic so the information can be attached and reattached to the paper screen. Our approach differed slightly from PICTIVE. Since we were primarily interested in the final layout of information of the computer screen, we only audio taped participants' discussion of how their interfaces worked. We also used paper instead of paper and plastic. The final screen layout that each participant created was retained and later analyzed in conjunction with the audio tapes for interface requirements.

The questionnaire and interview data revealed the characteristics of the developers and the tasks that they perform related to user interface design and development. Seven interface designers, four systems analysts, three system support personnel, three information systems/data processing managers, and three engineers were interviewed. Participant job responsibilities included user interface design; programming, debugging, testing, maintaining, and installing software; troubleshooting; and solving hardware and software problems. Participant age ranged from 23 to 51 years. Most participants had no formal training in interface design, but all agreed that interface design is crucial to the design process. Participants worked on a variety of platforms including MS-DOS, Microsoft Windows, and OSF Motif. All were familiar with a variety of software including word processors, spreadsheets, and graphics packages. All were involved in interface design, but the amount of time spent designing the interface varied from minimal time to most of the time spent at work.

Results

The audio tapes and screens from the design task provided an account of how the participants (developers) perform the task of software design. From this task analysis a general user model of how the participants used examples in interface design was formulated. Most participants were very pragmatic in that they wanted only information relevant to the current interface problem. They wanted to specify the kind of information and examples retrieved, and be able to browse through it for relevance. In addition, participants mentioned that although they currently use interface examples to get ideas, they have to recreate the example in their own application.

The user interface requirements are based upon the necessary information that designers reported they needed to get their jobs done and what would satisfy the needs of the general user model. The main focus of this phase was to discover how examples should be represented in an IDGS. Some of the suggested ways of implementing requirements from the secondary research were confirmed and new requirements for IDGSs were identified. These new requirements are numbered consecutively from the previous three requirements from the secondary research section so that the first new requirement from this phase is numbered four.

Confirmed Implementations

- Provide design advice tailored to the developer's current design problem.

- Provide design rationale for design issues with examples of good and bad implementations.

- Provide the source code for user interface examples and a way to integrate the examples into the interface under development.

New Requirements

4. An IDGS should allow the developer to view information such as user interface examples, design rationales, design rules, version evolution, guidelines, principles, requirements, user profiles, and code to implement the example.

    - Interface examples and information should be represented in different forms (e.g., audio, textual, and active interfaces).

5. An IDGS should allow easy specification of what information and examples are of interest in order to allow the developer to focus on relevant information.

6. An IDGS should provide a mechanism to expand the base of examples and design guidelines provided.

    - An IDGS should provide some type of note pad to record ideas for the new interface which were generated from user interface examples.

Discussion

Although the PICTIVE method was useful for discovering user interface requirements, it unfortunately constrained the design solutions generated. One benefit was that participants could quickly and easily state their preferences for what information to include in an interface, design and modify their interface, and discuss how information within their interface interacted. Also, the PICTIVE method provided us with a screen layout for information which participants deemed relevant in representing examples. One drawback was that the users' prior experience influenced their design and how it functioned. Many designs were constrained by a participant's experience with a particular graphical user interface such as Microsoft Windows. For example, participants with Microsoft Windows experience used buttons, scroll bars, and menus and did not introduce new interface objects or information. As a result, the way the interface functioned was also constrained by the way these objects functioned. Rather than creating novel interface designs and functions, participants created systems that fit into the interface environment in which they work. Despite the constrained design solutions, many interesting design ideas were generated which are reflected in the prototypes presented next.

14.3 Rapid Prototyping

This section describes four different approaches to the issues and requirements that have been raised in the secondary research and requirements analysis phases previously reported. While only Prototype D meets all of the defined requirements for an effective IDGS, Prototypes A, B, and C show four different techniques which were prototyped and aimed at meeting specific requirements in different ways. Prototypes A and B show how two different applications were designed to allow a designer or developer to access information about low-level interface aspects, such as the elements of an "Open..." dialog box. They differ from each other in that Prototype A does not allow the user to interact with the user interface example, whereas Prototype B allows the user to click on objects within the user interface example to show the behavior associated with each object. Prototype C shows how design guidance about higher-level aspects of an interface could be presented based upon characteristics such as the users, environment of use, and task of the proposed user. Prototype D is our closest effort at specifying

Characteristic	Type of Interface Design Guidance System					
	Design Guide-lines	Software Tools	Prototype A	Prototype B	Prototype C	Prototype D
1. Ensures cognitive compatibility by supporting human factors techniques.	○	○	–	–	●	●
2. Works with accepted software development practices and tools.	–	●	●	●	●	●
3. Makes development easier and faster.	–	○	●	–	–	●
4. Provides user profiles, design rationales, principles, and requirements.	●	○	○	○	●	●
5. Can specify examples and other information for relevancy.	–	–	–	○	●	●
6. Provides a mechanism to expand the base of examples and design guidelines.	–	○	–	–	○	●

Table 14.1 *Attributes of different types of IDGSs. Legend:* ● *Yes,* ○ *Somewhat,* – *No.*

what the optimal IDGS would contain. Parts of Prototypes A, B, and C would be contained within modules of Prototype D. By coupling an understanding of the interface designer's task with existing approaches to IDGSs and appropriate new technologies (e.g., multimedia, expert systems, animation), we can supply a new and highly effective form of IDGS. Table 14.1 represents which requirements are met by each of the forms of design guidance previously reviewed (Design Guidelines and Software Tools), and which requirements are met by each of the prototypes (to follow). The prototypes, labeled A, B, C, and D, are presented in the following sections.

Prototype A

Figure 14.1 (Prototype A) shows a screen from a prototype IDGS system that uses animation to represent specific design rules through good and bad examples. It provides the code to generate each of the screens within the user interface examples. The user is presented a list of user interface elements and high-level concepts (not shown) on which design advice is available. In the example shown in Figure 14.1 the developer chose to get information on "Open" dialog boxes from the list. The user was then presented with an example of a bad dialog box (with one scroll list for both drives and files with a long title). When the user clicked on the "Continue" button, the screen changed through animation to show the improved screen (Figure 14.1) along with a rationale about an element such as "Scroll Box Titles" that was changed to make the interface better. If the user clicked on the "Continue" button again, another yellow box would pop up next to another aspect of the interface that was changed along with the rationale for doing so. By representing the before and after screens, the developer or designer sees an example of a good and bad solution to the same design problem. If the developer or designer desires to use the example in an interface, a click on the "Dump code to disk" button would produce the real code that created the object. Although this prototype could speed up development because it provides the code for the examples, it does have several limitations. It doesn't support cognitive compatibility between the end user and the developed interface, nor does it allow specification of examples. It also fails to allow the user to add new examples or guidelines to the IDGS.

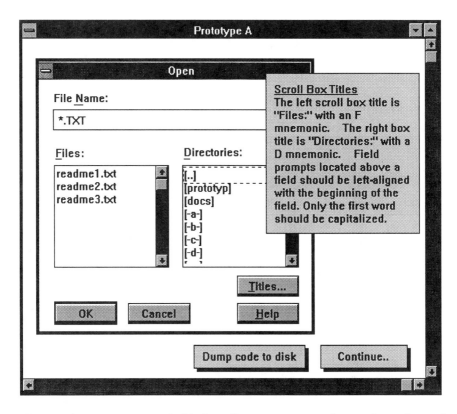

Figure 14.1 *A prototype IDGS that allows comparison of examples and use of code (Prototype A).*

Prototype B

Figure 14.2 (Prototype B) shows a screen from a prototype IDGS that allows a developer or designer to interact with an example application. As the user clicks on the various parts of the application, a help window updates to provide information about the relevant control. In Figure 14.2 the developer has clicked on the "Open" dialog box and has been supplied with information about that box. This interface shows some advantage over Prototype A in that the user can actually choose the interface object about which information is wanted rather than merely watching the slide-show-like animation in Prototype A. The "Topic Menu" buttons provide another means to access more in-depth information on specific topics. Prototype B is similar to the

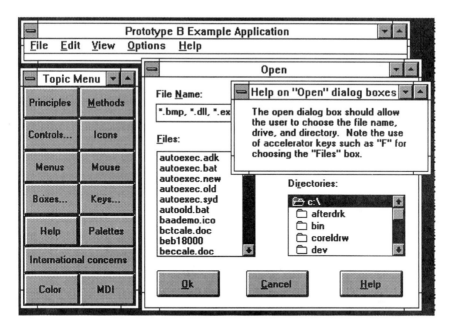

Figure 14.2 *A prototype IDGS that allows interaction with an example interface (Prototype B).*

example interface provided with Microsoft's® *The Windows Interface: An Application Design Guide* (1992). Like Microsoft's example interface, this prototype allows for interaction, but it does not provide the developer or designer with the code as a feature of the IDGS interface in a manner as easy as in Prototype A. In addition, it doesn't ensure cognitive compatibility by supporting human factors techniques. Although it provides some design rationales and principles, it doesn't allow consideration of particular types of users or tasks. No mechanism exists to make additions to the example and guideline base of this IDGS.

Prototype C

Figure 14.3 (Prototype C) shows a window from the prototype system called ASKJEF (Barber et al. 1991). Design principles and guidelines are displayed on the right-hand portion of the screen with arrows to the pertinent interface attributes. A history of viewed examples is logged in the window at the bottom of the screen automatically. In Figure 14.3 the developer has specified an interest in designing a touch screen application for ordering food in a

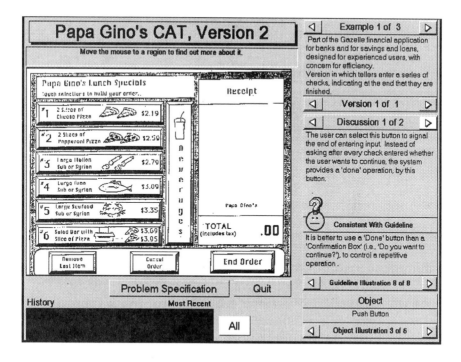

Figure 14.3 *A prototype IDGS with examples that addresses cognitive compatibility (Prototype C).*

restaurant that will be used by people who have little experience with computers. The example interface shown in the large window of Figure 14.3 is from the interface for the "Papa Gino's CAT" application. It allows developers and designers to specify end-user and environment characteristics to receive examples of interface screens that relate to their specific design problem. Examples were collected from products that had already been developed and for which data was available. The examples were combined with design principles and guidelines derived from an interface design course taught by Jef Raskin, one of the original designers of the Apple Macintosh. This prototype was developed in response to the expressed request by developers who wanted to see examples relevant to their own design problem. Unlike Prototypes A and B, prototype C allows the developer or designer to specify parameters about the design problem in order to retrieve design examples that are relevant to the current problem, such as intended environment, user's experience, and the task description. Another important

Figure 14.4 *A prototype IDGS that incorporates all characteristics listed earlier (Prototype D).*

aspect of this prototype is that it provides a design rationale for the suggested design solutions. As Carroll et al. (1991) point out, one advantage to using a tool like design rationale is that it allows descriptions and abstractions of principles and issues which can be tracked as technology changes. The system uses case-based reasoning to store and retrieve examples of interfaces which best match the user's specification of the design problem. In many cases the interface displays before and after examples of how the interface was made more usable through interface testing and redesign. The usability issues identified are described in windows that surround the example screen.

Prototype D

This final prototype (Figure 14.4) was designed to fulfill all of the requirements of an effective IDGS shown in Table 14.1. It supports the implementation of several well-defined human factors methods as well as user interface examples and high-level guidelines and principles. Each task area that a designer or developer would perform during an user-centered design approach to interface design is represented by an icon on the main menu bar shown in Figure 14.4. The small size of the main menu bar allows the IDGS to be running at the same time as the user's preferred development or prototyping tool in a windowed environment. Users could use any of the seven modules (Library Services, Requirements Analysis, Usability Testing, Icon and Menu Services, Prototyping, Expert Evaluation, or Help) while they are developing their interface. Moving the cursor over an icon makes the label for the module visible and selecting an icon brings the user into the selected module. Each module would have a tutorial on the implementation and appropriateness of the methods supported within that module. Although this prototype IDGS is not currently functional, it serves as a specification of the interface requirements for a comprehensive IDGS.

For a design question a developer or designer may want to start by reviewing the literature or guidelines on certain topics. This would be done by selecting the Library Services module (depicted by the books icon). This would bring up a window which allows the designer or developer to search for information on human-computer interaction topics from online databases, CD-ROMs, and in-house libraries. In addition, forms that are used for methods described in the other modules (Requirements Analysis, Usability Testing, Icon and Menu Services, Expert Evaluation) would be accessible in this module.

For assistance to determine the specific needs of the end user of the to-be-developed interface, the developer could select the Requirements Analysis module (notebook and pencil icon). This would bring up a window which explains methods for determining the needs of the end user and provides tools for each method. Tools provided are: a database of questions for conducting interviews, forms for structuring a task analysis, and a method for deriving user interface requirements through user interviews, focus groups, and consideration of system constraints. The outputs of these methods would be things such as an end-user profile, environment profile, and task descriptions. A tutorial would show the developer methods of translating these descriptions into user interface requirements.

The Usability Testing module (hand pushing a button icon) explains methods for testing the developer's or designer's design through usability testing techniques. It provides training to set up and run a usability test as well as how to analyze and interpret the resulting data. The tutorial takes the user of the IDGS through such topics as developing task scenarios, choosing test participants, techniques for running the test, rationale for the different types of tests, methods for the analysis of the data, and how the results can impact the design of the tested software. Templates for such things as task scenarios, participant questionnaires, consent forms, and data collection sheets would be provided. In addition, should the user of the IDGS want to collect data real-time during a usability test, there would be a data logging system which outputted the results in a form that is easily interpreted immediately following the test.

The Icon and Menu Services module (forms icon) explains methods for determining the structure and appearance of menus and icons for the interface, and provides tools for each method. Included would be online icon tests for how memorable, identifiable, recognizable, and appropriate the icons are for the targeted domain and end user. A tutorial on how to choose and recruit participants for tests is also available. An icon library should also be provided to log the results of previous tests. Menu tests would provide methods for testing existing menu structures as well as provide assistance to the developer in the implementation of appropriate and useful menu structures.

The Prototyping module (computer icon) provides access to the developer's or designer's preferred prototyping tool and a Critic that will evaluate designs for standards and guideline consistency. The need for the Critic comes from the secondary and requirements analysis research (reported earlier) which found that developers required that the guesswork be taken out of which standard or rule be implemented in what context. The Critic would analyze the designer's current prototype, identify areas that may be troublesome for the end user, and provide design solution alternatives. The critic idea was previously reviewed under software tools at the beginning of this chapter. As part of the proposed solution to interface problems, libraries of actual code should be provided. In addition to providing design solutions, the Critic would provide an added benefit—education on better interface design.

To support the creative process, the Prototyping module would provide the ability to create and arrange custom controls. This would allow developers to create a new widget and add it to a library for appropriate reuse. For example, a developer may find that the environment does not support a noneditable text widget. The inability for end users to discriminate between editable and noneditable text could cause them to try to edit text when they are not permitted to do so. The developer could create a widget that looked as if the text was etched into stone, store it in the library, and link it to an example topic. This would allow the developer to specify the end-user task as "reading text" and receive this widget as an example.

The Expert Evaluation module (magnifying glass icon) is intended to help the developer to conduct assessments based upon user interface style guides, industry standards, and theory related to human-computer interface design. This module would provide access to online style guides for LAF consistency as well as tutorials on assessment techniques for cognitive compatibility. Tutorials on methods like requirements analysis, task analysis, heuristic evaluation (Nielsen, Chapter 2), usability walkthrough, and cognitive walkthrough (Wharton et al., Chapter 5) would all be provided as well as software tools to assist in using them. Several tools have already been developed to assist in usability assessments (Rieman et al. 1991; Montaniz and Mack 1993a). This module would not only serve as an informational source to learn about methods of assessment, but also as a tool to support the developer in doing those assessments. This module is in response to the trend for many companies to rely upon experts to perform usability tests. Although these experts employ usability engineering methods, they are often only usable by people trained in the technique. In other words, the typical software developer is either not aware of the technique or unable to practice it. These methods are also inappropriately used after the interface has been developed, rather than early in the development cycle. In a competitive marketplace where time to market and development cost drive schedules, an analysis like usability assessment should be supported for use early in design to allow designers and developers to make their best attempts at the interface from the concept stage of product development. However, without the proper support, this will not occur. By supporting usability assessment methods in this module, it will help to integrate usability assessment techniques into the software development process.

The Help module ("i" icon) provides help on how to use the IDGS. It also provides assistance as to which methods are appropriate given the developer's specific system, interface, goals, end users, and schedule. This module should be well integrated and accessible from the other modules.

The last icon on the menu bar allows the user to exit the prototype.

Discussion

In order to positively affect design, future IDGSs should provide the features included in Table 14.1. Several approaches to those features were explored in Prototypes A through C which ultimately lead to the design of Prototype D. To test whether the concepts proposed in Prototype D met the needs of its potential users and to get a sense of possible alternative solutions, we conducted the focus group research reported next.

14.4   Focus Group Research

Phase four in our research was a focus group activity that took place to get user feedback on the concept and proposed interface in the earliest stages of the IDGS design. This research enabled us to determine if there was a qualitative demand for such a product by developers. By soliciting the candid feedback from developers on the role of human factors in the development process, as well as on IDGSs, we were able to determine if the prototype IDGS was a viable product concept. In addition, we hoped to confirm and discover requirements that would make the IDGS work well with the task of software development. The assumption was that if we could create an IDGS that was more closely suited for use during software development than the guideline documents and tools provided today, then human factors guidance may have a greater chance of affecting software design. It could also make software development faster and cheaper, producing designs from a user-centered perspective.

Method

Four focus groups, consisting of a total of 38 participants, were conducted. Two groups were held in New York City, one group was held in San Francisco, California, and one group was held in Santa Clara, California. Twenty participants were software development consultants. The remaining eighteen participants were in-house developers from several large companies (e.g. Citibank, Cyanamide, Prudential Insurance, and Bank of New York). Typical titles of the participants were: Systems Development Manager, Director of Systems Development, Senior Analyst, Senior Programmer, and Director or Vice-Presidents of MIS.

The focus group sessions consisted of the following steps: a group discussion about the current state of user interface design, presentation of a single-page introduction to the IDGS concept, a group discussion on the single page description and concept, a demonstration of the example IDGS, a follow-up discussion, and a questionnaire about user interface design practices in their respective companies. The following general issues were explored during the group discussions and questionnaires:

- What is the role of the end user and user interface in the application development cycle?

- What are developers' current frustrations with designing user interfaces and what tools did they currently use?
- What is the general reaction to the concept of an IDGS?
- What are the requirements for an IDGS to be both adopted and optimally useful in software development?

Overall Results

The focus group activity resulted in participant comments and questionnaire answers in relationship to the IDGS, as well as current user interface design practices. Overall, there was an expressed need to specify interfaces at the task level rather than at the level of individual widgets. This would mean that the developer could merely specify the end-user, environment, and task characteristics and the IDGS application would present the skeleton (or a semi-complete) interface design. Based upon experiences from the use of several other online tools, there was considerable skepticism towards the IDGS prototype. There was certainly a range of development philosophies, from primarily (computer) system-driven design to primarily user-centered design. Those who primarily considered the system in development felt that there was no problem with how user interfaces were developed and tended to get little feedback on their designs during development. These developers often expressed an adversarial relationship with end users. Primarily user-centered designers took their user interface designs to probable end users for feedback. Both groups used examples from commercially developed software packages, often inappropriately. There was a strongly expressed requirement that the IDGS would only be useful if kept current with the latest developments in interface design. The next section lists the basic conclusions, supported with the quotations and questionnaire data that led to those conclusions.

What is the Role of the End User and User Interface in the Application Development Cycle?

Based upon our sample of developers, several similarities were found. Developers currently consider the look-and-feel of the user interface at the concept and specification stage of the product development cycle. Although participants agreed that user interface is important, some participants felt that users will use what they design and that design support in the form of consultation was unneeded. Many participants did not perceive a problem worth solving with user interface design. One participant commented that he generally writes the interface without much reference to the users and that "they generally accept the result because when you give them an application, the way it looks is the way it is." Another said, "I would not send my developers to a course or buy (an IDGS) because I view the whole interface thing as a matter of stressing 'creeping elegance,' and not useful enough to spend money on." Still another stated, "I have never created an interface that I did not like."

There was also some consensus as to the tools used in development. The majority of development is occurring in the Microsoft Windows and OSF Motif environments. Microsoft's Software Development Kit (SDK) is by far the number one tool for developing applications. X toolkits are the number two tools used to develop product. Code generators and rapid prototypers were used by about 20 percent of the participants. The biggest frustration with user interface tools was that they do not generate usable code and ironically were depicted as difficult to learn and use.

Usability testing seems to be relatively popular; however, it was difficult to determine the extent to which this method is actually practiced. For instance, although 55 percent of the participants reported that they practice usability testing as part of their design process, only 14 percent had a facility or equipment to do so. The number one concern for practicing usability testing and other human factors methods was time. In addition, developers felt that usability was more important if there are large numbers of users, and if the users are nontechnical.

What Are Developers' Current Frustrations with Designing User Interfaces and What Tools Do They Currently Use?

Several limitations of current IDGSs, identified earlier in this chapter from the secondary research, were confirmed in the focus group. These are listed below followed by supporting quotes.

- Current style guidelines do little to ensure cognitive compatibility.

  "You better talk to the (end users) before you start (coding) to find out what your business requirements are."

  "In my shop, it (the GUI design) is driven by the user."

- Current style guidelines are not well suited for use during interface development.

"If (the user interface design guidance system prototype) was interactive with you on the computer as you are designing, even better. If it could interact with the developer rather than being just a knowledge base on a CD-ROM that must be searched and nobody uses."

- Current style guidelines are often too general.

"(A Major problem in developing user interfaces is) deciding on the standards."

"Because the CUA standard is loosely defined, we find ourselves simply going into those packages and seeing how they handle certain situations . . . and mimicking that behavior."

- Current style guidelines are often difficult to use.

"Word and Excel are the kind of applications that really set the standards for style and so on . . . (we) use these as a base point, rather than any particular set of rules, whether it's CUA or anything else."

- Current style guidelines are perceived as limiting creativity.

Forty-seven percent of respondents indicated that current user interface design standards inhibit flexibility and that was their number one problem.

- Developers use examples to make user interface design decisions.

"We've spent a lot of time looking at Word and Excel and exactly how they do things and making sure we follow their procedures . . . because (our end users) are familiar with it."

"(To design a GUI), we usually take existing Windows programs and see how they work. We take Excel and say, Well, Excel has this grid down here and the data field up there, and we try to emulate that as much as possible."

What Is the General Reaction to the Concept of an IDGS?

Although views were mixed, there is a strong preference for the adoption of an IDGS. Some respondents wanted a full toolset whereas others wanted selected pieces of the interface that they were shown.

- Overall, there was a perceived need for an IDGS.

Seventy-seven percent of participants thought that their company would benefit from employment of an online IDGS.

". . . it looks like something like this is packaging that whole kind of intuitive understanding process into one unit that just makes it a lot easier to access the information you need."

"I like the testing capabilities. It sounds like in here that there's a high emphasis on what works, in making sure what you design works."

"If it works to help deliver an improved needs-finding (requirements definition) process assisted by expert analysis, then I'm for it. There is too much isolation in development."

- Some thought that the scope is too broad.

"Break it apart, because as a whole, it's too ambitious to be practical."

- Interest was shown in a library product.

"There are certain things in the product that I would like today that have nothing to do with helping me program. I would like the library search, independent of the tools that will do anything for me. . . I would like to do look ups on specific design ideas. So, I am separating the product into two parts—the library part which they could turn out a lot faster."

". . . the human factors library on CD-ROM I would certainly find valuable."

"I really thought the library was the best idea. I mean as a separate product I think that is great and I would love that, because again I would like to see other peoples' experience looking at types of buttons, the way things are set up. To be able to get that database, that is great. And it does not even have to generate code from that, because just to be able to see it as a library book. I think a library where individuals' experiences and design ideas reside is the single most valuable piece."

- Course work was suggested as an alternative.

"Don't write a software program; it will take too long and you won't make any money. Create a course, maybe a one-week course, and at the end of it you get a CD-ROM with your knowledge base, with human factors literature on it for free. Because, obviously these guys have their act together when it comes to psychology. They know the psychology of visuals, and that's great. And what we need more of is trained programmers, not tools to help us do something."

- Many participants felt all that was needed was a magazine or book.

"I think that a good book on the technique might be valuable. . . If I want to get an understanding of something, I want to take a book home, sit in my chair, and read it to gain an overview. I'm not quite convinced that this is such a product."

"I was thinking more of a magazine, a subscription, because then you could have quarterly, bimonthly, monthly updates on the latest things happening in a particular area."

"It could be a magazine like the *WordPerfect* magazine, that comes out monthly with the latest updates and happenings, and even includes a little disk of macros that you can feed into your system if you want.

- Integration with a computer assisted software engineering (CASE) tool was seen as a viable alternative.

Most of the respondents could see value to the tool being an add-in GUI design tool to a more complete CASE environment, especially if it were integrated, offering direct input into the development environment.

- The IDGS could also serve as a tutorial on interface design or standards.

"The system could be of use to novices who are just beginning development, and perhaps for maintaining standards across several applications within an organization."

"But with parts of it online for frequent updating, it would be a useful tool to those people who are just starting to develop GUI applications."

What Are the Requirements for an IDGS to be Both Adopted and Optimally Useful in Software Development?

There was confirmation on some of the requirements identified earlier in the secondary research and requirements analysis. The numbers preceding these requirements correspond to those in Table 14.1. Requirements are listed below with supporting quotations from respondents in the focus group.

1. Ensure that the developed user interface is congruent with how end users perform tasks (cognitive compatibility) by supporting the use of well-defined human factors methods.

"We think it's intuitive and then it gets to the user and it's not intuitive to them."

"We've had to go back and redo a lot of our initial thoughts in terms of what we thought would be a really good interface."

"Sometimes we're programming for ourselves instead of the user. We have to realize who our users are, if they're sophisticated or not."

"Sometimes, as a GUI designer, you design things one way and a user will come around with a completely different approach to using it that you hadn't even thought of."

Specific methods:

Usability Testing

> Respondents felt that if the IDGS could be used to build test cases for GUIs where they could do usability tests based upon models of users, it would be "very helpful" because the current products are either lacking this capability or do not perform this task very well.

Requirements Analysis

> Respondents felt that this function was considered "ideal" because requirements gathering is an important part of the development cycle and would be beneficial for ensuring that all of the "gaps" have been filled.

Prototyping

> The ability to present a model early in the development process, before making any commitments, could prevent wasted development time and effort in the end.

Expert Analysis

> "Certainly, products like this that help to build test model type systems really quick are very helpful."

> "The thing that differentiates this from what's currently out there is the expert human processing to understand the cognitive analysis."

2. An IDGS must be online and be designed to work with the accepted software development practices and tools.

"I would like it better if it were online within my development environment, sort of like a spell-checker DLL that I can call on for advice at key points in development, rather than a totally separate product."

"If you could use it for both design and development, it could really speed up development."

"I think it would be better to use the knowledge (about human-machine interface design) and come up with widgets or parts that people can put into their applications."

"Without the ability to produce something I can use, it's not very useful to me from a productivity standpoint."

"What they are describing is effectively a person looking over your shoulder who constantly knows the newest and the best ideas about design, saying nah, you really don't want to do that, you do this. It combines library with the consultant idea."

"If it were interactive with you on the computer as you are designing, even better. If it could interact with the developer rather than being just a knowledge base on a CD-ROM that must be searched and nobody uses."

3. An IDGS must make development easier and faster, not just improve the quality of the interface.

"I see the distinction between design and development. However, I would be interested only if the tool could be used for both design and development. If it speeded up development, then I think you'd finding a lot more interest than in a more abstract kind of design tool."

4. Provide design advice tailored to the developer's current design problem.

"It always seems like the basics are covered very well and the intricate things are not covered at all." . . . "Right, Not even documented."

"I don't know how they can keep it up-to-date with this type of information (such as the latest on pen-based interfaces) for me to be able to use it. . . (For) me to use it, they need to already have all that pen information in (the library) . . ."

5. Provide a mechanism to expand the base of examples and design guidelines.

One participant wanted "a little more than was described" with actual modules of objects for events, association of events with code. "It should have entry points for programmers, so unique code can be added to an existing library of user interface code."

"I think the idea of creating the 'Experience Library,' also letting you add in your system, saying what your own experiences have been, adding that information to the body of knowledge is good, especially if you can then distribute this information throughout the corporation."

Two new requirements were also identified.

6. There is a need for task-based examples that are reused in development.

"I see the distinction between design and development. However, I would be interested only if the tool could be used for both design and development. If it speeded up development, then I think you'd finding a lot more interest than in a more abstract kind of design tool."

7. An IDGS system must be kept current.

"The main thing is not only how relevant but how up-to-date, because . . . it all changes so often."

"Can they keep the system current? . . . How current can the examples be, because (interfaces) are changing all the time."

"The main thing is not only how relevant but how up-to-date, because of course it all changes so often."

"If (some vendor) adopted (human factors methods) . . . offered this type of tool set and demonstrated that indeed they had successfully applied it, and improved their product offerings and now were making it available for you also to buy into, then I think that would be one scenario for establishing (human factors) and the tool set and proving its success."

Future Direction

Supporting developers and designers in interface design is perhaps the ultimate challenge for a human factors professional. We must not only describe all that is known about interface principles, guidelines, and design rules, but we must also practice human factors in the creation of the system. If designed and implemented correctly, IDGSs are a way for human factors to get interface design guidance into the mainstream of software development. This research must be considered by human factors professionals who are serious about trying to introduce methods and design principles into the mainstream of software development. The trend of creating tools for developers without consideration of the developers, their tasks, and environment of use is not congruent with the user-centered design approach that is preached by the human factors community. This research will serve to provide requirements for a tool that will fit designers' and developers' needs. This is one step toward more effectively linking design and evaluation.

The data from all phases of this research is being used to generate further product concepts. Based upon the results of the previously reported research a functional prototype needs to be designed and evaluated. Further studies need to be performed to evaluate how effective the proposed IDGS (Prototype D) is in affecting the efficiency of the development process and the quality of the resulting interface relative to one designed and developed with traditional methods of software design.

Bibliography

A

Ackerman, A. F., Buchwald, L. S., and Lewski, F. H. 1989. Software inspections: An effective verification process. *IEEE Software* **6**, 3 (May): 31–36.

Anderson, J. R. 1987. Skill acquisition: Compilation of weak-method solutions. *Psychological Review* **94**: 192–211.

Anderson, J. R. 1993. *Rules of the mind.* Hillsdale, NJ: Lawrence Erlbaum Associates.

Anderson, J. R., Farrell, R., and Sauers, R. 1984. Learning to program in LISP. *Cognitive Science* **8**: 87–130.

Anderson, J. R., Boyle, C. F., and Yost, G. 1985. The geometry tutor. *Proceedings of the Ninth International Joint Conference on Artificial Intelligence,* 1985 (Los Angeles, CA, August 18–23), Vol. **1**: 1–7. Los Altos, CA: Morgan Kaufmann Publishers, Inc.

Anderson, J. R., Conrad, F. G., and Corbett, A. T. 1989. Skill acquisition and the LISP Tutor. *Cognitive Science* **13**: 467–506.

Anderson, J. R., Boyle, C. F., Corbett, A., and Lewis, M. W. 1990. Cognitive modelling and intelligent tutoring. *Artificial Intelligence* **42**: 7–49.

Anderson, J. R., Corbett, A. T., Fincham, J., Hoffman, D., and Pelletier, R. 1992. General principles for an intelligent tutoring architecture. In *Cognitive Approaches to Automated Instruction,* edited by Regian, J. W., and Shute, V. J., 81–106. Hillsdale, NJ: Lawrence Erlbaum Associates.

Andriole, S. J. 1987. Storyboard prototyping for requirements verification. *Large Scale Systems Information Decision Technology* **12**: 231–247.

B

Barber, J., Bhatta, S., Goel, A., Jacobson, M., Pearce, M., Penberthy, L., Shankar, M., Simpson, R., and Stroulia, E. 1991. AskJef: Integration of case-based and multimedia technologies for interface design support. *Proceedings of the 2nd Inter. Workshop on Artificial Intelligence in Design* (Pittsburgh, PA, June 22–25). Kluwer Academic Publishers.

Barnard, P. 1991. Bridging between basic theories and the artifacts of human-computer interaction. In *Designing Interaction: Psychology at the Human-Computer Interface*, edited by Carroll, J. M., 103–127. New York: Cambridge University Press.

Barnard, P., Hammond, N., Morton, J., Long, J., and Clark, I. 1981. Consistency and compatibility in human-computer dialogue. *International Journal of Man-Machine Studies* **15**: 87–134.

Bastien, C., and Scapin, D. L. 1991. A validation of ergonomic criteria for the evaluation of user interfaces. *SIGCHI Bulletin* **23**, 4 (October): 54–55.

Bellotti, V. 1988. Implications of current design practice for the use of HCI techniques. In *People and Computers IV*, edited by Jones, D. M., and Winder, R., 13–34. Cambridge: Cambridge University Press.

Bellotti, V. M. E. 1993. Integrating theoreticians' and practitioners' perspective with design rationale. *Proceedings ACM/IFIP INTERCHI'93 Conference* (Amsterdam, The Netherlands, April 24–29): 101–106.

Bell, B. 1992. Using programming walkthroughs to design a visual language. *Technical Report CU-CS-581-92*. Ph.D. diss., University of Colorado, Boulder, CO.

Bell, B., Citrin, W., Lewis, C., Rieman, J., Weaver, R., Wilde, N., and Zorn, B. (1994). The programming walkthrough: a structured method for assessing the writability of programming languages. *Software Practice and Experience* **24**, 1 (January): 1–25.

Bennett, J. 1984. Managing to meet usability requirements: Establishing and meeting software development goals. In *Visual Display Terminals*, edited by Bennett, J., Case, D., Sandelin, J., and Smith, M., 161–184. Englewood Cliffs, NJ: Prentice-Hall.

Bias, R. 1991. Walkthroughs: Efficient collaborative testing. *IEEE Software* **8**, 5 (September): 94–95.

Bias, R. G., and Mayhew, D. J. 1994. *Cost-Justifying Usability*. Boston: Academic Press.

Bias, R. G., Lanzetta, T. M., and Scanlon J. 1993. Consensus requirements: Low- and high-tech methods for discerning system requirements from groups of users. In the *Proceedings of the IEEE International Conference on Systems, Man, and Cybernetics* (Le Touquet, France, October).

Booth, P. A. 1990. Identifying and interpreting design errors. *International Journal of Human-Computer Interaction* **4**, 2: 307–332.

C

Card, S. K., Moran, T. P., and Newell, A. 1983. *The Psychology of Human-Computer Interaction*. Hillsdale, NJ: Erlbaum.

Card, S., Robertson, G., and Mackinlay, J. 1991. The information visualizer, an information workspace. *Proceedings ACM CHI'91 Conference* (New Orleans, LA, April 28–May 2): 181–188.

Carroll, J. M. 1994. *Use-Oriented Design Representations*. Reading, MA: Addison-Wesley.

Carroll, J. M, and Kellogg, W. A. 1989. Artifact as theory nexus: Hermeneutics meets theory-based design. *Proceedings ACM CHI'89 Conference* (Austin, TX, April 30–May 4): 7–14.

Carroll, J., and Mack, R. 1984. Actively learning to use a word processor. In *Cognitive Aspects of Skilled Typewriting*, edited by Cooper, W. New York: Springer-Verlag.

Carroll, J. M., and Rosson, M. B. 1987. The paradox of the active user. In *Interfacing Thought: Cognitive Aspects of Human-Computer Interaction*, edited by Carroll, J. M., 80–111. Cambridge: Bradford Books/MIT Press.

Carroll, J. M., and Rosson, M. B. 1990. Human-computer interaction scenarios as a design representation. *Proc. IEEE HICSS-23, 23rd Hawaii International Conference on System Sciences* (Hawaii, January 2–6), **Vol. II**: 555–561.

Carroll, J. M., and Rosson, M. B. 1991. Deliberated evolution: Stalking the View Matcher in design space. *Human-Computer Interaction* **6**, 3&4: 281–318.

Carroll, J. M., and Rosson, M. B. 1992. Getting around the task-artifact cycle: How to make claims and design by scenario. *ACM Transactions on Information Systems* **10**, 2 (April): 181–212.

Carroll, J., Mack, R., and Kellogg, W. 1987. Interface metaphors and user interface design. In *Handbook of Human-Computer Interaction*, edited by Helander, M., 67–85. Amsterdam: Elsevier Science Publishers.

Carroll, J. M., Kellogg, W. A., and Rosson, M. B. 1991. The task-artifact cycle. In *Designing Interaction: Psychology at the Human-Computer Interface*, edited by Carroll, J. M., 74–102. New York: Cambridge University Press.

Carroll, J. M., Singley, M. K., and Rosson, M. B. 1992. Integrating theory development with design evaluation. *Behaviour & Information Technology* **11**, 5: 247–255.

Chapanis, A., and Budurka, W. J. 1990. Specifying human-computer interface requirements. *Behaviour & Information Technology* **9**, 6: 479–492.

Chignell, M. H., and Valdez, J. F. 1991. Truncated experiments and field experiments in usability engineering. In *Proceedings of the IEEE International Conference on Systems, Man, and Cybernetics*: 1349–1353.

Clarke, L. 1991. The use of scenarios by user interface designers. In *People and Computers VI*, edited by Diaper, D., and Hammond, N., 103–115. Cambridge: Cambridge University Press.

Conklin, P. 1991. Bringing Usability Effectively into Product Development. Paper presented at the workshop on *Human-Computer Interface Design: Success Cases, Emerging Methods, and Real World Context* (Boulder, CO, July 24–26).

Cool, C., Fish, R. S., Kraut, R. E., and Lowery, C. M. 1992. Iterative design of video communication systems. *Proc. ACM CSCW'92 Conf. Computer-Supported Cooperative Work* (Toronto, Canada, November 1–4): 25–32.

Cuomo, D. L., and Bowen, C. D. 1992. Stages of user activity model as a basis for user-system interface evaluations. In *Proceedings of the Human Factors Society 36th Annual Meeting* (Atlanta, GA, October 12–16): 1254–1258.

D

de Souza, F., and Bevan, N. 1990. The use of guidelines in menu interface design. *Proc. IFIP INTERACT'90 Third Intl. Conf. Human-Computer Interaction* (Cambridge, U.K., 27–31 August): 435–440.

Desurvire, H. 1989. Usability Testing Results for the Project Database. *Internal Document TM-TAP-014420.* Piscataway, NJ: Bell Communications Research.

Desurvire, H. W., and Thomas, J. C. 1993. Enhancing the performance of interface evaluators. *Proc. Human Factors and Ergonomic Society 37th Annual Meeting* (Seattle, WA, October 11–15).

Desurvire, H., Lawrence, D., and Atwood, M. 1991. Empiricism versus judgment: Comparing user interface evaluation methods on a new telephone-based interface. *ACM SIGCHI Bulletin* **23**, 4 (October): 58–59.

Desurvire, H. W., Kondziela, J. M., and Atwood, M. E. 1992. What is gained and lost when using evaluation methods other than empirical testing. In *People and Computers VII*, edited by Monk, A., Diaper, D., and Harrison, M. D., 89–102. Cambridge: Cambridge University Press. A shorter version of this paper is available in the *Digest of Short Talks presented at CHI'92* (Monterey, CA, May 7): 125–126.

Douglas, S., and Moran, T. 1983. Learning text-editing semantics by analogy. *Proceedings ACM CHI'83 Conference* (December 12–15, Boston, MA): 207–211.

Dykstra, D. J. 1993. *A Comparison of Heuristic Evaluation and Usability Testing: The Efficacy of a Domain-Specific Heuristic Checklist.* Ph.D. diss., Department of Industrial Engineering, Texas A&M University, College Station, TX.

E

Eason, K. D. 1983. Methodological issues in the study of human factors in tele-information systems. *Behaviour & Information Technology* **2**: 357–364.

Egan, D. E. 1988. Individual differences in human-computer interaction. In *Handbook of Human-Computer Interaction*, edited by Helander, M., 543–568. Amsterdam: Elsevier Science Publishers.

Ehn, P. 1988. *Work-Oriented Design of Computer Artifacts.* Stockholm, Sweden: Arbetlivs-centrum.

Engelbeck, G. E. 1986. Exceptions to generalizations: Implications for formal models of human-computer interaction. *Unpublished Masters Thesis*, Department of Psychology, University of Colorado, Boulder.

F

Fagan, M. E. 1976. Design and code inspection to reduce errors in program development. *IBM Systems Journal* **15**, 3: 182–211.

Fagan, M. E. 1986. Advances in software inspection. *IEEE Transactions on Software Engineering* **12**, 7 (July): 744–751.

Fischer, G. 1987. A critic for Lisp. *Proceedings of the 10th International Joint Conference on Artificial Intelligence*: 177–184.

Fischer, G. 1991. Supporting learning on demand with design environments. *Proceedings of the International Conference on the Learning Sciences, 1991* (Evanston, IL, August): 165–172. Charlottesville, VA: Association for the Advancement of Computing in Education.

Fischer, G., Lemke, A. C., Mastaglio, T., and Morch, A. I. 1990. Using critics to empower users. *Proceedings ACM CHI'90 Conference* (Seattle, Washington, April 1–5): 337–346.

Fitts, P. M., and Posner, M. I. 1967. *Human Performance.* Basic Concepts in Psychology Series. Belmont, CA: Wadsworth Publishing Company, Inc. Brooks/Cole Publishing Company.

Fox, J. 1992. The effects of using a hypertext tool for selecting design guidelines. *Proceedings of the Human Factors Society 36th Annual Meeting* (Atlanta, GA, October 12–16): 428–432.

Freedman, D., and Weinberg, G. M. 1990. *Handbook of Walkthroughs, Inspections, and Technical Reviews: Evaluating Programs, Projects, and Products,* Third Edition. New York: Dorset House.

Frost, R. J. 1930. *The Complete Poems of Robert Frost.* Holt, Rinehart & Winston, Inc.

G

Gilb, T. 1988. *Principles of Software Engineering Management.* Wokingham, England: Addison-Wesley.

Golembiewski, G. 1987. On and off the playing field. *Circuits Manufacturing* **27**: 37–38.

Good, M. 1988. User Interface Consistency in the DECwindows Program, *Digital Equipment Corporation Technical Report* **DEC-TR 564**, July 1988.

Good, M. 1989a. Developing the XUI style. In *Coordinating User Interfaces for Consistency,* edited by Nielsen, J., 75–88. Boston: Academic Press.

Good, M. 1989b. Seven experiences with contextual field research. *ACM SIGCHI Bulletin* **20**, 4: 25–33.

Good, M. 1992. Participatory design of a portable force feedback device. *Proceedings ACM CHI'92 Conference* (Monterey, CA, May 3–7): 439–446.

Good, M., Spine, T. M., Whiteside, J., and George, P. 1986. User-derived impact analysis as a tool for usability engineering. *Proceedings ACM CHI'86 Conference* (Boston, April 13–17): 241–246.

Gould, J. D., and Lewis, C. H. 1983. Designing for usability: Key principles and what designers think. *Proceedings ACM CHI'83 Conference* (Boston, MA, December 12–15): 50–53.

Gould, J. D., and Lewis, C. H. 1985. Designing for usability: Key principles and what designers think. *Communications of the ACM* **28**, 3 (March): 300–311.

Gould, J., Boies S. J., and Lewis, C. 1991. Making usable, useful, productivity-enhancing computer applications. *Communications of the ACM* **34**, 1 (January): 74–85.

Gray, W. D., John, B. E., and Atwood, M. E. 1992. The précis of project Ernestine or an overview of a validation of GOMS. *Proceedings ACM CHI'92 Conference* (Monterey, CA, May 3–7): 307–312.

Greenbaum, J., and Kyng, M. 1991. *Design at Work*. Hillsdale, NJ: Lawrence Erlbaum.

Greeno, J. G., and Simon, H. A. 1988. Problem solving and reasoning. In *Steven's Handbook of Experimental Psychology*, edited by Atkinson, R. C., Herrnstein, R., Lindzey, G., and Luce, R. D. New York: John Wiley and Sons.

Grudin, J. 1989. The case against user interface consistency. *Communications of the ACM* **32**, 10 (October): 1164–1173.

Grudin, J. 1991. Systematic sources of suboptimal interface design in large product development organizations. *Human-Computer Interaction* **6**: 147–196.

Grudin, J., and Poltrock, S. E. 1989. User interface design in large corporations: Coordination and communication across disciplines. *Proceedings ACM CHI'89 Conference* (Austin, TX, April 30–May 4): 197–203.

H

Hackman, G. S., and Biers, D. W. 1992. Team usability testing: Are two heads better than one? In *Proceedings of the Human Factors Society Annual Meeting*: 1205–1209.

Hackman, J. R., and Morris, C. G. 1975. Group tasks, group interaction process, and group performance effectiveness: A review and proposed integration. In *Advances in Experimental Social Psychology*, **8**, edited by Berfkowitz, L. New York: Academic Press.

Heidegger, M. 1962. *Being and Time* (Trans. J Macquarrie and E. Robinson). New York: Harper and Row.

Hellriegel, D., and Slocum, J. W. 1992. *Management*, 6th Edition. Reading, MA: Addison-Wesley.

Hewlett-Packard Company, Corporate Human Factors Engineering 1990. *SoftGuide: Guidelines For Usable Software*. Palo Alto, CA.

Holleran, P. A. 1991. A methodological note on pitfalls in usability testing, *Behaviour & Information Technology* **10**, 5: 345–357.

Holtzblatt, K., and Jones, S. 1990. Contextual Inquiry: Principles and Practice, *Digital Equipment Corporation, Technical Report* **DEC-TR 729**, Oct 1990.

HUSAT 1990. *The HUFIT Planning, Analysis and Specification Toolset*. HUSAT Research Institute of Technology, Loughborough, U.K.

Hutchins, E., Hollan, J., and Norman, D. 1986. Direct manipulation interfaces. In *User Centered System Design: New Perspectives on Human-Computer Interaction*, edited by Norman, D., and Draper, S., 87–124. Hillsdale, NJ: Erlbaum.

I

IBM 1991. *Systems Application Architecture, Common User Access, Guide to User Interface Design*. International Business Machines Corporation, Armonk, NY. (Order #: **SC34-4289**.)

International Standards Organization 1990. Working Paper of *ISO 9241 Part 10*, Dialogue Principles, Version 2, ISO/TC 159/SC4/WG5 N155, 1990.

J

Jeffries, R. J., and Desurvire, H. W. 1992. Usability testing vs. heuristic evaluation: Was there a contest? *ACM SIGCHI Bulletin* **24**, 4 (October): 39–41.

Jeffries, R., Miller, J. R., Wharton, C., and Uyeda, K. M. 1991. User interface evaluation in the real world: A comparison of four techniques. *Proceedings ACM CHI'91 Conference* (New Orleans, LA, April 28–May 2): 119–124.

Johnson, J., Roberts, T. L., Verplank, W., Smith, D. C., Irby, C. H., Beard, M., and Mackey, K. 1989. The Xerox Star: a retrospective. *IEEE Computer* **22**, 9 (September):11–29.

Johnson, J. A., Nardi, B. A., Zarmer, C. L., and Miller, J. R. 1993. ACE: Building interactive graphical application. *Communications of the ACM* **36**, 4: 41–55.

Jørgensen, A. H. 1990. Thinking-aloud in user interface design: A method promoting cognitive ergonomics. *Ergonomics* **33**, 4: 501–507.

K

Karat, C. 1990a. Cost-benefit analysis of iterative usability testing. *Proc. IFIP INTERACT'90 Third International Conference on Human-Computer Interaction* (Cambridge, U.K., August 27–31): 351–356.

Karat, C. 1990b. Cost-benefit analysis of usability engineering techniques. *Proceedings of the Human Factors Society Annual Conference* (Orlando, FL, October): 839–843.

Karat, C. 1991. Cost-benefit and business case analysis of usability engineering. *Proceedings ACM CHI'91 Conference* (New Orleans, LA, April 28–May 2), Tutorial Notes.

Karat, C. 1992. Cost-justifying human factors support on development projects. *Human Factors Society Bulletin* **35**, 11: 1–4.

Karat, C. 1994. A business case approach to usability cost justification. In *Cost-Justifying Usability*, edited by Bias, R., and Mayhew, D. Boston: Academic Press.

Karat, C., Campbell, R. L., and Fiegel, T. 1992. Comparison of empirical testing and walkthrough methods in user interface evaluation. *Proceedings ACM CHI'92 Conference* (Monterey, CA, May 3–7): 397–404.

Karat, J. 1988. Software evaluation methodologies. In *Handbook of Human-Computer Interaction*, edited by Helander, M., 891–903. Amsterdam: Elsevier Science Publishers.

Karat, J. 1994. Scenario use at various stages of a product's development. In *Scenario-Based Design: Envisioning Work and Technology in System Development*, edited by Carroll, J. M. Book under preparation.

Karat, J., and Bennett, J. 1991a. Working within the design process: Supporting effective and efficient design. In *Designing Interaction: Psychology at the Human Computer Interface*, edited by Carroll, J. M., 269–285. Boston: Cambridge University Press.

Karat, J., and Bennett, J. L. 1991b. Using scenarios in design meetings—A case study example. In *Taking Software Design Seriously: Practical Techniques for Human-Computer Interaction Design*, edited by Karat, J., 63–94. Boston: Academic Press.

Kepner-Tregoe, Inc. 1982. *Workshop on Problem Solving and Decision Making.*

Kieras, D. E., and Polson, P. G. 1985. An approach to the formal analysis of user complexity. *International Journal of Man-Machine Studies* **22**: 365–394.

Knight, J. C., and Myers, E. A. 1993. An improved inspection technique. *Communications of the ACM* **36**, 11 (November): 51–61.

Kuhn, T. 1962. *The Structure of Scientific Revolutions.* Chicago: University of Chicago Press.

L

Langlotz, C. P., and Shortliffe, E. H. 1983. Adapting a consultant system to critique user plans. *International Journal of Man-Machine Studies* **19**: 479–496.

Lewis, C. 1982. Using the 'thinking-aloud' method in cognitive interface design, *IBM Research Report* **RC 9265 (#40713)**, IBM Thomas J. Watson Research Center, Yorktown Heights, NY.

Lewis, C. 1988. How and why to learn why: Analysis-based generalization of procedures. *Cognitive Science* **12**: 211–256.

Lewis, C., and Mack, R. 1982. Learning to use a text editor: Evidence from thinking aloud protocols. *Proceedings ACM CHI'82 Conference* (Gaithersburg, MD, March 15–17): 387–392.

Lewis, C., and Norman, D. 1986. Designing for error. In *User Centered System Design: New Perspectives on Human-Computer Interaction*, edited by Norman, D., and Draper, S., 411–432. Hillsdale, NJ: Erlbaum.

Lewis, C., and Polson, P. G. 1991. Cognitive walkthroughs: A method for theory-based evaluation of user interfaces. Tutorial Notes for *CHI'91* (New Orleans, LA, April 27 – May 2).

Lewis, C., Polson, P., Wharton, C., and Rieman, J. 1990. Testing a walkthrough methodology for theory-based design of walk-up-and-use interfaces. *Proceedings ACM CHI'90 Conference* (Seattle, WA, April 1–5): 235–242.

Lewis, C., Polson, P. G., and Rieman, J. 1991a. Cognitive walkthrough forms and instructions. Institute of Cognitive Science *Technical Report #ICS 91-14*. University of Colorado, Boulder, CO, 80309.

Lewis, C., Rieman, J., and Bell, B. 1991b. Problem-centered design for expressiveness and facility in a graphical programming system. *Human-Computer Interaction* **6**, 3&4: 319–355.

Lewis, C., Polson, P., Rieman, J., Wharton, C., and Wilde, N. 1992. *CHI'92 Tutorial Notes. Cognitive walkthroughs: A method for theory-based evaluation of user interfaces.* Presented at CHI'92, Conference on Human-Computer Interaction (Monterey, CA, May 4).

Lewis, J., Henry, S., and Mack, R. 1990. Integrated office system benchmarks: a case study. *Proc. IFIP INTERACT'90: Third Intl. Conference on Human-Computer Interaction* (Cambridge, U.K., August 27–31): 337–343.

M

MacIntyre, F., Estep, K. W., and Sieburth, J. M. 1990. Cost of user-friendly programming. *Journal of Forth Application and Research* **6**, 2: 103–115.

Mack, R. 1991. Understanding and learning text-editing skills: Observations on the role of new user expectations. In *Cognition, Computing and Cooperation*, edited by Robertson, S., Black, J., and Zachery, W., 304–337. Norwood, NJ: Ablex.

Mack, R. 1992. Questioning design: Toward methods for supporting user-centered software engineering. In *Questions and Information Systems*, edited by Lauer, T., Peacock, E., and Graesser, A., 101–130. Hillsdale, NJ: Erlbaum.

Mack, R., and Montaniz, F. 1990. A comparison of touch and mouse interaction techniques for a graphical windowing software environment. *Proceedings of the 35th Annual Meeting of the Human Factors Society* (San Francisco, CA, September 2–6): 286–289.

Mack, R. L., and Nielsen, J. 1993. Usability inspection methods. *ACM SIGCHI Bulletin* **25**, 1 (January): 28–33.

Mack, R., Lewis, C., and Carroll, J. 1983. Learning to use a word processor: Problems and prospects. *ACM Transactions on Office Information Systems* **1**, 3: 254–271.

MacLean, A., and McKerlie, D. 1994. Design space analysis and use-representations. In *Scenario-Based Design: Envisioning Work and Technology in System Development*, edited by Carroll, J. M. Book under preparation.

MacLean, A., Young, R. M., and Moran, T. P. 1989. Design rationale: The argument behind the artifact. *Proceedings ACM CHI'89 Conference* (Austin, TX, April 30–May 4): 247–252.

MacLean, A., Bellotti, V., Young, R. M., and Moran, T. P. 1991a. Reaching through analogy: A design rationale perspective. *Proc. ACM CHI'91* (New Orleans, LA, 28 April–2 May): 167–172.

MacLean, A., Young, R. M., Bellotti, V. M. E., and Moran, T. P. 1991b. Questions, options, and criteria: Elements of design space analysis. *Human-Computer Interaction* **6**, 3&4: 201–250.

MacLean, A., Bellotti, V., and Shum, S. 1993. Developing the design space with design space analysis. In *Computers, Communication and Usability: Design Issues, Research and Methods for Integrated Services*, edited by Byerley, P., Barnard, P., and May, J., 197–220. Amsterdam: Elsevier Science Publishers.

Martin, J., and McClure, C. 1983. *Software Maintenance: The Problem and Its Solution.* Englewood Cliffs, NJ: Prentice-Hall.

Mayhew, D. 1992. *Principles and Guidelines in User Interface Design.* Englewood Cliffs, NJ: Prentice-Hall.

McGinnis, D. R., and Sass, C. J. 1988. Modified design walkthroughs and their effect on program correctness of solutions in business courses utilizing third and fourth generation programming languages. *Proceedings of the 1988 North American Conference of the International Business Schools Computer Users Group*: 86–90.

McGrath, J. E. 1984. *Groups: Interaction and Performance.* Englewood Cliffs, NJ: Prentice-Hall.

Microsoft 1992. *The Windows Interface: An Application Design Guide.* Redmond, WA: Microsoft Press.

Molich, R., and Nielsen, J. 1990. Improving a human-computer dialogue. *Communications of the ACM* **33**, 3 (March): 338–348.

Montaniz, F., and Mack, R. 1993a. *A usability logging tool built out of Microsoft Windows applications and macrolanguage.* (Research Report **82056**). Hawthorne, NY: IBM Thomas J. Watson Research Center.

Montaniz, F., and Mack, R. 1993b. *A comparison of the effectiveness of two usability inspection methods: cognitive walkthrough and intuitive inspection.* (Research Report **83674**). Hawthorne, NY: IBM Thomas J. Watson Research Center.

Mosier, J. N., and Smith, S. L. 1986. Application of guidelines for designing user interface software. *Behaviour & Information Technology* **5**, 1 (January–March): 39–46.

Morrison, G. R., and Ross, S. M. 1988. A four stage model for planning computer-based instruction. *Journal of Instructional Development* **11**: 6–14.

Muller, M. J. 1991. PICTIVE: An exploration in participatory design. *Proceedings ACM CHI'91 Conference* (New Orleans, La, April 28–May 2): 225–231.

Muller, M. J., Wildman, D. M., and White, E. A. 1993. 'Equal opportunity' PD using PICTIVE. *Communications of the ACM* **36**, 4: 64–66.

Myers, B. A., and Rosson, M. B. 1992. Survey on user interface programming. *Proceedings ACM CHI'92 Conference* (Monterey, CA, May 3–7): 195–202.

N

Newell, A. 1990. *Unified Theories of Cognition.* Cambridge: Harvard University Press.

Newell, A., and Rosenbloom, P. S. 1981. Mechanisms of skill acquisition and the law of practice. In *Cognitive Skills and Their Acquisition,* edited by Anderson, J. R., 1–55. Hillsdale, NJ: Lawrence Erlbaum Associates, Publishers.

Newell, A., and Simon, H. A. 1972. *Human problem solving.* Englewood Cliffs, NJ: Prentice-Hall.

Nielsen, J. 1987. Using scenarios to develop user friendly videotex systems. *Proc. NordDATA'87 Joint Scandinavian Computer Conference* (Trondheim, Norway, June 15–18): 133–138.

Nielsen, J. 1989a. Prototyping user interfaces using an object-oriented hypertext programming system. *Proc. NordDATA'89 Joint Scandinavian Computer Conference* (Copenhagen, Denmark, June 19–22): 485–490.

Nielsen, J. 1989). Usability engineering at a discount. In *Designing and Using Human-Computer Interfaces and Knowledge Based Systems,* edited by Salvendy, G., and Smith, M. J., 394–401. Amsterdam: Elsevier Science Publishers.

Nielsen, J. 1989c. *Coordinating User Interfaces for Consistency.* Boston: Academic Press.

Nielsen, J. 1990a. *Hypertext and Hypermedia.* Boston: Academic Press. Paperback edition published 1993.

Nielsen, J. 1990b. Big paybacks from 'discount' usability engineering. *IEEE Software* 7, 3 (May): 107–108.

Nielsen, J. 1990c. Paper versus computer implementations as mockup scenarios for heuristic evaluation. *Proc. IFIP INTERACT'90 Third Intl. Conf. Human-Computer Interaction* (Cambridge, U.K., August 27–31): 315–320.

Nielsen, J. 1990d. Traditional dialogue design applied to modern user interfaces. *Communications of the ACM* **33**, 10 (October): 109–118.

Nielsen, J. 1990e. *Designing User Interfaces for International Use.* Amsterdam: Elsevier Science Publishers.

Nielsen, J. 1992a. Finding usability problems through heuristic evaluation. *Proceedings ACM CHI'92 Conference* (Monterey, CA, May 3–7): 373–380.

Nielsen, J. 1992b. Evaluating the thinking aloud technique for use by computer scientists. In *Advances in Human-Computer Interaction* Vol. **3**, edited by Hartson, H. R., and Hix, D., 69–82. Norwood, NJ: Ablex.

Nielsen, J. 1992c. Reliability of severity estimates for usability problems found by heuristic evaluation. In *Digest of CHI'92 Posters and Short Talks* (Monterey, CA, May 3–7): 129–130.

Nielsen, J. 1992d. The usability engineering life cycle. *IEEE Computer* **25**, 3 (March): 12–22.

Nielsen, J. 1993a. *Usability Engineering.* Boston: Academic Press.

Nielsen, J. 1993b. Iterative user-interface design. *IEEE Computer* **26**, 11 (November): 32–41.

Nielsen, J. 1993c. Is usability engineering really worth it? *IEEE Software* **10**, 6 (November): 90–92.

Nielsen, J. 1994a. Guerrilla HCI: Using discount usability engineering to penetrate the intimidation barrier. In *Cost-Justifying Usability*, edited by Bias, R. G., and Mayhew, D. J., 245–272. Boston: Academic Press.

Nielsen, J. 1994b. Scenarios in discount usability engineering. In *Scenario-Based Design: Envisioning Work and Technology in System Development*, edited by Carroll, J. M. Book under preparation.

Nielsen, J. 1994c. Enhancing the explanatory power of usability heuristics. *Proceedings ACM CHI'94 Conference* (Boston, MA, April 24–28).

Nielsen, J., and Landauer, T. K. 1993. A mathematical model of the finding of usability problems. *Proceedings ACM/IFIP INTERCHI'93 Conference* (Amsterdam, The Netherlands, April 24–29): 206–213.

Nielsen, J., and Molich, R. 1989. Teaching user interface design based on usability engineering. *ACM SIGCHI Bulletin* **21**, 1 (July): 45–48

Nielsen, J., and Molich, R. 1990. Heuristic evaluation of user interfaces. *Proceedings ACM CHI'90 Conference* (Seattle, WA, April 1–5): 249–256.

Nielsen, J., and Phillips, V. L. 1993. Estimating the relative usability of two interfaces: Heuristic, formal, and empirical methods compared. *Proceedings ACM/IFIP INTERCHI'93 Conference* (Amsterdam, The Netherlands, April 24–29): 214–221.

Nielsen, J., Bush, R. M., Dayton, T., Mond, N. E., Muller, M. J., and Root, R. W. 1992. Teaching experienced developers to design graphical user interfaces. *Proceedings ACM CHI'92 Conference* (Monterey, CA, May 3–7): 557–564.

Nielsen, J., Desurvire, H., Kerr, R., Rosenberg, D., Salomon, G., Molich, R., and Stewart, T. 1993. Comparative design review: An exercise in parallel design. *Proceedings ACM/IFIP INTERCHI'93 Conference* (Amsterdam, The Netherlands, April 24–29): 414–417.

Nilsen, E., Jong, H., Olson, J. S., and Polson, P. G. 1992. Method engineering: From data to model to practice. *Proceedings ACM CHI'92 Conferences* (Monterey, CA, May 3–7):313–320.

Norman, D. A. 1983. Design rules based on analysis of human error. *Communications of the ACM* **26**, 4 (April 1983): 254–258.

Norman, D. A. 1986. Cognitive engineering. In *User Centered System Design: New Perspectives on Human-Computer Interaction*, edited by Norman, D., and Draper, S., 31–61. Hillsdale, NJ: Erlbaum.

Norman, D. A. 1988. *The Psychology of Everyday Things*. New York: Basic Books. The paperback edition was published under the title *The Design of Everyday Things*.

O

Olson, J. S., and Olson, G. M. 1990. The growth of cognitive modeling in human-computer interaction since GOMS. *Human-Computer Interaction* **5**, 2&3: 221–265.

OSF 1992. *OSF/Motif Style Guide.* New York: Prentice Hall.

P

Perlman, G. 1989. Asynchronous design/evaluation methods for hypertext technology development. *Proceedings ACM Hypertext'89 Conference* (Pittsburgh, PA, November 5–8): 61–81.

Polson, P., and Lewis, C. 1990. Theory-based design for easily learned interfaces. *Human-Computer Interaction* **5**, 2&3: 191–220.

Polson, P. G., and Olson, J. S. 1992. An approximate method for estimating total learning time: An example of a usability inspection method derived from cost/benefit considerations. Paper presented at *Human-Computer Interaction Consortium Annual Winter Conference*, Pittsburgh, PA, January 28, 1992.

Polson, P., Lewis, C., Rieman, J., and Wharton, C. 1992a. Cognitive walkthroughs: A method for theory-based evaluation of user interfaces. *International Journal of Man-Machine Studies* **36**: 741–773.

Polson, P., Rieman, J., Wharton, C., and Olson, J. 1992b. Usability inspection methods: rationale and examples. *Proceedings of 8th Symposium on Human Interface* (Kawasaki, Japan, October 21–23): 377–384.

Potter, S. S., Cook, R. I., Woods, D. D., and McDonald, J. S. 1990. The role of human factors guidelines in designing usable systems: A case study of operating room equipment. *Proceedings of the Human Factors Society 34th Annual Meeting* (Orlando, FL, October 8–12): 392–395.

Pressman, R. S. 1992. *Software Engineering: A Practitioner's Approach.* New York: McGraw-Hill.

R

Rettig, M. 1993. Cooperative software. *Communications of the ACM* **36**, 4: 23–28.

Rieman, J., Davies, S., Hair, D. C., Esemplare, M., Polson, P. G., and Lewis, C. 1991. An automated cognitive walkthrough. *Proceedings ACM CHI'91 Conference* (New Orleans, LA, April 28–May 2): 427–428.

Rosenbaum, S. 1989. Usability evaluations vs. usability testing: When and why? *IEEE Transactions on Professional Communications* **32**, 4 (December): 210–216.

Rosenberg, D. 1989. A cost-benefit analysis for corporate user interface standards: What price to pay for a consistent look and feel? In *Coordinating User Interfaces for Consistency*, edited by Nielsen, J., 21–34. Boston: Academic Press.

Rowley, D. E., and Rhoades, D. G. 1992. The cognitive jogthrough: a fast-paced user interface evaluation procedure. *Proceedings ACM CHI'92 Conference* (Monterey, CA, May 3–7): 389–395.

Russell, G. W. 1991. Experience with inspection in ultralarge-scale developments. *IEEE Software* **8**, 1 (January): 25–31.

S

Scapin, D. L. 1990. Organizing human factors knowledge for the evaluation and design of interfaces. *International Journal of Human-Computer Interaction* **2**, 3: 203–229.

Schön, D. 1983. *The Reflective Practitioner.* New York: Basic Books.

Shneiderman, B. 1982. Designing computer system messages. *Communications of the ACM* **25**, 9 (September): 610–611.

Shneiderman, B. 1987. *Designing the User Interface.* Reading, MA: Addison-Wesley.

Silverman, B. G. 1992. Survey of expert critiquing systems: Practical and theoretical frontiers. *Communications of the ACM* **35**, 4 (April): 106–127.

Smith, D. C., Irby, C., Kimball, R., Verplank, W., and Harslem, E. 1982. Designing the Star user interface. *Byte* **7**, 4 (April): 242–282.

Smith, S. L., and Mosier, J. N. 1986. *Design Guidelines for Designing User Interface Software.* Technical Report **MTR-10090**, The MITRE Corporation, Bedford, MA 01730, USA.

Snyder, K. 1991. *A Guide to Software Usability.* IBM Corporation, White Plains, NY (order #: **SC34-4289-00**).

Stasko, J., Badre, A., and Lewis, C. 1993. Do algorithm animations assist learning? An empirical study and analysis. *Proceedings ACM/IFIP INTERCHI'93 Conference* (Amsterdam, The Netherlands, April 24–29): 61–66.

Steele, R. 1988. Cell-based VLSI design advice using default reasoning. *Proceedings of 3rd Annual Rocky Mountain Conference on AI*, RMSAI, Denver: 66–74.

Stevens, S. M. 1989. Intelligent interactive video simulation of a code inspection. *Communications of the ACM* **32**, 7 (July): 832–843.

T

Temple, Barker, and Sloan 1990. *The Benefits of the Graphical User Interface: A Report on New Primary Research.* **Technical report. 098-10794**. Cosponsored by Microsoft Corporation and Zenith Data Systems.

Tetzlaff, L., and Schwartz, D. R. 1991. The use of guidelines in interface design. *Proceedings ACM CHI'91 Conference* (New Orleans, LA, April 28–May 2): 329–333.

Thomas, J. C. 1976. A method for studying natural language dialogue. *IBM Research Report* **RC 5882**. Yorktown Heights, NY: IBM T. J. Watson Research Center.

Thomas, J. C., and Gould, J. D. 1975. A psychological study of Query by Example. Presented at the National Computer Conference (Anaheim CA, May), *AFIPS Conference Proceedings* **44**: 439–445.

Thovtrup, H., and Nielsen, J. 1991. Assessing the usability of a user interface standard. *Proceedings ACM CHI'91 Conference* (New Orleans, LA, April 28–May 2): 335–341.

Tognazzini, B. 1989. Achieving consistency for the Macintosh. In *Coordinating User Interfaces for Consistency*, edited by Nielsen, J., 57–73. Boston: Academic Press.

Tullis, T. S. 1988. Screen Design. In *Handbook of Human-Computer Interaction*, edited by Helander, M., 377–411. Amsterdam: Elsevier Science Publishers.

V

Vessey, I., Jarvenpaa, S. L., Tractinsky, N. 1992. Evaluation of vendor products: CASE tools as methodology companions. *Communications of the ACM* **35**, 4: 106–127.

W

Wasserman, A. 1991. Can research reinvent the corporation? *Harvard Business Review* **69**, 2: 164–175.

Weller, E. F. 1993. Lessons from three years of inspection data. *IEEE Software* **10**, 5 (September): 38–45.

Wharton, C. 1992. Cognitive Walkthroughs: Instructions, Forms, and Examples. Institute of Cognitive Science *Technical Report* **CU-ICS-92-17.** University of Colorado, Boulder, CO 80309.

Wharton, C., Bradford, J., Jeffries, R., and Franzke, M. 1992. Applying cognitive walkthroughs to more complex user interfaces: Experiences, issues, and recommendations. *Proceedings ACM CHI'92 Conference* (Monterey, CA, May 3–7): 381–388.

Whiteside, J. A. 1986. Usability engineering. *UNIX Review* **4**, 6: 22–37.

Whiteside, J., Bennett, J., and Holtzblatt, K. 1988. Usability Engineering: Our Experience and Evolution. In *Handbook of Human-Computer Interaction*, edited by Helander, M., 791–818. Amsterdam: Elsevier Science Publishers.

Whitten, N. 1990. *Managing Software Development Projects: Formula for Success.* New York: John Wiley & Sons. 203–223.

Wixon, D., and Jones, S. 1991. Usability for Fun and Profit: A Case Study of the Design of VAX Rally version 2. Presented at NASA sponsored Conference: *Human Computer Interface Design: Success Cases, Emerging Methods and Real World Context.* July 1991. University of Colorado, Boulder (available from Dennis Wixon).

Wixon, D., Holtzblatt, K., and Knox, S. 1990. Contextual design: An emergent view of system design. *Proceedings ACM CHI'90 Conference* (Seattle, April 1–5): 329–336.

Wolf, C., and Rhyne, J. 1987. A taxonomic approach to understanding direct manipulation. *Proceedings of the Human Factors Society 31st Annual Meeting.* 576–580.

Wright, P. C., and Monk, A. F. 1991a. The use of think-aloud evaluation methods in design. *ACM SIGCHI Bulletin* **23**, 1: 55–71.

Wright, P., and Monk, A. 1991b. A cost-effective evaluation method for designers. *International Journal of Man-Machine Studies* **35**: 891–912.

Y

Yourdon, E. 1989. *Structured Walkthroughs* (4th ed.). Englewood Cliffs, NJ: Yourdon Press.

Author Index

Subject Index